PRAXIS®
CORE AND
PLT PREP

THIRTEENTH EDITION

© 2021 by Kaplan, Inc.

Published by Kaplan Publishing, a division of Kaplan, Inc.
750 Third Avenue
New York, NY 10017

ISBN: 978-1-5062-6619-0

10 9 8 7 6 5 4 3 2

Kaplan Publishing books are available at special quantity discounts to use for sales promotions, employee premiums, or educational purposes. For more information or to purchase books, please call the Simon & Schuster special sales department at 866-506-1949.

Studying for the Praxis: Where Do I Start?

Studying for the Praxis means taking a big step toward a new and meaningful career as a teacher. But figuring out how to most effectively prepare for the exam can be stressful. Our goal is to give you the tools and strategies you need to feel calm and confident on test day.

You're getting not just the content in this book—and there's a lot to cover here—but also access to a wealth of practice through your online resources, including full-length computer-based tests that simulate the real online test environment.

You can customize these materials to your individual needs. You don't have to—indeed, you probably shouldn't—work through the book in the order it is written. If you are studying for any (or all) of the Praxis Core exams, Part I of this book covers those. If you are prepping for one of the Principles of Learning and Teaching tests, Part II addresses them. In either case, you'll start with a pre-test to assess your strengths and your areas of greatest opportunity. After reviewing your results to identify your personal patterns, you'll get into the chapters covering the tests you are taking to learn how expert test takers tackle each topic and question type. At the end of each chapter, Practice Sets will help you build on what you've learned. And finally, full-length practice tests in your book and in your online resources will let you put it all together.

Taking into account the information you learn from your pre-tests, use the advice and study aids discussed below to make the most of your practice time.

What's Included in My Online Resources?

Your online resources give you access to the following additional content. There are six additional full-length practice exams, all accompanied by complete explanations:

- Two full-length Core Academic Skills for Educators (Reading, Mathematics, and Writing) practice exams
- One full-length Principles of Learning and Teaching (PLT) (Grades K–6) practice test
- Two full-length Principles of Learning and Teaching (PLT) (Grades 5–9) practice tests
- One full-length Principles of Learning and Teaching (PLT) (Grades 7–12) practice test

As a special bonus for those of you who are studying for Praxis Core Math (or who may have a mathematics content test for your state's licensing requirements), you'll also find the following in your online resources:

- Kaplan's *Math Foundations*. This is a course designed specially for adult learners who need to reacquaint themselves with the foundations of arithmetic, algebra, and geometry. It has 5 hours of video lessons and 225 practice questions designed to restore your skill level and confidence in these areas of math.

Take a moment right now to register your online companion using these simple steps:

1. Go to **kaptest.com/moreonline**.
2. Follow the on-screen directions. Have your copy of this book available.

GO ONLINE

kaptest.com/moreonline

Please note that access to the online portal is limited to the original owner of this book.

Once you've registered your book, go to **kaptest.com/login** anytime to log in with your email and password.

What's Included in My Book?

Throughout this book, you'll find the following notable features.

Time-Tested Strategies for Every Question Type

Kaplan has spent decades researching the Praxis and teaching thousands of students the effective methods they need to succeed. This book contains detailed instructions on how to analyze and correctly answer the various question types you will encounter on the specific Praxis exam for which you are studying.

Pre-Tests

At the beginning of Chapters 1–3 (covering the three Praxis Core tests) and of Chapter 5 (covering the Principles of Learning and Teaching (PLT) tests), you'll find pre-tests that are between one-third and one-half the length of the corresponding full tests for which you are preparing. We recommend that you take these pre-tests before you start working through the Kaplan Methods and strategies for taking the full tests. The pre-tests are accompanied by full explanations for each problem, and they break down your performance by content area to help you identify your strengths and opportunities. Having this information will let you work in an efficient and focused way.

Practice Sets

At the ends of Chapters 1–3 and 5, you'll find sets of practice questions in the same format as the questions you'll see on the full-length practice tests and official exams. The explanations for these questions immediately follow each practice set. Take the practice sets without putting time pressure on yourself. They are designed to provide you with an opportunity to check your skills after reading the material in each chapter, but before assessing your overall performance with a full-length in-book or online test.

Full-Length Practice Exams

You have three full-length practice exams in your book. You'll find one in Chapter 4—a full-length Praxis Core exam including the Reading, Math, and Writing tests. You'll find two more in Chapter 6—one each for the PLT (Grades K–6) and PLT (Grades 7–12) tests. These are complete testing experiences, just like you'll have on your official tests. We've put one of each of these major Praxis tests in your book so that you can conveniently test when you're away from your computer.

As noted above, your online resources contain additional full-length practice exams: two each for the three Core tests, and one or two for each of the PLT grade bands. These computer-based practice tests are designed to replicate the official test day experience as closely as possible. Treat them as you would the actual exam: clear off your work space, turn off your cell phone, and remove any other distractions. The practice tests are timed in the same manner as the official tests, so make sure you have enough uninterrupted time to complete the test before you begin.

After you complete the test, you'll find complete answers and explanations (either in the book or online, depending on where you took the test). Moreover, for your online tests, you can see a Performance Summary that analyzes your strengths and weaknesses by question type and content area. Use this feedback to prioritize any area that needs significant improvement and return early and often to study the relevant portions of this book.

There's a Lot of Material to Review. How Will I Remember Everything I'll Need to Ace the Test?

In addition to providing you with the best practice questions and test strategies, Kaplan's team of learning scientists is dedicated to researching and testing the best methods for getting the most out of your study time. Here are their top five tips for improving retention.

Tip 1: Start or End Each Study Session by Reviewing Practice Questions

Practice questions provide focus for each study session by showing what you still need to learn and by helping you draw connections between what you already know and what you will be studying. Studies show that students who tackle test-like questions at the beginning of a practice session will perform better on test-like questions after studying than students who don't begin a session with test-like practice. Take the time to read all explanations carefully. Familiarity with the structure of the questions and answers will help you feel more comfortable during the official test.

Tip 2: Review Multiple Topics in One Study Session

This may seem counterintuitive, as we're used to practicing one skill at a time, but research shows that weaving topics together leads to increased learning by creating semantic connections in long-term memory. Not only that, but testmakers often include more than one topic in a single question. Studying in an integrated manner is the most effective way to prepare for this test.

Tip 3: Customize the Content

Drawing attention to difficult or critical content can ensure you don't overlook it as you read and re-read sections. The best way to do this is to make it more visual—highlight, make tabs, use stickies, whatever works. We recommend highlighting only the most important or difficult topics. Targeted highlighting is a great way to emphasize parts of the text, but over-highlighting can have the opposite effect.

Tip 4: Repeat Topics over Time

Many people try to memorize concepts by repeating them over and over again in succession. Research shows, however, that retention is improved by spacing out the repetition over time (a technique sometimes called "spaced learning" or "boosting") and mixing up the order in which you study content. For example, try reading the chapters in a different order the second (or third!) time around. Try following a new sequence when revisiting practice questions that you previously answered incorrectly. As you continue to study and learn more about the test, you will find that it becomes easier to understand questions that you may have previously answered incorrectly.

Tip 5: Take a Moment to Reflect

When you finish reading a section for the first time, stop and think about what you've just read. Jot down a few thoughts about why the content is important or what topics came to mind when you read it. Thinking about what you've just learned activates a part of your memory called metacognition and can help long-term memories form more clearly. Associating new learning with a memory you already have is another fantastic way to retain information.

This also works when answering questions. After answering a question, take a moment to think through each step you took to arrive at a solution. What led you to the answer you chose, even if it wasn't correct? Understanding the steps you took will help you make good decisions when answering future questions.

What's in the Appendix?

At the end of this book, in the section titled "Praxis Resources," you'll find helpful information about furthering your occupation as a teacher. When you're done studying, make sure to read through the "Getting Started: Advice for New Teachers" section. In addition, in your online resources, you'll find a list of links to state licensing requirements websites and other contact information for state teacher certification offices.

The Praxis and You

First things first: the Praxis isn't a single exam; it's a series of exams. This book, along with your online resources, provides preparation for four of the most commonly required tests in the Praxis series. Chapters 1–4 of the book cover the three Core Academic Skills for Educators tests (one each for Reading, Mathematics, and Writing). Chapters 5–6 address the Principles of Learning and Teaching (PLT) tests.

It is essential that you know which tests are required in the state(s) where you plan to teach before registering for the tests and beginning your preparation. Understanding these requirements will guide your use of this book and your online resources. To learn which tests you need to take, contact your state's department of education. You can find contact information and web addresses for each state in the State Certification Information table in this book's online resources.

The Tests and the Differences Between Them

Praxis Core Academic Skills for Educators

The first part of this book deals with the Praxis Core Academic Skills tests—three tests covering reading (5713), mathematics (5733), and writing (5723) skills. These tests are often required for undergraduates entering education programs. Some states also require them for non–education major applicants seeking jobs in the classroom.

If you need to take tests from the Praxis Core series, then the first three chapters of this book will provide you with the content review you need. Each chapter in this part contains a set of practice questions for one of the three Core tests. In Chapter 4, you'll find full-length practice tests for each of the Praxis Core tests. In your online resources, you'll find two more full-length practice tests for each of the three Praxis Core tests. Additionally, you'll find Kaplan's complete *Math Foundations* course to help you remove the rust from your foundational arithmetic, algebra, and geometry skills.

Praxis Principles of Learning and Teaching

The second part of the book is dedicated to the Praxis Principles of Learning and Teaching (PLT) tests. Chapter 5 introduces the format and structure of the PLT tests, and it also contains an outline of key subject matter components of the tests. In addition to strategy and content review, Chapter 5 contains three sets of practice questions: one for each of the three grade-level bands (K–6, 4–9, and 7–12) tested on the PLTs.

Chapter 6 contains two full-length practice tests: one each for PLT: Grades K–6 (5622) and PLT: Grades 7–12 (5624). Those are the two most commonly tested grade-level bands nationwide, but there is also a PLT: Grades 5–9 middle school test (5623). For that one, you'll find two full-length tests in your online resources, along with an additional full-length practice test for each of the K–6 and 7–12 tests.

To determine which of these tests you will need to take, please refer to the requirements for the state where you plan to teach. You can find a list of links to state licensing requirements websites and other contact information for state teacher certification offices in your book's online resources.

Computer-Delivered Tests

Aside from Braille Proficiency (0633), all Praxis tests are offered exclusively via computer-delivered formats, and all of the full-length tests in the online companion accompanying this book are computer-delivered tests. The question sets in the printed book contain questions in formats that correspond to those you'll see on the computer-delivered exams.

Note: In the past, Praxis distinguished between computer-delivered tests (whose test numbers began with a 5) and paper-based tests (whose test numbers began with a 0). If you are using Praxis materials or references written before 2018, you may see the same test referred to by both types of numbers, as paper-based testing persisted longer in some regions and on some tests than others. To make sure you are preparing for the most up-to-date test formats, visit **ets.org/praxis**.

A Note About Scoring

A passing score on a Praxis test will vary depending on which state is requiring you to take the test. What's more, your state may change the passing score on a particular test from year to year. For information on passing scores in your state, consult **ets .org/praxis/scores**. However, for the most up-to-date information about score requirements, please contact the state licensing board, organization, institution, or teacher-training program that will receive your scores.

Registering for Praxis

The easiest way to register for Praxis tests is online at **ets.org/praxis/register**. You may also register by printing out and mailing in a Test Authorization Voucher Request Form (this document can be found on the registration website), or by calling **1-800-772-9476**. As of this writing, there is a $35 fee if you use the phone registration service. If you intend to take a Praxis test while outside the United States, visit the registration website and follow the instructions there.

Depending on your method of registration, you will either receive a test admission ticket in the mail or you will need to print out an e-ticket from the online registration site. Bring this ticket with you to the testing site—without it, you will not be admitted to the test.

Whichever route you choose, be sure to check the test dates and locations and choose a location where you will feel the most comfortable. Also, look at up-to-date information about the state where you plan to teach. A helpful list of relevant state addresses and websites appears in your book's online resources.

Note: Historically, the Praxis could only be taken at certain testing centers approved by ETS. However, in 2020, due to the closure of testing centers resulting from COVID-19, ETS approved an at-home testing option. As you prepare to take the Praxis, research your testing options at the official site, **ets.org/praxis**.

If you are a test taker who requires accommodations for a disability or other health-related issue, you will need to provide documentation to support your request. You can find official information about the process of submitting a request for accommodations at **ets.org/praxis/register/disabilities** or by contacting ETS.

Phone: 1-609-771-7780; 1-866-387-8602 (toll-free for test takers in the United States, U.S. Territories, and Canada)

Fax: 1-609-771-7165

Email: stassd@ets.org (general inquiries)

Mail: ETS Disability Services

P.O. Box 6054

Princeton, NJ 08541-6054 USA

Please note that the information in this book is current as of the time of publication. It is recommended that you supplement your review with information from the Praxis website (**ets.org/praxis**), as test names, codes, content, and procedures are subject to change.

Kaplan wishes you all the best during your preparation for the Praxis series of exams!

PART ONE

PRAXIS CORE ACADEMIC SKILLS FOR EDUCATORS

INTRODUCING THE PRAXIS CORE ACADEMIC SKILLS FOR EDUCATORS TESTS

The Praxis Core Academic Skills for Educators tests (Praxis Core tests) consist of three exams: one in Reading, one in Mathematics, and one in Writing. These tests measure basic academic skills and are normally taken by undergraduates in education programs. Also, some non–education majors are required to take these exams to be certified to teach in some states.

In a nutshell, most teachers must pass the Praxis Core tests to be certified to teach.

This section is devoted to preparing you for the Praxis Core tests. The review sections and practice tests that follow provide comprehensive and thorough preparation for each of these tests. Be sure to understand your strengths and weaknesses as a test taker before working through these sections. You will need to pass all three tests to be certified to teach in many Praxis states. As a result, it's important to know where you need the most help so that you can focus your preparatory energies where they are most needed.

CORE TEST	QUESTIONS	TIME
Reading	56	85 minutes
Mathematics	56	90 minutes
Writing	40	40 minutes
	2 essays	60 minutes

CHAPTER 1

PRAXIS CORE READING

LEARNING OBJECTIVES

By the end of this chapter, you will be able to do the following:

- Describe the structure and format of the Praxis Core Academic Skills for Educators: Reading test
- Outline and use the Kaplan Method for Praxis Core Reading
- Apply Praxis Reading Strategies
- Use the Praxis Core Reading practice test to assess your performance

---

Taking Your Core Reading Pre-Test

Before you begin studying and practicing Praxis Core Reading, take a pre-test to assess your initial strengths and areas of greatest opportunity on the test. With 25 questions to complete in 38 minutes, the pre-test is a little less than half the length of the official exam. Find time to complete the pre-test in one sitting and strictly time yourself as you take it.

The purpose of the pre-test is self-assessment. Some test takers hesitate to take pre-tests because they haven't studied yet, or they want to try the questions without time restrictions so that they can get them all correct. However, those approaches defeat the purpose of the pre-test, which is to give test takers a clear-eyed look at their performance and skill level on all that the test entails.

Part of the test's challenge is its timing. Some of the questions may seem easy, and some may strike you as really difficult. When you encounter hard questions on the pre-test, don't be afraid to skip them or make your best guess. It's more valuable to get a broad view of your performance on different question types than to spend several minutes struggling to get one question right.

So, do your best, but don't get too excited or worried about your score on the pre-test. There's a lot of learning and practice to come, and your performance on the pre-test does not predict your official score. That will be the result of your study and effort.

Core Reading Pre-Test

38 Minutes—25 Questions

Directions: You have 38 minutes to complete this pre-test. Read the instructions for each question carefully and circle the correct answer(s) in your book. If a question asks you to "Select all that apply," then more than one answer could be right and you should select all of the choices you believe to be correct. You may use blank scratch paper to take notes during this pre-test.

Questions 1–4 refer to the following stimulus.

Most people think that the Hula Hoop was a fad born in the 1950s, but in fact, people were doing much the same thing with circular hoops made from grapevines and stiff grasses all over the ancient world. More than 3,000 years ago, children in Egypt played with large hoops of dried grapevines. The toy was propelled along the ground with a stick or swung around at the waist. During the 14th century, a "hooping" craze swept England and was as popular among adults as kids.

The word *hula* became associated with the hoop toy in the early 1800s, when British sailors visited the Hawaiian Islands and noted the similarity between hooping and hula dancing. In 1957, an Australian company began making wood rings for sale in retail stores. The item attracted the attention of Wham-O, a fledgling California toy manufacturer. The plastic Hula Hoop was introduced in 1958 and was an instant hit.

1. According to the passage, all of the following statements are true EXCEPT

   A. Most people do not appreciate the ancient origins of the Hula Hoop.

   B. The earliest prototypes of the Hula Hoop were made of grape leaves and stiff grasses.

   C. Precursors of the Hula Hoop were only used by children.

   D. The Hula Hoop was an early success for the toy company Wham-O.

   E. The name of the Hula Hoop was partly inspired by a popular dance of the Hawaiian Islands.

2. The author's primary purpose in this passage is to

   A. describe the way that fads like the Hula Hoop come and go

   B. discuss the historical origins of the Hula Hoop

   C. explain how the Hula Hoop got its name

   D. question the reasons for the Hula Hoop's popularity

   E. use the example of the Hula Hoop to illustrate a point about fads

3. Which of the following can be inferred from the information provided in the passage?

   A. Human beings have generally managed to find some time for play.

   B. The ancient version of the Hula Hoop was introduced to Egypt from Hawaii.

   C. In some medieval and ancient civilizations, the Hula Hoop's ancestor was even more popular than the Hula Hoop itself.

   D. The idea for the plastic Hula Hoop originated in Hawaii.

   E. Practicing with a Hula Hoop is a good way to learn the hula dance.

4. Which of the following best describes how this passage is organized?

   A. Presentation of evidence followed by the conclusion drawn from the evidence

   B. Presentation of a conclusion followed by evidence in support of it

   C. Chronologically

   D. Geographically

   E. Holistically

Although the Industrial Revolution heralded an age of consumer ease and excess, it also invited a cyclical process of destruction and reduced resources. Greenhouse gases were released into the atmosphere while carbon dioxide–consuming trees were cut down to make way for new living space. Numerous health problems caused by substandard working conditions prevented people from thriving after they emigrated to the city from rural areas. And the environment that had cradled humankind since its inception was slowly being degraded—all in the name of progress.

5. In this passage, what is the writer's view of the Industrial Revolution?

   A. It was a boon to humanity because it made great improvements to people's standard of living.

   B. It was praiseworthy because it provided material comforts, despite its somewhat negative impact on the environment.

   C. It allowed some to live a life of ease, but harmed the health and working lives of many while destroying much of the environment.

   D. It allowed great progress in science and technology, resulting in better lives for most people.

   E. It provided new opportunities to many who had been living in rural poverty by providing jobs for them in new industries.

Although acorns are the quintessential foodstuff for common squirrels, many humans would never consider consuming these tough-looking nuts with their little protective hats. And indeed, if a human did try to crunch on a raw acorn, its tannic acids would most likely not only leave a bitter taste but also cause stomach ailments. However, Native Americans of California have eaten acorns for centuries, either by carrying out extensive processes to remove the offending acids or by identifying trees that produce sweeter acorn varieties.

6. Which of the following best reflects the organization of the passage?

   A. Problems with a food are described, and then ways that some people have overcome the problems are listed.

   B. Arguments against eating a type of food are listed, and then arguments in favor of eating the type of food are listed.

   C. The passage compares, and then contrasts, the types of foods humans eat with those typically consumed by squirrels.

   D. An idea about a type of food commonly believed to be a misconception is discussed, and then the idea is confirmed with evidence.

   E. Examples of features of a type of food are listed, and then methods for eating the food are evaluated.

The question of whether a child's personality is the result of genetic material inherited from the parents or the nurturing and environment provided by the parents is a perennial subject of debate. Whereas no one would deny that environment and upbringing play a limited role, the genetic traits that a child inherits provide some sort of basic blueprint for who and what that child becomes. After all, if one plants tomatoes, _____.

7. Which of the following best completes this passage?

    A. one must tend them carefully in order to gather good vegetables

    B. one had better choose the variety and location with equal care

    C. one will get tomatoes, but not necessarily good tomatoes

    D. one must expect tomatoes to grow, not cucumbers or daffodils

    E. one must be sure to tend them well, regardless of the quality of the seeds

Although some researchers have linked the modern game of basketball to Mesoamerican games that date back thousands of years, the current version of the game is generally credited to Dr. James Naismith, who "invented" the game in Springfield, Massachusetts, in 1891. In his initial version of the game, players would attempt to throw soccer balls into peach baskets perched at a standard height—hence, the name *basketball*.

8. The main idea of this passage is that

    A. basketball was first played in Springfield, Massachusetts

    B. Naismith invented the current version of basketball in 1891

    C. basketball is most popular in Mesoamerica

    D. basketball gets its name from peach baskets

    E. basketball is a combination of soccer and other Mesoamerican games

Questions 9–11 refer to the following stimulus.

Meter in poetry refers to verses' basic rhythmic structure. This important component of poetry is specifically studied by people called prosodists. One of the most frequently used of all meters is iambic pentameter. An *iamb* is a grouping (also known as a *foot*) of two syllables with the stress on the second syllable. *Pentameter* refers to a line of poetry with five feet of syllables, where each foot is an iamb. William Shakespeare is perhaps the most famous writer of iambic pentameter, having composed hundreds of poems in this meter and popularizing it for the masses.

9. According to the passage, a foot is

    A. a grouping of syllables

    B. similar to a meter

    C. named after William Shakespeare

    D. rarely used in poetry

    E. none of the above

10. The author would most likely agree with which of the following about poetry?

    A. Iambic pentameter is the most effective meter for conveying drama and emotion.

    B. The study of poetry is not a worthwhile pursuit.

    C. Writers other than Shakespeare wrote poems in iambic pentameter.

    D. Shakespeare wrote poems in meters other than iambic pentameter.

    E. Use of pentameter requires putting stress on the first syllable of every group of two syllables.

11. It can be inferred from the passage that which of the following is true of Shakespeare's work?

    A. Shakespeare wrote plays as well as poetry.

    B. Shakespeare wrote over 300 poems in iambic pentameter.

    C. The author's favorite poet is Shakespeare.

    D. The upper classes were particular fans of Shakespeare's poetry.

    E. Many people were exposed to and became fans of Shakespeare's poems.

Proxemics is defined as the study of spatial distances between individuals in different cultures and situations. Edward Hall, founder of this field of study, coined the term. Hall studied how different cultures use space and spatial boundaries. His findings have influenced how diplomats are trained to engage members of different cultures.

12. Which of the following can be inferred from the passage?

    A. Edward Hall was an important diplomat.

    B. Most cultures have the same norms for space and spatial boundaries.

    C. The use of space and spatial boundaries is important to diplomats.

    D. Proxemics is a field of study with few practical applications.

    E. Diplomats are trained to engage all members of different cultures in the same way.

Tungsten is a metal with numerous industrial uses. One of its main uses is as a filament in electric lights. It was discovered in 1783 in Spain by Fausto and Juan Jose de Elhuyar. Its name comes from the Swedish *tung sten,* or heavy stone. Surprisingly, tungsten's symbol on the periodic table is W. This symbol comes from the German word for tungsten, *Wolfram.*

13. According to the passage, tungsten's name comes from

    A. the names of its discoverers

    B. the German language

    C. its industrial uses

    D. the Swedish language

    E. its symbol on the periodic table

Questions 14–16 refer to the following stimulus.

Children have an almost unbelievable talent for learning vocabulary. Between the ages of 1 and 17, the average person learns the meaning of about 80,000 words—about 14 per day.
(5) Dictionaries and traditional classroom vocabulary lessons only account for part of this spectacular knowledge growth. More influential are individuals' reading habits and their interaction with people whose vocabularies are larger than
(10) their own. Reading shows students how words are used in sentences. Conversation offers several extra benefits that make vocabulary learning engaging—conversation supplies visual information, offers frequent repetition of new
(15) words, and gives students the chance to ask questions.

14. The passage suggests that a child is most receptive to learning the meaning of new words

    A. when the child reaches high school age
    B. when the child is talking to other students
    C. when the child is assigned vocabulary exercises
    D. when the child is regularly told that he or she needs to improve
    E. when vocabulary learning is made interesting

15. The author's attitude toward children's vocabulary acquisition can best be described as one of

    A. amazement
    B. skepticism
    C. reverence
    D. apathy
    E. surprise

16. The author mentions that "the average person learns . . . about 14 words per day" (lines 3–4) most likely in order to

    A. argue that conversation is the most effective way for children to learn new vocabulary
    B. provide evidence that children learn vocabulary at an incredible rate
    C. supply evidence to discredit the idea that learning vocabulary in a traditional classroom setting actually helps students learn
    D. support the claim that children learn about 80,000 words between the ages of 1 and 17
    E. argue against the idea that adults possess a more impressive range of vocabulary than children

Questions 17–18 refer to the following stimulus.

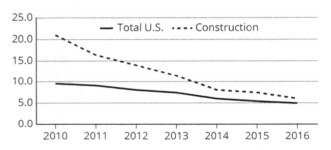

**Total Unemployment Rate &
Construction Unemployment Rate
(U.S. Annual Average, 2010–2016)**

Each month, the U.S. Bureau of Labor Statistics (BLS) publishes information about the unemployment rate (percentage of workforce unemployed) for both individual industries and the nation as a whole. The chart plots the average annual unemployment rates for the entire nation and the construction industry from 2010 to 2016. The BLS publishes both unadjusted and seasonally adjusted figures. The data in this chart are unadjusted.

17. Given the information provided in the chart, which of the following is a true statement?

    A. Between the years of 2010 and 2016 inclusive, the unemployment rate for the U.S. construction industry never exceeded 20 percent.

    B. The difference in the unemployment rates of the U.S. construction industry and the U.S. workforce as a whole remained very nearly the same from 2010 to 2016.

    C. The unemployment rate for the U.S. workforce as a whole never exceeded 8 percent during the years 2010 to 2016 inclusive.

    D. The difference between the unemployment rates of the construction industry and the total U.S. workforce shrank between 2010 and 2016.

    E. There are two years in the 2010–2016 period during which the total U.S. workforce unemployment rate did not decrease.

18. If the most recent trend shown in the total U.S. workforce unemployment rate continued for 2017–2019,

    A. the unemployment rate would start climbing toward its 2012 level

    B. the unemployment rate would stay at nearly the same level as it was in 2016

    C. the total workforce unemployment rate would fall to nearly zero within the next few years

    D. the gap between the construction industry unemployment rate and the total workforce unemployment rate would begin to widen again

    E. the construction industry unemployment rate would fall to nearly zero within a few years

Animals that use coloring to safeguard themselves from predators are said to have *protective coloration*. Many animals change their protective pigmentation with the seasons. The caribou sheds its brown coat in winter, replacing it with white fur. The stoat, a member of the weasel family, is known as the ermine in winter, when its brown fur changes to the white fur prized by royalty. The chameleon, even more versatile than these, changes color in just a few minutes to match whatever surface it happens to be lying on or clinging to.

19. The feature of the chameleon discussed in this passage is its ability to

    A. camouflage itself despite frequent changes in location

    B. cling to surfaces that are hidden from attackers

    C. adapt easily to seasonal changes

    D. use disruptive coloring to confuse predators

    E. change the colors of surfaces it is resting on

Hernan Cortez came to the New World in search of gold, but his interest was also fired by the Aztecs' strange drink, which was made from cacao beans. When Cortez returned to Spain, his ship's cargo included three chests of cacao beans. It was from these beans that Europeans experienced their first taste of what seemed to be a very unusual beverage.

20. In the first sentence, the word *fired* most nearly means

    A. burned

    B. stimulated

    C. removed

    D. surprised

    E. dulled

Questions 21–25 refer to the following stimulus.

Passage 1

Yawning is the human body's way of crying out for more oxygen in the bloodstream. Most yawns occur when a person is tired or bored. At such times, the body is not functioning at its optimal level and requires an increase in oxygen to return to normal activities. The respiratory system responds to this need by producing a yawn. The deep breath of a yawn provides a sudden increase in the amount of oxygen in the blood and simultaneously rids the body of the excess carbon dioxide that has accumulated because of oxygen deficiency.

Passage 2

Recent studies have shown that the number of times a person yawns is not affected by the amount of oxygen in the air he or she breathes. Oxygen-rich, oxygen-depleted, and normal air all lead to the same average number of yawns in a given time period. Respiration, therefore, is not the primary function of yawning. It is far more likely that yawning is actually a stretching mechanism. Both stretching and yawning most commonly occur during periods of tiredness. Particularly strong support for this theory is found in the behavior of people who are paralyzed on one side of their bodies from a stroke. It has been observed that such people can stretch limbs on the otherwise paralyzed sides of their bodies when they yawn.

21. There is no correlation between the amount of oxygen in the air and the number of times a person yawns in a day. This statement, if true, would best support the argument of

   A. Passage 1, because respiration is not a function of yawning

   B. Passage 1, because stretching is not a function of yawning

   C. Passage 2, because respiration is not a function of yawning

   D. Passage 2, because stretching is not a function of yawning

   E. Both passages, because neither respiration nor stretching is a function of yawning

22. The authors of Passage 1 and Passage 2 would agree that

   A. yawns are caused by tiredness or boredom

   B. the primary cause of yawns is biological, not social

   C. yawns are caused by a need to stretch

   D. yawning elevates the level of oxygen in the bloodstream

   E. nearly all scientists agree on the primary cause of yawning

23. In Passage 2, what could be the author's reason for including the final sentence?

   A. It proves that respiration is not a function of yawning.

   B. It shows how the tiredness of a yawning person can be measured.

   C. It supports the idea that a person partially paralyzed by a stroke can sometimes move a paralyzed limb.

   D. It suggests that higher levels of oxygen in the blood can improve mobility for paralyzed individuals.

   E. It supports the claim that stretching and yawning are closely associated.

24. A sleep center found that individuals who had been awake more than 24 hours yawned 1.5 times more frequently than those who had been awake for fewer than 12 hours. What conclusion would both authors draw from this information?

    A. The author of Passage 1 would conclude that a lack of sleep caused an increased need to stretch. The author of Passage 2 would conclude that a lack of sleep caused an increased need for oxygen.

    B. The author of Passage 1 would conclude that a lack of sleep caused an increased need for oxygen. The author of Passage 2 would conclude that the lack of sleep caused an increased need to stretch.

    C. The two authors would agree that lack of sleep caused an increased need for oxygen.

    D. The two authors would agree that lack of sleep caused an increased need to stretch.

    E. The two authors would conclude that a lack of sleep caused both an increased need for oxygen and an increased need to stretch.

25. According to the author of Passage 1, doing which of the following would keep a person from yawning?

    A. Increasing the amount of carbon dioxide in the bloodstream

    B. Stretching throughout the day

    C. Reducing pressure on the lungs

    D. Increasing the amount of oxygen in the bloodstream

    E. Finding a less boring job

Core Reading Pre-Test Answers and Explanations

1. C

The question asks which statement is *not true* according to the passage. The last sentence of the first paragraph states that during the 14th century, a "hooping" craze in England was popular with both kids and adults, making **(C)** untrue and thus correct. The other choices, all of which are supported by statements in the passage, can be eliminated.

2. B

The primary purpose of a passage must be supported by every part of the passage. Here, the purpose of the passage is to present the history of the Hula Hoop, **(B)**. While choice (C) is mentioned in the passage, it is simply a detail, not the primary purpose, and can be eliminated. The passage does not question why the Hula Hoop is popular, so (D) is out. And no broader thought related to other fads besides the Hula Hoop is presented, so eliminate (A) and (E).

3. A

Since you are being asked to infer the answer, it will not be directly stated in the passage. However, the correct answer will be based unambiguously on the information provided. Since nothing in the passage suggests that Hawaii is connected with the toy called the Hula Hoop—only that British sailors saw a resemblance between the hula dance and the motions of someone attempting to keep the hoop off the ground—choices (B) and (D) are wrong. And there is no comparison of degrees of popularity of the Hula Hoop and its forerunners, so (C) is also wrong. Choice (E) may be true, but it is not implied by the passage. In all of the time periods mentioned in the passage, humans were able to find time for play, which implies that engaging in play is a universal behavior of humans. That makes **(A)** correct.

4. C

The passage begins with the earliest forerunner of the Hula Hoop and gives examples of where hoop toys have been popular down through history. The passage presents these examples in the order in which they occurred, so choice **(C)** is correct. The passage draws no conclusions, so (A) and (B) are out. Although the passage mentions geographic locations, there is no clear pattern in their presentation, so (D) is wrong. And choice (E) makes no sense at all, since "holistically" does not describe a method of organization.

5. C

The writer's descriptions of the effects of the Industrial Revolution are almost entirely negative. While first acknowledging that the Industrial Revolution provided consumers with more goods, the writer then says that the era resulted in poor working conditions and pollution in cities when people emigrated from rural areas. In addition, it greatly harmed the natural environment. This characterization fits choice **(C)**. Because the writer has scant praise for the Industrial Revolution's increase in material comforts, rule out (A) and (B). The writer barely mentions scientific and technological advances, so eliminate (D). Finally, choice (E) distorts the writer's view of the lives of people who migrated from rural areas to the cities—while the Industrial Revolution may have provided job opportunities, the harsh realities of those jobs were not worth the benefits.

6. A

Be sure to read the question before the passage: think about the passage's organization as you read. Note Structural Keywords like "Although," "And indeed," and "However," which signal the flow of the passage. The author first provides reasons why people typically do not eat acorns even though squirrels do, and then the author changes directions ("However...") and explains how native Californians have found ways around these problems. This makes choice **(A)** correct. Choice (B) misconstrues the tone of the passage, which never presents "arguments." The passage never compares or contrasts "types of food" as in (C); it only discusses acorns. Although the first half of (D) sounds reasonable—as it could be considered a "misconception" that humans cannot eat acorns—the second half of (D) incorrectly states that the last part of the passage confirms, rather than disproves, this misconception. Finally, the passage does not list examples, nor does it "evaluate" any "methods," so (E) is out.

7. D

For this analogy question, you must select the answer that best completes the author's line of thought. Because the author clearly believes in the primacy of genetics, you need a completing statement that illustrates this belief. Only choice (**D**) does this; it states that if one plants tomatoes, one will get tomatoes, not some other plant. That's genetics.

8. B

The passage is about James Naismith's invention of the current version of basketball in 1891. Choice (**B**) is therefore correct. Choices (A) and (D) are both mentioned in the passage, but each is too narrow in scope to address the passage as a whole. Choice (C) is a distortion; basketball's popularity in Mesoamerica is never mentioned. Choice (E) is also a distortion that fails to address Naismith's role in creating the current version of the game.

9. A

To answer this Detail question, scan the passage for a reference to *foot* or *feet*. The first such mention is in the third sentence, which states: "An *iamb* is a grouping (also known as a *foot*) of two syllables…" Clearly, then, a foot is a grouping of syllables, and choice (**A**) is correct.

10. C

While you cannot make a specific prediction, keep in mind the author's explanatory tone as you evaluate the answer choices. The author makes no claims about what type of meter best conveys drama and emotion, as in (A), or whether the study of poetry is a worthwhile pursuit, (B). The author states that "Shakespeare is perhaps the most famous writer of iambic pentameter," so logically, there must be other writers who used this device. Choice (**C**) is therefore correct. Although it seems likely that Shakespeare wrote in other meters, the passage never states or implies this, so (D) is wrong. The passage states that iambs put stress on the *second* syllable, so (E) is incorrect.

11. E

Review what the author states about Shakespeare so you can determine which statement must logically follow. If Shakespeare did indeed *popularize* iambic pentameter "for the masses," it must be true that "many people" heard and liked his poems, choice (**E**). Although (A) is factually true, the question asks for something that can be inferred from the passage, which discusses Shakespeare only as a poet and never hints at his being a playwright. Although he "composed hundreds of poems in this meter," you cannot determine from this that Shakespeare wrote "over 300" (B); perhaps he wrote 250. Nothing in the passage hints at the author's personal favorite poet, (C). Finally, rule out (D), since the passage's only mention of social class is that Shakespeare popularized iambic pentameter "for the masses."

12. C

This passage describes the field of proxemics and concludes by linking proxemics with how diplomats are trained to engage members of different cultures. This implies that the use of space and spatial boundaries is important to diplomats, so (**C**) is correct. Choice (A) is a distortion; the passage does not suggest that Hall was a diplomat. (B) is contradicted by the passage, which states that cultures vary in their use of space and spatial boundaries. (D) is contradicted by the fact that Hall's findings have influenced the training diplomats receive—a practical application of proxemics. Finally, there is no support for choice (E) in the passage.

13. D

According to the passage, the word *tungsten* comes from the Swedish language, in which *tung sten* means "heavy stone." Choice (**D**) is correct.

14. E

There is no sentence in the passage that directly states "Children are most receptive to learning new words…" Look for the evidence that is provided to answer this Inference question. In lines 7–10, the author mentions that reading and conversation are particularly helpful. Lines 13–16 note how conversation is engaging. These claims are consistent with (**E**)—children learn "when vocabulary learning is made interesting." There is nothing in the passage to suggest that children learn more at high school age (A). Choice (B) might be tempting, but it is too specific. There's no reason to believe that talking to students is more helpful than talking to anyone else. In fact, the passage implies students learn more when speaking with older individuals "whose vocabularies are larger than their own" (lines 9–10). Choice (C) contradicts the passage, and (D) is never mentioned at all.

15. A

Research the passage for hints about the author's view of vocabulary acquisition. The author refers to children's "almost unbelievable talent" (line 1) and their "spectacular knowledge growth" (lines 6–7), and the author cites data about the average number of words children learn per day. Predict that the author is strongly favorably impressed by children's ability to learn words. This prediction matches "amazement," (**A**). The author never expresses doubt, or "skepticism," about vocabulary acquisition, (B), nor is the author *surprised*, (E), by it. The author's forceful language means he is certainly not *apathetic*, (D). The word "reverence," (C), is a strongly positive word but means "a feeling of awed respect"; while the author is impressed by children's abilities, he is not deferential or worshipful of them.

16. B

Before looking at the answer choices, predict why the author includes the detail mentioned in the question stem. In the first sentence of the passage, the author claims that "Children have an almost unbelievable talent for learning vocabulary." The next sentence provides data to support this claim, including the detail mentioned in the question stem. Therefore, (**B**) is correct. Choices (A) and (E) incorrectly state that the author is making an argument—while the author does claim children have an "almost unbelievable talent," the overall passage is not argumentative. And although the author later claims that conversation (A) "offers several extra benefits" (lines 11–12), the detail in the question stem does not relate to this claim. The detail in the question stem also does not relate to children's learning in traditional classrooms, (C), and is just another way of restating choice (D) rather than evidence to support that claim.

17. D

This question requires a careful look at the trends shown in the chart. Construction industry unemployment exceeded 20 percent in 2010, so choice (A) is incorrect. The difference between the two unemployment rates decreased steadily throughout this period, so eliminate (B). The total workforce unemployment rate was nearly 10 percent (and certainly higher than 8 percent) in 2010, so rule out (C). And since total workforce unemployment declined through the period, (E) is incorrect. That leaves (**D**), and indeed, the space between the two trendlines decreased throughout the period so that, by 2016, it was only a fraction of what it had been in 2010.

18. B

To answer this question, extend the total workforce unemployment line according to its trend over the last couple of years shown—which was definitely leveling off. Thus, choice (**B**) is correct. There is no indication that unemployment would start to increase or fall significantly, so rule out (A) and (C). You have been tasked only with extending the total workforce unemployment trend, so there is no evidence for either (D) or (E).

19. A

The answer to this Detail question is explicitly stated in the passage: "The chameleon...changes color in just a few minutes to match whatever surface it happens to be lying on or clinging to." Choice (**A**) is correct. There is no evidence in the passage to support any of the other answer choices.

20. B

Cover the word *fired*, read the sentence, and predict the answer choice that best fits the context. It's obvious that Cortez's interest was made *stronger*. The only choice that fits is (**B**). Choice (D), "surprised," might have been tempting because the beverage is described as "very unusual" in the last sentence, but while Europeans and Cortez himself likely were surprised by the drink, the word *fired* refers to Cortez's *interest* in the drink, not to Cortez.

21. C

Passage 1 states clearly that the purpose of yawning is to increase the amount of oxygen in the bloodstream—a respiratory function. Therefore, if there is no correlation between the amount of oxygen in the area and the number of times a person yawns, then respiration would not appear to be a function of yawning, and choice (A) must be wrong. Since Passage 2 states that respiration is *not* the purpose of yawning, choice (**C**) is correct. The evidence cited does not rule out stretching as a function of yawning, so (B), (D), and (E) are all incorrect.

22. B

Neither author suggests that there might be a social cause of yawning, so choice (**B**) is correct. Although Passage 1 mentions that most yawns occur when a person is tired or bored, and Passage 2 says they usually occur during periods of tiredness, neither suggests tiredness or boredom as a cause—so eliminate (A). Only the author of Passage 2 might agree with (C), and only the author of Passage 1 would agree with (D), so both of those choices are wrong. Finally, (E) is incorrect because the two authors disagree with each other.

23. E

The author of Passage 2 doesn't suggest that this evidence proves anything, so choice (A) is incorrect. Neither (B) nor (D) is a subject of the passage, so rule them out. Since choice (C) simply restates the last sentence of the passage, it provides no support for it. The evidence that a person paralyzed on one side of the body can stretch limbs on the paralyzed side of the body during yawns suggests that yawning and stretching are very closely related—making (**E**) correct.

24. B

Because Passage 1 claims that yawning is caused by an increased need for oxygen, rule out choices (A) and (D). Passage 2, on the other hand, maintains that yawning is a stretching mechanism, so (**B**) is correct. Choices (C) and (E) can be ruled out because the authors disagree on the cause of yawning.

25. D

Because the author of Passage 1 argues that yawning is caused by the need to raise the oxygen level in the bloodstream, it logically follows that increasing the amount of oxygen in the bloodstream would help prevent yawning, so choice (**D**) is correct. Choice (A) is the opposite, (B) is consistent with Passage 2, and (C) and (E) are not mentioned in either passage.

Introducing Praxis Core Reading

Reading comprehension tests are the "bread and butter" of standardized tests, and the Praxis Core Academic Skills for Teachers: Reading test is no exception. According to ETS, the Praxis Core Reading test measures "academic skills in reading needed to prepare successfully for a career in education." That sounds straight-forward enough. In fact, if you're reading this book, you're demonstrating skills in reading. But success on this test is about more than just reading and comprehending. It's about reading to answer multiple-choice questions.

There are three basic components of this reading test: the passages, the questions, and the answer choices. Each component can be handled strategically—you can squeeze the test for all it's worth to get maximum points.

Know What to Expect

Test Format

The Praxis Core Reading test contains several passages of varying lengths. The lengthier passages are approx-imately 200 words each, followed by four to seven questions. The shorter passages, about 100 words each, are followed by two or three questions. The test will include a set of paired passages on related topics, which total about 200 words, followed by four to seven questions. You will also encounter some brief statements, each followed by a single question. Finally, about three questions will accompany information presented in a chart or graph. Altogether, you will be required to answer 56 multiple-choice questions in 85 minutes. As with all Praxis exams, there is no penalty for incorrect answers, so be sure to answer every question, even if you have to guess.

PRAXIS CORE READING
Format: Computer-delivered
Number of Questions: 56 Time: 85 minutes
Question Types: multiple-choice (called "selected-response" by the testmaker) with one correct answer; multiple-choice with one or more correct answers Questions will be based either on statements or passages or on a chart or graph
Test may include questions that do not count toward your score
No penalty for incorrect answers
Scratch paper is available during the exam (it will be destroyed before you leave the testing center)

Regardless of the length of the passage, the multiple-choice questions will be based exclusively on the passage's content. You will never be expected to bring any outside knowledge to bear on the questions. In fact, it can be dangerous to mentally add material to the passage, as doing so may make wrong answer choices seem more tempting. Keep your focus exclusively on what is stated in the passage. You may be required to make infer-ences or identify assumptions on the test, but even the answers to these questions will be based entirely on what is written in the passage and not on any outside knowledge you might have.

The vast majority of questions on the Praxis Core Reading test require you to select one answer from among five choices. Expect to see at least one question that requires you to choose all the answers that apply; to get credit for the question, you must select all the answers that are accurate, which could be anywhere from one to all of the answer choices. To indicate the difference, these questions will always include the special "Select all that apply" instruction and will have a box, instead of an oval, in front of each answer choice.

The questions in Core Reading fall into one of three basic categories: 1) Key Ideas and Details; 2) Craft, Structure, and Language Skills; and 3) Integration of Knowledge and Ideas. According to ETS, each category will comprise about a third of the questions on the Core Reading test, although Craft, Structure, and Language Skills will account for slightly fewer questions.

Key Ideas and Details questions require you to both understand the content of the passage itself and comprehend the implications of the passage's content. For instance, you may have to identify the main idea or purpose of the passage or identify a specific detail within the passage. Some of these questions are relatively straightforward; the challenge is to find the correct answer as quickly and efficiently as possible. The Kaplan Method for Reading and the Reading Strategies in the following pages will teach you how to do just that. Trick answers on these questions generally distort the meaning of the passage or focus on a scope that is broader or narrower than what appears in the passage. Additionally, Key Ideas and Details questions may ask you to apply your understanding of the passage's broad ideas and details by determining inferences that logically proceed from the passage content.

Craft, Structure, and Language Skills questions test your ability to understand the mechanics of a passage: how an author uses words, organization, and writing techniques to convey the passage's intended meaning. For instance, you may be asked what a particular word means in a given context or what a word reveals about the author's viewpoint or tone. You may have to provide an explanation of the structure of a passage. You may also be asked how the author uses information or writing techniques and what functions they fulfill in achieving the author's purpose. Finally, these questions may ask what all these features of writing mechanics reveal about the author's particular viewpoint.

Integration of Knowledge and Ideas questions require you to pull together information from multiple sources or multiple ideas from within one passage, then interpret or apply that integrated information. Some of these questions will require you to read and interpret information presented visually in a chart or graph. Others will ask you to analyze the parts of an argument made in a passage, perhaps assessing the strengths, weaknesses, assumptions, evidence, and/or relevance of the argument. They may ask you to determine how ideas within a passage relate, or apply ideas from the passage to new situations. Finally, these questions may test your ability to integrate ideas by comparing and contrasting the approaches of different authors in paired passage sets.

Regardless of the nature of the material you encounter on your test, a systematic approach to handling the passages, questions, and answer choices will help you move through the test with confidence, efficiency, and accuracy.

How to Approach Praxis Reading

As we already mentioned, you have 85 minutes to complete 56 questions about passages of varying lengths. That translates to about a minute and a half per question. When you consider the fact that while you are reading the passage, you are not answering questions, you quickly realize that this test does not give you a lot of time to work on each passage and question.

The lack of time makes it essential to move forward steadily on this test. Spending more than two or three minutes on a single question will jeopardize your ability to get a good look at every question. If a question gives you trouble, mark the question for review and move on. If you have time, return to the question, eliminate any answer choices you can, and guess. However, learn to let go of a question if need be, especially if there are other questions and passages you haven't seen yet.

Because there is no penalty for wrong answers on this exam, you should never leave any questions unanswered, even if that means taking random guesses at the end of the exam. Ideally, you will manage your time such that you get a decent look at every question and eliminate at least some wrong answer choices. However, if you are pressed for time, guessing is the best option.

Also, be aware that short passages are normally accompanied by a single question. Longer passages may have four or more questions associated with them. That means you should spend more time on the passages that translate to the most points. You can quickly skim short passages and passages with only one or two questions.

How to Read for Points

The passages on the Praxis Core Reading test are drawn from a wide variety of topics—everything from art and science to business, politics, biography, and history. If you were reading them out of personal interest, you might take your time and re-read confusing portions or jargon. But on this test, you're reading for points, which is an entirely different proposition.

Almost all reading passages on the Praxis Core Reading test, no matter what the length or subject matter, share one important characteristic: compared to typical reading material, these passages are dense with information. This is one reason why they can be difficult to slog through when you apply a normal reading approach. Not only is it useless to try to absorb everything you read on a Praxis reading passage, but doing so is likely to slow you down and hurt your score.

How Not to Read

1. Don't try to understand the passage thoroughly. Doing so is a waste of time.
2. Don't get caught up in the details.
3. Don't treat every part of the passage as equally important. Search for the answer you are looking for, find it, and move on.

Never forget that your goal in this section is to answer the questions correctly. You get no points for having an especially thorough understanding of the passage. To get the score you're aiming for, you need to develop a method for handling questions quickly without getting bogged down with your reading of the passages. In fact, you need to learn to spend less time reading the passages so that you can spend more time understanding the questions and finding the correct answers. Let's quickly take a look at the components of a typical Reading passage and question.

The Taj Mahal was built by the Mughal
emperor Shah Jahan as a burial place for his
favorite consort, Arjumand Banu Begum. She
was known as Mumtaz Mahal, "the Elect of
(5) the Palace." Construction began soon after
her death in 1631. The Taj Mahal and the
surrounding complex of buildings and gardens
were completed around 1653. However, the
Taj Mahal is much more than an expression of
(10) love and loss. It's a breathtakingly symmetrical
representation of heaven.

1. The passage is primarily concerned with

    A. the Taj Mahal as an expression of love and loss

    B. the history of the building of the Taj Mahal

    C. the Taj Mahal as an architectural representation of heaven

    D. the balance between the building and the gardens in the Taj Mahal complex

    E. the importance of the Taj Mahal to the Mughal empire

This passage is full of dates, names, and all sorts of other information. All those details are not worth sweating over unless there is a question about them, in which case you'd zero in on the specific detail to answer the question. However, this question isn't focused on the details; this question asks about the passage as a whole.

Each of the wrong answer choices focuses too narrowly on a detail. Only choice (**B**) is broad enough to address the whole passage, which is about the history of the building of the Taj Mahal.

Now that we've covered the basics of how to read for points, it's time to look in detail at the Kaplan Method for Reading.

The Kaplan Four-Step Method for Praxis Reading

If you approach every passage the same way, you will work your way through the Reading test efficiently.

THE KAPLAN METHOD FOR PRAXIS READING

STEP 1: Read the passage

STEP 2: Decode the question

STEP 3: Research the detail

STEP 4: Predict the answer and evaluate the answer choices

The Kaplan Method for Reading requires you to do most of your work before you actually get around to answering the questions. It's very tempting to read the questions and immediately jump to the answer choices. Don't do this. The work you do up front not only saves you time in the long run but also increases your chances of avoiding the tempting wrong answers.

Step 1. Read the Passage

The first thing you're going to do in most cases is read the passage itself. This should not come as a big surprise. It's important to realize that while you don't want to memorize or dissect the passage, you do need to read it. If you try to answer the questions without reading it, you're likely to waste time and make mistakes. Although you'll learn more about how to read passages later in this chapter, keep in mind that the main things you're looking for when you read a passage are the Main Idea and the paragraph topics, both of which are often indicated by keywords.

For example, the following sample passage has the Main Idea and some keywords underlined and annotated:

The <u>first detective stories</u>, written by Edgar Allan Poe and Arthur Conan Doyle, emerged in the mid-19th century, at a time when there was an <u>enormous public interest</u> in scientific progress.	**This passage is basically about detective stories and science.**
(5) The newspapers of the day continually publicized the latest scientific discoveries, and scientists were <u>acclaimed as the heroes</u> of the age. Poe and Conan Doyle shared this fascination with the step-by-step, logical approach used by scientists in their (10) experiments. These writers instilled their detective heroes with <u>outstanding</u> powers of scientific reasoning.	**Poe and Conan Doyle seem to be important.**
The character of Sherlock Holmes, for <u>example</u>, illustrates Conan Doyle's <u>admiration</u> for the scientific (15) mind. In each case that Holmes investigates, he is able to use the most insubstantial evidence to track down his opponent. Using only his restless eye and <u>ingenious</u> reasoning powers, Holmes pieces together the identity of the villain from such unremarkable (20) details as the type of cigar ashes left at the crime scene or the kind of ink used in a handwritten letter. <u>In fact</u>, Holmes's painstaking attention to detail often reminds the reader of Charles Darwin's *On the Origin of Species*, published some 20 years earlier.	**Holmes is an example of a detective with a scientific mind.** **Ways that Holmes uses a scientific approach.** **Author/Doyle thinks Holmes is impressive.** **Comparison between Holmes and Darwin**

Again, you'll spend more time a little later learning how to read the passage. The point here is that the first thing you'll do is read through the entire passage, noting the major themes and a few details.

Step 2. Decode the Question

The first thing you'll need to do with each question is to decode it. In other words, you need to figure out exactly what the question is asking before you can answer the question. Basically, you need to make the question make sense to you.

> Which of the following is implied by the statement that Holmes was able to identify the villain based on "unremarkable details"?

Essentially, this question is asking what the author means by mentioning "unremarkable details." Looking at it in this way makes the answer clearer.

Exception: Check the instructions before reading a passage. If you see there is only one question related to the passage (a common occurrence with short statement passages), read the question stem before reading the passage so you know precisely what you need to get out of the text. This will save time, because you can often skim or ignore portions of the passage as you search for the information you need to answer the single question.

Step 3. Research the Details

This does not mean that you should start re-reading the passage from the beginning to find the reference to "unremarkable details." Focus your research. Where does the author mention Holmes? You should have noted when you read the passage that the author discusses Holmes in the second paragraph. So scan the second paragraph for the reference to "unremarkable details." (Hint: you can find the reference in lines 19–20.)

A common mistake to avoid is answering questions based on memory. Go back and do the research. Generally, if you can answer most questions correctly based on memory, you have spent too much time on the passage.

Step 4. Predict the Answer and Evaluate the Answer Choices

When you find the detail in the passage, think about the purpose that it serves. Why does the author mention "unremarkable details"? If you read the lines surrounding the phrase, you should see that the author is discussing how amazing it is that Holmes can solve mysteries based on so little evidence (as he is "able to use the most insubstantial evidence to track down his opponent" in lines 16–17). Therefore, the reason the author mentions "unremarkable details" is to show how impressive Holmes is. And now that you have predicted the answer, scan your answer choices.

- A. Holmes's enemies left no traces at the crime scene.
- B. The character of Holmes was based on Charles Darwin.
- C. Few real detectives would have been capable of solving Holmes's cases.
- D. Holmes was particularly brilliant in powers of detection.
- E. Criminal investigation often involves tedious, time-consuming tasks.

While you can quickly dismiss most of the answers because they do not match your prediction, choice (**D**) should leap out at you as a perfect match. Predicting an answer allows you to briskly eliminate incorrect answer choices, avoid tempting wrong answer choices, and zero in on the correct answer. Now that you've seen how to apply the Kaplan Method, it's time to back up a little and look more specifically at how to approach passages.

The Passage

As you learned earlier, reading for points is not exactly like the reading you do in school or at home. As a general rule, you read to learn or you read for pleasure. It's a pretty safe bet that you're not reading Praxis Reading passages for the fun of it. If you happen to enjoy it, that's a fabulous perk, but most people find these passages pretty dry. You should also be clear about the fact that you are not reading these passages to learn anything. You are reading these passages so that you can answer questions. That's it. Reading to answer a few questions is not the same thing as reading to learn.

The main difference between reading to learn and reading to answer questions is that the former is about knowledge and the latter is only about earning points. Anything that doesn't get you points is a waste of time for the purposes of the test. The Praxis Reading test is not a place to learn anything new. Therefore, your goal is to read in such a way that you maximize your chances of getting points on the questions. The questions will ask you about the Main Idea, a few details, a few inferences, and the author's writing strategy. You need to get enough out of the passage to deal with these questions.

Seven Praxis Reading Strategies

1. **Look for the Main Idea**
   The most important thing to pick up is the gist of the passage (i.e., the Main Idea and the paragraph topics). Praxis Reading passages are chosen because they are well organized; this means you will likely find the Main Idea very early in the passage text and the topic of each paragraph within the first one or two sentences of the paragraph. The remainder of a paragraph is likely to be more detail heavy. Remember that you can research the details as you need them later, using your paragraph notes to guide you to them.

2. **Take Paragraph Notes**
   You are provided scratch paper, so use this to your advantage. Do not take a lot of notes, but do jot down a very brief paraphrase of each paragraph. If you do not take any notes, you are putting yourself at a disadvantage. These passages can be dull and difficult to remember. Make it easy to find the stuff you'll need to answer the questions.

3. **Don't Sweat the Details**
   Don't waste time reading and re-reading parts you don't understand. As long as you have a general idea of where the details are, you don't have to really know what they are. Remember, if you don't get a question about a detail, you don't have to know it. Furthermore, as long as you have made a note of the paragraph topic, you should be able to go back and find the details. Details will always be consistent with the paragraph topics.

4. **Find Structural Keywords**
   Within each paragraph, some of the most important words are ones that you might typically gloss over: Structural Keywords. These are words that indicate the structure and direction of the passage. For instance, keywords such as *but*, *however*, and *although* indicate a contrast is coming. *As*, *and*, and *moreover* signal the continuation of an idea. Keywords such as *because* and *resulting in* may indicate a cause-and-effect relationship. An author may also use keywords to indicate the passage's organization; these keywords include *first*, *next*, and *in conclusion*. While you might typically skim over these words,

they are invaluable for answering Praxis questions because they reveal the structure of a passage and, therefore, the content of the paragraph notes you should take. Many Praxis questions center on Structural Keywords.

5. **Locate Opinions**

Some questions, including Global, Writer's View, and Connecting Ideas questions, will require you to understand the author's viewpoint. Therefore, it is important to note any opinions the author expresses in the passage. The most helpful indicator of the author's view is, again, keywords. Some Opinion Keywords—such as *excellent*, *remarkable*, or *horrifying*—obviously indicate a positive or negative view. Other Opinion Keywords are subtler, but if you practice looking out for words that signal the author's viewpoint, you will notice these too. Note that some passages may include the views of others (such as the views of people with whom the author disagrees), so be sure to keep viewpoints straight. Also be on the lookout for Emphasis Keywords (for instance, *enormous*, *outstanding*, and *ingenious* in the Holmes passage), which might not necessarily indicate an opinion but do signal important ideas in the passage.

6. **Make It Simple**

Sometimes, you'll come across difficult language and technical jargon in the passages. As much as possible, try not to get bogged down by language you find confusing. The underlying topics are generally pretty straightforward. It can be very helpful to put confusing-sounding language into your own words. You don't have to understand every word in order to summarize or paraphrase. All you need is a general understanding.

7. **Keep Moving**

Aim to move quickly through each passage. Remember, just reading the passage doesn't get you any points.

Reading Strategies Practice

Now it's time to see how one puts the Method into action on a passage. As you read the following passage, keep in mind the Reading Strategies. Remember not to focus on the details but rather to zero in on the Main Idea. As you work through the passage, think about why particular words are underlined as keywords and read the accompanying paragraph notes.

Greek Poetry Passage

The poems of the <u>earliest</u> Greeks, like those of other ancient societies, consisted of magical charms, mysterious predictions, prayers, and traditional songs of work and war. These

(5) poems were intended to be sung or recited, not written down, because they were created before the Greeks began to use writing for literary purposes. All that remains of them are fragments mentioned by later Greek writers.

(10) Homer, <u>for example</u>, quoted an ancient work song for harvesters, and Simonides adapted the ancient poetry of ritual lamentation (i.e., songs of mourning for the dead) in his writing.

The different forms of early Greek poetry

(15) all had something in <u>common</u>: they described the way of life of a whole people. Poetry expressed ideas and feelings that were shared by everyone in a community—their folktales, their memories of historical events, and their religious

(20) speculation. The poems were wholly impersonal, with little emphasis on individual achievement. It never occurred to the earliest Greek poets to tell us their names or to try to create anything completely new.

(25) In the "Age of Heroes," <u>however</u>, the content and purpose of Greek poetry changed. By this later period, Greek communities had become separated into classes of rulers and ruled. People living in the same community, <u>therefore</u>,

(30) had different, even opposed, interests; they shared fewer ideas and emotions. The particular outlook of the warlike upper class gave poetry a new content, one that focused on the lives of individuals. Poets were assigned a new task: to

(35) celebrate the accomplishments of outstanding characters, whether they were real or imaginary, <u>rather than</u> the activity and history of the community.

In the heroic age, poets became singers of

(40) tales who performed long poems about the fates of warriors and kings. One need only study Homer's *Iliad* and *Odyssey*, which are recorded examples of the epic poetry that was sung in the heroic age, to understand the influence that

(45) the upper class had on the poet's performance. <u>Thus</u>, the poetry of the heroic age can no longer be called folk poetry. <u>Nor</u> was the poetry of the heroic age nameless, and in this period, it lost much of its religious character.

Notice some of the keywords that signal the structure of this passage. "Earliest" in line 1 indicates the passage will begin by discussing early poetry, while "however" in line 25 indicates the switch to later poetry. Other keywords likewise signal the contrast between earlier and later Greek poetry: "rather than" in line 37 and "Nor" in line 47.

Now let's see how the Reading Strategies help with answering questions.

1. The passage is primarily concerned with

   A. how the role of early Greek poetry changed

   B. how Greek communities became separated into classes

   C. the superiority of early Greek poetry

   D. the origin of the *Iliad* and the *Odyssey*

   E. why little is known about early Greek poets

2. The author most likely mentions Homer and Simonides at the end of paragraph 1 in order to

    A. provide examples of early Greek poets

    B. demonstrate that such writers were ahead of their time

    C. illustrate the use of an oral tradition by later Greek writers

    D. criticize the simplicity of some poets' styles in Greek oral poetry

    E. honor two legendary Greek writers

3. Which of the following discoveries would strengthen the author's claims about Greek poetry in paragraph 2?

    Select all that apply.

    A. An early Greek poem about a village's collective praises to a god after a good harvest

    B. An early Greek poem celebrating the exploits of the warrior Diocles

    C. An undated Greek poem relaying an instructive fable

4. According to the passage, which of the following did poetry of the heroic age primarily celebrate?

    A. Community life

    B. Individuals

    C. Religious beliefs

    D. The value of work

    E. Common people

5. Which of the following best describes the organization of the passage?

    A. Two opposing views about poetry interpretation are presented, and one is rejected.

    B. A claim about historical poetry is presented, then undermined with evidence.

    C. The similarities among three historical periods are described.

    D. The poetry of two historical periods is explained chronologically in order to show the contrasts.

    E. The commonalities between the poems of two historical eras of the same culture are elucidated.

Notice that by using the Reading Strategies, you can answer many questions with the aid of your paragraph notes and the Main Idea you identified. You should research specific details only when you need to. Practice using these Reading Strategies on every Praxis Reading passage you encounter. You'll minimize the time you need to spend on each passage while maximizing your understanding of the material necessary to correctly answer questions.

Reading Strategies Practice Answers and Explanations

Main Idea: changes in ancient Gr. poetry

Paragraph 1:   intro early Gr. poetry, oral

Paragraph 2:   early: about community

Paragraph 3:   later: age of heroes, classes, individuals

Paragraph 4:   later cont'd: Homer, upper class, secular

1.   A

Remember to predict an answer to the question before looking at the answer choices! In this case, the question asks for the Main Idea of the passage. You should not need to re-read any of the passage text. Instead, look to the Main Idea identified in your notes. The Main Idea perfectly matches choice (**A**). (B) is outside the scope of this passage. (C) expresses an opinion that the author never expresses. (D) mentions the *Iliad* and the *Odyssey*, which are discussed only in paragraph 4. Likewise, (E) does not address the purpose of the entire passage.

2.   C

This question asks why the author decided to include a particular detail. Notice that the passage text includes the Structural Keywords "for example" in relation to these writers: questions often center on these types of keywords. This phrase indicates that the author included the writers as examples of "later Greek writers" who mentioned early Greek poetry. This matches choice (**C**). (A) distorts the intention of this detail, as Homer and Simonides are not themselves early Greek poets. (B), (D), and (E) each misrepresent the author's viewpoint, which is objective throughout the passage (note the lack of any Opinion Keywords); the author never claims any poets were "ahead of their time," criticizes, or seeks to honor anyone.

3.   A

The question stem asks which discoveries would support the author's description of Greek poetry in the second paragraph. Rather than wasting time re-reading paragraph 2, check the paragraph note: it may contain all you need to answer the question. The note indicates the paragraph discusses early Greek poetry and its emphasis on the community. Therefore, (B) can be eliminated because it is about an individual person, and (C) can be eliminated because it cannot be attributed to early poetry. (**A**) is the only match and is therefore correct. Only if your paragraph note is insufficient to answer the question should you research the paragraph text for additional information, using the note as the foundation of your thinking.

4.   B

This question stem asks for the subject of poetry during the heroic age. The paragraph notes indicate the answer will be found in paragraph 3 or 4, and they state that poetry of the heroic period was about individuals, the upper classes, and secular material. This matches choice (**B**). Choices (A), (C), and (E) all reflect early Greek poetry as described in the first two paragraphs. Choice (D) is outside the scope of the passage.

5.   D

To review the structure of the overall passage, consult the paragraph notes. The first two paragraphs describe early Greek poetry, while the last two paragraphs describe late Greek poetry. This matches choice (**D**). The other answer choices either do not match the organization identified in the notes or miss the Main Idea of the passage. (A) incorrectly identifies two opposing views. Notice that there were no Opinion Keywords in the passage text; the passage never discusses opposing viewpoints, and thus the author never rejects one. Likewise, the passage only describes periods of poetry; it does not attempt to undermine a claim, as in choice (B). (C) incorrectly identifies three periods instead of two. (E) focuses on the similarities rather than the differences between the passages.

The Questions

As you already know, Praxis Core Reading points come from answering the questions, not from absorbing everything in the passages. This doesn't mean that it is not important to approach the passage strategically—it is. However, if you do not answer the questions correctly, the passage hasn't done you much good.

Recall that there are three categories of question types on the Core Reading Test: Key Ideas and Details; Craft, Structure, and Language Skills; and Integration of Knowledge and Ideas. Before analyzing the types of questions you will encounter in each category, take three to four minutes to read the following passage. As always, read it with the goal of answering questions afterward: look for the Main Idea, take paragraph notes, locate keywords, and don't stress the details.

The <u>first</u> truly American art movement was formed by a group of landscape painters who emerged in the early 19th century and were called the Hudson River School. The

(5) first works in this style were created by Thomas Cole, Thomas Doughty, and Asher Durand—a trio of painters who worked during the 1820s in the Hudson River Valley and surrounding locations. Heavily

(10) influenced by European Romanticism, these painters set out to convey the remoteness and splendor of the American wilderness. The <u>strongly</u> nationalistic tone of their paintings caught the spirit of the times, and

(15) within a generation, the movement had mushroomed to include landscape painters from all over the United States. Canvases <u>celebrating</u> such typically American scenes as Niagara Falls, Boston Harbor, and

(20) the expansion of the railroad into rural Pennsylvania were greeted with <u>enormous popular acclaim</u>.

<u>One factor</u> contributing to the success of the Hudson River School was the rapid

(25) growth of American nationalism in the early 19th century. The War of 1812 had given the United States a new sense of pride in its identity, and as the nation continued to grow, there was a desire to compete with Europe

(30) on both economic and cultural grounds. The vast panoramas of the Hudson River School fit the bill perfectly by providing a new movement in art that was <u>unmistakably</u>

American in origin. The Hudson River School

(35) <u>also</u> arrived at a time when writers in the United States were turning their attention to the wilderness as a unique aspect of their nationality. The Hudson River School profited from this nostalgia because they

(40) effectively represented the continent the way it used to be. The view that the American character was formed by the frontier experience was widely held, and many writers were concerned about the future of

(45) a country that was becoming increasingly urbanized.

<u>In keeping</u> with this nationalistic spirit, <u>even</u> the painting style of the Hudson River School exhibited a strong sense of American

(50) identity. Although many of the artists studied in Europe, their paintings show a desire to be free of European artistic rules. Regarding the natural landscape as a direct manifestation of God, the Hudson River School painters

(55) attempted to record what they saw as accurately as possible. <u>Unlike</u> European painters, who brought to their canvases the styles and techniques of centuries, they sought neither to embellish nor to idealize

(60) their scenes, portraying nature with the care and attention to detail of naturalists.

Main Idea: describe HRS subject, success, and style (Am. nationalism)

Paragraph 1:   describe HRS = 1st Am. art movement

Paragraph 2:   reason success = nationalism: pride identity & value frontier

Paragraph 3:   style = Am. identity; not Eur.

Hopefully, you caught that this passage was about why the Hudson River School became so successful. You should have also noted that the second paragraph addresses how American nationalism contributed to the success of the Hudson River School, and the third paragraph discusses how nationalist sentiment was evident in the Hudson River School painting style. Now use this passage to learn about the characteristics and strategies of each of the question types that appear on the Praxis Reading test.

Key Ideas and Details Questions

Global Questions

A Global question asks you to summarize the topic, theme, or purpose of the passage. Keywords such as *primary*, *purpose*, or *main idea* can signal a Global question. The key strategy for Global questions is to look for an answer choice that captures the entire passage. Usually, the testmakers will try to distract you by having one or more answer choices focus on a detail or single paragraph. You need to recognize the choice that deals with the passage as a whole. As previously suggested, read every passage with the task of identifying the Main Idea in mind and include it in your notes; rarely, if ever, should you have to return to the passage text to answer a Global question.

> The passage is primarily concerned with
>
> A. the history of American landscape painting
> B. why an art movement caught the public imagination
> C. how European painters influenced the Hudson River School
> D. why writers began to romanticize the American wilderness
> E. the origins of nationalism in the United States

Do you see which one of these answers describes the entire passage without being too broad or too narrow?

(A) is too broad, as is (E). The passage is not about *all* American landscape painting; it's about the Hudson River School. Nationalism in the United States is a much larger topic than the role of nationalism in a particular art movement. On the other hand, (C) and (D) are too narrow. European painters did influence the Hudson River School painters, but that isn't the point of the whole passage. Similarly, writers are mentioned in paragraph 2, but the passage is about an art movement. Only **(B)** captures the essence of the passage—it's about an art movement that caught the public imagination.

Detail Questions

Detail questions are straightforward—all you have to do is locate the needed information in the passage. While Detail questions can be worded in various ways, the phrase *according to the passage* often signals a Detail question. The correct answer will be directly stated, though perhaps worded differently, in the passage text; you can put your finger on the information that answers the question. The key strategy is to use your notes to locate the relevant paragraph and research that portion of the text. Remember to predict an answer in your own words before looking at the answer choices.

Which of the following is NOT mentioned as contributing to the success of the Hudson River School?

A. American nationalism increased after the War of 1812.

B. Americans were nostalgic about the frontier.

C. Writers began to focus on the wilderness.

D. The United States wanted to compete with Europe.

E. City dwellers became concerned about environmental pollution.

Before reading the answer choices, paraphrase some of the reasons for the Hudson River School's success: nationalism, postwar pride, a desire to be equal with Europe, and the nostalgic appeal of the frontier. The passage mentions four of the five answer choices explicitly. (A) is mentioned in lines 23–30. (B) appears in line 39. (C) shows up in lines 35–37. (D) is mentioned in lines 28–29. Only (E) does not appear in the passage. Since you need the choice that is NOT mentioned, (E) is correct.

Inference Questions

An Inference question, like a Detail question, asks you to find relevant information in the passage. However, once you've located the detail, you've got to go one step further to figure out the underlying meaning of a particular phrase or example. The passage will not directly state the correct answer, but you can put your finger on evidence in the passage that directly supports the answer. The correct answer to an Inference question logically follows the information in the passage text. Wrong answer choices will often contain information beyond the subject matter of the passage. You can often spot Inference questions because they contain keywords such as *implies*, *suggests*, or *infers*.

Which of the following best describes what is suggested by the statement that the Hudson River School paintings "fit the bill perfectly" (line 32)?

A. The paintings depicted famous battle scenes.

B. The paintings were very successful commercially.

C. The paintings reflected a new pride in the United States.

D. The paintings were favorably received in Europe.

E. The paintings were accurate in their portrayal of nature.

The keyword "suggested" signals an Inference question. Remember that the passage text will not directly state the answer, but you will use the evidence in the passage to predict what the author means by the phrase. First, read the lines surrounding the quote to put the quote in context. Paragraph 2 discusses the reason for the Hudson River School's success: its portrayal of American identity when Americans were highly nationalistic. That's why the paintings "fit the bill." The previous sentence refers to America's "new sense of pride in its identity" and "desire to compete with Europe on…cultural grounds." (C) summarizes the point nicely. Note that this question revolves around the interplay between the Main Idea of the passage and certain details within it. The detail in the question stem supports the topic of the paragraph—the growing sense of nationalism in America. (A) superficially relates to the War of 1812 but does not answer the question. (B) and (D) are way off base; (E) includes a detail that is found to be relevant later on in the passage, but it does not capture the gist of the inference.

Craft, Structure, and Language Skills Questions

Vocabulary-in-Context Questions

While Vocabulary-in-Context questions do require you to possess a college-level vocabulary, they are less about definitions and more about understanding how a word is used in the context of an overall passage—hence, Vocabulary-*in-Context* questions. The key strategy is to locate the word in the passage text, pretend the word is a blank, and then predict a word to substitute for the blank *before looking at the answer choices*. Base your prediction on the context of the surrounding text; sometimes you may need to re-read before and after the relevant sentence to truly understand the context. Sometimes, your prediction will actually match one of the choices; select it and you're done. Even if your prediction doesn't exactly match an answer choice, making a prediction will still help you know what type of word you need. Trap answers on Vocabulary-in-Context questions are often common meanings of the word that do not fit the context of the passage. Therefore, take a moment to re-read your word choice back into the passage text to make sure it fits in context before selecting your answer choice.

> Which of the following words, if substituted for the word "celebrating" in line 18, would introduce the LEAST change in the meaning of the sentence?
>
> A. praising
> B. portraying
> C. worshipping
> D. observing
> E. partying

Remember the strategy: pretend the word is a blank and then predict a word to substitute for the blank. Consider the context: the paragraph describes how the Hudson River School paintings captured the "strongly nationalistic tone" (line 13) of the times, leading to their being received with "enormous popular acclaim" (lines 21–22). Some of these Emphasis Keywords may have stuck out when you first read the text. Since the passage uses the word "celebrating" to describe how Hudson River School painters depicted nationalistic scenes like Boston Harbor in a way that would draw public approval, predict that the word must mean *positively portraying*. This matches choice (**A**). Choices (B) and (D) are too neutral in tone for the contextual meaning of "celebrating." (C) is too extreme, while (E) uses a common meaning of the word that does not fit in context.

Function Questions

Rather than asking you about the meaning of content in a passage, Function questions ask you about *how* the author uses elements of the passage. In other words, what *function* does something serve in the passage? Key phrases such as *the author mentions* and *in order to* often signal a Function question. Function questions may ask about the use of a particular word, phrase, paragraph, or writing device—or even about the organization of the entire passage. The key strategy for Function questions is to locate the relevant portion of the text and use your notes to determine what role the text in question serves in the context of the entire passage. For instance, a portion of text could provide evidence, supply an example, provide a contrasting viewpoint, or contribute to an author's Main Idea. Trap answers may include an actual detail or point of the passage but not represent the function of the particular text in question. For Function questions that ask about the overall organization of the passage, use your notes to review the purpose of each paragraph and then find the answer choice that matches your prediction.

The passage most likely mentions the War of 1812 (line 26) in order to

A. refute the perceived inferiority of America

B. criticize European interference in America

C. provide an example of the Hudson River School's subject matter

D. identify a source of American nationalism

E. praise American nationalism

For Function questions, be sure to keep the author's overall purpose in mind: to describe the Hudson River School's subjects, success, and style. The correct function of a portion of the passage must be in line with the author's overall purpose. The cited text appears in paragraph 2, so use your notes to determine the purpose of this phrase in context. Paragraph 2 identifies the growth of American nationalism as contributing to the success of the Hudson River School, and it describes sources of this sentiment. The context around line 26 states that the War of 1812 "had given the United States a new sense of pride in its identity" (lines 26–28), so this must be the author's reason for mentioning the War of 1812: as a source of the growing nationalism. Choice (**D**) perfectly matches that prediction. Choices (A), (B), and (E) can be eliminated because they do not match the author's overall purpose: the author does not "refute" or "criticize," and while the author seems to have a positive view of the Hudson River School, he does not expressly "praise" it. Choice (C) misrepresents the function of the cited phrase. Although the War of 1812 could have provided subject matter for the painters, the passage does not identify it as such; its mention instead functions to identify a source of nationalism.

Writer's View Questions

Writer's View questions require you to understand the nuances of the author's viewpoint and his or her approach to the passage's subject matter. These questions may contain key phrases such as *author's attitude*, as they ask you about the attitude of the author toward a portion or Main Idea of the text. The key strategy for these questions is to develop an understanding of the author's view when first reading the passage, then predict and choose answers that match this viewpoint. To identify the author's view, remember to look for Opinion and Emphasis Keywords when reading the passage; these words will help you determine a Main Idea that aligns with the author's viewpoint. For instance, keywords may indicate that the author favors something, opposes something, is merely describing something, or perhaps takes a more nuanced view. Trap answers for Writer's View questions often misrepresent the author's attitude (for instance, stating the author favors a view while the author only reports on it objectively) or present the view of someone else in the passage.

The author's attitude toward the Hudson River School can be described by which of the following statements?

Select <u>all</u> that apply.

A. Its artwork represents the best painting style to ever originate in America.

B. Its style differed from the style of contemporary European artwork.

C. It was artistically superior to contemporary European artwork.

It can be difficult to make specific predictions for questions that ask about the author's attitude, but keep in mind the author's overall purpose: to describe the subjects, success, and style of the Hudson River School. The correct answer will likely be similarly objective in tone, as the author does not express opinions about the art in the passage. With the overall view in mind, evaluate each answer choice. Eliminate (A), as the author never expresses a view about the superiority of the Hudson River School, saying only that it was the "first truly

American art movement" (line 1). Use your notes to research choice (B). Paragraph 3 contrasts the Hudson River School style with the European style: though "influenced by European Romanticism" (line 10), the American "paintings show a desire to be free of European artistic rules" (lines 51–52), and the painters were "unlike European painters" (lines 56–57). Therefore, the author would likely agree with (B). Evaluate (C) as well, as more than one answer could be correct. You can eliminate (C) for the same reason as with (A); the author never claims the artwork is "superior." Therefore, **(B)** alone is correct.

Integration of Knowledge and Ideas

Infographics Questions

One way you may be asked to integrate ideas is by reading and interpreting information presented in visual form in a graph, chart, or other diagram. Typically, an infographic will be accompanied by three questions. Some Infographics questions may simply ask you to read information from an infographic, while others may ask you to draw conclusions based on the information presented. When answering Infographics questions, pay careful attention to the labels and titles on the infographic; reading the infographic incorrectly will make it difficult, if not impossible, to correctly answer the related questions. Note that you may not need the entire infographic to answer a question, so focus only on the portion of the infographic required to answer the question. As on all Core Reading questions, predict the answer before looking at the answer choices. This will help you avoid trap answers that go further than is warranted by the information presented in the infographic. Additionally, be careful not to confuse causation with mere correlation of data.

The Hudson River School emerged in the mid-1800s in America, and it typically depicted natural American landscapes in a way that celebrated America's unique national identity. The timeline below displays the names and dates of some famous Hudson River School paintings, along with the artists who created them.

Selected Paintings of Hudson River School Artists

1836 *The Oxbow (The Connecticut River near Northampton)*, Thomas Cole

1857 *Niagara Falls*, Frederic Edwin Church

1859 *The Catskills*, Asher Brown Durand

1868 *Among the Sierra Nevada Mountains, California*, Albert Bierstadt

1869 *Mount Washington*, John Frederick Kensett

1872 *Great Canyon of the Sierra, Yosemite*, Thomas Hill

Which conclusion about the art of the Hudson River School is best supported by the data presented in the timeline above?

A. The majority of Hudson River School paintings were created in the 1850s.

B. Hudson River School paintings may depict mountains or water features.

C. Thomas Cole was the first Hudson River School painter.

D. Albert Bierstadt's paintings are the best examples of Hudson River School art.

E. The Hudson River School had fallen out of popularity by the 1880s.

Before reading the answer choices, remember to evaluate the infographic and make a general prediction if possible. The infographic is a timeline listing some Hudson River School paintings and artists. Don't skip the title of the timeline; the graphic only displays *selected* artists. This timeline does not contain every possible Hudson River School artwork, so keep that in mind when it comes to drawing conclusions about the infographic. Now evaluate the answer choices. Eliminate (A); although some paintings were created in the 1850s, they do not constitute the majority of paintings represented on the graphic, let alone the majority of *all* paintings. (B) seems more likely, as it is supported by the names of the paintings. Additionally, the presence of the weaker word "may" makes this answer easier to support. Eliminate (C), as the timeline does not necessarily include *every* Hudson River School painting. Likewise, eliminate (E); if the timeline depicted the entirety of Hudson River School art, we might be able to draw this conclusion, but we do not know whether more paintings followed the one recorded in 1872. Also eliminate (D), as the timeline provides no viewpoints about Hudson River School art. Choice (**B**) is correct. Be careful to verify that the answer you choose for an Infographics question is fully supported by the information contained in the graphic.

Logical Reasoning Questions

Logical Reasoning questions require you to both identify and evaluate the parts of arguments that appear in a passage. You can identify these questions by their use of argument-related terms in the question stem: *evidence, strengthen, weaken, assumption, conclusion, argument*, etc. Keep in mind that these questions are not asking for *your* opinion of the argument. Rather they require a logical analysis of the claim in question. For instance, they may ask you to evaluate whether given evidence is relevant to an argument's conclusion, what types of information could strengthen or weaken an argument, and what unstated assumptions may underlie the author's claim. These questions may also ask about additional conclusions that one can logically draw from the passage's claims, such as identifying statements with which an author is "most likely to agree." For more complicated Logical Reasoning questions, it may be helpful to jot down the argument's components: the evidence, the conclusion, and the unstated assumption(s). When evaluating evidence, remember that it must be logically relevant to the argument's conclusion, while evidence that strengthens or weakens an argument must impact the likelihood of the argument's assumptions being true. Trap answers will typically contain information that may be related to the overall subject matter but is logically irrelevant to the argument in question.

Which of the following, if true, would most strengthen the claims presented in the passage?

A. The subjects of many Hudson River School paintings were classical European landmarks.

B. Several renowned European painters were using the American West as the subject of their landscape paintings in the early 19th century.

C. During the time of the Hudson River School, poetry about living in American urban settings flourished.

D. The landscapes depicted in many Hudson River School paintings later became American national parks.

E. Based on the content of personal letters of the period, most Americans after the War of 1812 desired to emulate European culture.

While you cannot make a specific prediction for this question, you should review the author's claims before looking at the answer choices to determine the *type* of evidence that would strengthen the argument. While the author is not opinionated about the Hudson River School, the passage describes its subject matter (natural scenes depicting American nationalism), success (capturing the prevailing spirit of nationalism), and style (detailed depictions of nature). Use this prediction of the passage's purpose to evaluate the answer choices, looking for information that would provide further evidence for the author's claims. Eliminate choices that either weaken the argument or are irrelevant to the argument. Eliminate (A), as this would weaken, rather than strengthen, the author's claims that the Hudson River School depicted "the American wilderness" (line 12). Eliminate (B), as Europeans painting American scenes would not support the author's claims about the Hudson River School; this choice would perhaps undermine the claim that the movement "was unmistakably American in origin" (lines 33–34). Likewise, (C) does not strengthen the author's claims about the Hudson River School's primarily natural subjects; rather, it weakens the claim that writers "were turning their attention to the wilderness" (lines 36–37) and "were concerned about the future of a country that was becoming increasingly urbanized" (lines 44–46). Choice (D) would strengthen the author's claims about the movement's subject matter, as locations that "convey the remoteness and splendor of the American wilderness" (lines 11–12) would likely be valued as future national parks; **(D)** is therefore correct. Finally, choice (E) also weakens the author's claims that the prevailing American attitude was a "pride in its identity" and a "desire to compete with Europe" (lines 27–29).

Connecting Ideas Questions

A final category of questions asks you to evaluate the various ways in which ideas may be related. For instance, questions that accompany paired passages fall into this category since they ask you to compare and contrast the views and techniques of two authors. Questions that accompany paired passages may also ask you to identify how information from one passage relates to that from the other passage; for instance, perhaps one passage provides evidence for or against an idea in the other passage. Most questions that accompany paired passages are actually question types you have already encountered (Global, Inference, Function, etc.), but since they may ask about one or both passages, they require more careful attention to keeping the ideas straight.

Other Connecting Ideas questions may ask you to describe the relationship (such as compare/contrast or cause/effect) between ideas presented in a single passage or apply the information in the passage to a new situation. As always, make a strong prediction for Connecting Ideas questions before looking at the answer choices.

> According to the passage, European Romantic painters differed from American Romantic painters of the Hudson River School in that European Romantic painters
>
> A. desired to emulate naturalists
>
> B. ignored painting traditions
>
> C. may not have depicted scenes realistically
>
> D. rejected religious inspiration
>
> E. celebrated the nationalism of their homelands

Since it asks how two groups mentioned in the passage differ, this is a Connecting Ideas question. As always, use your notes to locate the relevant portion of the passage to research. Be especially careful to keep the characteristics of the different groups straight. Paragraph 3 discusses the contrasts between the American and European artists. The paragraph describes the Americans artists as desiring to be "free of European artistic rules" (line 52), considering nature a "manifestation of God" (line 54), and painting realistically (lines 55–56 and 61–62). Since the passage describes Americans as being "unlike" the Europeans (line 56), by logical extension, it depicts the Europeans as following "rules" and the "techniques of centuries" (lines 52 and 56–58), and willing to "embellish" and "idealize" their scenes (lines 59–60). Note that the question stem asks for a characteristic of *European* painters, so choice **(C)** is correct. The slightly weaker wording of (C), "might," makes the choice easier to support from the text and therefore more likely to be correct. Choices (A) and (B) are incorrect because they depict the behaviors of the Americans, who are said to be "unlike" the European painters. Choice (D) distorts the passage: the Americans are said to regard nature as "a direct manifestation of God" (lines 53–54), but the passage never states that Europeans differed in this practice. Finally, the passage never identifies the subject matter of the Europeans' art, so (E) is incorrect.

Reading Questions Practice

Now it's time to practice some Praxis Reading questions. Make sure to use Kaplan's Four-Step Method when working through this quiz.

Questions 1–7

O'Keeffe Passage

The painter Georgia O'Keeffe was born in Wisconsin in 1887 and grew up on her family's farm. At 17, she decided she wanted to be an artist and left the farm for schools in Chicago
(5) and New York, but she never lost her bond with the land. Like most painters, O'Keeffe painted the things that were most important to her, and nearly all her works are simplified portrayals of nature.

(10) O'Keeffe became famous when her paintings were discovered and exhibited in New York by the photographer Alfred Stieglitz, whom she married in 1924. During a visit to New Mexico in 1929, O'Keeffe was so moved by the bleak
(15) landscape and broad skies of the Western desert that she began to paint its images. Cows' skulls and other bleached bones found in the desert figured prominently in her paintings. When her husband died in 1946, she moved to New Mexico
(20) permanently and used the horizon lines of the desert, colorful flowers, rocks, barren hills, and the sky as subjects for her paintings. Although O'Keeffe painted her best-known works in the 1920s, '30s, and '40s, she continued to produce
(25) tributes to the Western desert until her death in 1986.

O'Keeffe is widely considered to have been a pioneering American modernist painter. Whereas most early modern American artists were
(30) strongly influenced by European art, O'Keeffe's position was more independent. She established her own vision and preferred to view her painting as a private endeavor. Almost from the beginning, her work was more identifiably American than
(35) that of her contemporaries in its simplified and idealized treatment of color, light, space, and natural forms. Her paintings are generally considered "semi-abstract" because even though

they depict recognizable images and objects, the
(40) paintings don't present those images in a very detailed or realistic way.

Rather, the colors and shapes in her paintings are often so reduced and simplified that they begin to take on a life of their own, independent
(45) of the real-life objects from which they are taken.

1. Which of the following best states the main idea of the passage?

    A. O'Keeffe was the best painter of her generation.

    B. O'Keeffe was a distinctive modern American painter.

    C. O'Keeffe liked to paint only what was familiar to her.

    D. O'Keeffe never developed fully as an abstract artist.

    E. O'Keeffe used colors and shapes that are too reduced and simple.

2. The author most likely mentions "most early modern American artists" (line 29) in order to

    A. demonstrate the superiority of O'Keeffe's landscape art

    B. explain that other American artists were influenced by Europeans

    C. show how O'Keeffe's inspiration and art were unique

    D. argue that O'Keeffe's American upbringing influenced her artistic style

    E. criticize O'Keeffe's contemporaries as artistically old-fashioned

3. The passage suggests that Stieglitz contributed to O'Keeffe's career by

   A. bringing her work to a wider audience

   B. supporting her financially for many years

   C. inspiring her to paint natural forms

   D. suggesting that she study the work of European artists

   E. requesting that she accompany him to New Mexico

4. Which of the following is most similar to O'Keeffe's relationship with nature as portrayed in the passage?

   A. A photographer's relationship with a model

   B. A writer's relationship with a publisher

   C. A student's relationship with a part-time job

   D. A sculptor's relationship with an art dealer

   E. A carpenter's relationship with a hammer

5. According to the passage, why have O'Keeffe's paintings been described as "semi-abstract" (line 38)?

   A. They involve a carefully realistic use of color and light.

   B. They depict common, everyday things.

   C. They show familiar scenes from nature.

   D. They depict recognizable things in an unfamiliar manner.

   E. They refer directly to real-life activities.

6. As used in line 43, "reduced" most nearly means

   A. decreased

   B. cheapened

   C. streamlined

   D. miniaturized

   E. humbled

7. The author would describe the "colors and shapes" (line 42) in O'Keeffe's paintings as

   A. dynamic

   B. realistic

   C. ornate

   D. unrecognizable

   E. abstract

Questions 8–10

Chaos Passage

Whether as a result of some mysterious tendency in the collective psyche or as a spontaneous reaction to their turbulent historical experience after the breakup of the Mycenaean
(5) world, the Greeks felt that to live with changing, unmeasured, seemingly random impressions— to live, in short, with what was expressed by the Greek word *chaos*—was to live in a state of constant anxiety.
(10) If the apparent mutability of the human condition was a source of pain and bewilderment to the Greeks, the discovery of a permanent pattern or an unchanging substratum by which apparently chaotic experience could be measured
(15) and explained was a source of satisfaction, even joy, which had something of a religious nature.

8. The primary purpose of the passage is to

   A. evaluate conflicting viewpoints

   B. challenge an accepted opinion

   C. question philosophical principles

   D. enumerate historical facts

   E. describe a cultural phenomenon

9. The function of the first five lines in the passage ("Whether as a result . . . the Mycenaean world") is to

   A. supply a detailed context for the worldview of the ancient Greeks

   B. argue that the fragmentation of Mycenae led to the negative ancient Greek view of *chaos*

   C. describe the general mentality of the ancient Greek community

   D. present the religious underpinnings of the Greek view of *chaos*

   E. provide two possible explanations for the ancient Greek tendency to react to unpredictability with anxiety

10. Which of the following, if true, would most strengthen the argument presented in the passage?

   A. Ancient Greek artwork often depicted an admiration for the orderly movement of the constellations.

   B. The breakup of Mycenaean society actually resulted in the creation of a unique Greek cultural identity.

   C. Archaeologists discovered poems by numerous ancient Greek authors celebrating excitement associated with uncertainty about the future.

   D. The Greek work *chaos* means "quiet tranquility."

   E. An ancient Greek philosopher's determination that earthquakes could be attributed to three observable causes was met with widespread disdain and fear.

Questions 11–13

Katie spends some of her leisure time streaming shows. Last year, Katie decided to track her viewing habits. The table below shows the time, in hours, that Katie spent watching each of five show genres for each month. Katie watched no other shows than what she recorded in the table, and she watched shows only on her laptop.

Genre	J	F	M	A	M	J	J	A	S	O	N	D	Total
Comedy	7	6	8	10	8	9	5	10	11	11	9	8	102
Documentary	3	4	4	3	5	2	3	5	6	2	3	5	45
Drama	5	5	6	4	5	6	2	4	6	3	7	5	58
News	12	12	12	12	12	12	12	12	12	12	12	12	144
Reality	4	5	4	0	1	2	2	2	8	9	9	3	49
Total	31	32	34	29	31	31	24	33	43	37	40	33	398

11. Which of the following show genres did Katie watch more than the others during the first three months of last year?

    A. Comedy

    B. Documentary

    C. Drama

    D. Reality

    E. Katie watched all genres equally.

12. Given the information provided, which of the following best accounts for Katie's total hours of viewing last July and September?

    A. Katie's laptop was broken in the month of July, but by September it was fixed.

    B. In July, Katie watched fewer hours of shows in each genre than she averaged for previous months.

    C. Katie watched the usual amount of programming in July, but she increased her average viewing hours in every genre in September.

    D. Katie spent more hours of her leisure time in July on outdoor activities than in other months, but in September, she spent most of her leisure time watching new episodes of her favorite shows.

    E. There were very few shows that Katie wanted to watch in July and September.

13. Which of the following statements is best supported by the information provided?

    A. Katie watched a consistent amount of news programming every month last year.

    B. Katie watched more hours of documentaries than of either comedy or drama last year.

    C. Katie watched the most hours of programming last year in May.

    D. Katie watched a consistent number of reality programming hours every month last year.

    E. Katie's favorite genre is comedy.

Questions 14–18

Panda Passage

Ever since the giant panda was discovered in the middle of the 19th century, a debate has raged over its relation to other species. Whereas the general public tends to view the panda as a
(5) kind of living teddy bear, biologists have not been sure how to classify this enigmatic animal. At different times, the panda has been placed with bears in the Ursidae family, with raccoons in the Procyonidae family, and in its own Ailuropodidae
(10) family.

Biologists who classify animal species have tried to categorize the panda according to whether its traits are homologous or merely analogous to similar traits in other species.
(15) Homologous traits are those that species have in common because they have descended from a common ancestor. For instance, every species of cat has the homologous trait of possessing only four toes on its hind foot because every member
(20) of the cat family descended from a common feline ancestor. The greater the number of such traits that two species share, the more closely they are related. An analogous trait is a trait that two species have in common not because
(25) they are descended from a common ancestor, but because they have different ancestors that developed in similar ways in response to similar environmental pressures. A cat and a lion have more homologous traits between them than a
(30) cat and a human, for example. So cats and lions are more closely related than cats and humans. A whale and a fish have analogous tail fins because they both evolved in aquatic environments, not because they share a common ancestor. The
(35) questions surrounding the classification of the giant panda are linked to whether certain traits are homologous or simply analogous.

14. According to the passage, which of the following is true of the classification of the giant panda?

   A. The correct classification of the giant panda is in the Ursidae family.

   B. The classification of the giant panda is based on analogous traits.

   C. The classification of the giant panda has changed because of the rapid evolution of the species.

   D. The classification of the giant panda has proved difficult for biologists because of traits pandas share with several other types of animals.

   E. The giant panda is best classified by biologists as a kind of giant teddy bear.

15. Which of the following is NOT possible using the homologous/analogous classification scheme?

   A. Two species sharing more than one homologous trait

   B. Two species sharing more than one analogous trait

   C. Two species sharing an analogous trait but having no common ancestor

   D. Two species sharing a homologous trait but having no common ancestor

   E. Two species sharing no analogous or homologous traits

16. Which of the following best describes the organization of the second paragraph?

   A. Two terms are defined using examples.

   B. Two theories are contrasted.

   C. A hypothesis is proven.

   D. Two arguments are presented with evidence.

   E. Examples of species are listed.

17. The author's attitude toward the panda classification debate can best be described as one of

    A. disdain

    B. incredulity

    C. objectivity

    D. elation

    E. concern

18. The passage suggests that which of the following is true about animal classification?

    Select all that apply.

    A. Giant pandas share traits with both bears and raccoons.

    B. Homologous traits are more significant for classification purposes than analogous traits.

    C. Cats and lions did not develop under similar environmental pressures.

Despite their amazing architectural and cultural achievements, including extensive roadway systems, none of the pre-Columbian civilizations of Mesoamerica developed a wheel for transport. However, archeologists have discovered wheeled toys used by Mesoamerican children. Since they never applied wheel technology to vehicles, the Mesoamericans must not have had the need to carry heavy loads.

19. Which of the following, if true, would suggest an alternative to the author's hypothesis?

    A. The wheeled toys used by Mesoamerican children often featured an animal pulling a toy wagon.

    B. The Mesoamericans' environment lacked any native animals capable of pulling heavy loads, so wheeled vehicles, such as carts, were unusable.

    C. The Mesoamericans did not engage in long-distance trade.

    D. Mesoamerican road systems connected villages only within the same geographic location.

    E. The Mesoamericans adopted the wheel for transport when it was later introduced by Europeans.

Questions 20–23

Stem Cells: Paired Passage Set

Passage 1

Stem cells are science's miracle cure. Since these undifferentiated cells have not yet chosen what type of cell to become, they can be nudged into becoming whatever type of cell is needed
(5) to replace damaged cells in a person who has a degenerative disease or a serious injury.

Scientists obtain stem cells primarily from discarded embryos. Stem cells can also be obtained from the blood or organs of healthy
(10) adults, but these are not as adaptable as embryonic stem cells. Using embryonic stem cells can mean a revolutionary change in quality of life for patients suffering from debilitating diseases such as Parkinson's or Alzheimer's. With stem
(15) cell research, the benefits for living, breathing, sentient people outweigh any debate regarding the origins of the cells themselves.

Passage 2

Stem cell research has the potential to assuage or completely halt the advance of devastating
(20) diseases. However, scientists assault the dignity of life when they use embryonic stem cells for their work. By taking cells from discarded embryos, we start down a slippery slope. It is all too easy to transition from using discarded
(25) embryos to creating embryos solely for the purpose of stem cell medicine.

Since we can obtain stem cells from healthy adults with no cost to life, this is the path on which we should be progressing. These stem
(30) cells, safely obtained, can have a life-changing impact on patients.

20. The authors of both passages would most likely agree with which of the following statements about stem cell research?

   A. The medical benefits of stem cell research outweigh ethical concerns.

   B. Embryonic stem cells have greater potential than do adult stem cells.

   C. Stem cell research could lead to benefits for human health.

   D. Stem cell research is the only promising route to combat debilitating human diseases.

   E. The benefits of stem cell research must be weighed against ethical concerns.

21. The attitude of the author of Passage 2 toward the use of embryonic stem cells can best be described as one of

   A. excitement

   B. disapproval

   C. indifference

   D. uncertainty

   E. ignorance

22. Which best describes the relationship between Passage 1 and Passage 2?

    A. Passage 1 recounts a narrative that Passage 2 analyzes.

    B. Passage 1 provides evidence that Passage 2 undermines.

    C. Passage 1 introduces a theory that Passage 2 expands upon.

    D. Passage 1 proves an idea that Passage 2 celebrates.

    E. Passage 1 presents a viewpoint Passage 2 counters.

23. Which of the following could be substituted for the word "assuage" in line 18 with the least change in meaning?

    A. decrease

    B. cure

    C. heighten

    D. satisfy

    E. aggravate

Reading Questions Practice Answers and Explanations

O'Keeffe Passage

1. B

Global. Use as your prediction the main idea you identified in your notes. The main idea here is that the passage describes the inspiration, subject matter, style, and uniqueness of O'Keeffe's art. This matches choice **(B)**, which is both accurate and general enough without being so general that the meaning of the passage is lost—making it exactly the kind of answer you want on Global questions. (A) is incorrect because the author never claims O'Keeffe was the best painter of her generation. (C) is potentially tricky. It's true that O'Keeffe liked to paint things that were familiar to her (lines 5–9)—primarily certain nature images—but this is just one point about O'Keeffe discussed in the passage, rather than the reason the passage was written. (D) is never suggested by the passage. (E), like (C), focuses too much on a detail. (E) also distorts the author's view, as she never criticizes O'Keeffe.

2. C

Function. For Function questions, research the context of the cited portion of the text while keeping in mind the author's purpose for both the relevant paragraph and the passage as a whole: the function of a particular part of the passage will always be to serve the purpose of the entire passage. The overall passage describes O'Keeffe's background and particular artistic style; paragraph 3 discusses O'Keeffe's particular legacy as a painter by differentiating her from other contemporary American artists. In the sentence in question, the Structural Keyword "whereas" indicates the author's intent to contrast O'Keeffe's "independent" position with the European influences of "most early modern American artists" (lines 28–31). This matches choice **(C)**. Choices (D) and (E) incorrectly identify the author's purpose; while the author clearly takes a positive view of O'Keeffe's work, the author never goes so far as to "argue" or "criticize" anything. Likewise, the author identifies O'Keeffe's work as "pioneering" (line 28) but never claims it is

"superior" to any other art, so (A) is incorrect. Choice (B) correctly states the author's view that other American artists were influenced by "European art" (lines 29–30), but it does not identify the author's specific purpose for mentioning other artists, which is to show how O'Keeffe was unique.

3. A

Inference. Research Stieglitz: the first sentence of paragraph 2 states that O'Keeffe "became famous" when Stieglitz "discovered and exhibited" her work in New York City. You can infer, then, that Stieglitz helped O'Keeffe by introducing her work to more people—making choice **(A)** correct. Whatever financial arrangement, if any, existed between Stieglitz and O'Keeffe, (B) is not mentioned in the passage. Paragraph 1 strongly implies that O'Keefe was inspired to paint natural forms long before she met Stieglitz, making (C) inaccurate. Choice (D) contradicts paragraph 3, which states that O'Keeffe was not strongly influenced by European artists. Finally, (E) is incorrect because the passage does not describe the circumstances leading to O'Keeffe's visit to New Mexico.

4. A

Connecting Ideas. First, ask yourself what O'Keeffe's relationship to nature was. O'Keeffe painted from nature—it was the subject of her work. Of the choices offered, which is most similar to the relationship between a painter and her subject? Choice **(A)** is correct because a model is the subject of a photographer's work. (B) is incorrect because a publisher is not the subject of a writer's work; a publisher simply prints and distributes a writer's work. Similarly, (C) is out because a part-time job is not a student's subject. Choice (D) is incorrect because an art dealer buys and sells a sculptor's work, but the art dealer is not the subject of the sculptor's work. Finally, a hammer is simply a carpenter's tool; it doesn't provide a carpenter with a subject or model, so (E) is out.

5. D

Detail. Research around the cited reference to find the context of this potentially unfamiliar term. Note the Structural Keyword "because" in the sentence containing the term, which indicates that a cause-and-effect relationship will be explained: her work is considered "semi-abstract" *because* it depicts "recognizable images" in a way that is not "very detailed or realistic." Choice **(D)** simply restates this idea. Choice (A) is incorrect because it refers to "realistic" qualities, contradicting the passage's definition of *semi-abstract*. Choices (B) and (E) can both refer to a component of the semi-abstract style—its portrayal of "recognizable" subjects—but neither one accounts for the unrealistic depiction of such subjects that constitutes the other component of semi-abstract art. Choice (C) accurately describes the subject matter of O'Keeffe's work, but it is not a reason for her style being classified as semi-abstract.

6. C

Vocab-in-Context. Read the surrounding lines for context and then predict a word that you can substitute for the cited word. The relevant sentence begins with the Structural Keyword "rather," which indicates the contrast between presenting "images in a very detailed or realistic way" and the "reduced and simplified" style of O'Keeffe. Notice that the word in question must therefore contrast with "detailed" and be a synonym for "simplified"; predict a word like *minimal*. Choice **(C)** matches this prediction. Choices (A) and (D) are both words that mean "small in size," which is not suggested by the context. Choice (B) incorrectly refers to either low monetary value or a negative view of O'Keeffe's art, neither of which the author indicates. Choice (E) does not fit in context, as it does not make sense that "colors and shapes" could be "humbled."

7. A

Writer's View. Research the context of the cited phrase. Your paragraph notes should indicate that in the fourth paragraph, the author identifies O'Keeffe's "colors and shapes" as "simplified" and taking "on a life of their own" (lines 42–44). The previous paragraph provides more clues: the author refers to O'Keeffe's art as "semi-abstract" depictions of regular things in unrealistic ways (lines 37–41). It again refers to the "color" and "space" as "simplified and idealized" (lines 35–36). Use these references as your prediction for how the author describes the "colors and shapes." This matches choice **(A)**, which reflects the author's description of the features as "tak[ing] on a life of their own" (line 44). Choices (B), (C), and (D) are all the opposite of the author's description of O'Keeffe's paintings. Choice (E) distorts the author's view, as the passage instead describes O'Keeffe's work (and not her colors and shapes in particular) as "*semi*-abstract."

Chaos Passage

8. E

Global. There is only one answer choice that captures the purpose of the two paragraphs. This passage is simply a description of a cultural phenomenon—the desire to seek out order and avoid chaos—that was prevalent in ancient Greece. Choice **(E)** reflects the Main Idea.

(A) misses the point of the passage because the author does not mention any conflicting viewpoints. Instead, he describes two aspects of a single cultural phenomenon. (B) and (C) are out because the passage is not challenging or questioning anything. It simply attempts to describe a perspective on Ancient Greek culture. Finally, (D) is out because it misses the point. This passage is less concerned with delineating historical facts than with the overall zeitgeist or collective spirit of a society.

9. E

Function. Consider how the first five lines in particular serve the author's purpose for the overall passage: to describe ancient Greek culture's collective drive to avoid chaos and seek order. The lines in question include the Structural Keywords "as a result," indicating that they provide a reason for what follows: the Greeks viewing "*chaos*" with "anxiety." The first five lines also include the Structural Keywords "whether…or," indicating two possible reasons for this view. So the first lines of the passage present two possible explanations for the Greek view of chaos, which matches choice **(E)**. The first lines do not provide a "detailed context," so (A) is incorrect. Choice (B) inappropriately identifies the author's purpose as argumentative, and it also misrepresents the author's statement that there were *two* possible reasons (not only the fragmentation of Mycenae) for the Greek view of chaos. Choice (C) is incorrect, as the lines in question provide *reasons* for the Greek view, not a description of the mentality itself. Choice (D) is incorrect because the lines include no mention of "religious underpinnings."

10.   A

Logical Reasoning. Before looking at the answer choices, paraphrase the author's argument: the ancient Greeks collectively viewed perceived chaos with anxiety, and they valued order. An answer choice that provides evidence that would strengthen this argument will be correct; eliminate answers that either weaken or are irrelevant to the argument. Choice (**A**) is correct because it provides an example of the Greek tendency, described in lines 12–15, to view the discovery of order positively. Although the passage does mention the breakup of Mycenae, as in choice (B), the passage does not argue that the Greek viewpoint it describes was "unique." Nor does this fact provide evidence to support the passage's main claim. Choices (C) and (D) would weaken, rather than strengthen, the author's argument that the Greeks viewed uncertainty with "constant anxiety" (lines 5–9). Choice (E) would also weaken the author's argument that "the discovery of a permanent pattern" would be met with "satisfaction, even joy" (lines 12–16).

11.   A

Infographic. Research only the relevant portions of the table, making a prediction before looking at the answer choices. To determine the number of hours watched, you will need to add together the hours listed for January, February, and March, across the row for each genre. A quick assessment of the table reveals that Katie watched more hours of news than anything else, but since "News" is not an answer choice, evaluate the other genres. Exact numbers are not necessary; since the table shows Katie watched more hours of comedy than any genre except news, (**A**) is correct.

12.   D

Infographic. Before looking at the answer choices, research the relevant portions of the table. Katie's total monthly hours of watching shows were the lowest for

the entire year in July and the highest in September. These trends also held true for individual genres (for the most part), with the notable exception of news programs, which held steady at 12 hours a month for the entire year. With this information in mind, evaluate the answer choices. Choice (A) is incorrect because Katie still watched shows in July, and the paragraph before the table indicates she only watches programs on her laptop. (B) is incorrect because Katie watched the same number of news programming hours as in previous months. (C) is incorrect because, while Katie did increase her viewing in September, her total hours in July were lower. (D) could account for the lower than average total hours in July and the higher than average total hours in September, so (**D**) is correct. (E) is incorrect because it does not describe Katie's viewing in September.

13.   A

Infographic. Although you cannot make a specific prediction, keep in mind the overall trends of the table when evaluating the answer choices. Choice (**A**) is correct; Katie watched 12 hours of news programming every month of last year. Choice (B) is incorrect because Katie watched more hours of comedy and of drama than she did of documentaries. Choice (C) is incorrect because Katie watched the most total hours in September. (D) is incorrect because Katie's hours spent watching reality programs varied from month to month. Choice (E) is incorrect because even if Katie had watched more hours of comedy than anything else, you could not reach the conclusion that Katie's favorite genre necessarily corresponds with whichever one she watched the most.

Panda Passage

14.   D

Detail. Check your paragraph notes for the location of this detail. The classification of the giant panda is discussed in the first paragraph. The answer to this question can be found in the second sentence of the first paragraph. According to this sentence, "biologists have not been sure how to classify this enigmatic animal." This is right in line with (**D**).

(A) contradicts the passage because the author never states which classification is correct. (B) is also incorrect because classification should be based on homologous, not analogous traits. (C) is never discussed in the passage. (E) is a comical distortion of the passage. Although the passage does state that the general public may view the panda as a giant teddy bear, that does not correspond to the biological classification of the animal, which is the focus of this question.

15. D

Connecting Ideas. The second paragraph discusses homologous and analogous traits in depth. The second sentence of the second paragraph defines homologous traits as those linked to a common ancestor. Consequently, **(D)** is the correct answer, because two species with a homologous trait by definition possess a common ancestor.

(A), (B), (C), and (E) are all possible based on the description given in the second paragraph. Two species can share numerous homologous traits, as in choice (A). That would simply mean that they inherited multiple traits from a common ancestor. Similarly, two species can share numerous analogous traits, as in (B). This would simply mean that they did not share a common ancestor but developed under similar environmental pressures. (C) is consistent with the definition of analogous traits, so it can be eliminated. Finally, (E) can be eliminated because nowhere does the passage state that two species must have analogous or homologous traits.

16. A

Organization. Check your paragraph notes and paraphrase the organization before looking at the answer choices. The second paragraph explains the difference between homologous and analogous traits, using examples of various animals to illustrate the definitions, and concludes that panda classification is difficult because it is uncertain what types of traits this animal exhibits. This matches choice **(A)**. Choices (B), (C), and (D) are incorrect because the paragraph never presents any theories, hypotheses, or arguments; rather, the passage merely explains why it is difficult to classify the panda due to the ambiguity of its traits. (E) is incorrect because although

the paragraph does list examples of animals, the paragraph's organization and purpose center on explaining the two categories of traits.

17. C

Writer's View. Review the purpose and Main Idea of the passage before looking at the answer choices. Does the author express an opinion regarding the panda debate? The author acknowledges the debate in paragraph 1 and concludes the passage by stating that the classification is questionable due to the uncertainty regarding the panda's traits. Therefore, predict that the author thinks the debate is legitimate but does not take a particular side. This matches choice **(C)**; the author objectively explains the debate. Choices (A) and (D) are incorrect because they present the author as either rejecting or rejoicing over the debate; the passage presents neither of these views. (B) is also incorrect; the author does not question the legitimacy of the debate but rather acknowledges it by concluding that the panda's classification is questionable. The author never expresses concern about the debate, so (E) is also incorrect.

18. A, B

Inference. It is not possible to make a specific prediction for some Inference questions, but keep in mind the overall Main Idea of the passage when evaluating the answer choices. The first paragraph states that pandas have been classified with both bears and raccoons; the second paragraph states that classification can be based on shared traits, so the panda must share at least some traits with both bears and raccoons. **(A)** is therefore correct. Evaluate the remaining answer choices, as the question asks you to select all that apply. Choice **(B)** is also correct; the passage concludes that "the questions surrounding the classification of the giant panda are linked to whether certain traits are homologous or simply analogous" (lines 34–37). Choice (C), however, is incorrect; although the passage explains in lines 28–30 that cats and lions share homologous traits (and therefore, by definition, a common ancestor), it states nothing about the environments in which they developed. They may have developed in similar or differing situations, and the passage makes no claim about either possibility.

19. B

Logical Reasoning. Be sure to identify the components of the author's argument and make a prediction of what could constitute an alternate hypothesis before looking at the answer choices. The author concludes that the Mesoamericans did not have a need to carry heavy loads, based on the evidence that Mesoamericans used wheels for toys but not for transport vehicles. The author makes the assumption that the only reason the Mesoamericans would not have applied wheel technology to transport vehicles is that there was no need to carry heavy loads. Predict that an alternate hypothesis would assume a different reason for not applying wheel technology to transport. This matches choice (B), which provides another reason for not applying wheel technology: lack of animals capable of pulling a heavy wheeled vehicle. Choice (A) is incorrect because it provides information about children's toys but does not give an alternative hypothesis for not applying wheel technology to transport. (C) is incorrect because there could be other reasons for using the wheel for transport (such as farming or short-distance trade) besides long-distance trade. (D) is irrelevant as a reason for not applying the wheel to transport. (E) only serves as a potential weakener to the author's original hypothesis (rather than providing a potential alternative hypothesis) in its suggestion that Mesoamericans actually did have a need to transport heavy loads using the wheel.

Stem Cells: Paired Passage Set

20. C

Connecting Ideas/Logical Reasoning. Be sure to predict before reading the answer choices. The correct answer must be quite general, since the two authors disagree. Author 1 argues that the use of embryonic stem cells will likely help combat disease, while Author 2 claims adult cells should be used. On what point do the authors agree? Stem cell research (regardless of the stem cells' origin) can significantly aid in the fight against disease; this matches choice (C). Be careful of answer choices that only represent one of the two authors' views. Choices (A) and (B) represent Author 1's views, while (E) reflects Author 2's views. While both authors

consider stem cell research promising, neither goes so far as to claim it is the "only" possible route to combating disease, as in (D).

21. B

Connecting Ideas/Writer's View. Carefully consider only the attitude of the author of Passage 2. The author strongly disapproves of using embryonic stem cells, stating that when scientists do so, they "assault the dignity of life" (lines 20–21) and "start down a slippery slope" (line 23). This prediction matches choice (B). Choice (A) incorrectly provides the opposite of the author's view. (C) incorrectly indicates the author lacks an opinion, while (D) and (E) convey, respectively, that the author's position is ambivalent or nonexistent; in fact, the author is firmly against the use of embryonic stem cells.

22. E

Connecting Ideas/Global. Paraphrase the Main Idea of each passage before evaluating the answer choices. Passage 1 claims stem cells are a "miracle cure" (line 1) and argues for the superiority of using embryonic stem cells, despite any possible debate about the cells' origin. Passage 2 also praises the use of stem cell research, but argues the cells should be obtained from adults due to ethical concerns. This prediction matches choice (E). Choice (A) misrepresents Passage 1, which is not a "narrative." Passage 1 provides some evidence that using embryonic stem cells can provide superior results relative to using stem cells from adults, and while Passage 2 disagrees with Passage 1's conclusion, Passage 2 never counters this evidence; (B) is therefore incorrect. For choice (C), Passage 1 could be said to introduce the theory that stem cells are a "miracle cure," but Passage 2 does not so much "expand" the theory as affirm it while disagreeing about how to act on it. Choice (D) is incorrect because while Passage 1 makes claims and provides some evidence, it does not actually "prove" anything; moreover, Passage 2 certainly does not "celebrate" the claim of Passage 1.

23.   A

Connecting Ideas/Vocabulary-in-Context. Remember to predict a word to substitute for the word in context. The first sentence of Passage 2 claims "stem cell research has the potential to *assuage* or completely halt the advance of devastating diseases." "Assuage" must mean something related to stopping the advance of diseases, but less than "*completely* halting" them. Predict a word like *reduce.* This matches choice (**A**). Choice (B) is too extreme to match the word *assuage;* it is too close in meaning to "completely halt." Choices (C) and (E) have the opposite of the intended meaning and make no sense in context. (D) also does not work in context; "assuage" can mean "satisfy" in some contexts (as in "assuaging hunger"), but it does not make sense that the "advance of…diseases" can be "satisfied."

[CHAPTER 2]

PRAXIS CORE MATHEMATICS

LEARNING OBJECTIVES

By the end of this chapter, you will be able to do the following:

- Describe the structure and format of the Praxis Core Academic Skills for Educators: Mathematics test
- Outline and use the Kaplan Method for Praxis Mathematics
- Apply Praxis Mathematics Strategies
- Apply basic math concepts and rules
- Use the Praxis Core Mathematics practice test to assess your performance

---

Taking Your Core Math Pre-Test

Before you begin studying and practicing Praxis Core Math, take a pre-test to assess your initial strengths and areas of greatest opportunity on the test. With 28 questions to complete in 45 minutes, the pre-test is half the length of the official exam. Find time to complete the pre-test in one sitting and time yourself strictly as you take it.

The purpose of the pre-test is self-assessment. Some test takers hesitate to take pre-tests because they haven't studied yet, or they want to try the questions without time restrictions so that they can get them all correct. Those approaches, however, defeat the purpose of the pre-test, which is to get a clear-eyed look at your performance and skill levels on all that the test entails.

Part of the test's challenge is its timing. Some of the questions may seem easy, and some may strike you as really difficult. When you encounter hard questions on the pre-test, don't be afraid to skip them or make your best guess. It's more valuable to get a broad view of your performance on different question types than to spend several minutes struggling to get one question right.

So, do your best, but don't get too excited or worried about your score on the pre-test. There's a lot of learning and practice to come, and your performance on the pre-test does not predict your official score. That will be the result of your study and effort.

Core Math Pre-Test

45 Minutes—28 Questions

Directions: You have 45 minutes to complete this pre-test. Read the instructions for each question carefully and circle the correct answer(s) in your book. If a question asks you to "Select all that apply," then more than one answer could be right and you should select all of the choices you believe to be correct. If a question is followed by a box instead of answer choices, write your response directly into the box. You may use blank scratch paper to take notes during this pre-test.

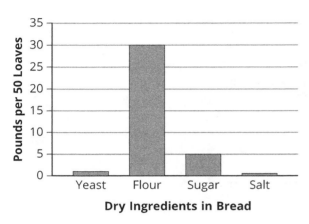

Dry Ingredients in Bread

1. The bar graph above shows the amounts of dry ingredients a bakery needs to produce 50 loaves of bread. If 50 loaves contain 30 pounds of flour, how many pounds of sugar will the bakery need to produce 100 loaves of bread?

   A. 30
   B. 20
   C. 15
   D. 12
   E. 10

2. A warehouse worker is packing boxes of shoes into crates. Each crate can hold 15 boxes. If the worker is packing the 63rd box, which crate is currently being filled?

   A. Third
   B. Fourth
   C. Fifth
   D. Sixth
   E. Seventh

$$\frac{17}{3}, \ \frac{21}{5}, \ \sqrt{3}, \ x, \ \frac{5}{8}$$

3. The numbers in the list above are arranged in decreasing order, and each number in the list is different. Which of the following could be the value of x?

   Select all that apply.

   A. $\frac{7}{3}$

   B. $\frac{14}{5}$

   C. $\sqrt{2}$

   D. $\frac{1}{2}$

   E. $\frac{15}{16}$

Train X traveled on a straight railroad track for 60 minutes without stopping. Train X traveled the first 36 minutes at a constant speed of 35 kilometers per hour, and then Train X traveled for the final 24 minutes at a constant speed of 70 kilometers per hour.

4. Which of the following graphs correctly shows the total distance s, in kilometers, that Train X traveled at the time of z minutes, where $0 \leq z \leq 60$?

    A.
    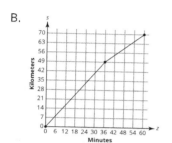

    B.
    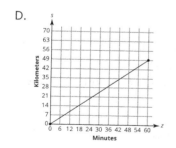

    C.

    D.
    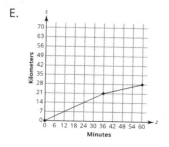

    E.

A student did the following conversion:

$$8 \text{ grams} \times \frac{2.2 \text{ pounds}}{1,000 \text{ grams}} \times \frac{16 \text{ ounces}}{1 \text{ pound}}$$

5. Which of the following best describes the conversion?

    A. Grams to pounds

    B. Ounces to pounds

    C. Pounds to grams

    D. Grams to ounces

    E. Pounds to ounces

6. X is 3 more than 4 times Y, and Y is 7 less than 12 times Z. Which of the following equations correctly describes the relationship between X and Z?

    A. X is 25 less than 48 times Z.

    B. X is 28 less than 48 times Z.

    C. X is 28 more than 48 times Z.

    D. X is 31 less than 36 times Z.

    E. X is 31 more than 24 times Z.

7. At a certain store, the price of every folding chair is $40, and the price of every card table is $54. What percent greater than the price of a folding chair is the price of a card table?

    A. 25%

    B. 30%

    C. 35%

    D. 46%

    E. 50%

Distribution of the Profits of Company _J_ in 2019

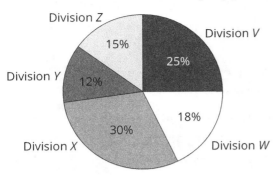

8. The pie chart above shows the distribution of the profits of Company _J_ in 2019 among its five divisions. The total profits of Company _J_ in 2019 were $164,000,000. The total profits of Company _J_ in 2020 were $240,000,000, with the sum of the profits of Division _W_ and Division _X_ in 2020 being 39 percent of the total profits of Company _J_ in 2020, and the sum of the profits of Division _Y_ and Division _Z_ in 2020 being 46 percent of the total profits of Company _J_ in 2020. How much less were the profits of Division _V_ in 2020 than the profits of Division _V_ in 2019?

A. $5,000,000

B. $7,000,000

C. $10,000,000

D. $14,000,000

E. $24,000,000

9. In the final step of a calculation, Evelyn divided by 7 when she should have multiplied by 7. By what number should Evelyn multiply her incorrect final result of 458 in order to obtain the correct result?

A. 7

B. 14

C. 49

D. 70

E. 343

10. Which of the following is equivalent to $8n - 15 > 49$?

A. $n > 15$

B. $8n > 34$

C. $n < 4$

D. $8n > 32$

E. $n > 8$

11. If $3x + 3 = 6(y + 2)$, then $x - 2y =$

A. $-\dfrac{1}{3}$

B. 0

C. 3

D. 5

E. 9

12. Bill has _c_ cards in his baseball card collection. Jason has 25 more baseball cards than Bill. Charlie has one-fifth the number of baseball cards that Jason has. Which of the following represents the number of baseball cards that Charlie has?

A. $\dfrac{c}{5} + 25$

B. $c + 25 - 5$

C. $(c + 25) \times 5$

D. $\dfrac{c}{5} + 5$

E. $25(c - 5)$

Peggy washes cars for 10 weeks during her summer vacation. It takes her about 1 hour to wash a car. She washes a total of 123 cars during her vacation and earns $8 for every car that she washes.

13. Which of the following numbers are needed to calculate the total amount of money Peggy earns washing cars during her vacation?

A. 10, 123, and 1

B. 10, 123, and $8

C. 10, 1, and $8

D. 10, 1, 123, and $8

E. 123 and $8

14. A vendor who takes only $5 bills charges the following prices: $10 for one pizza and $5 for three sodas. Nabila wants to buy two pizzas and nine sodas for her friends. How many $5 bills will she need?

    A. 5

    B. 7

    C. 11

    D. 22

    E. 35

15. Bruno and Mitch both run hot dog stands. On Friday afternoon, Bruno sold t hot dogs and received $20 in tips. Mitch sold $\frac{4}{5}$ as many hot dogs as Bruno and received $6 less in tips. If each vendor charges $2 for a hot dog, which of the following represents the number of dollars Mitch earned?

    A. $\frac{4t}{5} - 6$

    B. $\frac{4t}{5} + 6$

    C. $\frac{8t}{5} + 14$

    D. $\frac{8t}{5} + 26$

    E. $\frac{t}{10} - 14$

16. Which of the following shows a right triangle whose area is 8 and whose right angle has a vertex that is located at (3, 4)?

    A.
    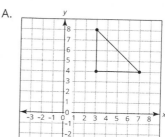

    B.
    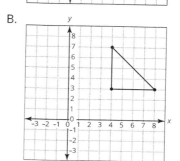

    C.
    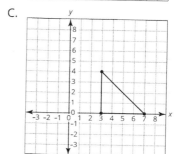

    D.
    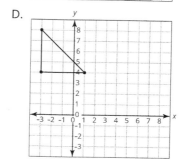

    E.
    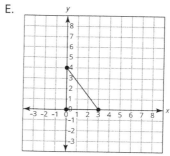

A certain machine that Company *X* makes requires 375 widgets. Company *X* wants to make 80 of these machines. Company *X* will buy 360 containers of widgets from Company *Y*, which only sells these widgets in containers that each contain the same number of widgets. The number of widgets in each container is *N*, where *N* is a positive integer.

17. What is the smallest possible value of *N* so that Company *X* will buy enough widgets for the 80 machines?

    A. 83

    B. 84

    C. 85

    D. 86

    E. 88

18. The formula $p = 75n + 250$ represents the amount *p*, in dollars, that a salesperson is paid in a week when the salesperson sells *n* brand-*A* televisions. What is the smallest number of televisions that a salesperson must sell in a week in order to be paid at least $3,010?

    A. 27

    B. 34

    C. 36

    D. 37

    E. 41

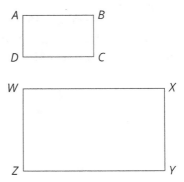

19. Rectangles *ABCD* and *WXYZ* are drawn to scale. If rectangle *ABCD* has an area of 12 square feet, which of the following is most likely the area of rectangle *WXYZ*?

    A. 20

    B. 24

    C. 36

    D. 48

    E. 96

Given a point *C* in three dimensions, a sphere is the set of all points in three dimensions that are the same distance from the center *C*. A sphere is the result of rotating a semicircle completely about its diameter. When a line goes through the center of a sphere, the line segment whose endpoints are the two points where the line intersects the sphere is a diameter of the sphere.

20. Which of the following could be the set of points that are on the intersection of a sphere and a plane, if the center of the sphere is not a point on that plane?

    A. An ellipse with an area less than the surface area of the sphere

    B. An ellipse with an area equal to the surface area of the sphere

    C. A circle with a diameter less than the diameter of the sphere

    D. A circle with a diameter equal to the diameter of the sphere

    E. A circle with a diameter greater than the diameter of the sphere

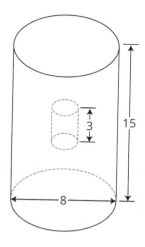

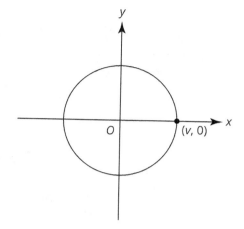

In the figure above, there is a smaller right circular cylinder completely contained in a larger right circular cylinder. The diameter of the circular base of the larger right circular cylinder is 8, and the height of the larger right circular cylinder is 15. The diameter of the circular base of the larger right circular cylinder is 4 times the diameter of the circular base of the smaller right circular cylinder, and the height of the smaller right circular cylinder is 3.

21. What fraction of the volume of the larger right circular cylinder is the volume contained in the larger right circular cylinder that is outside of the smaller right circular cylinder? (The volume V of a right circular cylinder with a circular base having a radius r and a height h is given by the formula $V = \pi r^2 h$.)

22. In the *xy*-plane above, the origin *O* is the center of the circle shown. The point at coordinates $(v, 0)$ is a point on the circumference of the circle. If the circumference of the circle is 100, which of the following is the best approximation of *v*?

A. 10

B. 16

C. 20

D. 24

E. 48

23. The length of one side of a triangle is 8. The length of another side of the triangle is 12. Which of the following could be the perimeter of the triangle?

Select <u>all</u> that apply

A. 23

B. 25

C. 33

D. 37

E. 41

{25, 27, 27, 27, 32, 32, 42, 46, 46}

24. In the above list of numbers, what is the average of the median and mode?

    A. 27

    B. 28.25

    C. 29.5

    D. 35.5

    E. 37

25. Twenty-five people take a survey. Five people say that they own both a smartphone and a tablet, whereas 6 people say that they own neither. If 17 people own a smartphone, how many own a tablet?

    A. 7

    B. 9

    C. 11

    D. 15

    E. 17

26. A container contains 7 orange disks, 14 green disks, x purple disks, and nothing else. When one disk is selected at random from the container, the probability that the selected disk is purple is $\frac{3}{8}$ greater than the probability that the selected disk is green. What is the value of x?

    A. 21

    B. 26

    C. 27

    D. 35

    E. 41

27. The average (arithmetic mean) of nine numbers is 12. What is the sum of those numbers?

    A. 18

    B. 27

    C. 108

    D. 120

    E. 1,008

28. Jackie puts 50 slips of paper into a hat. The slips of paper are numbered 1 through 50. If Jackie pulls a slip of paper out at random, what is the probability that the number on the slip will be a factor of 20?

    A. $\frac{6}{50}$

    B. $\frac{20}{50}$

    C. $\frac{2}{50}$

    D. $\frac{40}{50}$

    E. $\frac{15}{50}$

Core Math Pre-Test Answers and Explanations

1.   E

In this problem, you are given a bar graph that displays information about the weight (in pounds) of certain ingredients, including sugar, required to make 50 loaves of bread. You are then asked to use this information to calculate the number of pounds of sugar required to make 100 loaves of bread. From the graph, you can see that it takes 5 pounds of sugar to make 50 loaves. Set up the following proportion:

$$\frac{\text{Sugar}}{\text{Loaves}} = \frac{5}{50} = \frac{x}{100}$$

Cross-multiply and solve for x as follows:

$$50x = 500$$
$$x = 10$$

It will take 10 pounds of sugar to make 100 loaves of bread.

2.   C

The question asks for the ordinal number of the crate that is currently being filled. This is equal to the number of crates that are completely filled, plus one. Because each crate holds 15 boxes of shoes, the 60th box completes the fourth crate. This means that the 63rd box is going into the fifth crate.

3.   C, E

The question is looking for numbers that are less than $\sqrt{3}$ and greater than $\frac{5}{8}$.

Find the decimal equivalents of $\sqrt{3}$ and $\frac{5}{8}$ using a calculator: 1.73 and 0.625. Next, find the decimal equivalents of all the answer choices: (A) 2.333, (B) 4.2, (C) 1.41, (D) 0.5, (E) 0.9375. The only two that fall between the desired range are 1.41 and 0.9375, so choose (**C**) and (**E**).

4.   A

First, convert the times of the two distinct parts of the trip from minutes to hours.

First part: $36 \div 60 = 0.6$ hours

Second part: $24 \div 60 = 0.4$ hours

Then, to find the distance traveled for each part of the trip, multiply the time of each period by the speed of the train during that period.

First part: 0.6 hours $\times$ 35 km/hour = 21 km

Second part: 0.4 hours $\times$ 70 km/hour = 28 km

Total: $21 + 28 = 49$ km

Note that kilometers are given on the y-axis. The graph that shows (1) the first time period ending at 21 km and (2) the total trip being 49 km is (**A**).

5.   D

The only "real" unit in the expression is 8 grams (the rest are conversion factors as fractions), so grams must be the starting point. Eliminate (B), (C), and (E).

When doing unit conversions, remember that if a given unit is in both the numerator and denominator, that unit cancels out. The expression has grams and pounds in both the numerator and the denominator, so the unit remaining at the end of the conversion is ounces. Thus, the expression converts grams to ounces.

6.   A

Translate the information given into algebra. First, work with the information that X is 3 more than 4 times Y. You can write 4 times Y as $4Y$. Then 3 more than 4 times Y is $4Y + 3$. Since X is 3 more than 4 times Y, $X = 4Y + 3$.

Now work with the information that Y is 7 less than 12 times Z: 12 times Z is $12Z$. Then 7 less than 12 times Z is $12Z - 7$. Since Y is 7 less than 12 times Z, $Y = 12Z - 7$.

You have now found that $X = 4Y + 3$ and $Y = 12Z - 7$. Substitute $12Z - 7$ for Y in the equation $X = 4Y + 3$. Then $X = 4(12Z - 7) + 3 = 4(12Z) - 4(7) + 3 = 48Z - 28 + 3 = 48Z - 25$. Thus, $X = 48Z - 25$. This says that X is 25 less than 48 times Z.

7. C

The formula for percent increase is

$$\text{Percent increase} = \frac{\text{New value} - \text{Original value}}{\text{Original value}} \times 100\%$$

So the percent that $54 is greater than $40 is

$$\frac{54 - 40}{40} \times 100\% = \frac{14}{40} \times 100\%$$
$$= \frac{7}{20} \times 100\%$$
$$= 7 \times 5\%$$
$$= 35\%$$

8. A

To find the difference between Division V's 2019 and 2020 profits, find each year's profit separately.

2019: According to the pie chart, in 2019, Division V made 25% of the 164,000,000 profit: $(0.25)164,000,000 = 41,000,000$.

2020: According to the text, the other divisions made 39% and 46% of the profit, respectively.

$100\% - 39\% - 46\% = 15\%$ left for Division V in 2020. So $(0.15)240,000,000 = 36,000,000$.

Compare: 41 million − 36 million = 5 million difference.

9. C

Evelyn needs to do two things: correct the error and apply the original correct calculation.

Correcting the error: to "cancel out" the error of dividing by 7, multiply by 7.

Applying the original correct calculation: multiply by 7.

Multiplying by 7 two times is equivalent to multiplying by 49.

10. E

Solve inequalities just as you would solve an equation. You are trying to isolate the variable. First isolate $8n$. This yields $8n > 64$. Now divide by 8, which gives $n > 8$. The only wrinkle to look out for in inequalities is that if you multiply or divide by a negative number, you need to reverse the inequality sign. However, no such operation is involved here.

11. C

This question requires you to rearrange the equation until you have $x - 2y$ isolated on one side. Start with the parentheses and use the distributive property: $3x + 3 = 6y + 12$. Now, get all the numbers on the right side by subtracting 3 from both sides: $3x = 6y + 9$. Then you need the y's on the same side as the x's, so subtract $6y$ from both sides: $3x - 6y = 9$. Lastly, because you want to know what $x - 2y$ is equal to, divide both sides of the equation by 3: $x - 2y = 3$.

12. D

Follow the information one step at a time to build up the expression the question asks for. The variable c represents the number of cards that Bill owns. Use this to write an expression for Jason. Because Jason has 25 more cards than Bill, the number of cards that Jason has can be expressed as $c + 25$. Now look at what it says about Charlie: he has $\frac{1}{5}$ as many cards as Jason. Divide the expression representing the number of cards that Jason has by 5:

$$\frac{c + 25}{5} = \frac{c}{5} + \frac{25}{5} = \frac{c}{5} + 5$$

13. E

The question asks you to identify which of the given numbers you need to determine how much money Peggy earns washing cars. There are four numbers: 10 weeks, 1 hour, 123 cars, and $8 per car. You only need to know the number of cars and the rate she earns per car to determine the total amount she earns. That means you only need 123 and $8.

14. B

Nabila needs two $5 bills for every pizza she buys, and since she buys two pizzas, she needs four $5 bills for pizza. She needs one $5 bill for every three sodas she buys, and since she buys nine sodas, she needs three $5 bills for soda. Four $5 bills for pizza plus three $5 bills for soda means Nabila needs seven $5 bills in total.

15. C

To solve this type of problem, begin with the information about the first element and apply what you learn about the second. You know that Bruno sold t hot dogs and received $20 in tips. Mitch sold $\frac{4}{5}$ as many hot dogs. This can be expressed as $\frac{4t}{5}$. You also learn that Mitch received $6 less in tips, which means that he received $14 in tips. The last piece of information allows you to express the whole thing in terms of dollars. Because each hot dog sells for $2, the money Mitch earned from selling hot dogs equals $2 \times$ number of hot dogs. Mitch therefore earned $2 \times \frac{4t}{5} + 14 = \frac{8t}{5} + 14$ dollars.

16. A

A coordinate is written in the form (x, y), where x is the number of spaces left or right of the origin, and y is the number of spaces up or down from the origin. Only (A) and (C) have a vertex at $(3, 4)$: that is, 3 to the right and 4 up from the origin. **(A)** is the one that has its right angle at that point. (C)'s right angle is at $(3, 0)$, with a different corner at $(3, 4)$. Note that you do not have to consider area at all.

17. B

First, calculate the total number of widgets Company X needs: 375 widgets/machine $\times$ 80 machines = 30,000 widgets needed.

One of the answer choices must be correct, so backsolving will be efficient. Start with (C): 85 widgets/container $\times$ 360 containers = 30,600. This is enough widgets, but the question asks for the *smallest* number of widgets per container.

Test (B): 84 widgets/container $\times$ 360 containers = 30,240.

Choice (A), 83, will be too small, so the correct choice is **(B)**. (Note that you could have tested choice (A) instead of (B) to find that out.)

18. D

Rather than turning this into a complicated inequality, simply solve the given equation for $3,010:

$$3,010 = 75n + 250$$
$$2,760 = 75n$$
$$36.8 = n$$

Logically, this means 36 will be under $3,010, and 37 will slightly exceed $3,010, so the answer must be 37.

19. D

The rectangle $WXYZ$ looks like its length is twice that of the smaller rectangle, and its width also looks like twice the width of the smaller rectangle. If you were to draw the smaller rectangle $ABCD$ inside the larger rectangle $WXYZ$, you would be able to fit four of them inside. Thus, the area of the larger rectangle must be approximately 4 times the area of the smaller one, or $4 \times 12 = 48$.

20. C

When a plane and a sphere have at least one point of intersection, there is no way that the intersection could be an ellipse. The intersection must be a circle or a single point. Eliminate choices (A) and (B).

If the plane intersects the sphere at more than one point and the plane does not contain the center of the circle, the diameter of the circle of intersection must be a circle whose diameter is less than the diameter of the sphere. Choice **(C)** is correct, and you can eliminate (D) and (E).

21. 79/80

Since the question asks you to compare the volumes of the large and small cylinders, find each of these separately.

Large cylinder: The diameter is 8, so the radius is 4. The height is given as 15. Therefore, $V = (4)^2 \times 15 \times \pi = 240\pi$.

Small cylinder: The diameter is one-fourth that of the large cylinder, so the diameter is 2, making the radius 1. The height is given as 3. Therefore, $V = (1)^2 \times 3 \times \pi = 3\pi$.

The problem specifically asks for the fraction of the large cylinder that is NOT occupied by the small cylinder. The volume of the large cylinder not occupied by the small cylinder is $240\pi - 3\pi = 237\pi$.

The fraction of the large cylinder not occupied by the small cylinder is therefore $\frac{237\pi}{240\pi} = \frac{237}{240} = \frac{79}{80}$.

22. B

Point O is the origin, which mean its coordinates are $(0, 0)$. Since O is also the center of the circle and the point $(v, 0)$ is on the circumference of the circle, the radius of the circle is the distance from $(0, 0)$ to $(v, 0)$. In other words, v is the radius of the circle.

The circumference of a circle is $2\pi r$, where r is the radius and π can be approximated as 3.141. Since the circumference of the circle is given as 100, $100 = 2 \times 3.141 \times r$. Then solve for r: $50 = 3.141 \times r$, and $15.9 = r$. The closest value in the choices is 16.

23. B, C, D

The triangle inequality theorem states that the length of any side of a triangle must be less than the sum of the lengths of the other two sides of the triangle. If the lengths of two sides of the triangle are 8 and 12, then the length of the third side (call it z) must be less than the sum of the lengths of the other two sides. So $z < 8 + 12 = 20$. Thus, $z < 20$.

The triangle inequality theorem also states that the length z of the third side of a triangle must be greater than the positive difference of the other two sides of the triangle. So $z > 12 - 8 = 4$. Thus, $z > 4$.

Combine the two pieces of information you know about z to establish a range of possible values for z: $4 < z < 20$. Since the perimeter of any polygon is the sum of the lengths of its sides, the perimeter of a triangle is the sum of the lengths of its three sides. So the perimeter of the triangle in this question is $8 + 12 + z = 20 + z = z + 20$.

Since z is greater than 4 and less than 20, the perimeter $20 + z$ of the triangle can be any number that is greater than 24 and less than 40. Looking at the choices, three fall in this range: 25, 33, and 37.

24. C

The values in the list are already in order. The value 27 shows up three times, more often than any other number, so 27 is the mode. The median is 32, the middle number of the list. To find the average of 27 and 32, add the two numbers and divide by 2, resulting in 29.5.

25. A

Solving this type of problem requires three steps. First, subtract the number of people who have neither a smartphone nor a tablet from the total. This leaves you with 19. From this number, subtract the number who own a smartphone: 17. This gives you 2 for the number of people who own *only* a tablet. Finally, add 5 (the number of people who own both) to 2 to get the total number of people who own a tablet. Sketching a Venn diagram may help to understand how these numbers are related.

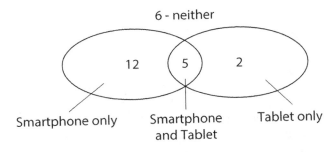

26. D

Translating English to math, the equation given in the problem is $P(\text{purple}) = P(\text{green}) + \dfrac{3}{8}$.

The probability formula is:

$$\text{Probability} = \frac{\text{Number of desired outcomes}}{\text{Number of possible outcomes}}.$$

$$P(\text{purple}) = \frac{x}{7 + 14 + x} = \frac{x}{21 + x}$$

$$P(\text{green}) = \frac{14}{7 + 14 + x} = \frac{14}{21 + x}$$

The equation $P(\text{purple}) = P(\text{green}) + \dfrac{3}{8}$ becomes

$$\frac{x}{21 + x} = \frac{14}{21 + x} + \frac{3}{8}.$$

Multiply both sides by $(21 + x)$ and solve for x:

$$x = 14 + \frac{3}{8}(21 + x)$$

$$x = 14 + 7.875 + 0.375x$$

$$0.625x = 21.875$$

$$x = 35$$

27.　C

This question requires you to think in terms of rearranging the average formula, usually written as $\dfrac{\text{Sum of numbers}}{\text{Number of numbers}} = \text{Average}$. In this question, you are given the average and the number of items. To find the sum of those numbers, write the formula this way: Sum = Number of numbers $\times$ Average. Multiply the average by the number of items: $12 \times 9 = 108$.

28.　A

This question tests probability, as well as factors. The factors of 20 are 1, 2, 4, 5, 10, and 20. There are six factors. Probability is the ratio of the number of desired outcomes to the number of total possible outcomes. Because the desired outcomes are the factors of 20 and the total possible outcomes are all numbers from 1 to 50, the probability is $\dfrac{6}{50}$.

Introducing Praxis Core Mathematics

Few people are neutral on the subject of mathematics. Math tests generate strong reactions, both from students in school and from Praxis test takers. Whether you are looking forward to the Praxis Core Academic Skills for Educators: Mathematics test or you're dreading it, there is good news: becoming familiar with the test's structure and format, along with doing some solid review of math fundamentals, will put you in a position to succeed.

The subject matter of the Praxis Core Mathematics test should be familiar. The test covers arithmetic, data analysis and statistics (e.g., averages and probability), and middle school–level algebra and geometry. For those who feel out of practice with this material, this chapter contains a substantial math review section. If you haven't already done so, start by taking the Core Math pre-test to identify the topics where you need a refresher.

Even those who feel rock-solid with their math skills set can benefit from practice on Praxis Core Mathematics questions. That's because the standardized test format rewards those who can answer questions quickly *and* accurately. A large majority of the questions on the Praxis Core Mathematics test are multiple-choice questions. This format has two important implications.

First, you need not show your work. In some cases, it may be faster to work backward by testing the answer choices than to work forward by doing lengthy calculations. This chapter will show you how to spot such cases to improve your efficiency.

Second, the presence of wrong answer choices can lead to mistakes, especially for a math whiz. Imagine a simple algebra problem that asks you to solve for the value of $2x$. You might dive right in, set up the equation, and determine that $x = 4$. You then glance at the answer choices and see that the first one is 4. "Piece of cake," you think. But be careful. The question asked you to solve for $2x$, so the correct choice is 8. Success on Praxis Core Mathematics requires you to learn how to avoid careless errors like that one, even when you have no trouble completing the math.

In this chapter, we'll show you an approach to test taking that takes advantage of the nature of the Praxis test's format to increase your score.

Know What to Expect

Test Format

The Praxis Core Mathematics test covers a wide range of math topics. More on that shortly. First, here are the basics of the test's format.

PRAXIS CORE MATHEMATICS
Format: Computer-delivered
Number of Questions: 56 Time: 90 minutes
Question Types: multiple-choice (called "selected-response" by the testmaker) with one correct answer; multiple-choice with one or more correct answers; numeric entry (enter the correct answer in a blank box on the screen)
On-screen four-function calculator available

(*continued*)

PRAXIS CORE MATHEMATICS
Test may include questions that do not count toward your score
No penalty for incorrect answers
Scratch paper is available during the test (it will be destroyed before you leave the testing center)

There are a few ways to take advantage of the test format to improve your score:

- Manage your time effectively. With 56 questions in 90 minutes, you have just over $1\frac{1}{2}$ minutes per question. Make sure to give yourself time to see every question.

- Guess strategically. There is no penalty for selecting a wrong answer. If a question has you thoroughly confused, or if you feel that it will take you too long to answer, eliminate any clearly incorrect answer choices, make your best guess, and move on. The next question may be one you can answer quickly and confidently.

- You can answer questions in any order. You should plan to move through the test more or less in order, but you may skip or guess on a question that is confusing or threatens to take too much time. Be sure to note any questions you skip or guess on so that you can return to them if you have time left at the end of the section.

Test Content

According to ETS, the Praxis Core Mathematics exam "measures academic skills in mathematics needed to prepare successfully for a career in education." While the test covers a range of math subjects, most of the content will be familiar. The test draws primarily from math content that corresponds to material you learned in eighth- or ninth-grade math classes. For some test takers, that's great news. For those of you who haven't looked at these concepts since middle school, the "Mathematics Content Review" section of this chapter will allow you to reacquaint yourself with the basics and practice with this content as it is tested on the Praxis Core Mathematics exam.

The following table provides a quick breakdown of the math content that appears on the Praxis Core Mathematics test. It shows the approximate number of questions per content area and the percentage of the test they represent.

PRAXIS CORE MATHEMATICS CONTENT	
Number and Quantity	20 questions: 36%
Algebra and Geometry	18 questions: 32%
Data Interpretation and Representation, Statistics, and Probability	18 questions: 32%

While the content is familiar, the question types on the Praxis Core Mathematics exam are different from the questions you remember from math tests you took in school. Rather than asking you to show your work and demonstrate mastery of concepts, Praxis Core Mathematics is all about results. You don't have to show your work, and you're not graded on how you approach the problems—all that matters is that you get to the correct answer, and get there quickly.

In short, Praxis Core Mathematics is a standardized exam, largely composed of multiple-choice questions. That means that there will be opportunities throughout the test to use the answer choices to help you solve problems, especially when you're in a pinch. Since there is no penalty for incorrect answers, you have a one-in-five chance of selecting the right answer, even without reading the question. After reading the question and plugging in an answer or two, you're well on your way to finding the correct answer, even on questions that cause you trouble. We'll discuss how to make the most of these "backdoor" strategies later in the chapter.

As you work through this chapter, pay attention to the material with which you are already comfortable and those topics that give you any difficulty. For questions you have a natural knack for, it makes sense to work out your answers in a more straightforward fashion. For questions in areas that give you trouble, think about using the answer choices and working backward. Praxis Core Mathematics is all about results, and the only results that matter are correct answer choices.

Question Types

On Praxis Core Mathematics, you'll see three question types: Multiple-Choice Single-Select, Multiple-Choice Select-One-or-More Answer Choices, and Numeric Entry. Let's take a look at an example of each.

Multiple-Choice Single-Select. By far the most common is the familiar multiple-choice question with five answer choices and one correct answer. Of the 56 questions on the test, approximately 49 will be of this type.

Answer the following question by selecting the correct response.

> The town of Spartaville is 500 km away from the town of Pleasantville. A map of the county is drawn to a scale of 1 cm = 2.5 km. How many centimeters apart are the two towns on the map?
>
> A. 50
>
> B. 200
>
> C. 250
>
> D. 1,000
>
> E. 2,500

To solve this problem, you can use a proportion to determine the distance on the map. The relationship between map and actual kilometers is given in the scale 1 cm = 2.5 km. The ratio is always the same. So $\frac{1 \text{ cm}}{2.5 \text{ km}} = \frac{x \text{ cm}}{500 \text{ km}}$. Cross-multiply and solve for the number of centimeters: 200. Choice (**B**) is correct. Notice that you can also solve this problem by testing the answer choices. Choice (A) would give you $50 \times 2.5 = 125$. That's too small. Choice (B) gives $200 \times 2.5 = 500$, which is correct. It's now clear that the remaining choices would all be too large. You'll see more about how to use Backsolving strategies like this in the next section.

Multiple-Choice Select-One-or-More Answer Choices. Occasionally, the testmaker will give you a multiple-choice question in which more than one answer choice may be correct. Sometimes, a question of this type will ask you to choose the "correct response(s)," meaning that one or more answer choices may work. You get credit for a question of this type only if you select all of the correct answer choices and none of the incorrect ones. At other times, the instructions for a question of this type may specify the number of correct answer choices. If, for example, a question gives you four answer choices and tells you to click on "two correct responses," you will get credit for that question only if you select the two correct choices and neither of the incorrect ones. While the instructions may sound a little complicated, you will get used to these questions with a little practice. Moreover, you are unlikely to see more than three or four questions of this type on the test.

Answer the following question by selecting the correct response(s).

Which of the following values are equal to 760?

Select all such values.

A. 0.76×10^3

B. 7.6×10^2

C. 7.6×10^3

D. $7,600 \times 10^{-1}$

E. $7,600 \times 10^{-2}$

This question tests your knowledge of exponents. When multiplying by powers of 10, simply move the decimal point the number of places indicated in the exponent of 10 to the left if the exponent is negative, and move it to the right if the exponent is positive. Convert the values this way:

(A) $0.76 \times 10^3 = 760$

(B) $7.6 \times 10^2 = 760$

(C) $7.6 \times 10^3 = 7,600$

(D) $7,600 \times 10^{-1} = 760$

(E) $7,600 \times 10^{-2} = 76$

Because you are asked to select all of the applicable choices, you must select answers **(A)**, **(B)**, and **(D)**, and not select (C) and (E), to get credit for this question.

Numeric Entry. The third question type you'll see on the Praxis Core Mathematics test is the one that is most like the typical questions on math tests in school. These problems present you with a question and then a box in which to type your answer. If the answer is meant to be a fraction, you'll see two boxes: one for the numerator and one for the denominator. Although there are no answer choices to select, you still don't have to show your work. You may do your work on scratch paper and type in your answer. If you use the on-screen calculator, it has a button marked "Transfer Display" that will automatically enter whatever is on the calculator screen into the answer box. (If you use that feature, make sure you are at your final answer before clicking "Transfer Display.")

Enter the correct answer in the box.

Donald's daily commute is 20 miles. Marta's daily commute is 24 miles. What percent longer is Marta's daily commute than Donald's daily commute?

Marta's commute is [   ] % longer than Donald's commute.

To solve this problem, you need to find the difference between Marta's and Donald's commutes and then determine what percent of Donald's commute that difference represents. The formula you'll use here is as follows:

$$\text{Percent greater} = \frac{\text{Higher value} - \text{Lower value}}{\text{Lower value}} \times 100\%$$

Apply the numbers from the story problem to this formula.

$$\frac{24 - 20}{20} \times 100\% = \frac{4}{20} \times 100\% = \frac{1}{5} \times 100\% = 20\%$$

So, to get the question right, enter **20** into the box.

Calculator

For the Praxis Core Mathematics test, you will have access to an on-screen four-function calculator. This calculator has buttons for the primary arithmetic operations, parentheses, square roots, and positive/negative numbers. As previously mentioned, it also has a button labeled "Transfer Display" that will enter the number on the calculator screen into the blank box for numeric-entry questions.

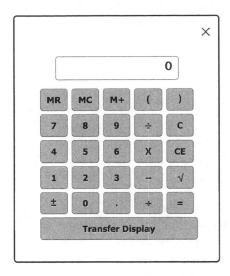

You will have the opportunity to work with a calculator that has the same functionality when you are doing the practice tests or exercises in this book's online resources.

While the calculator may be helpful and save you time on some questions, don't use the calculator unnecessarily. Here are a few tips to make the most of the calculator:

- Most of the questions on Praxis Core Mathematics will not require the calculator.
- The calculator is most helpful on questions that require lengthy calculations or those that contain large numbers.
- The calculator will display fractions as numbers with decimal points. You might have to translate the result to a fraction to answer some multiple-choice and numeric-entry questions.
- Opening the calculator and typing in numbers could actually cost you time if the calculations are simple enough to do in your head or on scratch paper, so be judicious with your calculator use.

One caution: Some Praxis tests, such as Mathematics: Content Knowledge (5161) and Algebra I (5162), provide scientific or graphing calculators that have additional functionality. For any test in the Praxis series that contains mathematics, check **ets.org/praxis/test_day/policies/calculators** for information about the type of calculator provided or permitted, for tutorials on its use, and for tips on using the appropriate calculator efficiently and effectively.

How to Approach Praxis Core Mathematics

The two most important things to remember when it comes to Praxis Mathematics are that Praxis Mathematics is not high-school mathematics and that you should never leave a question unanswered.

If you have not taken the Praxis Core Mathematics pre-test at the beginning of this chapter, do so now. Completing the pre-test and reviewing your results will give you a sense of the content areas with which you are most comfortable and those that give you trouble. You'll be able to refresh your familiarity with those content areas in the "Mathematics Content Review" section of this chapter.

Managing Your Time

Once you know your strengths and weaknesses, you can make more strategic use of your time on the test. If a question looks like one you can readily handle using a straightforward "textbook approach," work through it in a straightforward manner. But also be on the lookout for alternative, time-saving approaches, such as using the answer choices to work backward or estimating to avoid lengthy calculations.

Plan to work through the section more or less in order. If you are strong with the math content on this test and have completed sufficient practice, you may be able to complete all of the questions with time remaining. If so, use the extra time to double-check any questions on which you were not entirely confident. You can mark questions within the test interface or keep a list on your scratch paper of questions you'll revisit, time permitting.

While rolling through the entire test quickly and confidently is the ideal goal, chances are that most test takers will feel some degree of time pressure and will run into a handful of questions that cause them some doubt or confusion. If you fall into this latter group, taking the advice that follows can have a big impact on your score.

Skip and Guess Strategically

To take full advantage of the test format, keep three things in mind:

- With 56 questions in 90 minutes, you have just over a minute and a half per question.
- Your goal is to answer as many questions correctly as possible.
- There is no wrong-answer penalty.

All of this means that mismanaging just two or three questions can impact your score. If you confront a very difficult or confusing question and respond by taking two (or three, or four, or more) minutes to solve it, you will have eaten up the time that you could have used to get two or three or more questions correct. That trade-off is bad for your score (even if finally getting that tough question right is psychologically satisfying).

To be a great test taker, follow these simple guidelines to skip questions and guess strategically to improve your score:

- When you encounter a question that you know you are unlikely to answer correctly (or that is likely to take you more than a minute and a half to answer), skip it immediately.
- When you skip a question, mark it in the test interface (and/or on your scratch paper) so that you can return to it after answering all other questions.
- Before skipping to the next question, select an answer. You don't want to inadvertently run out of time and leave a question blank. Even making a random guess gives you a chance of getting the question right.

- If there are some answer choices you can eliminate through estimation or critical thinking (e.g., "I know that the right answer will be a positive number, but (D) and (E) are negative"), do so. Then guess from among the choices that remain.

Following these tips will help you maintain control of the test. If you allow a question to cost you time and increase your frustration, you sacrifice that control. A good way to think about it is this: "I won't guess because I fail and give up; I will guess when it is the smart and strategic thing for me to do to improve my score." Sometimes, when you skip a question and come back to it at the end, you discover that it was simpler than you thought at first. That's great. Even if you still find it hard or confusing, you'll be happy that you managed the test in a way that allowed you to get to all of the easiest questions with time to answer them, and you'll know you've done your level best throughout.

The Kaplan Three-Step Method for Praxis Mathematics

> **THE KAPLAN METHOD FOR PRAXIS MATHEMATICS**
>
> **STEP 1:** Read through the question
>
> **STEP 2:** Do it now or guess
>
> **STEP 3:** Look for the fastest approach

Step 1. Read Through the Question

This step may sound comically obvious. "Of course, I'm going to read through the question! How else can I solve the problem?" In reality, this step is not as self-evident as it seems. Many test takers will start doing calculations after reading the first part of the question's first sentence. Expert test takers, however, read the entire question carefully before they start solving the problem. Doing this helps them spot the most efficient approach to the question, and it helps them avoid careless mistakes. Consider the following problem:

> At Blinky Burgers restaurant, two hamburgers and five orders of french fries cost the same as four hamburgers and two orders of french fries. If the restaurant charges $1.50 for a single order of french fries, how much does it charge for two hamburgers?
>
> A. $2.25
>
> B. $3.00
>
> C. $4.50
>
> D. $5.00
>
> E. $6.00

Pay close attention to what the question is asking. This question contains a pitfall for test takers who don't read carefully. Can you spot it?

The question asks for the cost of two hamburgers, not one. Many students will get this question wrong by finding the price of one hamburger and then forgetting to double it. It's a careless mistake, but it's easy to be careless when you're working quickly. Always make sure you know what's being asked.

Step 2. Do It Now or Guess

Another reason to read carefully before answering is that you probably shouldn't solve every problem on your first pass. As discussed previously, taking control of your Praxis test experience involves deciding which problems to answer and which ones to guess on and come back to later.

Before you try to solve the problem, decide whether you want to do it now. In our sample problem about Blinky Burgers, this will likely depend on how comfortable you are setting up algebraic equations or, possibly, whether you've spotted an alternative approach to the problem. If you have no idea how to solve the problem, or if you think the problem will take a long time to solve, take your best guess, mark the question, and make note of it on your scratch paper. After you've answered the remaining questions, you can return to the questions you've marked and spend more time on them.

Don't worry about "the ones that got away." It feels good to try to answer every question on a test, but if you end up not getting back to a question or two, don't feel bad. Make quick, strategic guesses; bank your time; and let go. By spending more of your time on the questions you can answer, you'll improve your chances of getting a great score.

Step 3. Look For the Fastest Approach

Once you have understood what a question is asking and have decided to tackle it, look for any alternative approaches that may be more efficient. Sometimes the "obvious" or "classroom" way of solving a problem is the long way. Take another look at the Blinky Burgers problem.

> At Blinky Burgers restaurant, two hamburgers and five orders of french fries cost the same as four hamburgers and two orders of french fries. If the restaurant charges $1.50 for a single order of french fries, how much does it charge for two hamburgers?
>
> A. $2.25
> B. $3.00
> C. $4.50
> D. $5.00
> E. $6.00

Many students would turn this word problem into two algebraic equations: $2h + 5f = 4h + 2f$ and $f = 1.50$. From there, they would substitute 1.50 for f in the first equation and solve for h. Finally, they would multiply that answer by 2 to identify the correct answer choice. There is nothing wrong with that algebraic approach, and it would definitely produce the correct answer.

With a little critical thinking, however, you may spot an even faster approach here. The story problem tells you that two hamburgers and five orders of fries cost the same as four hamburgers and two orders of fries. Take away all of the like items from the two orders, and you're left with a helpful equation: three orders of fries cost the same as two hamburgers. Because one order of fries costs $1.50, three orders cost $4.50, and so $4.50 must also be the cost of two hamburgers. You can select **(C)** with confidence, and you didn't even have to set up any algebraic equations.

Textbook Approaches Versus Backdoor Strategies

We've mentioned a few times that the Praxis Core Mathematics test is not like the math tests you took in high school. That's because on most high-school tests, you were expected to show your work to demonstrate the ability to work step-by-step from the information given to the correct answer.

Praxis Core Mathematics doesn't work like that. While you're welcome to work through a problem in a straightforward way, you are by no means required to do so. Frequently, in fact, it pays to use an alternative approach. Let's apply the Kaplan Method for Praxis Mathematics to a few practice problems to see alternative strategies in action.

The questions that make up the Praxis Mathematics test contain many word problems with five answer choices containing numbers: integers, percents, or fractions. Praxis Core Mathematics also tests basic algebra, so occasionally, the answer choices will contain variables. In either case, it's important to note that the answer is right in front of you—you just have to find it.

Two methods in particular are extremely useful when you don't see how to use—or would rather not use—the textbook approach to solving the question. We call these strategies Backsolving and Picking Numbers. These strategies can help to make confusing problems more concrete. But even when you know how to solve using the "traditional approach," solving strategically may be faster.

Backsolving

Backsolving is a strategy that you can use on questions in which all of the answer choices contain nothing except numbers (no variables and no operations). In questions like these, it is sometimes easier to work backward from the answer choices than to work forward from the question.

Here's how Backsolving works. Once you note that all of the answer choices are exclusively numbers, note whether they are arranged from smallest to largest (more common) or from largest to smallest (less common). In either case, start with choice (C). If that number works when you plug it into the problem, then that's the correct answer, and you're done. If choice (C) does not work, then you can usually see whether it is too large or too small. If choice (C) is too large, try the next smallest choice. In other words, if the choices are arranged from smallest to largest, you would next test choice (B). If it is correct, you're done. If choice (B) is still too large, you know that choice (A) must be correct, and again, you're done. If you use Backsolving strategically, you usually don't have to try out more than two answer choices before zeroing in on the correct answer. To make this idea concrete, apply the strategy to the following problem.

> In a certain school, all students study exactly one language, either Chinese or Spanish. The ratio of students studying Chinese to those studying Spanish is 3:7. If there are 84 more students in Spanish classes than in Chinese classes, how many students study Chinese?
>
> A. 48
>
> B. 54
>
> C. 63
>
> D. 84
>
> E. 147

The correct answer should yield a ratio of Chinese learners to Spanish learners of 3:7. Note that the answer choices are arranged from smallest to largest and begin by testing out choice (C).

If there are 63 students in Chinese classes, there are $63 + 84 = 147$ Spanish learners, so the ratio of students of Chinese to students of Spanish is $\frac{63}{147} = \frac{9}{21} = \frac{3}{7}$, which is correct. You're done.

With choice (**C**) as the correct answer, this question took almost no time at all. Of course, the answer isn't always the first choice you pick. But usually, when you start with (C) and that answer doesn't work, you'll know which direction to go. Choice (C) will be too big or too small, leaving you with only two answers that could possibly be correct.

Try another one.

> A tailor has 20 yards of shirt fabric. How many shirts can she make if each shirt requires $2\frac{3}{4}$ yards of fabric?
>
> A. 6
> B. 7
> C. 8
> D. 10
> E. 14

You can, of course, find the correct answer by dividing 20 by $2\frac{3}{4}$. If that calculation gives you pause, Backsolving can get you to the correct answer efficiently and effectively. Note that the answer choices are arranged from smallest to largest. Now, start by testing choice (C). If the tailor could make 8 shirts, that would require at least $2\frac{3}{4} = \frac{11}{4} \times 8 = 22$ yards of fabric. That's too much fabric, so the correct answer must be less than 8. Eliminate (C), (D), and (E). You could multiply $2\frac{3}{4}$ by 7 at this point, or you could reason out the problem. If 8 shirts require 22 yards of fabric, and each shirt takes $2\frac{3}{4}$ yards, you know that 7 shirts would take less than 20 yards of fabric because $22 - 2\frac{3}{4}$ would be less than 20. (**B**) is therefore correct.

Let's quickly recap the steps involved in Backsolving:

Step 1: Start with choice (C) and plug it in. If the numbers work out, choose (C) and move on.

Step 2: If (C) doesn't work, eliminate it along with other choices you know are too big or too small.

Step 3: Keep going until you find the choice that works.

Picking Numbers

Some problems on the Praxis Core Mathematics test may initially strike you as vague or abstract, particularly when they contain variables or test the properties of numbers. Picking a number to stand in for a variable can make questions of this type far more concrete. Just make sure that the number you pick meets the criteria described in the question. Consider the following example, which tests remainders.

> When n is divided by 14, the remainder is 10. What is the remainder when n is divided by 7?
>
> A. 1
> B. 2
> C. 3
> D. 4
> E. 5

To pick a number that can stand in for n in this problem, add the remainder given in the problem to the divisor given in the problem and substitute that number for n. Because $14 + 10 = 24$, substitute 24 for n. Now, divide 24 by 7: $24 \div 7 = 3r3$ (in other words, "3 with a remainder of 3"). Thus, the answer is (**C**).

Note, too, that Backsolving would not have provided any help in this problem. That's because the problem is about the properties of an unknown number. As you practice, take note of the characteristics of problems for which various strategies are or are not useful so that you can spot those cases when you're taking the official exam.

Another case in which Picking Numbers can be helpful is on questions in which the answer choices contain variables. This is great news because, for some test takers, these problems are among the most confusing on the Praxis Core Mathematics test. Give the following example a try:

> Four years from now, Ron will be twice as old as his sister will be then. If Ron is R years old now, how many years old is his sister now?
>
> A. $\dfrac{R - 4}{2}$
>
> B. $R - 4$
>
> C. $\dfrac{R + 4}{2}$
>
> D. $R - 2$
>
> E. $R + 2$

If you are comfortable translating word problems into algebra, you may be confident tackling this problem with the "classroom approach." Keep in mind, however, that Picking Numbers can be easier and quicker on questions like this one. Here's how you would pick numbers in this case: Begin by picking a number for R, Ron's age now. Choose a simple number that is easy to add to, subtract from, and divide. We'll use $R = 10$. Now, substitute 10 for R in the question and the answer choices, and you're left with the following, much simpler problem:

> Four years from now, Ron will be twice as old as his sister will be then. If Ron is 10 years old now, how many years old is his sister now?
>
> A. $\dfrac{10 - 4}{2}$, or 3
>
> B. $10 - 4$, or 6
>
> C. $\dfrac{10 + 4}{2}$, or 7
>
> D. $10 - 2$, or 8
>
> E. $10 + 2$, or 12

Now, let's see: Ron is 10 years old *now*, so in four years, he'll be 14, which means his sister will be 7 years old *then*. Because she'll be 7 in four years, that means she must be 3 years old *now*. The correct answer is (**A**).

Picking Numbers is also an effective strategy on percent questions that do not specify a value. On these questions, pick 100 as your value because it is easy to calculate percents of 100.

Give this question a try:

> The value of a certain stock rose by 30 percent from March to April and then decreased by 20 percent from April to May. The stock's value in May was what percent of its value in March?
>
> A. 90%
>
> B. 100%
>
> C. 104%
>
> D. 110%
>
> E. 124%

Notice that while the question involves the value of a certain stock, the question does not give that value. Picking a number to stand in for the initial value of the stock will make the question more concrete and manageable. Since you must determine a percentage of the initial value, use 100 to stand in for the initial value of the stock. If the stock price was initially $100 per share, then after it rose by 30 percent from March to April, its value in April was $130. When that value decreased by 20 percent in May, that decrease was $0.20 \times \$130 = \$26$. Subtract $26 from $130 to find the value of the stock in May: $\$130 - \$26 = \$104$. Because the March value was $100, the May value of $104 is 104% of the March value. Choice (**C**) is therefore correct.

Picking Numbers can also come in handy on questions about number properties, such as evens and odds or positives and negatives. The following example may be easy if you've memorized the rules about even and odd numbers, but if you haven't (or if you suddenly draw a blank on test day), Picking Numbers to stand in for the variables will help you answer the question quickly and confidently.

> If a and b are odd integers and m and n are even integers, then which one of the following must be an odd integer?
>
> A. $a + b$
>
> B. $m + n$
>
> C. $b \times n$
>
> D. $a \times b$
>
> E. $m \times n$

To pick numbers here, simply assign an appropriate number to each variable; for example, $a = 1$, $b = 3$, $m = 2$, and $n = 4$. This makes it easy to evaluate the choices. (A) $a + b = 1 + 3 = 4$. Incorrect. (B) $m + n = 2 + 4 = 6$. Incorrect. (C) $b \times n = 3 \times 4 = 12$. Incorrect. (**D**) $a \times b = 1 \times 3 = 3$. Correct. (E) $m \times n = 2 \times 4 = 8$. Incorrect.

When using a Picking Numbers strategy, make sure you're choosing stand-ins that fit the description of the variables in the question stem. Pay attention to terms such as *positive* and *negative* (you can't pick zero in those cases), *integer* (you can't pick a fraction), and *even* and *odd*. Remember the rules of the number line, too. Students sometimes forget that -1 is greater than -2, or that $-\frac{1}{4}$ is greater than $-\frac{1}{2}$. As long as you remain aware of what the question is asking and how it's defining the variables, Picking Numbers can be quite helpful in number properties questions.

To sum up: Picking Numbers can be useful when 1) there are variables in the question or answer choices, 2) the question asks about percentages but doesn't supply real numbers, and 3) the question asks about number properties.

The preceding examples show how Backsolving and Picking Numbers can come in handy on Praxis Core Mathematics questions. Get comfortable with these strategies and be flexible in your approach to new problems. It's essential that you figure out which techniques work best for you for the wide range of problems you'll see on the test.

The next section of this chapter provides a review of the basic mathematical concepts that are tested on the Praxis Core Mathematics test. Use your results from the pre-test to help you determine which areas are especially important for you to review, but don't hesitate to work through the entire *Content Review* section. After that, the chapter closes with a practice set of questions in the formats you'll see on test day. You may choose to refresh your memory on the Backsolving and Picking Numbers strategies before you work through that set.

Introducing the Mathematics Content Review

Now that you've learned the Kaplan Method for the question types on the Praxis Core Mathematics test, take some time to review the math concepts and rules that you're expected to know for the exam before practicing these questions in format. Keep a few things in mind as you work through the content review.

First, quite a bit of content is covered in this review. Depending on your strengths and weaknesses, you may be able to move quickly through some areas but may need to slow down and focus on others that give you trouble.

Second, before working through this review, be sure that you have taken the Praxis Core Mathematics pre-test to note the areas in which you have the greatest difficulty.

Third, on the test, you'll probably use the on-screen calculator for most complex addition, subtraction, multiplication, and division. In the Content Review, however, you're encouraged to work out the majority of examples longhand to reinforce your understanding of the underlying concepts.

Finally, note that the questions that follow each section of the review are not in test-like format. That's intentional. Here, you'll want to focus on the math content. You'll have additional opportunities to practice using strategic approaches in the test-like Practice Set at the end of the chapter and, of course, in the in-book and online practice tests. First, though, shore up your content weaknesses so that you'll be ready to play to your strengths when test day rolls around.

Mathematics Review One—Number and Quantity

The Decimal System

Decimals are numbers that use place values to show amounts less than 1. You already use decimals when working with money. For example, in the amount $10.25, you know that the digits to the right of the **decimal point** represent cents, or hundredths of a dollar.

The first four decimal place values are labeled on the chart below.

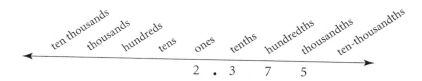

The number 2.375 is on the chart above. When reading a decimal out loud or in your head, read *and* in the place of the decimal point. After reading the decimal part, say the place value of the last decimal digit. So, you would read this number as "Two *and* three hundred seventy-five *thousandths*."

Comparing and Ordering

Comparing decimals is similar to comparing whole numbers.

> Matt ran the 400-meter race in 45.8 seconds. Alonzo ran the same race in 45.66 seconds. Which runner had the faster time?

- Line up the decimal points. Add a zero at the end of 45.8 so that both times have the same number of digits after the decimal.

  45.80
  45.66

- Since the whole numbers are the same, now compare the decimal parts of the numbers as though they were whole numbers. Doing this shows that **Alonzo's time was faster**.

  80 is greater than 66, so 45.8 is greater than 45.66

When you compare more than two numbers, it is helpful to compare one place-value column at a time, working left to right.

> Arrange the numbers 0.85, 1.8, 0.8, and 0.819 in order from greatest to least.

- Write the numbers in a column, lining up the decimal points. Add zeros so that the numbers have the same number of decimal places.

  0.850
  1.800
  0.800
  0.819

- Compare the digits, working from left to right. Only 1.8 has a whole-number part—a number greater than zero to the left of the decimal point—so it is the greatest. The remaining numbers each have 8 in the tenths column. Looking at the hundredths column, 0.85 is next, followed by 0.819. The least number is 0.8.

  In order:
  1.8
  0.85
  0.819
  0.8

Decimal Operations

Addition and Subtraction

Adding decimals is much like adding whole numbers. The trick is to make sure you have lined up the place-value columns correctly. You can do this by writing the numbers in a column and carefully lining up the decimal points.

Add 0.37 + 13.5 + 2.638:

- Write the numbers in a column, lining up the decimal points.

- You may add placeholder zeros so that the decimals have the same number of decimal places.

$$\begin{array}{r} 0.370 \\ 13.500 \\ +2.638 \\ \hline \end{array}$$

- Add. Starting on the right, add up each column. Regroup, or carry, as you would with whole numbers.

- Place the decimal point in the answer directly below the decimal points in the problem.

$$\begin{array}{r} ^{1\ \ 1} \\ 0.370 \\ 13.500 \\ +2.638 \\ \hline 16.508 \end{array}$$

To subtract decimals, write the numbers in a column with the greater number on top. Make sure the decimal points are in a line.

Find the difference between 14.512 and 8.7.

- Write the numbers in a column, lining up the decimal points. Add placeholder zeros so that the numbers have the same number of decimal places.

$$\begin{array}{r} 14.512 \\ -8.700 \\ \hline \end{array}$$

- Subtract. Regroup, or borrow, as needed. Place the decimal point in the answer directly below the decimal points in the problem.

$$\begin{array}{r} ^{13\ 15} \\ 1\!\!\!/4.\!\!\!/5 12 \\ -8.700 \\ \hline 5.812 \end{array}$$

The greater number may have fewer or no decimal places. In the next example, a decimal is subtracted from a whole number.

What does 9 minus 3.604 equal?

- Line up the place-value columns. Put a decimal point after the whole number 9 and add placeholder zeros.

$$\begin{array}{r} 9.000 \\ -3.604 \\ \hline \end{array}$$

- Subtract, regrouping as needed. Place the decimal point in the answer directly below the decimal points in the problem.

$$\begin{array}{r} ^{8\ \ 9\ \ 9\ 10} \\ \!\!\!/9.\!\!\!/0\ \!\!\!/0\ \!\!\!/0 \\ -3.6\ 0\ 4 \\ \hline 5.3\ 9\ 6 \end{array}$$

Multiplication and Division

You can use the same rules to multiply decimals that you use to multiply whole numbers. You don't have to line up the decimal points. You should wait until you are finished multiplying before placing the decimal point in the answer. The number of decimal places in the answer equals the sum of the number of decimal places in the numbers you are multiplying. On test day, use the on-screen calculator to save time and avoid mistakes. For now, though, make sure you understand the rules of these operations.

Find the product of 2.6 and 0.45.

- Set up the problem as though you were multiplying the whole numbers 26 and 45.

$$\begin{array}{r} 2.6 \\ \times 0.45 \\ \hline \end{array}$$

- Ignore the decimal points while you multiply.

- Now, count the decimal places in the numbers you multiplied. The number 2.6 has one decimal place, and 0.45 has two decimal places, for a total of three.

$$\begin{array}{r} 2.6 \\ \times 0.45 \\ \hline 130 \\ 1040 \\ \hline 1.170 \end{array}$$

- Starting from the right, count three decimal places to the left and insert the decimal point.

When you divide decimals, you must figure out where the decimal point will go in the answer before you divide.

Divide 14.4 by 6.

- Set up the problem. Because the divisor (the number you are dividing by) is a whole number, place the decimal point in the answer directly above the decimal point in the dividend (the number you are dividing).

- Divide. Use the rules you learned for dividing whole numbers.

$$\begin{array}{r} 2.4 \\ 6{\overline{\smash{\big)}\,14.4}} \\ \underline{-12} \\ 24 \\ \underline{-24} \\ 0 \end{array}$$

If the divisor is also a decimal, you must move the decimal points in both the divisor and the dividend before you divide.

Divide 4.9 by 0.35.

- Set up the problem. There are two decimal places in the divisor, which is 0.35. Move the decimal point in both the divisor and the dividend two places to the right. Note that since the dividend is 4.9, you need to add a zero to it to move the decimal two places.

$$0.35{\overline{\smash{\big)}\,4.90}}$$

- Place the decimal point in the quotient directly above the decimal point in the dividend.

- Divide.

$$\begin{array}{r} 14. \\ 35{\overline{\smash{\big)}\,490.}} \\ \underline{-35} \\ 140 \\ \underline{-140} \\ 0 \end{array}$$

Fractions

A fraction uses two numbers to represent part of a whole. The bottom number, called the **denominator**, indicates how many equal parts the whole is divided into. The top number, called the **numerator**, indicates how many parts of the whole you are working with.

- There are 4 equal parts in this rectangle. Because 3 are shaded, we say that $\frac{3}{4}$ of the rectangle is shaded.

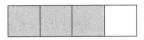

In a proper fraction, the numerator is less than the denominator. A **proper fraction** represents a quantity less than 1. An **improper fraction** is equal to or greater than 1.

- There are 6 equal parts in the figure below, and 6 are shaded; therefore, $\frac{6}{6}$ of the figure is shaded: $\frac{6}{6} = 1$.

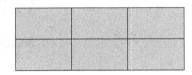

- In this grouping, each figure is divided into 2 equal parts or halves, so the denominator of the fraction is 2. A total of 3 parts are shaded, so the fraction of the shaded area of the figures is $\frac{3}{2}$.

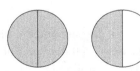

A **mixed number** is another way to show an amount greater than 1. It consists of a whole number and a proper fraction. Another name for the shaded portion in the last figure is $1\frac{1}{2}$. The improper fraction $\frac{3}{2}$ equals the mixed number $1\frac{1}{2}$.

You can also change an improper fraction to a whole number or mixed number.

Change $\frac{16}{5}$ to a mixed number.

- Divide the numerator (16) by the denominator (5). Because 16 is not evenly divisible by 5, there is a remainder. In this case, the remainder is 1.

$16 \div 5 = 3r1$

- The answer becomes the whole number, and the remainder becomes the numerator of the proper fraction. The denominator is the same as that of the original fraction.

$\frac{16}{5} = 3\frac{1}{5}$

You can also change a mixed number to an improper fraction.

Change $7\frac{2}{3}$ to an improper fraction.

- Multiply the whole number (7) by the denominator of the fraction (3). Then add the numerator (2).

  $7 \times 3 = 21$
  $21 + 2 = 23$

- Write the sum over the denominator of the original fraction.

  $7\frac{2}{3} = \frac{23}{3}$

To perform operations with fractions, you need to be able to write equal fractions in higher or lower terms. The terms are the numerator and the denominator. A fraction is **reduced to lowest terms** when the two terms do not have any common factor except 1.

- To **raise** a fraction, multiply both terms by the same number:

  $\frac{3}{4} = \frac{3 \times 3}{4 \times 3} = \frac{9}{12}$

- To **reduce** a fraction, divide both terms by the same number:

  $\frac{10}{15} = \frac{10 \div 5}{15 \div 5} = \frac{2}{3}$

Fraction Operations

Addition and Subtraction

You can add or subtract **like fractions**. Like fractions have a **common denominator**, which means the numbers below the fraction bar are the same.

Add $\frac{3}{10} + \frac{5}{10}$.

- Because the denominators are the same, add the numerators.

  $\frac{3}{10} + \frac{5}{10} = \frac{8}{10}$

- Reduce the answer to lowest terms.

  $\frac{8}{10} = \frac{8 \div 2}{10 \div 2} = \frac{4}{5}$

Subtract $\frac{2}{9}$ from $\frac{7}{9}$.

- Subtract the numerators. The answer is already in lowest terms.

  $\frac{7}{9} - \frac{2}{9} = \frac{5}{9}$

If the denominators are not the same, convert one or both fractions to equivalent fractions so that they become like fractions.

Add $\frac{5}{6} + \frac{1}{4}$.

- One way to find a common denominator is to list some multiples of both denominators.

  Multiples of 6: 6, $\boxed{12}$, 18

  Multiples of 4: 4, 8, $\boxed{12}$, 16

  The lowest common multiple of the denominators is 12.

$$\frac{5 \times 2}{6 \times 2} = \frac{10}{12}, \frac{1 \times 3}{4 \times 3} = \frac{3}{12}$$

- Convert each fraction to an equivalent fraction with a denominator of 12.

$$\frac{10}{12} + \frac{3}{12} = \frac{13}{12}$$

- Add the like fractions.

Multiplication and Division

It is not necessary to find a common denominator to multiply and divide fractions. To multiply fractions, simply multiply the numerators and then the denominators. Reduce the answer to lowest terms, if necessary.

What is the product of $\frac{7}{8}$ and $\frac{1}{2}$?

- Multiply the numerators and then multiply the denominators.

$$\frac{7}{8} \times \frac{1}{2} = \frac{7 \times 1}{8 \times 2} = \frac{7}{16}$$

Before multiplying a mixed number, change it to an improper fraction.

What is $\frac{1}{3}$ of $3\frac{3}{4}$?

- Change $3\frac{3}{4}$ to an improper fraction.

$$3\frac{3}{4} = \frac{15}{4}$$

- Multiply the numerators and the denominators.

$$\frac{1}{3} \times \frac{15}{4} = \frac{1 \times 15}{3 \times 4} = \frac{15}{12}$$

- Change to a mixed number and reduce to lowest terms.

$$\frac{15}{12} = 1\frac{3}{12} = 1\frac{1}{4}$$

To divide fractions, **invert** the divisor (the fraction you are dividing by) by switching its numerator and denominator. Then, multiply the fractions.

Jim has an 8-pound bag of nuts. He wants to fill smaller, $\frac{1}{2}$-pound bags using the nuts. How many $\frac{1}{2}$-pound bags can he fill?

- Divide 8 by $\frac{1}{2}$. Set up the division problem. Always write the whole or mixed numbers as improper fractions.

$$8 \div \frac{1}{2} = \frac{8}{1} \div \frac{1}{2} =$$

- Invert the fraction you are dividing by and change the operation sign to multiplication. Then multiply, following the rules for multiplying fractions. The result shows that Jim can fill **16 smaller bags**.

$$\frac{8}{1} \times \frac{2}{1} = \frac{16}{1} = 16$$

Ratios

Ratios represent the proportion of one quantity to another.

Ratios are usually written in the form *c:d*. A ratio does not, by itself, tell you the number of each item present.

> The ratio of blue marbles to green marbles in a bag is 5:3.

This does *not* necessarily mean that there are 5 blue marbles and 3 green marbles in the bag. All it means is that for every 5 blue marbles, there are 3 green marbles. It is possible that there are 10 blue marbles and 6 green marbles, 50 blue marbles and 30 green marbles, or any other combination in which the proportion of blue marbles to green marbles is 5:3.

Ratios can also be written as fractions. To write a ratio as a fraction, put the number associated with the word *of* in the numerator (on top) and put the number associated with the word *to* in the denominator (on the bottom) and reduce.

> The ratio of 20 apples to 12 oranges is $\frac{20}{12}$, which reduces to $\frac{5}{3}$, or 5:3 when expressed as a ratio.

Part-to-Part Ratios Versus Part-to-Whole Ratios

A ratio can express the relationship of a part to the whole, or it can express the relationship of a part to another part.

The previous examples both express part-to-part ratios. In the case of the marbles, there are two parts: blue marbles and green marbles. If all marbles in the bag are either blue or green, they make up the whole, that is, all the marbles in the bag. If we wanted to express the ratio of blue marbles to all the marbles in the bag, we would have to add the blue and green marbles together.

> If the ratio of blue marbles to green marbles in a bag is $\frac{5}{3}$, then the ratio of blue marbles to all marbles is $\frac{5}{3+5} = \frac{5}{8}$.

Proportions

A **proportion** is an equation that shows that two ratios are equal. The cross products in a true proportion are equal. In other words, when you multiply diagonally across the equal sign, the products are equal.

> The directions on a can of powdered drink mix say to add 3 cups of water to every 2 scoops of drink mix. Mike adds 12 cups of water to 8 scoops of drink mix. Did he make the drink correctly?

- Write the proportion, making sure the terms of the ratios are in the same order.

$$\frac{\text{Cups}}{\text{Scoops}} = \frac{3}{2} = \frac{12}{8}$$

- Cross-multiply and compare the products. Because the products are the same, the ratios are equal. This means **Mike made the drink correctly**.

$$3 \times 8 = 24$$
$$2 \times 12 = 24$$

Most proportion problems ask you to solve for a missing term.

A map scale says that 2 inches = 150 miles. What actual distance would a map distance of 5 inches represent?

- Write a proportion with both ratios in the same form: inches to miles. The variable x represents the unknown distance in miles.

$$\frac{\text{Inches}}{\text{Miles}} = \frac{2}{150} = \frac{5}{x}$$

- Locate the term in the first ratio that is diagonal from the known term in the second ratio. Cross-multiply.

$$\frac{2}{150} = \frac{5}{x}$$
$$150 \times 5 = 750$$

- Divide the result by the remaining known term to find the value of x.

$$x = 750 \div 2 = \mathbf{375}$$

Rates

Some proportion problems ask you to find a **rate**. A rate compares the number of units of one item to one unit of another item. When a rate is written in fraction form, its denominator is always one unit. In word form, rates are often expressed using the word *per*.

Connie drove 276 miles on 12 gallons of gasoline. How many miles per gallon did she get on the trip?

- Gas mileage is one kind of rate. You need to find how many miles Connie drove on 1 gallon of gasoline.

$$\frac{\text{Miles}}{\text{Gallons}} = \frac{276}{12} = \frac{x}{1}$$

- Solve. Connie got **23 miles per gallon** on the trip.

$$(276)(1) = 12x$$
$$x = 276 \div 12 = 23$$

On test day, remember to pay attention to each question stem and make calculations accordingly. If a bullet train travels 360 kilometers in 2 hours, it's easy to see that its rate is 180 kilometers per hour. If the question stem asks for the rate in kilometers per minute, however, you'll need to divide by 60 to get 3 km/min as the correct answer.

Percents

Percent means "per hundred" or "out of one hundred." For example, if you have $100 and you spend $25, you've spent $25 out of $100 or 25% of your money.

Because a percentage is a way of showing part of a whole, it has much in common with fractions, decimals, and ratios. In fact, a percentage is just a specific type of fraction: one in which the denominator is 100.

To convert a percent to a fraction, write the percent over 100 and reduce. To convert percents to decimals, drop the percent symbol and move the decimal point two places to the left.

Percent to Fraction

$$25\% = \frac{25}{100} = \frac{1}{4}$$

Percent to Decimal

$$25\% = 0.25$$

In any percent problem, there are three elements: the whole, the part, and the percent. The **whole** is the amount that the problem is about. The **part** is a portion of the whole. The **percent** is a number followed by the percent symbol (%).

> At a restaurant, Janice's bill is $20. She gives the waiter a tip of $3, which is 15% of her bill. Identify the whole, part, and percent in this situation.

- The entire bill of $20 is the whole. The $3 tip is the part, and the percent is 15%.

- One way to think of a percent problem is as a proportion. In this example, there are two ratios. The $3 tip is figured as a part of the $20, and 15% is the same as $\frac{15}{100}$. Because the two ratios are equal, they can be written as a proportion.

$$\frac{\text{Part}}{\text{Whole}} = \frac{3}{20} = \frac{15}{100}$$

- Cross-multiply to prove that the ratios are equal.

$$20 \times 15 = 300$$
$$3 \times 100 = 300$$

You can solve percent problems by using the equation $\text{Percent} = \frac{\text{Part}}{\text{Whole}}$ and solving for the missing element. Sometimes you will want to use the equation in the form $\text{Part} = \text{Percent} \times \text{Whole}$. Just remember to express the percent as a fraction with the percent value over 100, or as a decimal.

> At a plant that manufactures lighting fixtures, it is expected that approximately 2% of the fixtures assembled each day will have some type of defect. If 900 fixtures are completed in one day, how many of these are expected to be defective?

- You are given the percent and the whole, and you want to find the part. So use the equation $\text{Part} = \text{Percent} \times \text{Whole}$. Here, 2% = 0.02.

- Find the part: 2% of 900 = 0.02 × 900 = 18. **The company can expect to have 18 defective fixtures.**

There is a formula for percent change that may be handy for you to remember on test day:

$$\text{Percent change} = \frac{\text{New value} - \text{Original value}}{\text{Original value}} \times 100\%$$

If Charlie's rent was $1,400 per month last year and it has gone up to $1,620 per month this year, by what percentage did Charlie's rent increase from last year to this year?

$$\frac{1,610 - 1,400}{1,400} \times 100\% = \frac{210}{1,400} \times 100\% = 0.15 \times 100\% = 15\%$$

Charlie's rent went up 15% from last year to this year.

Note: When calculating a percent decrease, reverse the order of terms in the numerator (i.e., *original value − new value*) to avoid dealing with negative numbers.

Factors, Primes, and Divisibility

Multiples

An integer that is divisible by another integer with no remainder (see below) is a **multiple** of that integer.

- 12 is a multiple of 3 because 12 is divisible by 3; $\frac{12}{3} = 4$.

You can think of the multiples of a number as those numbers that you would get if you "counted" by that number. For example, if you counted by sixes, you would get 6, 12, 18, 24, 30, 36, 42, 48, and so on. All of these numbers, including 6, are multiples of 6.

Remainders

The **remainder** is what is left over in a division problem. A remainder is always smaller than the number you are dividing by.

- 17 divided by 3 is 5, with a remainder of 2.

This means that you can divide 17 into 5 equal parts (all of which have 3 units) plus 2 leftover units.

Factors

The **factors** of a number are the positive integers that evenly divide into that number.

- 36 has nine factors: 1, 2, 3, 4, 6, 9, 12, 18, and 36.

These factors can be grouped into pairs:

$$1 \times 36 = 2 \times 18 = 3 \times 12 = 4 \times 9 = 6 \times 6$$

Divisibility Tests

There are simple tests to determine whether a number is divisible by 2, 3, 4, 5, 6, or 9.

A number is divisible by 2 if its last digit is divisible by 2.

- 138 is divisible by 2 because 8 is divisible by 2.

A number is divisible by 3 if the sum of its digits is divisible by 3.

- 4,317 is divisible by 3 because $4 + 3 + 1 + 7 = 15$, and 15 is divisible by 3.
- 239 is *not* divisible by 3 because $2 + 3 + 9 = 14$, and 14 is not divisible by 3.

A number is divisible by 4 if its last two digits are divisible by 4.

- 1,748 is divisible by 4 because 48 is divisible by 4.

A number is divisible by 5 if its last digit is 0 or 5.

- 2,635 is divisible by 5, but 5,052 is *not* divisible by 5.

A number is divisible by 6 if it is divisible by both 2 and 3.

- 4,326 is divisible by 6 because it is divisible by 2 (last digit is 6) and by 3 ($4 + 3 + 2 + 6 = 15$).

A number is divisible by 9 if the sum of its digits is divisible by 9.

- 22,428 is divisible by 9 because $2 + 2 + 4 + 2 + 8 = 18$, and 18 is divisible by 9.

Prime Number

A **prime number** is an integer greater than 1 that has no factors other than 1 and itself. The number 1 is not considered prime. The number 2 is the first prime number and the only even prime. (This is fairly evident. Every other even number is divisible by 2 and therefore is not prime.) The first ten prime numbers are 2, 3, 5, 7, 11, 13, 17, 19, 23, and 29.

Powers and Roots

Powers constitute a special way to show repeated multiplication. For example, suppose you need to multiply $5 \times 5 \times 5 \times 5$. This series of operations can be expressed as "five raised to the fourth power." In other words, the number 5 appears in the expression 4 times.

We can write these operations using **exponents**. In the expression $5 \times 5 \times 5 \times 5$, the number 5 is the base. The exponent, a number written slightly above and to the right of the base, indicates how many times the base is repeated: $5 \times 5 \times 5 \times 5 = 5^4$.

To evaluate an expression, perform the multiplication indicated by the exponent.

Find the value of 2^5.

Write out the base the number of times indicated by the exponent and multiply.

$2^5 = 2 \times 2 \times 2 \times 2 \times 2 = 32$

Some specific exponents have properties to make note of:

1. A number raised to the exponent 1 equals itself. For example, $8^1 = 8$.
2. A number other than zero raised to the exponent zero equals 1. Example: $6^0 = 1$.
3. A number raised to a negative exponent is equal to a fraction, with a numerator of 1 and the term with a positive exponent in the denominator. Example:

$$4^{-2} = \frac{1}{4^2} = \frac{1}{4 \times 4} = \frac{1}{16}$$

A **square root** of a number n is a number that, when squared, equals the number n. Every positive number has two square roots. One square root of a positive number is positive, and the other square root of a positive number is negative. For example, the square roots of 25 are 5 and -5. This is because $5^2 = 25$ and $(-5)^2 = 25$. The number 0 has only one square root, 0.

By convention, if x is positive, $\sqrt{x}$ means the positive square root of x. Whenever there is a $\sqrt{\ }$ symbol, this means the positive square root. We have mentioned that 25 has two square roots, which are 5 and -5. However, $\sqrt{25}$ is unambiguous; it means the positive square root of 25. Therefore, we write $\sqrt{25} = 5$.

Find the value of $\sqrt{144}$.

- You know that $12 \times 12 = 144$.
- So $\sqrt{144} = 12$.
- Note that $\sqrt{144}$ is unambiguous. It means **12**.

The English System of Measurement

We use measurements to describe an object's length, weight, or volume. We also use measurement to describe a quantity of time. The United States uses the English, or standard, system of measurement. Study the lists below to learn the common standard units and their abbreviations.

Measurement Equivalencies

Length

1 foot (ft) = 12 inches (in.)
1 yard (yd) = 3 ft

Volume

1 cup (c) = 8 fluid ounces (fl oz)
1 pint (pt) = 2 c
1 quart (qt) = 2 pt
1 gallon (gal) = 4 qt

Weight

1 pound (lb) = 16 ounces (oz)
1 ton (t) = 2,000 lb

To change a larger unit of measurement to a smaller one, you need to multiply.

A picture frame is 3 feet 8 inches long. What is the length of the frame in inches?

- Change 3 feet to inches, using the fact that 1 foot = 12 inches. $3 \text{ ft} \times 12 = 36 \text{ in.}$

- Add the remaining 8 inches. The picture frame is **44 inches** in length. $36 + 8 = 44 \text{ in.}$

To change a smaller unit of measure to a larger one, divide using the appropriate measurement equivalency.

A package weighs 84 ounces. What is the weight of the package in pounds?

- Change 84 ounces to pounds. Because 1 pound = 16 ounces, divide by 16.

$$\begin{array}{r} 5 \\ 16\overline{)84} \\ -80 \\ \hline 4 \end{array}$$

- The remainder is in ounces, which are the same units of measure you started with. Therefore, the package weighs **5 lb 4 oz.** You can also express the remainder as a fraction: $5\dfrac{4 \text{ oz}}{16 \text{ oz}} = 5\dfrac{1}{4}$ lb.

In a measurement problem, you may need to add, subtract, multiply, or divide measurements. When finding a sum or a difference, remember that you can only add or subtract like measurement units.

A deck requires pieces of railing that are 5 feet 9 inches, 15 feet 4 inches, and 8 feet 6 inches. What is the total length of railing needed?

- Write the measurements in a column, aligning like units of measure.

- Add like units.

- Simplify the answer. Change 19 inches to 1 foot 7 inches and add this result to 28 feet. The deck requires **29 feet 7 inches** of railing.

$$\begin{array}{rr} 5 \text{ ft} & 9 \text{ in.} \\ 15 \text{ ft} & 4 \text{ in.} \\ +8 \text{ ft} & 6 \text{ in.} \\ \hline 28 \text{ ft} & 19 \text{ in.} \end{array}$$

When you subtract, you may need to regroup (also known as borrowing).

How much more is 4 pounds 3 ounces than 2 pounds 8 ounces?

- Align the values in the problem. Because you cannot subtract 8 ounces from 3 ounces, regroup 1 pound from the pounds column and add it to the ounces column as 16 ounces.

- Subtract. The difference is **1 pound 11 ounces**.

$$\begin{array}{rr} \overset{3}{\cancel{4}} \text{ lb} & \overset{19}{\cancel{3}} \text{ oz} \\ -2 \text{ lb} & 8 \text{ oz} \\ \hline 1 \text{ lb} & 11 \text{ oz} \end{array}$$

To multiply a measurement by a whole number, multiply the units of measure separately. Then simplify the result.

Tony has five lengths of plastic pipe, each measuring 6 feet 10 inches. What is the combined length of the five pieces of pipe?

- Multiply each part of the measurement by 5.

- Simplify using the fact that 1 foot = 12 inches. The combined length is **34 feet 2 inches**.

$$\begin{array}{r} 6 \text{ ft } 10 \text{ in.} \\ \times \quad 5 \\ \hline 30 \text{ ft } 50 \text{ in.} = \\ 30 \text{ ft} + 4 \text{ ft } 2 \text{ in.} = \\ 34 \text{ ft } 2 \text{ in.} \end{array}$$

To divide a measurement, you can divide each part of the measurement and then add the results. However, it will usually be faster to rewrite the measurement in terms of the smallest unit of measure. Then divide and simplify.

> John has 1 pint 5 fluid ounces of liquid lawn fertilizer. He plans to mix one-third of the liquid with two gallons of water and apply it to his lawn. How many fluid ounces of fertilizer will he use?

- Change the amount to ounces.
- To find one-third, divide by 3. John will use **7 fluid ounces** of lawn fertilizer.

$$1 \text{ pt} = 2 \text{ c} = 16 \text{ fl oz}$$
$$1 \text{ pt} + 5 \text{ fl oz} =$$
$$(16 + 5) \text{ fl oz} = 21 \text{ fl oz}$$
$$21 \text{ fl oz} \div 3 = 7 \text{ fl oz}$$

The Metric System

The **metric system** is the measurement system used in most countries. The main unit of length in the metric system is the **meter** (m). The **gram** (g) is the basic metric measure of mass (or weight). The basic unit of volume is the **liter** (l).

The units of measurement in the metric system are named by adding prefixes to the basic units. The prefixes have specific meanings:

milli– means one-thousandth
centi– means one-hundredth
deci– means one-tenth
deka– or *deca*– means ten
hecto– means hundred
kilo– means thousand

Therefore, a kilometer (km) equals 1,000 meters, a milligram (mg) equals a one-thousandth of a gram, and a centiliter (cl) equals a one-hundredth of a liter.

As in the decimal place-value system, each column on the chart below shows a value that is 10 times that of the column to its right. To convert between metric units, count the number of times that you must move to the right or left from the unit you are converting from to the unit you are converting to. Then move the decimal point that number of place values in the same direction.

kilo–	hecto–	deka–	meter	deci–	centi–	milli–
(km)	(hm)	(dam)	(m)	(dm)	(cm)	(mm)
1,000 m	100 m	10 m	1 m	0.1 m	0.01 m	0.001 m

Note: Although the chart uses the meter as the basic unit, you can also use the chart with liters and grams.

> How many millimeters (mm) are equal to 3 centimeters (cm)?

- Find *milli*– and *centi*– on the chart. The prefix *milli*– is one place to the right of the prefix *centi*–; therefore, you need to move the decimal point one place to the right to convert from centimeters to millimeters.
- So, 3 cm = 3.0 cm = **30 mm**.

How many grams (g) are equal to 6,400 (mg)?

- Start in the *milli–* column. The basic unit is three columns to the left. Move the decimal point three place-value columns to the left.

- So, 6,400 mg = **6.4 g**.

Metric measurements are written as decimal numbers. Therefore, you can perform operations with metric measurements using the rules for adding, subtracting, multiplying, and dividing decimals.

Three metal rods measure 1.5 meters, 1.85 meters, and 450 centimeters. What is the total length of the rods in meters?

- The first two measures are in meters. Convert the third measure to meters: 450 cm = 4.5 m.

- Use the rules for adding decimals. The total is **7.85 meters**.

$$\begin{array}{r} \overset{1}{1}.5 \\ 1.85 \\ +4.5 \\ \hline 7.85 \end{array}$$

Follow the same steps to subtract.

Tanya is jogging in a city park. The park has a path for joggers that is 2 kilometers in length. When she reaches the 750-meter checkpoint, how many kilometers does she have left to run?

- Change 750 meters to kilometers: 750 m = 0.75 km.

- Subtract using the rules for subtracting decimals. Tanya has **1.25 kilometers** left to run.

$$\begin{array}{r} \overset{1}{}\overset{9}{}\overset{10}{} \\ \cancel{2}.\cancel{0}\,\cancel{0} \\ -0.75 \\ \hline 1.25 \end{array}$$

Multiplying and dividing is easy in the metric system. Follow the rules for multiplying and dividing decimals.

Alex is a buyer at Rugs Plus. He plans to order 25 acrylic rugs to sell in the store. The shipping weight of each rug is 7.8 kilograms. What is the shipping weight in kilograms of the entire order?

- Multiply the weight of one rug (7.8 kg) by 25.

- The weight of 25 rugs is **195 kilograms**. Notice that the answer has the same unit of measure as the number you multiplied.

$$\begin{array}{r} 7.8 \\ \times\,25 \\ \hline 39.0 \\ 156.0 \\ \hline 195.0 \end{array}$$

At a food-processing plant, a storage tank holds 92.4 liters of a fruit drink. It takes three hours for a machine to empty the tank into small containers. How many liters of fruit drink does the machine process per hour?

- To find the number per hour, divide 92.4 liters by 3.

- The machine can process **30.8 liters per hour**.

$$\begin{array}{r} 30.8 \\ 3\overline{)92.4} \\ 9 \\ \hline 24 \\ -24 \\ \hline 0 \end{array}$$

Mathematics Review One Practice

1. Round 3.75 to the tenths place.

2. Round 5.908 to the ones place.

3. Which number is greater: 0.45 or 0.449?

4. Which number is greater: 0.008 or 0.08?

For questions 5 and 6, write the numbers in order from least to greatest.

5. 5.6   5.08   5.8   5.802

6. 0.1136   0.12   0.2   0.115

7. $\begin{array}{r} 4.025 \\ +3.971 \\ \hline \end{array}$

8. $\begin{array}{r} 8.5 \\ -1.074 \\ \hline \end{array}$

9. $\begin{array}{r} 17.52 \\ +3.80 \\ \hline \end{array}$

10. James ran three miles. His times for the individual miles were 7.2 minutes, 6.8 minutes, and 8.25 minutes. How long did it take him, in minutes, to run the three-mile distance?

11. $\begin{array}{r} 5.3 \\ \times 0.5 \\ \hline \end{array}$

12. $8\overline{)28.8}$

13. $\begin{array}{r} 9.62 \\ \times 1.005 \\ \hline \end{array}$

14. One container of floor cleaner holds 3.79 liters. If Zachary bought 4 containers, how many liters of cleaner did he buy?

For questions 15 and 16, write the proper fraction for the shaded portion of each figure.

15.

16.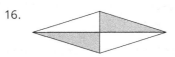

For questions 17 and 18, write an improper fraction and a mixed number for the shaded portion of each group of figures.

17.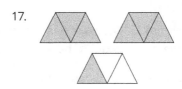

18.

For questions 19 and 20, write improper fractions as mixed numbers and mixed numbers as improper fractions.

19. $\dfrac{17}{3} =$

20. $2\dfrac{5}{12} =$

For questions 21 and 22, write an equal fraction with the given denominator.

21. $\dfrac{3}{4} = \dfrac{}{16}$

22. $\dfrac{3}{8} = \dfrac{}{40}$

For questions 23 and 24, reduce each fraction to lowest terms.

23. $\dfrac{21}{28} =$

24. $\dfrac{4}{24} =$

25. Eighteen of every 24 people surveyed say they went to at least one movie in December. What fraction of the people surveyed went to a movie in December? (Express your answer in the simplest fraction form.)

For questions 26 and 27, express the correct answer as a mixed number.

26. $5\dfrac{5}{6} + 2\dfrac{2}{3} =$

27. $\dfrac{3}{8} + \dfrac{7}{12} + 1\dfrac{2}{3} =$

28. To make the top of a dining room table, Cerise glues a piece of oak that is $\dfrac{5}{16}$ inch thick to a piece of pine that is $\dfrac{7}{8}$ inch thick. What is the total thickness, in inches, of the tabletop?

29. $\dfrac{2}{3} \times \dfrac{1}{4} =$

30. $2\dfrac{1}{3} \times 3\dfrac{2}{5} =$

31. A pygmy kangaroo needs to cross a highway that is 10 meters across. If the kangaroo covers exactly $1\dfrac{1}{4}$ meters each time it hops, how many hops would it take for the kangaroo to cross the highway?

For questions 32–34, write each ratio as a fraction in lowest terms.

32. Santiago made 24 sales in 6 hours. What is the ratio of sales to hours?

33. Carol's monthly take-home pay is $1,800. She spends $300 a month on food. What is the ratio of her food cost to her take-home pay?

34. A toy rocket travels 180 feet in 15 seconds. What is the rocket's speed expressed in feet per second?

35. Soan made a $400 down payment on a washer and dryer that cost a total of $1,200. What is the ratio of the down payment to the balance Soan owed after making the down payment?

For questions 36 and 37, find the value of the variable that completes the ratio.

36. $\dfrac{2}{3} = \dfrac{x}{18}$

37. $\dfrac{4}{\$2.12} = \dfrac{7}{x}$

38. The Bay City Cardinals have won 5 of 8 games. At the same rate, how many games will they have to play to win 60 games?

39. What is 20 percent of $25?

40. Find 90 percent of 200.

41. Pat called 120 customers to offer a software upgrade. Of those she called, 72 purchased the upgrade. What percentage of the customers whom Pat called agreed to the purchase?

For the situations described in questions 42 and 43, identify the whole, part, and percent.

42. Victor owed his uncle $1,000. Recently, he gave his uncle $200. That payment was 20 percent of the money he owed.

43. On a test with 80 problems, Sophie got 72 problems correct. In other words, she answered 90 percent of the problems correctly.

44. What is the greatest integer that will divide evenly into both 36 and 54?

45. List all factors of 168 between 20 and 29.

For questions 46–48, simplify each expression.

46. 3^2

47. 4^1

48. $\sqrt{49}$

49. How many inches are equal to 4 feet?

50. How many minutes are equal to 420 seconds?

Question 51 refers to the following information.

Portable Air Cooler
Duracool R612
3.75-gallon capacity
Runs 6 hours without refilling
Width: 27 in.; depth: 16 in.
Height: $13\frac{13}{4}$ in.
Shipping weight: 26 lb

51. Shoma wants to buy an air cooler. He knows the capacity of several other models in quarts. Write the expression Shoma could use to find the capacity for this model in quarts.

52.
```
    3 hr 30 min
    4 hr 20 min
  +2 hr 45 min
  ─────────────
```

53.
```
    3 gal 1 qt
   −1 gal 3 qt
  ─────────────
```

54. Nydia is working on an art project. She uses 1 pint 6 fluid ounces of film developer from a full container. If the capacity of the container is 3 quarts, how much developer is left in the container? (Express the answer in pints and fluid ounces.)

55. How many meters equal 5 kilometers?

56. Six hundred centimeters equal how many meters?

57. How many milligrams equal 4 grams?

58. In a vitamin supplement, each capsule contains 500 milligrams of vitamins. How many grams of vitamins are found in each capsule?

59. 5.4 cm + 19 cm + 2.85 cm = _____ cm

60. 12 kg + 10.5 kg + 120 g = _____ g

61. To make a carbonated punch, Kay Lynn adds 6 cans of club soda to 2 liters of cranberry juice. If each can holds 355 milliliters, how many liters of punch has Kay Lynn made?

Mathematics Review One Practice Answers and Explanations

1. 3.8

2. 6

3. 0.45

4. 0.08

5. 5.08, 5.6, 5.8, 5.802

6. 0.1136, 0.115, 0.12, 0.2

7. 7.996

8. 7.426

9. 21.32

10. 22.25

Add the times: $7.2 + 6.8 + 8.25 = 22.25$ minutes.

11. 2.65

12. 3.6

13. 9.6681

14. 15.16

Multiply 3.79 liters by 4: $3.79 \times 4 = 15.16$ liters.

15. $\frac{3}{5}$

16. $\frac{2}{4}$, or $\frac{1}{2}$

17. $\frac{7}{3}$, $2\frac{1}{3}$

18. $\frac{7}{2}$, $3\frac{1}{2}$

19. $5\frac{2}{3}$

20. $\frac{29}{12}$

21. $\frac{12}{16}$

22. $\frac{15}{40}$

23. $\frac{3}{4}$

24. $\frac{1}{6}$

25. $\frac{3}{4}$

Of those surveyed, $\frac{18}{24}$ went to at least one movie. Reduce the fraction to lowest terms: $\frac{18 \div 6}{24 \div 6} = \frac{3}{4}$.

26. $8\frac{1}{2}$

27. $2\frac{5}{8}$

28. $1\frac{3}{16}$

Add to find the total: $\frac{5}{16} + \frac{7}{8} = \frac{5}{16} + \frac{14}{16} = \frac{19}{16} = 1\frac{3}{16}$ inches.

29. $\frac{1}{6}$

30. $7\frac{14}{15}$

31. 8

Divide 10 by $1\frac{1}{4}$ because the kangaroo needs to cover 10 meters with a series of jumps each $1\frac{1}{4}$ meters in length. When dividing by a mixed number like $1\frac{1}{4}$, it's easier to work with an improper fraction: $1\frac{1}{4} = \frac{5}{4}$, so divide 10 by $\frac{5}{4}$. Remember, when dividing by a fraction, you flip the divisor and then multiply. So, $10 \div \frac{5}{4} = 10 \times \frac{4}{5} = \frac{40}{5} = 8$. It would take the kangaroo exactly 8 hops to cross the highway.

32. $\frac{24}{6} = \frac{4}{1}$

In other words, Santiago made an average of 4 sales per hour.

33. $\frac{\$300}{\$1,800} = \frac{1}{6}$

34. $\frac{180}{15} = \frac{12}{1} = 12$

35. 1 to 2

Subtract to find the amount owed: $1,200 − $400 = $800. Write the ratio and reduce: 400 to 800 = 1 to 2.

36. 12

37. $3.71

38. 96

Set up the proportion: $\dfrac{\text{Games won}}{\text{Games played}} = \dfrac{5}{8} = \dfrac{60}{x}$. Then, cross-multiply to solve for x: $8 \times 60 = 5x$, and $480 \div 5 = 96$. Alternatively, you might see that 60 is 5 multiplied by 12, so x must be 8 multiplied by 12, and $8 \times 12 = 96$.

39. $5

40. 180

41. 60%

$72 \div 120 = 0.6 = 60\%$

42. whole = $1,000; part = $200; percent = 20%

43. whole = 80; part = 72; percent = 90%

44. 18

The largest integer factor of 36 is 36, but 54 does not divide evenly by 36. The next largest integer factor of 36 is 18, and $54 \div 18 = 3$. Therefore, 18 is the largest common integer factor of 36 and 54.

45. 21, 24, 28

Factors of a number are integers that the number divides into with no remainder. There are three numbers between 20 and 29 that divide into 168 with no remainder: 21, 24 and 28. Besides using the calculator to test numbers, one approach is to start by finding the prime factorization of 168: $2 \times 2 \times 2 \times 3 \times 7$. Any number with a prime factorization that is a subset of the prime factorization of 168 will be a factor of 168: $21 = 3 \times 7$; $24 = 2 \times 2 \times 2 \times 3$; and $28 = 2 \times 2 \times 7$. There are no other groupings of the prime factors that produce a number between 20 and 29.

46. 9

47. 4

48. 7

49. 48 in.

50. 7 min

51. 3.75 × 4

4 quarts = 1 gallon, so multiply the number of gallons by 4 to find the number of quarts.

52. 10 hr 35 min

53. 1 gal 2 qt

54. 4 pt 10 fl oz

There are 2 pints per quart, and there are 16 fluid ounces per pint. You need to subtract 1 pt 6 fl oz from the starting volume, so write the beginning volume of 3 quarts in pints and fluid ounces. First, 3 qt = 6 pt. Express one of these pints in ounces. So 3 qt = 5 pt 16 fl oz.

Now subtract:

$$
\begin{array}{r}
5\ \text{pt} \quad 16\ \text{fl oz} \\
-\quad 1\ \text{pt} \quad\ 6\ \text{fl oz} \\
\hline
4\ \text{pt} \quad 10\ \text{fl oz}
\end{array}
$$

55. 5,000 m

56. 6 m

57. 4,000 mg

58. 0.5 g

There are 1,000 milligrams in 1 gram. Solve: 500 mg ÷ 1,000 mg/g = 0.5 g.

59. 27.25 cm

60. 22,620 g

Convert all values to grams before attempting to add: 12 kg (1,000 g/kg) = 12,000 g; 10.5 kg (1,000 g/kg) = 10,500 g.

61. 4.13 L

Multiply the number of milliliters of soda in a can by the number of cans: 355 ml/can × 6 cans = 2,130 ml. Convert to liters: 2,130 ml ÷ 1,000 ml/L = 2.13 L. Add the liters of soda and juice: 2.13 L + 2 L = 4.13 L.

Mathematics Review Two—Algebra and Functions

The Order of Operations

When a mathematical expression contains more than one operation, its value may depend on the order in which the operations are performed. To avoid confusion, mathematicians have agreed to perform operations in a certain order:

1. Parentheses or any other grouping symbols that enclose operations

2. Exponents and roots

3. Multiplication and division, working from left to right

4. Addition and subtraction, working from left to right

Study the following example to see how to apply the **order of operations**. Notice that parentheses appear in two places in the expression; however, only the first set of parentheses encloses an operation.

Evaluate the expression $\dfrac{(5+3)^2}{4} + 3(-1)$.

- Perform the addition in parentheses.

- Raise 8 to exponent 2.

- Divide, then multiply.

- Add.

$$\dfrac{(8)^2}{4} + 3(-1)$$

$$\dfrac{64}{4} + 3(-1)$$

$$16 + (-3)$$

$$13$$

The value of the expression $\dfrac{(5+3)^2}{4} + 3(-1)$ is **13**.

The fraction bar is also a grouping symbol. Before you divide, perform any operations shown above and below the bar.

Evaluate the expression $\dfrac{15+25}{2(5)} + 6$.

- Perform the operations above and below the fraction bar.

- Divide, then add.

$$\dfrac{15+25}{2(5)} + 6$$

$$\dfrac{40}{10} + 6$$

$$4 + 6 = 10$$

Algebraic Expressions

An **algebraic expression** uses numbers, operations, and variables to show relationships between numbers. **Variables** are letters (such as x and y) that represent unknown numbers. Each time the same letter appears within the same expression, it represents the same number.

Here are some examples of algebraic expressions in both words and symbols:

Algebraic expressions in words	In symbols
the product of 5 and a number	$5x$
a number decreased by 12	$x - 12$
the sum of 3 and the square of a number	$3 + x^2$
6 less than the quotient of a number and 2	$\frac{x}{2} - 6$
one-half a number increased by 15	$\frac{1}{2}x + 15$
4 times the difference of -3 and a number	$4(-3 - x)$
a number less another number	$x - y$
10 less the square root of a number, plus 3	$10 - \sqrt{x} + 3$

Simplifying and Evaluating Expressions

Simplifying an expression means performing all the operations you can within an expression. When working with variables, you must remember an important rule: you can add or subtract like terms only.

A **term** is a number, a variable, or the product or quotient of numbers and variables. A term cannot include a sum or a difference. Here are some examples of terms:

$$5x \quad 3y^2 \quad 13 \quad x^3 \quad \frac{x}{2}$$

Like terms have the same variable raised to the same power. For example, $3x^2$ and $5x^2$ are like terms; $8y$ and $4y$ are also like terms. However, $4x$ and $4y$ are not like terms because they contain different variables. Likewise, $6x$ and $2x^2$ are not like terms because the variables are not raised to the same power.

To simplify an expression, combine like terms.

Simplify $2x - 5 + 4x^2 - 8 + 6x$.

- In the result, it is customary to write the term with the greatest exponent first and to continue in descending order.

$$2x - 5 + 4x^2 - 8 + 6x$$
$$= (2x + 6x) + (-5 + (-8)) + 4x^2$$
$$= 8x + (-13) + 4x^2$$
$$= 4x^2 + 8x - 13$$

The **distributive property** allows you to remove grouping symbols to simplify expressions. We can state the distributive property using symbols.

$$a(b + c) = ab + ac \text{ and } a(b - c) = ab - ac$$

In other words, multiply each term inside the parentheses by the term outside the parentheses, and add or subtract the results depending on the operation inside the parentheses. The next example applies the distributive property.

Simplify $4x - 3(x + 9) + 15$.

- Change the subtraction of $3(x + 9)$ to the addition of a negative number.

- Use the distributive property. Multiply -3 by each term in the parentheses.

- Combine like terms. (Note: $1x$ means x.)

$$4x - 3(x + 9) + 15$$
$$= 4x + \left[-3(x + 9)\right] + 15$$
$$= 4x + (-3x) + (-3)(9) + 15$$
$$= 4x + (-3x) + (-27) + 15$$
$$= (4x + -3x) + (-27 + 15)$$
$$= 1x - 12$$
$$= x - 12$$

Evaluating an expression means finding its value. To evaluate an expression, substitute a given number for each variable.

Find the value of the expression $\dfrac{3x + 2y}{4}$ when $x = 6$ and $y = 5$.

- Replace the variables with the corresponding values given in the problem.

$$\frac{3x + 2y}{4} = \frac{3(6) + 2(5)}{4}$$

- Perform the operations above the fraction bar.

$$\frac{3(6) + 2(5)}{4} = \frac{18 + 10}{4} = \frac{28}{4} = 7$$

Note: To remove parentheses from an operation that follows a minus sign, imagine that -1 precedes the parentheses. Then use the distributive property.

Simplify $-(2x + 3)$.

$$-(2x + 3)$$
$$= -1(2x + 3)$$
$$= -1(2x) + (-1)(3)$$
$$= -2x + (-3) \text{ or } -2x - 3$$

Equations

An **equation** is a mathematical statement that two expressions are equal.

$$3 + 5 = 4 \times 2 \qquad\qquad 10 - 1 = 3^2 \qquad\qquad 5(3 + 5) = 40$$

An equation can contain one or more variables. Solving an equation means finding a value for each variable that will make the equation true.

$$4 + x = 11 \qquad\qquad 3x = 24 \qquad\qquad x - 5 = -2$$
$$x = 7 \qquad\qquad\qquad x = 8 \qquad\qquad\qquad x = 3$$

The basic strategy for solving an equation is to isolate the variable on one side of the equation. You can do this by performing **inverse**, or opposite, operations. However, you must always follow one basic rule: whatever you do to one side of the equation, you must also do to the other side.

Solve $x - 23 = 45$.

- On the left side of the equation, the number 23 is subtracted from x. The inverse of subtraction is addition, so add 23 to both sides of the equation.

$$x - 23 = 45$$
$$x - 23 + 23 = 45 + 23$$
$$x = 68$$

- To check your work, replace the variable with your solution and simplify. When $x = 68$, the equation is true.

Check:
$$x - 23 = 45$$
$$68 - 23 = 45$$
$$45 = 45$$

The following examples use the inverse operations of multiplication and division.

Solve $\frac{x}{2} = 17$.

- The variable x is divided by 2. Because multiplication is the inverse of division, you must multiply each side of the equation by 2.

$$\frac{x}{2} = 17$$
$$2\left(\frac{x}{2}\right) = 2(17)$$
$$x = 34$$

- To check your work, replace the variable with your solution and simplify. When $x = 34$, the equation is true.

Check:
$$\frac{34}{2} = 17$$
$$17 = 17$$

Solve $5x = 75$.

- Because the variable x is multiplied by 5, divide both sides of the equation by 5.

$$5x = 75$$
$$\frac{5x}{5} = \frac{75}{5}$$
$$x = 15$$

Inequalities

An **inequality** is a mathematical statement that connects two unequal expressions. Here are the inequality symbols and their meanings:

> greater than

< less than

$\geq$ greater than or equal to

$\leq$ less than or equal to

You solve an inequality much like an equation. Use inverse operations to isolate the variable.

Solve for x in the inequality $3x + 2 < 8$.

- Subtract 2 from both sides.

- Divide both sides by 3.

$$3x + 2 < 8$$
$$3x < 6$$
$$x < 2$$

The solution $x < 2$ states that any number less than 2 makes the inequality true. Check by substituting 1 (a number less than 2) for x: $3(1) + 2 < 8$, which simplifies to $5 < 8$, a true statement.

Note that multiplying or dividing an inequality by a negative number reverses the direction of the inequality. For instance, if we multiply both sides of the inequality $-3x < 2$ by -1, the result is $3x > -2$.

Algebra Word Problems

Algebra problems describe the relationships between several numbers. One number is the unknown and is represented by a variable. Using the relationships described in the problem, you can write an equation and solve for the variable.

There are twice as many seniors as juniors in a class on auto repair. If there are 24 students in the class, how many are seniors?

- Express the numbers in the problem in terms of the *same* variable. Let x represent the number of juniors. Because there are twice as many seniors, let $2x$ represent the number of seniors.

- Write and then solve an equation. The total number of juniors and seniors is 24, so $x + 2x = 24$. Solve:

$$x + 2x = 24$$
$$3x = 24$$
$$x = 8$$

Because $x = 8$, $2x = 2(8) = 16$. There are 8 juniors and 16 seniors in the class.

Consecutive integers are numbers that are evenly spaced and follow each other in the order in which one would count them. For example, 1, 2, and 3 are consecutive integers. The numbers 2, 4, and 6 are consecutive even integers, and 1, 3, and 5 are consecutive odd integers.

The sum of three consecutive integers is 105. What is the greatest of the three numbers?

- Let x represent the first number and $x + 1$ and $x + 2$ represent the other numbers.

- Write an equation and solve for x.

- Find the answer. The variable x represents the first number in the sequence, so the three numbers are 34, 35, and 36. The problem asks for the greatest number, which is **36**.

$$x + (x + 1) + (x + 2) = 105$$
$$3x + 3 = 105$$
$$3x = 102$$
$$x = 34$$

The Number Line and Signed Numbers

Signed numbers include zero, all positive numbers, and all negative numbers. Zero is neither positive nor negative. On a number line, the positive numbers are shown to the right of zero, and the negative numbers are shown to the left.

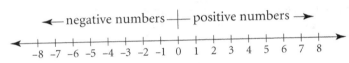

A positive number may be written with a plus (+) sign. If a number has no symbol, it is assumed to be positive. A negative number *must* be preceded by a minus (−) sign.

A signed number provides two important facts. The sign indicates the direction relative to zero on a number line, and the number indicates the distance from zero. For example, −5 lies five spaces to the left of zero, and +4 lies four spaces to the right of zero.

Adding and Subtracting Signed Numbers

You can use a number line to model the addition of signed numbers. This helps you remember the rules about how to add and subtract positive and negative numbers.

$1 + (-4) = -3$

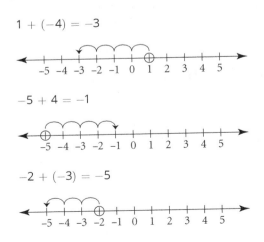

Begin at +1; move 4 units in a negative direction (left).

$-5 + 4 = -1$

Begin at −5; move 4 units in a positive direction (right).

$-2 + (-3) = -5$

Begin at −2; move 3 units in a negative direction (left).

To add without a number line, follow these steps:

- If numbers have like signs, add the numbers and keep the same sign.
- If the numbers have unlike signs, find the positive difference between the two numbers and use the sign of the larger number.

Add $15 + (-25)$.

- Because the numbers have unlike signs, subtract: $25 - 15 = 10$.

- Use the sign from the larger number: $15 + (-25) = \mathbf{-10}$.

Subtraction is the opposite of addition. To rewrite a subtraction problem as an addition problem, change the operation symbol to addition and change the sign on the number you are subtracting. Then apply the rules for adding signed numbers.

Subtract $3 - 8$.

- Change the operation and the sign of the number you are subtracting. So, $3 - 8$ becomes $3 + (-8)$.

- Add: $3 + (-8) = \mathbf{-5}$.

Inequalities on the Number Line

We can also use the number line to represent inequalities. For example:

$x < 2$

Note that the white circle indicates "less than," meaning that $x \neq 2$. The shading identifies all possible values of x.

$x \geq 2$

Note that the black circle indicates "greater than or equal to," meaning x could be 2. The circle and the shading identify all possible values of x.

The Coordinate Plane

A **coordinate grid** is a tool to help one locate points that lie in a **plane** or flat surface. The grid is formed by **two intersecting lines**: an *x*-**axis** and a *y*-**axis**. The *x*-axis is actually a horizontal number line, and the *y*-axis is a vertical number line. The point at which the two axes intersect is called the **origin**.

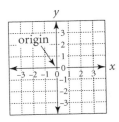

Each point on the grid can be named using a set of two numbers called an **ordered pair**. The first number is the distance from the origin along the *x*-axis. The second number is the distance from the origin along the *y*-axis. Write the numbers in parentheses and separate them with a comma: (x, y).

Write the ordered pairs for points *M* and *P*.

- Point *M* lies 2 spaces to the right of the origin along the *x*-axis and 3 spaces above the origin along the *y*-axis. The coordinates are (**2, 3**).

- Point *P* lies 1 space to the left along the *x*-axis and 3 spaces down along the *y*-axis. The coordinates are (**−1, −3**).

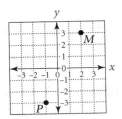

To plot points on the grid, use the number lines located at the axes. Remember that right and up are the directions for positive numbers, while left and down are the directions for negative numbers.

Point *A* is located at (−2, 1), and point *B* is located at (3, −2). Plot these points on a coordinate grid.

- To plot *A*, start at the origin. Count 2 spaces left along the *x*-axis. Count 1 space up along the *y*-axis.

- To plot point *B*, start at the origin. Count 3 spaces right along the *x*-axis. Count 2 spaces down along the *y*-axis.

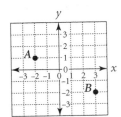

Basics of Lines and Slope

A line can be defined by the equation $y = mx + b$. The *y*-intercept of the line, *b*, is defined as where the line crosses the *y*-axis. This, by definition, is the point at which $x = 0$. The slope of the line, *m*, is defined as $\frac{\text{Rise}}{\text{Run}}$: in other words, how much the *y*-values change divided by how much the *x*-values change.

Here is the graph of the line: $y = \frac{2}{3}x + 5$:

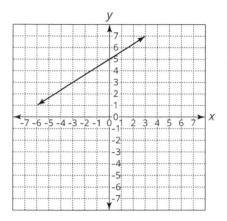

The y-intercept is 5, so you know that it crosses the y-axis at the point (0, 5).

You also know that the slope of the line is $\frac{2}{3}$, which means the y increases by 2 for every 3 units the x increases.

In order to calculate the slope of a line, use the slope formula: $\frac{\text{Change in } x}{\text{Change in } y}$. Another form of this equation is $\frac{y_2 - y_1}{x_2 - x_1}$.

For example, if you were given the points (1, 2) and (4, 8), you could find the slope:

$$\frac{\text{Change in } y}{\text{Change in } x} = \frac{y_2 - y_1}{x_2 - x_1} = \frac{8 - 2}{4 - 1} = \frac{6}{3} = 2$$

The slope is equal to 2.

Patterns and Functions

A **pattern** is a series of numbers or objects whose sequence follows a particular rule. You can figure out what rule determines the sequence by studying the terms you are given. Think: What operation or sequence of operations will always result in the next term in the series? Once you know the rule, you can continue the pattern.

Find the seventh term in the sequence: 1, 2, 4, 8, 16, . . .

- Determine the rule. Each number in the sequence is two times the number before it.
- Apply the rule. You have five terms and must find the seventh. Continue the pattern.
  The sixth term will be $16 \times 2 = 32$, and the seventh term will be $32 \times 2 = 64$.

A **function** is an algebraic rule that shows how the terms in one sequence of numbers are related to the terms in another sequence. For example, a sidewalk vendor charges $1.50 for a slice of pizza. The chart below shows how much it would cost to buy one to six slices.

NUMBER OF PIZZA SLICES	1	2	3	4	5	6
Cost	$1.50	$3.00	$4.50	$6.00	$7.50	$9.00

Each number of slices in the first row corresponds to a price in the second row. We could say that the amount a customer will pay is a function of (or depends on) the number of slices the customer orders. Therefore, you can write this function as follows:

$$\text{Cost} = \text{Number of slices} \times \$1.50, \text{ or } C = n(\$1.50)$$

If you know the function and a number in the first set of numbers, you can solve for its corresponding number in the second set. On the test, read $f(x)$ as "the function of x."

Using the function $y = 3x + 5$, what is the value of y when $x = -3$?

- Substitute the given value of x.

$$y = 3(-3) + 5$$
$$y = -9 + 5$$
$$y = -4$$

- Solve for y.

Using the function $n = 100 - 4(3 + m)$, what is the value of n when $m = 6$?

- Substitute the given value of m.

$$n = 100 - 4(3 + 6)$$
$$n = 100 - 4(9)$$
$$n = 100 - 36$$
$$n = 64$$

- Solve for n.

Solving Function Word Problems

Functions have many business applications. For instance, businesses use functions to calculate profits, costs, employee wages, and taxes.

Anderson Advertising is finishing a series of print ads for a client. Finishing the project will cost \$2,000 per day for the first seven days and \$3,500 per day after seven days. When finishing the project takes seven days or longer, Anderson can find the finishing costs by using the function $C = \$2,000d + \$1,500(d - 7)$, where $C =$ the cost of finishing the project and $d =$ the number of days. If the project takes 12 days to complete, what will the project cost?

Use the function to solve the problem.

$$C = \$2,000d + \$1,500(d - 7)$$
$$= \$2,000(12) + \$1,500(12 - 7)$$
$$= \$24,000 + \$1,500(5)$$
$$= \$24,000 + \$7,500$$
$$= \$31,500$$

Nita decides to join a health club. She gets brochures from two health clubs and compares the plans. No Sweat Fitness charges a one-time membership fee of $250 plus $8 per month. Freedom Health Center charges $25 per month. At both health clubs, the price (*P*) Nita will pay is a function of the number of months (*m*) she attends the club.

Nita plans to move in 18 months. If she attends a health club until she moves, which one offers the better price?

- Find the price at No Sweat Fitness.

$$P = \$250 + \$8m$$
$$= \$250 + \$8(18)$$
$$= \$250 + \$144$$
$$= \$394$$

- Find the price at Freedom Health Center.

$$P = \$25m$$
$$= \$25(18)$$
$$= \$450$$

- Compare the results. Even though Nita will have to pay a large amount up front, **No Sweat Fitness** offers the better price for 18 months of membership.

Mathematics Review Two Practice

1. $4(3) - 2 + (6 + 4 \times 2)$

2. $5^2 - (5 - 7)(2)$

3. Find the value of the expression
$5 + 2\left[7\left(\dfrac{10^2}{10}\right) + (6 - 2)(3)\right]$. Record each step in
the order of operations as you solve.

For questions 4–6, write an algebraic expression for each description. Use the variables x and y.

4. A number decreased by seven

5. The product of 3 and the square of a number, increased by that number

6. The amount by which -3 multiplied by a number is greater than the product of 2 and another number

7. A Minor League Baseball team is giving a local charity the sum of $1,500 plus $0.50 for each ticket over 2,000 sold for one game. Let x represent the number of tickets sold, where $x > 2,000$. Write the expression one could use to find the amount of the donation.

For questions 8 and 9, simplify the expressions.

8. $5 + x^2 - 3 + 3x$

9. $2y + 5 + 17y + 8$

10. Find the value of $6(x + 2) + 7$ when $x = 2$.

11. Find the value of $3x^2 + 3(x + 4)$ when $x = 3$.

12. Simplify the expression $3x^2 + 3(x - 3) + x + 10$.

For questions 13–16, solve for the variable in each equation.

13. $7x = 63$

14. $23 + m = 51$

15. $-13 = y - 12$

16. $\dfrac{x}{4} = -16$

17. When a number is divided by 4, the result is 32. What is the number?

18. Two houses are for sale on the same street. The square footage of the second is 1,000 less than twice the square footage of the first house. Together, the houses have 4,400 square feet. What is the square footage of the first house?

19. The Bulldogs won twice as many games as they lost. If they played a total of 36 games, how many did they win?

20. Sylvia scored 10 points better than Jamal on their science exam. Greg scored 6 points less than Jamal. Altogether, the students earned 226 points. How many points did Sylvia earn?

21. Which number should come next in the following pattern?

$-12, -9, -6, -3,$ _____ .

Question 22 refers to the following table.

Each term in the second row is determined by the function $f(x) = 2x - 1$.

x	1	2	3	4	5	...	12
y	1	3	5	7	9	...	

22. What number belongs in the shaded box?

Question 23 refers to the following information.

The price per scarf is a function of the number of scarves purchased. The original price per scarf, $5.00, is reduced by 25 cents with each additional scarf purchased, up to a total of four scarves. The table shows the price per scarf for purchases of up to four scarves.

Number (n) of scarves	1	2	3	4
Cost (c) per scarf	$5.00	$4.75	$4.50	$4.25

23. Write the equation that allows the information in the chart to be determined.

Questions 24 and 25 refer to the following information.

The Chimney Sweep charges $25 for a chimney inspection. If the customer purchases additional products or services, that customer receives a $15 discount on the inspection fee. Let s equal the cost of any additional services.

24. Jan has her chimney inspected and purchases a smoke guard for $89. How much will she pay in total?

25. After an inspection, Ahmed decides to have a new damper installed for $255. How much will he pay in total?

Question 26 refers to the following information.

Kamila is considering three job opportunities. At all three jobs, weekly pay (P) is a function of the number of hours (h) worked during the week. The functions are shown below:

Job 1: $P = \$9.75h$
Job 2: $P = \$70 + \$8.40h$
Job 3: $P = \$380 \times \dfrac{h}{38}$

26. If Kamila works 30 hours in a week, how much more will she earn at Job 2 than at Job 1?

For questions 27–29, solve for a specific value.

27. $8 + (-3) =$

28. $-1 + 2 =$

29. $6 - (-3) + (-5) + 8 =$

30. At noon, the temperature in the high desert was 92°F. A scientist observed the following temperature changes over the course of the next two hours: +12°, −5°, +6°, −3°, and +13°. What was the temperature at the end of the two-hour period?

For questions 31–33, simplify the inequalities.

31. $3x - 7 > 5$

32. $\dfrac{4 + x}{5} > 8$

33. $-4(x + 2) < 24$

34. When 3 is added to the product of −4 and a number *x*, the result is less than 5 added to the product of −3 and the number *x*. Graph the solution set of *x* on a number line.

For questions 35–42, write the ordered pair for each point.

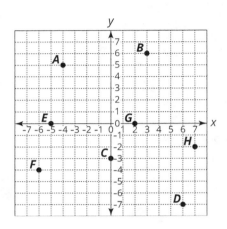

For question 43, plot the points on the coordinate grid.

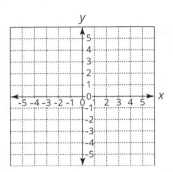

43. *J* at (−3, −2)

    K at (4, 0)

    L at (1, −3)

    M at (−4, 2)

35. Point *A*

36. Point *B*

37. Point *C*

38. Point *D*

39. Point *E*

40. Point *F*

41. Point *G*

42. Point *H*

Mathematics Review Two Practice Answers and Explanations

1. **24**

2. **29**

3. **169**

First, solve the parentheses inside the brackets: $5 + 2[7(10) + (4)(3)]$. Next, do the multiplication inside the brackets: $5 + 2[70 + 12]$. Third, do the addition inside the brackets: $5 + 2[82]$. Fourth, do the multiplication: $5 + 164$. Fifth, do the addition to find the correct answer: 169.

4. $x - 7$

5. $3x^2 + x$

6. $-3x - 2y$

7. $\$1,500 + \$0.50(x - 2,000)$

Here, x represents the number of tickets sold. The expression $x - 2,000$ is the number of tickets over 2,000 sold. Multiply this expression by \$0.50 to find the amount donated based on ticket sales. Add \$1,500 to this product.

8. $x^2 + 3x + 2$

9. $19y + 13$

10. **31**

11. **48**

12. $3x^2 + 4x + 1$

$$3x^2 + 3(x - 3) + x + 10$$
$$= 3x^2 + 3x - 9 + x + 10$$
$$= 3x^2 + 4x + 1$$

13. $x = 9$

14. $m = 28$

15. $y = -1$

16. $x = -64$

17. **128**

When x is divided by 4, the result is 32. Solve for x.

$$\frac{x}{4} = 32$$
$$4 \times \frac{x}{4} = 4 \times 32$$
$$x = 128$$

18. **1,800 sq ft**

Call the first house f and the second house s. Set up two equations with the information given: the first equation is $2f - 1,000 = s$, and the second equation is $f + s = 4,400$. Isolate s in the second equation: $s = 4,400 - f$. Now take the two expressions that are equal to s and set them equal to each other: $2f - 1,000 = 4,400 - f$. Add f and 1,000 to each side to get $3f = 5,400$. Finally, divide both sides by 3 to get $f = 1,800$.

19. **24 games**

Label the number of games that the Bulldogs lost as x and the number of games that they won as $2x$. The total number of games they played was 36, so $x + 2x = 36$. Combine like terms to get $3x = 36$. Divide both sides by 3 to get $x = 12$. The number of games they won equals $2x$, and $2(12) = 24$.

20. **84**

Let $x =$ Jamal's points, $x + 10 =$ Sylvia's points, and $x - 6 =$ Greg's points. Write and solve an equation:

$$x + x + 10 + x - 6 = 226$$
$$3x + 4 = 226$$
$$3x = 222$$
$$x = 74$$

The question asks for Sylvia's points, so $x + 10 = 74 + 10 = 84$.

21. **0**

22.   23

We're looking for the y value when x is 12. Plug 12 into the given function and solve for y.

23. $c = \$5.00 - \$0.25(n - 1)$

The price per scarf starts at $5.00 and decreases by $0.25 for every scarf after the first one. Represent this decrease as $\$0.25(n - 1)$, where n is the number of scarves being sold. Subtract this amount from the starting point, which is $5.00: $c = \$5.00 - \$0.25(n - 1)$.

24. $99

Simplifying the equation $C = (\$25 - \$15) + s$ yields $C = \$10 + s$. To find Jan's cost, add $10 to the service cost of $89.

25. $265

Again, work with the simplified equation $C = \$10 + s$. To find Ahmed's cost, add $10 to the service cost of $255.

26. $29.50

Use the functions for the two jobs, substituting 30 hours for h.

Job 1: $P = \$9.75h$

$= \$9.75(30)$

$= \$292.50$

Job 2: $P = \$70 + \$8.40h$

$= \$70 + \$8.40(30)$

$= \$70 + \$252$

$= \$322$

Subtract: $\$322 - \$292.50 = \$29.50$.

27.   5

28.   1

29.   12

30.   115°

Begin with 92°. Then perform the following operations: $92° + 12° - 5° + 6° - 3° + 13° = 115°$.

31. $x > 4$

32. $x > 36$

33. $x > -8$

Always remember to flip the direction of an inequality when you multiply or divide both sides by a negative number.

34.

Solve the inequality:

$$-4x + 3 < -3x + 5$$
$$-x < 2$$
$$x > -2$$

To graph the solution $x > -2$, place an open circle at -2 because -2 is not included in the solution. Then extend the line to the right to include all values greater than -2.

35.   (−4, 5)

36.   (3, 6)

37.   (0, −3)

38.   (6, −7)

39.   (−5, 0)

40.   (−6, −4)

41.   (2, 0)

42.   (7, −2)

43.

Mathematics Review Three—Geometry

Points, Lines, and Angles

A **point** is a single location in space. We assign a name to a point by writing a letter next to it. A **plane** is a two-dimensional flat surface. In the drawing, point A lies in plane P.

A **line** is a one-dimensional straight path that extends indefinitely in two directions. A line can be named with a single letter or with the letters designating two points on the line.

line s or $\overleftrightarrow{CD}$

A **ray** is part of a line that begins at the endpoint and extends indefinitely in one direction. A portion of a line with two endpoints is called a **line segment**. Both rays and line segments are named using the letters designating two points.

ray: $\overrightarrow{FG}$ segment: $\overline{FG}$

When two rays share an endpoint, they form an **angle**. The shared endpoint is the **vertex** of the angle. We can name an angle in different ways: with a number or letter written inside the angle, with the letter designating the point at the vertex, or with the letter designating the vertex followed by two letters that designate points on each ray. The symbol $\angle$ means "angle."

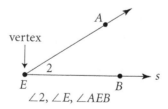

$\angle 2, \angle E, \angle AEB$

Angles are measured in **degrees**, indicated by a number and the degree symbol ($^\circ$).

A **right angle** forms a square corner and measures 90°. A right angle is often identified by a small square drawn inside it.

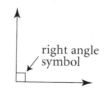

right angle symbol

An **obtuse angle** is greater than 90° but less than 180°.

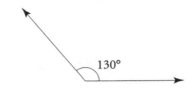

An **acute angle** is less than 90°.

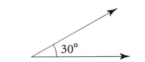

A **straight angle** measures 180°.

A **reflex angle** measures greater than 180° but less than 360°.

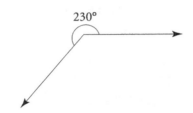

When the sum of two angles is 90°, the angles are **complementary**. When the sum of two angles is 180°, the angles are **supplementary**. You can use this information to solve for a missing angle measure.

In the drawing, ∠AOB and ∠BOC are complementary. What is the measure of ∠AOB?

- The measure of angle *BOC* is given as 23°, or *m*∠*BOC* = 23°. The sum of the angles is 90°. Therefore, ∠*AOB* measures **67°**.

$$m\angle AOB + 23° = 90°$$
$$m\angle AOB = 90° - 23°$$
$$m\angle AOB = 67°$$

In the drawing, ∠1 and ∠2 are supplementary. What is the measure of ∠1?

- It's given that ∠2 measures 45°. The sum of the angles is 180°. Thus, ∠1 measures 180° − 45° = **135°**.

Parallel Lines and Transversals

When two lines intersect, they form two pairs of vertical angles. **Vertical angles** have the same angle measure. In the drawing, ∠1 and ∠3 are vertical angles, as are ∠2 and ∠4.

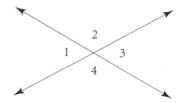

Intersecting lines also form adjacent angles. **Adjacent angles** share a common ray. For example, ∠1 and ∠2 are adjacent angles. The adjacent angles in this figure are supplementary angles because their sum is the measure of a straight angle.

If you know the measure of one angle, you can find the measure of the other three angles.

In the figure above, $m\angle 1 = 35°$. What are the measures of ∠2, ∠3, and ∠4?

- Because ∠1 and ∠2 are supplementary, their sum equals 180°. Solve for ∠2.

$$m\angle 2 + 35° = 180°$$
$$m\angle 2 = 145°$$

- Angles 1 and 3 are vertical, so both measure **35°**.
  Angles 2 and 4 are vertical, so both measure **145°**.

Parallel lines are lines that never intersect. This means that their distance from each other remains constant. The symbol for parallel is ||. A **transversal** is a line that intersects two or more other lines. When a transversal intersects two parallel lines, it forms special angle relationships.

In the drawing, $M||N$. The transversal, line P, forms eight angles.

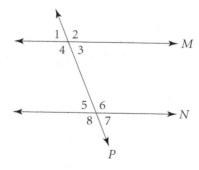

Each angle matches another angle in the same position on the transversal. These angles, called **corresponding angles**, always have the same measure. The corresponding angles are ∠1 and ∠5, ∠2 and ∠6, ∠3 and ∠7, and ∠4 and ∠8.

Alternate exterior angles, which are also equal in measure, are on opposite sides of the transversal and are on the outside of the parallel lines. One pair of alternate exterior angles is ∠1 and ∠7, and the other is ∠2 and ∠8.

Alternate interior angles are on opposite sides of the transversal and are inside the parallel lines. One pair of alternate interior angles is ∠3 and ∠5; the other is ∠4 and ∠6. Alternate interior angles are always equal in measure.

In the figure, $C \| D$. If $m\angle 4 = 48°$, what is the measure of ∠5?

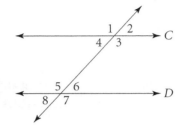

- There are many ways to solve the problem. Here is one way: ∠4 and ∠8 are corresponding angles, so $m\angle 8 = 48°$.

- Then ∠8 and ∠5 are supplementary angles, so $m\angle 5 + 48° = 180°$, and $m\angle 5 =$ **132°**.

Triangles

A **triangle** is a closed three-sided figure. From the definition, we can infer other properties. Because a triangle has three sides, it must also have three interior angles and three vertices.

We name a triangle by writing its vertices in any order, so you could name the triangle shown here $\triangle DEF$. Its sides are DE, EF, and DF.

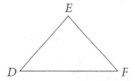

Triangles are classified by the lengths of their sides and by the measures of their angles. In the triangles in this section, sides with the same number of marks are equal.

Triangles Classified by Side Lengths

Equilateral triangle: All sides are equal in length. Note that the angles are equal as well.

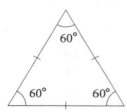

Isosceles triangle: Exactly two sides are equal in length. Note that the two angles opposite these sides are equal.

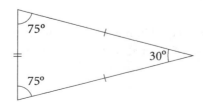

Scalene triangle: No sides are equal in length, and no angles are equal.

Triangles Classified by Angle Measures

Right triangle: One angle measures 90°.

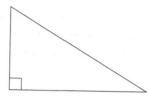

Acute triangle: All angles measure less than 90°.

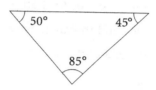

Obtuse triangle: One angle is greater than 90°.

Therefore, we can classify any triangle in two ways.

What kind of triangle is △*PQR*?

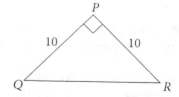

- Classify by its sides: Two sides have the same length, so △*PQR* is **an isosceles triangle**.
- Classify by its angles: ∠*P* is a right angle, so △*PQR* is a **right triangle**.
- △*PQR* is therefore a **right isosceles triangle**.

The sum of the measures of the interior angles of any triangle is 180°. You can use this fact to solve for a missing angle.

In $\triangle ABC$, $\angle A$ measures 55° and $\angle B$ measures 100°. What is the measure of $\angle C$?

- Write an equation and solve.

$$55° + 100° + \angle C = 180°$$
$$155° + \angle C = 180°$$
$$\angle C = \mathbf{25°}$$

Comparing Triangles

Figures are **congruent** (indicated by the symbol $\cong$) when they have exactly the same size and shape. In other words, two figures are congruent if their corresponding parts (the angles and sides) are congruent. You can often tell that two geometric shapes are congruent by sight. However, in geometry, you must be able to prove that figures are congruent.

Two triangles are congruent if the following corresponding parts are congruent:

Side-Side-Side (SSS)	The side measures for both triangles are the same.
Side-Angle-Side (SAS)	Two sides and the angle between them are the same.
Angle-Side-Angle (ASA)	Two angles and the side between them are the same.

Are triangles *ABD* and *BCD* congruent?

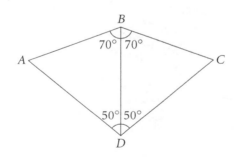

- Find the known corresponding parts: $\angle ABD \cong \angle CBD$ and $\angle ADB \cong \angle CDB$. Both triangles share side *BD*.

- Is this enough information to prove that the triangles are congruent? Yes, two angles and the side between them are equal. Using the ASA rule, $\triangle \mathbf{ABD} \cong \triangle \mathbf{BCD}$.

Understanding Similarity

Figures are **similar** (shown by the symbol $\sim$) when the corresponding angles are congruent and the corresponding sides are in proportion. In other words, similar figures always have the same shape, but they do not have to be the same size.

There are two rules that you can use to prove that two triangles are similar:

Rule 1:   If two angle measures in the first triangle are equal to two angle measures in the second triangle, the triangles are similar.

Rule 2:   If all corresponding sides have the same ratio, the triangles are similar.

Are triangles *JKL* and *MNO* similar?

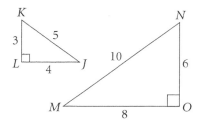

- Compare corresponding angles. Because only one angle measure is given, you cannot use Rule 1 to prove that the triangles are similar.

- Write ratios comparing the sides in the first triangle to the corresponding sides in the second triangle. Each ratio is equal to $\frac{1}{2}$.

$$\frac{\triangle JKL}{\triangle MNO} = \frac{3}{6} = \frac{4}{8} = \frac{5}{10} = \frac{1}{2}$$

- Because the ratios are equal, the triangles are similar: $\triangle JKL \sim \triangle MNO$.

Quadrilaterals

A **quadrilateral** is a closed shape with four sides.

A **rectangle** is a four-sided figure with four right angles. The opposite sides (sides across from each other) are the same length, and they are parallel.

A **square** is actually a kind of rectangle. It, too, has four right angles with parallel opposite sides. However, a square has one additional property: its four sides are all the same length.

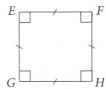

A **parallelogram** is a four-sided figure whose opposite sides are parallel and the same length. In addition, its opposite angles (the angles diagonally across from each other) are also equal in measure. A special parallelogram, called a **rhombus** (not shown), has four sides of equal length.

A **trapezoid** (not shown) is a four-sided figure with only two parallel sides.

All quadrilaterals have one important property in common: the sum of the measures of their interior angles is 360°. You can use this fact to find a missing angle measure.

In figure *ABCD,* the opposite sides are parallel. What is the measure of ∠A?

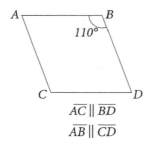

$$\overline{AC} \parallel \overline{BD}$$
$$\overline{AB} \parallel \overline{CD}$$

- Identify the figure. Because the opposite sides are parallel, the figure is a parallelogram.

- Find the measure of ∠C. The opposite angles of a parallelogram are equal in measure; therefore, $m\angle C = m\angle B$. Both ∠B and ∠C measure 110°.

- Because all of the angles in the figure must total 360° and ∠A and ∠D are equal, you can solve for ∠A.

$$2 \times m\angle A + 110° + 110° = 360°$$
$$2 \times m\angle A = 140°$$
$$m\angle A = 70°$$

Perimeter, Area, and Volume

Perimeter is the distance around a figure. To find the perimeter, simply add the lengths of the sides. For common figures, you can apply a formula to find the perimeter.

Square	Perimeter = 4 × Side	$P = 4s$
Rectangle	Perimeter = 2 × Length + 2 × Width	$P = 2l + 2w$
Triangle	Perimeter = Side$_1$ + Side$_2$ + Side$_3$	$P = a + b + c$

A rectangle is 16 inches long and 9 inches wide. What is the perimeter of the rectangle?

- Use the formula:

$$\text{Perimeter} = 2 \times \text{Length} + 2 \times \text{Width}$$
$$= 2 \times 16 + 2 \times 9$$
$$= 32 + 18$$
$$= 50 \text{ inches}$$

Area is the measure of the space inside a flat figure. Area is measured in square units. For example, if the sides of a figure are measured in inches, its area will be measured in square inches. The formulas for finding area are shown below.

Square	Area = Side^2	$A = s^2$
Rectangle	Area = Length × Width	$A = lw$
Parallelogram	Area = Base × Height	$A = bh$
Triangle	Area = $\frac{1}{2}$ × Base × Height	$A = \frac{1}{2}bh$
Trapezoid	Area = $\frac{1}{2}$(Base$_1$ + Base$_2$) × Height	$A = \frac{1}{2}(b_1 + b_2)h$

Three of the formulas mention two new measures: base and height. The **base** is one side of the figure. The **height** is the length from a vertex to the base, along a line segment forming a right angle to the base.

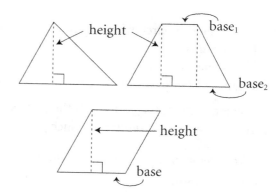

Find the area of polygon *ABCD*.

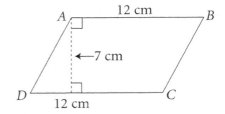

- Identify the figure. *ABCD* is a parallelogram.

- Find the data that you need. To use the formula for finding the area of a parallelogram, you need to know the height and the length of the base. You do not need to know the length of sides *BC* or *AD*.

- Use the formula: Area = Base × Height.

$$\text{Area} = 12 \times 7$$
$$= 84 \text{ sq cm or } 84 \text{ cm}^2$$

Circles: Circumference and Area

A **circle** is a closed, linear figure, all of whose points are the same distance from a single point: the center of the circle. The **circumference** of a circle is its perimeter, or the distance around the circle. The area of a circle is the space inside the circle.

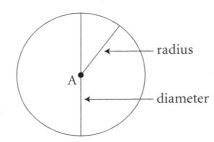

To find the circumference and area of a circle, you need to know certain measurements of the circle. The **diameter** is a line segment with endpoints on the circle that passes through the center of the circle. The **radius** is a line segment that connects the center of the circle to a point on the circle. The radius is one-half the diameter.

The formulas for the circumference and area of a circle use a special quantity called **pi (π)**. Pi is the ratio of the circumference to the diameter. Pi is approximately 3.14. The formula for the circumference C of a circle is $C = \pi \times \text{Diameter}$, or $C = \pi d$. The circumference of a circle is related to the radius r of the circle by $C = 2\pi r$. The formula for the area A of a circle is $A = \pi \times \text{Radius}^2$, or $A = \pi r^2$.

A china plate has a gold rim. If the plate's diameter is 10.5 inches, what is the distance around the rim to the nearest tenth of an inch?

- The diameter of the circle is 10.5 in.

- Use the formula $C = \pi d$:

- The circumference to the nearest tenth of an inch is **33 inches**.

$$C = \pi d$$
$$\approx 3.14(10.5)$$
$$= 32.97, \text{ or about 33 inches}$$

The circular surface of a satellite component must be covered with heat-resistant tiles. If the radius of the circular surface is 4 meters, what is the area of the circular surface in square meters?

- The radius of the circle is 4 m.
- Use the formula $A = \pi r^2$:
- The area of the surface is **50.24 square meters**.

$$A = \pi r^2$$
$$= 3.14\left(4^2\right)$$
$$= 3.14(16)$$
$$= 50.24 \text{ square meters}$$

What is the circumference of circle B to the nearest tenth of a centimeter?

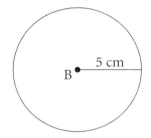

- The radius of the circle is 5 cm.
- Use the formula $C = 2\pi r$.
- The circumference to the nearest tenth of a centimeter is **31.4 cm**.

$$C = 2\pi r$$
$$\approx 2(3.14)(5)$$
$$\approx 3.14(10)$$
$$\approx 31.4 \text{ cm}$$

Volume

Volume is the measure of space inside a three-dimensional object. Volume is measured in **cubic units**. For example, if the sides of an object are measured in inches, the volume is the number of cubes with an edge length of one inch that would be needed to fill the object.

Many common three-dimensional objects have at least two identical and parallel **faces**. Think of a cereal box or soup can. Both objects have identical faces at the top and bottom. Either of these faces can be called the base of the object. To find the volume of any container with two identical bases, multiply the area of one base by the height of the object: volume = area of base × height.

Another way to find the volume of an object is to use the formula that applies specifically to that object. Three common regular solids are rectangular solids, cubes, and cylinders.

Rectangular solid	Volume = Length × Width × Height	$V = lwh$
Cube	Volume = Edge³	$V = e^3$
Cylinder	Volume = π × Radius² × Height	$V = \pi r^2 h$

A **rectangular solid** has two identical rectangular bases. The remaining sides of the solid are also rectangles.

A cardboard box has the dimensions shown in the diagram. What is the volume of the box in cubic feet?

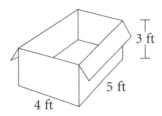

- Use the formula $V = lwh$:

$$V = lwh$$
$$= 5(4)(3) = 60 \text{ cubic feet}$$

A **cube** is a rectangular solid with six identical faces. In a cube, each edge is the same length.

A wood block measures 2 inches on each edge. What is the volume of the block?

- Use the formula $V = e^3$:

$$V = e^3$$
$$= 2^3 = 2 \times 2 \times 2 = 8 \text{ cubic inches}$$

A **cylinder** has two circular bases. The bases are connected by a curved surface. Cans, barrels, and storage tanks are often in the shape of cylinders.

A storage tank has a radius of 1.5 meters. What is the volume of the tank to the nearest cubic meter?

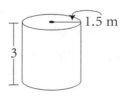

- Use the formula $V = \pi r^2 h$:

$$V = \pi r^2 h$$
$$\approx 3.14\left(1.5^2\right)(3) = 21.195 \text{ m}^3,$$

which rounds to **21 cubic meters**.

Working with Irregular Figures

An **irregular figure** combines geometric figures to form a new shape. To find the perimeter of an irregular figure, simply add the lengths of all the sides. You may need to deduce the lengths of some of the sides using the measures given for the other sides.

A family room has the dimensions shown in the diagram. All measurements are in feet. What is the perimeter of the room?

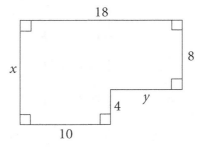

- Find the missing measurements. Measurement x equals the combined lengths of the two opposite walls: $x = 8 + 4 = 12$ ft. You also know that $18 - 10 = y$, so $y = 8$ ft.
- Add all the distances to find the perimeter: $12 + 18 + 8 + 8 + 4 + 10 =$ **60 ft**.

To find the area of an irregular figure, break the figure into parts. Then apply the correct formula to each part.

What is the area of this figure in square centimeters?

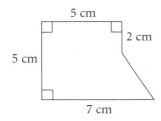 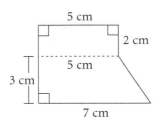

- Divide the figure into two shapes and find any missing measurements. Here, we have divided the figure into a trapezoid and a rectangle.

- Calculate the area of each shape.

Rectangle: $A = lw$
$$= 2(5) = 10 \text{ sq cm}$$

Trapezoid: $A = \frac{1}{2}(b_1 + b_2)h$
$$= \frac{1}{2}(5 + 7)(3) = \frac{1}{2}(12)(3)$$
$$= 6 \times 3 = 18 \text{ sq cm}$$

- Combine: $10 + 18 =$ **28 sq cm**.

Note that you could also solve for the area of a figure by dividing it into a square with sides of 5 and a triangle with a base of 2 and a height of 3. So, $5^2 + (2 \times 3) = 25 + 3 = 28$ square centimeters.

TRANSFORMATIONS

Though there are many types of graphical **transformations** (translations, reflections, rotations), the one most commonly tested on the Praxis is the translation. A **translation** occurs when points are shifted vertically, horizontally, or both. For example, if the point $(3, 5)$ were shifted upward by 2, the new point would be $(3, 7)$. If that point were then shifted leftward by 1, the new point would be $(2, 7)$.

If triangle *ABC* were translated 2 to the right and 3 down, where would point *C* be located?

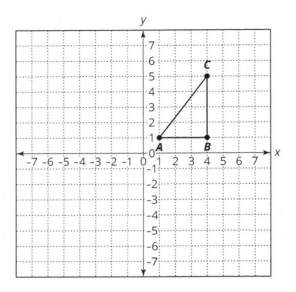

- Original point $C = (4, 5)$
- 2 to the right $= (6, 5)$
- 3 down $= (\mathbf{6, 2})$.

Mathematics Review Three Practice

1. A cube has an edge length of 6 inches. Express the volume of the cube using an exponent.

For questions 2 and 3, find the area and perimeter of each figure.

2.

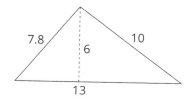

3.

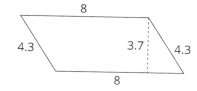

4. A right triangle has sides of lengths 9, 12, and 15. What is the area of the triangle?

Question 5 refers to the figure provided.

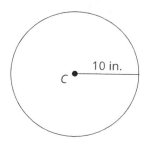

5. Find the approximate circumference and area of the circle. Round answers to the nearest whole number. Note: $\pi \approx 3.14$.

Question 6 refers to the following diagram.

6. If workers lay a tile border around the edge of the fountain shown in the diagram, how many feet long will the border be to the nearest foot? Note: $\pi \approx 3.14$.

Question 7 refers to the following information and figure.

On the target below, the 5- and 10-point bands are each 2 inches wide, and the inner circle has a diameter of 2 inches.

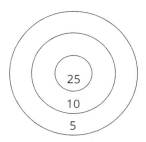

7. To the nearest inch, what is the outer circumference of the 10-point band? Note: $\pi \approx 3.14$.

For questions 8 and 9, find the volume of each object to the nearest whole unit.

8.

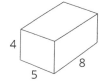

9.

10. A wooden crate measures 5 feet along each edge. What is the crate's volume in cubic feet?

11. Find the volume of the entire figure to the nearest cubic unit.

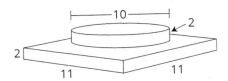

For questions 12 and 13, classify each angle based on its angle measure.

12. 55°

13. 270°

Questions 14 and 15 refer to the figure provided.

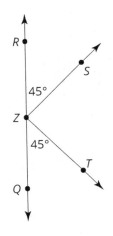

14. ∠QZR is a straight angle. What is the measure of ∠QZS?

15. What kind of angle is ∠SZT?

Questions 16–18 refer to the figure provided.

Note: lines *G* and *H* are parallel.

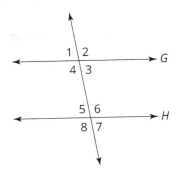

16. List two pairs of alternate interior angles.

17. Which angle corresponds to ∠7?

18. What can you determine about ∠4 and ∠8 from the diagram?

Question 19 refers to the following figure.

Note: lines *K* and *L* are parallel.

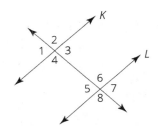

19. The measure of ∠7 is 115°. What is the measure of ∠4?

20. Classify the triangle in two ways.

21. Find the measure of the unknown angle in the triangle.

For questions 22 and 23, decide whether the pairs of triangles are congruent. Write *Yes*, *No*, or *Not enough information*.

22.

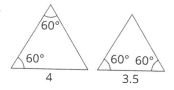

23.

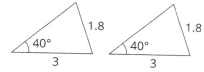

Question 24 refers to the figure provided.

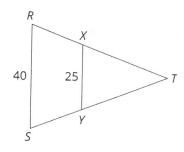

24. If $XY \parallel RS$, $m\angle S = 68°$, and $m\angle T = 48°$, then what is the measure of $m\angle TXY$?

For questions 25–27, list the names of all quadrilaterals that have the properties named in the question. Write *None* if no quadrilateral has the named properties.

25. Four right angles

26. Opposite sides are equal in length

27. Exactly one pair of parallel sides

Question 28 refers to the figure provided.

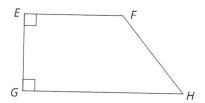

28. If $\angle F$ is 20° greater than three times the measure of $\angle H$, what is the measure of $\angle F$?

Mathematics Review Three Practice Answers and Explanations

1.   6 in.³

The volume of a cube is the length of an edge cubed. You can read 6 in.³ as "six inches cubed."

2.   Area: 39 sq units; perimeter: 30.8 units

Area of a triangle: $\frac{1}{2}(\text{Base})(\text{Height})$. Perimeter: Sum of the lengths of all sides.

3.   Area: 29.6 sq units; perimeter: 24.6 units

Area of a parallelogram: (Base)(Height)

4.   54

In any right triangle, one of the two shorter sides will be the base of the triangle and the other shorter side will be the height of the triangle. Thus, the area of the triangle described is $\frac{1}{2}(9 \times 12) = 54$.

5.   C = 63 in., A = 314 in.²

$A = \pi r^2$

$C = 2\pi r$

6.   38

Use the formula $C = \pi d$, where $d = 12$. Then $12(3.14) \approx 37.7 \approx 38$.

7.   19 in.

You need to find the circumference of the 10-point band. First, find the diameter that passes through the circle that includes the 10-point band (but not the outer 5-point band). Add the width of the 10-point band twice and the diameter of the inner circle: $2 + 2 + 2 = 6$ inches. Now use the formula for circumference to get $6(3.14) = 18.84$, which rounds to 19 inches.

8.   160 cubic units

$V = \text{length} \times \text{width} \times \text{height}$

9.   236 cubic units

$V = \pi r^2 h$

10.   125

If each edge measures 5 feet, then the crate is a cube. Use $V = e^3$, so $V = 5^3 = 125$.

11.   V ≈ 399 cubic units

Calculate the volume of the top solid (cylinder) and the bottom solid (rectangular solid) and add the volumes.

$$V_{\text{cyl}} = \pi r^2 h = \pi(5)^2(2) \approx 157$$
$$V_{\text{rect}} = lwh = (11)(11)(2) = 242$$
$$\text{Total volume} \approx 157 + 242 = 399$$

12.   Acute

13.   Reflex

14.   135°

$m\angle RZS + m\angle QZS = 180°$. Because $\angle RZS$ measures $45°$, $\angle QZS$ must measure $135°$.

15.   Right angle

Because $m\angle RZQ = 180°$, subtract the two known angles to find the measure of $\angle SZT$: $180° - 45° - 45° = 90°$. Because $\angle SZT$ measures $90°$, it is a right angle.

16.   ∠4 and ∠6, ∠3 and ∠5

17.   ∠3

18.   ∠4 and ∠8 are corresponding angles and thus have the same measure.

They are in the same position with respect to the parallel lines.

19.   65°

Because $\angle 7$ and $\angle 3$ are corresponding angles, $m\angle 7 = m\angle 3$; therefore, $m\angle 3 = 115°$. Because $\angle 3$ and $\angle 4$ are adjacent angles, $115° + m\angle 4 = 180°$; $m\angle 4 = 65°$.

20.   Equilateral, acute

21.   64°

22.   No

The angles in the two triangles are equal, but the sides are not.

23.   Not enough information

This is Angle, Side, Side, which is not one of the congruent structures; the triangles may or may not be congruent.

24. 64°

Because XY is parallel to RS and $m\angle S = 68°$, then $m\angle TYX = 68°$. Because they form a triangle, $m\angle TYX + m\angle T + m\angle TXY = 180°$. Substitute and solve: $68° + 48° + m\angle TXY = 180°$ and $m\angle TXY = 64°$.

25.   Rectangle, square

26.   Parallelogram, rectangle, square, rhombus

27.   Trapezoid

28.   140°

Let $x =$ the measure of $\angle H$. Then $3x + 20° = m\angle F$. The sum of the angles of a quadrilateral is 360°, so $3x + 20° + x + 90° + 90° = 360°$. Solve the equation:

$$4x + 200° = 360°$$
$$4x = 160°$$
$$x = 40°$$

So $3x + 20° = 140°$.

Mathematics Review Four—Statistics and Probability

Probability

Probability is the numerical representation of the likelihood of an event or events occurring.

Probability is expressed as the ratio of the number of favorable possible outcomes to the total number of possible outcomes. In fractional form, we express probability as follows:

$$\text{Probability (event)} = \frac{\text{\# of favorable outcomes possible}}{\text{\# of total possible outcomes}}$$

If you flip a coin, what are the odds that it will fall with the heads side up?

- The probability that the coin will land heads up is $\frac{1}{2}$, because there is one outcome favorable to your result (heads up) and there are two possible outcomes (heads or tails). You could also express this as 50%.

To find the probability that an event will *not* occur, simply change the numerator in the probability formula to represent the undesired outcomes. The chances that you will roll a 1 on a standard six-sided die are $\frac{1}{6}$. Thus, the probability that you will not roll a 1 is $\frac{5}{6}$.

To determine the probability of two independent results, multiply the probability of the first result by the probability of the second.

At a reception for biology majors, there are 12 freshmen, 15 sophomores, 9 juniors, and 14 seniors. At the end of the event, winners for two door prizes will be selected at random from among all students attending the reception. A given student can win only once. What are the chances that a freshman will win the first door prize and that a sophomore will win the second door prize?

The probability that a freshman will win the first door prize is $\frac{12}{50}$. There are 12 freshmen among a total of 50 students. The probability that a sophomore will then win the second door prize is $\frac{15}{49}$. (Remember that the first winner has been removed from the second drawing, so the number of students to pick from has been reduced by one.) Thus, the odds that a freshman will win the first door prize and that a sophomore will win the second door prize are as follows:

$$\frac{12}{50} \times \frac{15}{49} = \frac{180}{2,450} = \frac{18}{245}$$

Mean, Median, and Mode

Suppose you were asked how much money you usually spend on groceries in a week. Some weeks you may spend a great deal; other weeks, much less. You would probably choose an amount in the middle to represent what you typically spend. This middle value is called a **measure of central tendency.**

The most common measure of central tendency is the **mean**, or the arithmetic average.

> In five football games, a team scored 14, 21, 3, 20, and 10 points. What is the mean, or average, score per game?

- Add the values. $14 + 21 + 3 + 20 + 10 = 68$

- Divide by the number of items in the data set. $68 \div 5 =$ **13.6 points per game**

Although it is impossible for a football team to score 13.6 points in one game, the number represents the average of the scores from the five games.

Another measure of central tendency is the median. The **median** is the middle number in a list of data when the number of items in the list is odd.

> During a seven-hour period, a bookstore recorded the following numbers of sales per hour. Find the median number of sales per hour.

HOUR 1	HOUR 2	HOUR 3	HOUR 4	HOUR 5	HOUR 6	HOUR 7
43	28	24	36	32	37	48

- Arrange the values in ascending order.   24, 28, 32, 36, 37, 43, 48

- Find the middle number.   24, 28, 32, $\boxed{36}$, 37, 43, 48

If there is an even number of values, the median is the mean of the two middle values.

> Robert has the following test scores in his math class: 90, 72, 88, 94, 91, and 80.

- Arrange the values in ascending order and find the middle.   72, 80, $\boxed{88}$, $\boxed{90}$, 91, 94

- Find the mean of the two middle values. The median score is **89**.   Add: $88 + 90 = 178$
  Divide by 2: $178 \div 2 = 89$

The **mode** is the value that occurs most often in a set of data. A set of data could have more than one mode if two or more items occur the same number of times and these items occur more often than any other items. If each item of data occurs only once, there is no mode.

> Six weather stations recorded the following temperatures at 3:00 PM: 45°, 44°, 45°, 47°, 46°, and 45°. What is the mode of the data?

- The temperature 45° occurs the most often (three times), so the mode is **45°**.

Measures of Spread

Range and **standard deviation** are two statistical measures that tell how spread out the data is. For both range and standard deviation, the bigger the number, the more spread out the data.

Range: Calculate by finding the difference between the maximum and minimum values in the set: (maximum) − (minimum).

Standard deviation: The test will not ask you to calculate standard deviation by hand, but it is useful to know that data points that are far away from each other will have a higher standard deviation than data points that are clustered together.

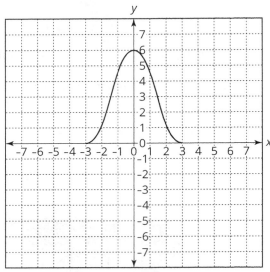

Small Standard Deviation

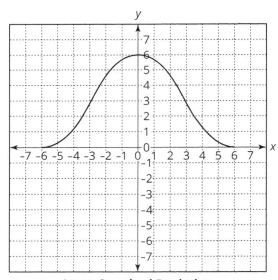

Large Standard Deviation

Calculate the range of this data set: {5, 2, 10, 0, −1, 9}.

Maximum value: 10

Minimum value: −1

10 − (−1) = 11

The range is **11**.

Statistical Questions and Sampling

Certain questions on the Praxis Core Math test may ask you to choose which of the answer choices is a "statistical question." Here's how you can distinguish arithmetic questions from statistical questions.

Arithmetic questions have only one answer. It may take multiple measurements to find this answer, but there is still one exact number that tells the whole story.

> What is the height of the tallest person in class? 6 feet.

> How many days in January were below freezing? 3 days.

Statistical questions have a range of answers or require you to determine an average. One specific number will not give an adequate explanation.

> When do students arrive at school? Between 8:00 AM and 8:30 AM.

> How many brothers do the math teachers have? You could either list all the results (0, 0, 3) or you could take the average (1). The single number 1 does not give an adequate explanation as to how many teachers were surveyed or what the spread of the data looks like.

Other questions on the Praxis will ask about whether a random sample of participants is "good" or "bad" for a study. The most important detail in these questions is the goal of the study.

> What population should a researcher survey if she wants to predict whom people will vote for in the next election?

The goal of the survey is to get information regarding an election. Thus, the researcher should only survey people who are eligible to vote. This would exclude people who cannot vote because they are too young, they are not registered, etc.

On the test, eliminate answer choices that are too broad (e.g., picking a random sample from all people) and those that are too narrow (e.g., picking a random sample from 30-year-old males).

Tables and Pictographs

Data are facts and information. By analyzing data, we can make predictions, draw conclusions, and solve problems. To be useful, data must be organized in some way. A **table** organizes data in columns and rows. The labels on the table help you understand what the data means.

> The table below shows population figures for selected counties in 2010 and 2020 and the land area in square miles for each county.

COUNTY	ADAMS	BELL	COOK	DAVIS	EVANS
2010 Pop.	11,128	25,199	6,532	82,204	139,519
2020 Pop.	15,295	22,707	6,518	90,834	130,748
Land Area in Sq. Miles	4,255	2,532	2,398	1,139	321

Which county showed the greatest percent increase in population from 2010 to 2020?

- **Read the labels.** The first row shows the county names. The second and third rows show population figures. The fourth row shows land area data. You do not need the land area data to answer this question.
- **Analyze the data.** Only Adams and Davis counties showed increases from 2010 to 2020.
- **Use the data.** Find the percent increases for Adams and Davis counties.

Adams:

$$\frac{15,295 - 11,128}{11,128} \approx 0.374 \approx 37\%$$

Davis:

$$\frac{90,834 - 82,204}{82,204} \approx 0.105 \approx 10\%$$

- **Adams County** showed the greatest percent increase in population from 2010 to 2020.

A **pictograph** is another way to display data. Pictographs use symbols to compare data. A key shows what value each symbol represents.

A city has three public library branches. A librarian kept track of the numbers of books checked out from each branch in a week. He used the data to create the pictograph below.

BRANCHES	BOOKS CHECKED OUT FROM 3/4 TO 3/10
North	📖 📖 📖 📖 📖 📖 📖
South	📖 📖 📖 📖 📖
West	📖 📖 📖 📖 📖 📖 📖 📖 📖

Key: 📖 = 150 books

From March 4 to March 10, how many books were checked out from the South and West branches combined?

- There are $4\frac{1}{2}$ symbols for the South branch and 9 symbols for the West branch. Add.

$$4\frac{1}{2} + 9 = 13\frac{1}{2} \text{ symbols}$$

- Find the value of the symbols. The key states that each symbol equals 150 books. Multiply $13\frac{1}{2}$ by 150.

$$13\frac{1}{2} \times 150 = \textbf{2,025 books}$$

Interpretation of Graphs

Bar Graphs

A **bar graph** uses bars to represent values. Bar graphs have two axis lines. One line shows a number scale, and the other shows labels for the bars. By comparing the length of a bar to the scale, you can estimate what value the bar represents.

A national corporation made a bar graph (shown below) to show the number of discrimination complaints made by employees during a six-year period. About how many more complaints were made in 1999 than in 1998?

- **Read the labels.** Each bar represents the number of complaints made within a year. The years are shown beneath the bars.

- **Analyze the data.** Compare the bars for 1998 and 1999 to the scale. There were 20 complaints in 1998 and about 32 complaints in 1999.

- **Use the data.** Subtract: 32 − 20 = 12. There were about **12 more complaints** in 1999 than in 1998.

A **double-bar graph** compares more than one type of data.

A studio released four films in one year. The graph below compares the cost of making each movie to its box office receipts, or ticket sales. Film *B*'s cost is approximately what percent of its box office receipts?

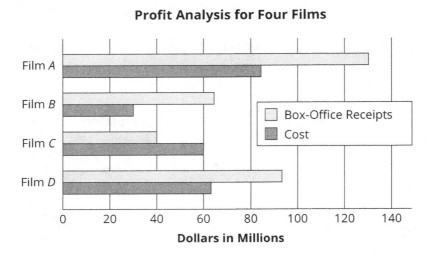

- **Read the labels.** Read the key to find the meaning of the bars. Notice that the scale represents millions of dollars.

- **Analyze the data.** Film *B*'s cost is about $30 million. It brought in about $65 million in receipts.

- **Use the data.** Find what percent $30 is of $65.

The percent that $30 is of $65 is

$$\frac{\$30}{\$65} = 0.462 \approx \mathbf{46\%}$$

Line Graphs

A **line graph** is useful for showing changes over time. By analyzing the rise and fall of the line, you can tell whether a value is increasing, decreasing, or staying the same. Like a bar graph, a line graph has two axis lines. One is marked with a scale; the other is (usually) marked in regular time intervals.

The graph below shows the number of patients who visited an emergency room for the treatment of scooter-related injuries.

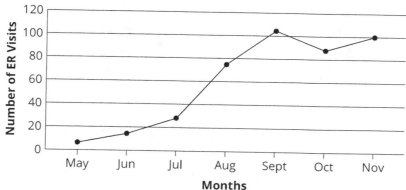

**Westside Hospital
Number of Emergency Room Visits
Related to Scooter Injuries**

During what month was there a decrease from the previous month in the number of emergency room visits for scooter-related injuries?

The points on the graph are positioned above the months, which are arranged in calendar order. By examining the line that connects the points, you can tell whether there was an increase or a decrease from one month to the next.

You can tell a lot about the information in a line graph even if you don't look at the exact values. Because the scale on the vertical axis increases from bottom to top, a line that slopes up from left to right shows an increase over time. Likewise, a line that slopes down from left to right shows a decrease during that period of time.

In this graph, there is only one segment that does not slope up from left to right—the segment from September to October. This means that there was a decrease in scooter-related injuries in **October** relative to September.

The steepness of a line can also be informative. A steeper line indicates a faster rate of change than a flatter line. In this graph, the line from July to August is the steepest, indicating that the largest one-month increase occurred during that period. (This can be confirmed by actually reading the values and comparing them.)

If a line graph has more than one line, a **key** will tell you what each line represents.

The graph below shows the changes in ticket prices for two amusement parks.

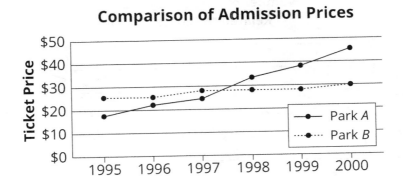

What was the last year in which the price of admission to Park *B* was greater than the price of admission to Park *A*?

- The admission prices for Park *A* are represented by a solid line. Park *B*'s prices are shown with a dotted line. The graph begins in 1995. In 1995, Park *B*'s ticket price is greater than Park *A*'s. Follow the two lines to the right. Between 1997 and 1998, the lines cross, and Park *A*'s prices climb higher than Park *B*'s. The year **1997** was the last time that Park *B* charged more than Park *A* for a ticket.

Circle Graphs

A **circle graph**, or **pie chart**, is used to show how a whole amount is broken into parts. The sections of a circle graph are often labeled with percents. The size of each section corresponds to the fraction it represents. For example, a section labeled 25% will be $\frac{1}{4}$ of the circle.

A graph below shows how a children's sports camp spends its weekly budget.

How much does the sports camp spend on lunches each week?

- **Analyze the graph.** According to the heading, the entire circle represents the camp's weekly budget of $2,250. Find the section labeled "lunches." According to the section label, lunches make up 35% of the weekly budget.

- **Use the data.** To find the amount spent on lunches, find 35% of $2,250: $2,250 × 0.35 = **$787.50**.

A circle graph may also be labeled using fractions or decimals. One common kind of circle graph labels each section in cents to show how a dollar is used.

According to the graph, what percentage of the average household's energy bills is spent on drying clothes, lighting, and heating water?

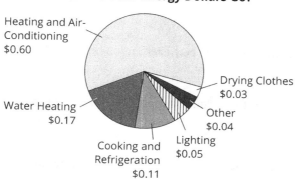

Where Do Your Energy Dollars Go?

- **Analyze the graph.** The entire circle represents $1. The amounts in the sections mentioned in the problem are $0.03, $0.05, and $0.17.

- **Use the data.** Add the amounts: $0.03 + $0.05 + $0.17 = $0.25. Because $0.25 is 25% of a dollar, **25%** of an average household's energy bills is spent on these items.

Scatterplots

A **scatterplot** is a graph with many points. Usually, it is accompanied by a line of best fit that follows the trend of the points. The x-axis and y-axis labels identify which variables are being related to each other, as in this example:

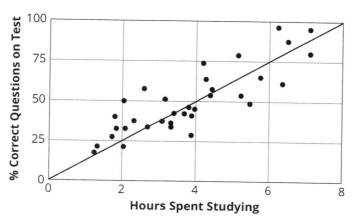

The most important detail to remember about scatterplots is the different types of correlation:

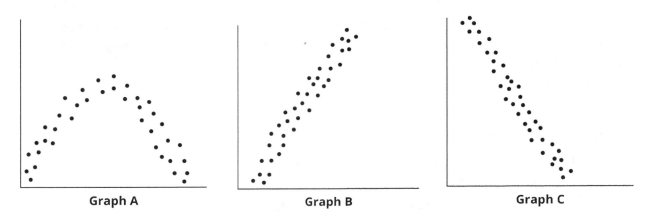

Graph A **Graph B** **Graph C**

Here we see three scatterplots.

Graph A shows no single correlation: there is no consistent trend between the *x* values and the *y* values.

Graph B shows positive correlation: as the *x* values increase, the *y* values increase as well.

Graph C shows negative correlation: as the *x* values increase, the *y* values decrease.

Estimation

Some questions ask for an **estimate**—which is an approximate value rather than an exact value. Here are some estimation techniques to practice.

> Approximately how many people attended the three-game series if attendance at each of the games was 33,541; 35,045; and 34,092; respectively?

> - The problem asks for the *approximate* number of people; therefore, you can estimate. Notice that all three amounts are close to 35,000.

$33{,}541 \approx 35{,}000$
$35{,}045 \approx 35{,}000$
$34{,}095 \approx 35{,}000$

> - Multiply 35,000 by 3 to find that the approximate attendance for the three-game series was **105,000**.

$35{,}000 \times 3 = 105{,}000$

> If Ambrose wants to save enough money to make a $1,159 purchase a year from now, approximately how much should he save per month?

> - The problem asks for the *approximate* amount; therefore, you can estimate. Divide to find how many equal parts are in the total amount of money Ambrose needs to save up. Because 1 year = 12 months, divide $1,159 by 12.

- Round one or both of the numbers so that they are easy to divide. Here, rounding $1,159 to $1,200 makes the division simple. Ambrose needs to save about **$100** a month.

$1,200 \div 12 = \$100$ per month

You can also use estimation to help you narrow down answer choices in multiple-choice questions, or to check your calculations.

Souvenir sales are $389, $205, and $276 at each of three booths. What is the total amount in sales?

A. $615

B. $870

C. $999

D. $1,523

E. $2,621

Strategy 1

You can estimate an answer by rounding values to the nearest hundred. The closest choice to $900 is **(B)** $870.

$400 + $200 + $300 = $900

Strategy 2

You can calculate an answer and then check it against an estimate to see whether your answer makes sense. Choice **(B)** $870 is close to an estimate of $900.

$389 + $205 + $276 = $870

Mathematics Review Four Practice

For the situations described in questions 1 and 2, express probability as a fraction, a decimal, and a percent.

1. A game has 50 wooden tiles. Players randomly draw tiles to spell words. If 20 of the tiles are marked with vowels, what is the probability of drawing a vowel from the tiles?

2. There are four red, four blue, and two green marbles in a bag. If one marble is drawn randomly from the bag, what is the probability that the marble will be green?

For each data set in questions 3 and 4, find the mean, median, and mode. Round calculations to the nearest hundredth or cent.

3. Golf scores for 18 holes: 76, 82, 75, 87, 80, 82, and 79

4. Sales totals for 6 weeks: $5,624; $10,380; $8,102; $6,494; $12,008; and $8,315

5. What is the median value of $268; $1,258; $654; $1,258; $900; $1,588; and $852?

Questions 6 and 7 refer to the following table.

County	Adams	Bell	Cook	Davis	Evans
Population (2010)	11,128	25,199	6,532	82,204	139,519
Population (2020)	15,295	22,707	6,518	90,834	130,748
Land area in sq miles	4,255	2,532	2,398	1,139	321

6. On average, Bell County had how many people per square mile in 2020? (Round your answer to the nearest integer.)

7. To the nearest percent, what was the percent decrease in Evans County's population from 2010 to 2020?

Question 8 refers to the following table.

Community A: Percentage of Three-Year-Old Children with School Readiness Skills for the Years 2014 and 2020		
	2014	**2020**
Recognizes all letters	13%	15%
Counts to 20 or higher	37%	41%
Writes own name	22%	24%
Reads or pretends to read	68%	70%

8. Community A had 350 three-year-old children in 2020. Based on the table, how many were able to write their own name?

Questions 9 and 10 refer to the following graph.

9. To the nearest ten, how many employee discrimination complaints were there in 1995 and 1996 combined?

10. About how many more complaints were there in 2000 than in 1995?

Questions 11 and 12 refer to the following graph.

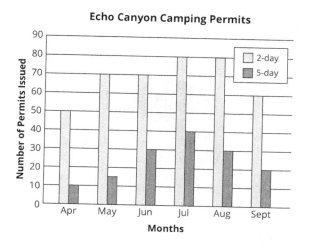

Echo Canyon Camping Permits

11. In May, what was the ratio of the number of 2-day permits to the number of 5-day permits issued?

12. In which month were a total of 80 permits issued?

Questions 13 and 14 refer to the following graph.

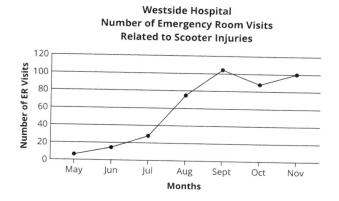

**Westside Hospital
Number of Emergency Room Visits
Related to Scooter Injuries**

13. In which month did the number of scooter-related injuries increase by the greatest amount over the previous month?

14. To the nearest ten, how many total emergency room visits were caused by scooter injuries in August, September, and October?

Questions 15 and 16 refer to the following graph.

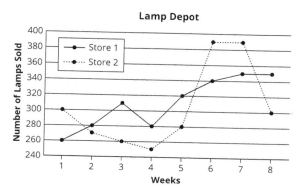

Lamp Depot

15. Approximately how many more lamps were sold at Store 2 than at Store 1 in week 6?

16. During which week did Store 1 experience the greatest increase in sales over the week immediately before?

Question 17 refers to the following graph.

Sports Camp Weekly Budget = $2,250

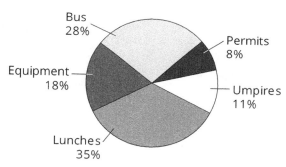

Bus 28%
Permits 8%
Equipment 18%
Umpires 11%
Lunches 35%

17. What percentage of the total sports camp budget is spent on equipment and umpires?

Question 18 refers to the following graph.

Where Do Your Energy Dollars Go?

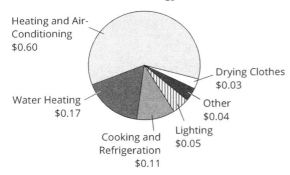

Heating and Air-Conditioning $0.60

Drying Clothes $0.03

Water Heating $0.17

Other $0.04

Cooking and Refrigeration $0.11

Lighting $0.05

18. Which expense is more than 50 percent of an energy dollar?

Question 19 refers to the following graph.

The employees of National Bank are given the following graph to explain how each dollar of their retirement fund is invested.

How Your Retirement Dollar Is Invested

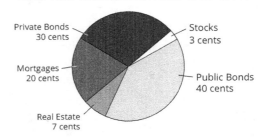

Private Bonds 30 cents

Stocks 3 cents

Mortgages 20 cents

Public Bonds 40 cents

Real Estate 7 cents

19. What percentage of each retirement dollar is invested in real estate and stocks?

Mathematics Review Four Practice Answers and Explanations

1. $\frac{2}{5}$, 0.4, 40%

2. $\frac{1}{5}$, 0.2, 20%

3. **Mean: 80.14; median: 80; mode: 82**

4. **Mean: $8,487.17; median: $8,208.50; mode: none**

5. **$900**
The median is the middle number. Arrange the amounts in order and find the middle value.

6. **9**
Divide Bell County's 2020 population by its land area: $22,707 \div 2,532 \approx 9$.

7. **6%**
Find the difference between Evans County's population in 2010 and 2020 and divide that number by the original (2010) population: $(139,519 - 130,768) \div 139,519 \approx 0.06$. That's approximately 6%.

8. **84**
In 2020, 24% of three-year-old children could write their own name. Find 24% of 350: $0.24 \times 350 = 84$.

9. **50**

10. **About 15**

11. **14:3**
Write a fraction and simplify: $\frac{70}{15} = \frac{14}{3}$. Then, express this as a ratio: 14:3.

12. **September**
Add the 2-day and 5-day permits for each month. Only September's permits equal 80: $60 + 20 = 80$ permits.

13. **August**

14. **270**

15. **50**
There were 390 sales at Store 2 and 340 sales at Store 1 in the sixth week. Find the difference: $390 - 340 = 50$.

16. **Week 5**
The steepest line segment is for the time period between week 4 and week 5, representing an increase of 40 sales.

17. **29%**

18. **Heating and air-conditioning**

19. **10%**
Add: 3 cents + 7 cents = 10 cents. Then 10 cents out of 100 cents is $\frac{10}{100}$, or 10%.

Mathematics Mixed Practice

Directions

Each of the questions in this practice is a multiple-choice question with one correct answer unless otherwise indicated. Practice is not timed, but remember that, on the official exam, you will have approximately one and one-half minutes per question on average. Be on the lookout for alternative approaches that may save you time on some questions.

Note: Just as on the exam, the figures accompanying problems in this practice set are intended to provide information useful in solving the problem. The figures are drawn as accurately as possible unless the problem indicates that the figure is not drawn to scale. Figures can be assumed to lie in a plane unless the problem states otherwise. Lines shown as straight can be assumed to be straight, and the position of points can be assumed to be in the order shown. A right angle is denoted by the symbol ⌐.

1. Eight paper slips are placed in a bag to be drawn as a science assignment. Each slip is labeled with the name of a different planet: Mercury, Venus, Earth, Mars, Jupiter, Saturn, Uranus, and Neptune. What is the probability of drawing at random a slip labeled with the name of a planet that does NOT start with the letter *M*?

   A. $\frac{1}{4}$

   B. $\frac{1}{3}$

   C. $\frac{3}{8}$

   D. $\frac{3}{4}$

   E. $\frac{5}{6}$

2. The user's manual for a stereo set includes a scale diagram in which 2 scaled inches represent 8 actual inches. If the speakers of the stereo set measure 6 inches tall in the diagram, how tall are they in reality?

   A. 1 foot 6 inches

   B. 1 foot 8 inches

   C. 1 foot 10 inches

   D. 2 feet

   E. 2 feet 2 inches

Peterson Family Estimated Expenditures 2000

Annual Income = $42,000

3. The pie chart shown above represents the estimated expenditures of the Peterson family in 2000. How much did the Petersons manage to save that year?

   A. $5,000

   B. $6,000

   C. $7,000

   D. $8,000

   E. $9,000

4. If the area of the rectangle above is 15, what is its perimeter?

   A. 5

   B. 8

   C. 15

   D. 16

   E. 21

5. If $26 - y = 2x + 14 + y$, what is the value of $x + y$?

   A. 1

   B. 2

   C. 3

   D. 6

   E. 8

Questions 6–7 refer to the following graph.

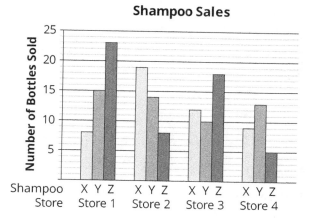

Shampoo Sales

6. In how many of the stores studied were there at least twice as many bottles of shampoo X sold as there were of shampoo Z?

   A. None

   B. One

   C. Two

   D. Three

   E. Four

7. What fraction of the total number of shampoo bottles sold at store 3 were bottles of shampoo Y?

   A. $\frac{1}{4}$

   B. $\frac{1}{5}$

   C. $\frac{1}{6}$

   D. $\frac{1}{8}$

   E. $\frac{1}{10}$

8. What value times 0.15 is 525?

   A. 3.5

   B. 35

   C. 350

   D. 3,500

   E. 35,000

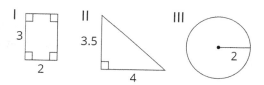

9. Which of the figures above has an area of 6?

   A. I only

   B. I and II

   C. II and III

   D. I and III

   E. I, II, and III

10. Which of the following, when divided into 137, leaves a remainder of 5?

   A. 12

   B. 10

   C. 9

   D. 8

   E. 4

11. Which of the following is greater than 1.25?

   A. 125%

   B. $\frac{3}{2}$

   C. 0.125

   D. 12.5%

   E. $\frac{2}{3}$

12. A bus carries 15 sixth graders, 18 seventh graders, 12 eighth graders, and no other students. What fraction of the total number of students on the bus are seventh graders?

   A. $\frac{1}{5}$

   B. $\frac{2}{7}$

   C. $\frac{2}{5}$

   D. $\frac{3}{7}$

   E. $\frac{3}{5}$

13. To find 36 times 4, you could multiply what number by 12?

   A. 8

   B. 10

   C. 12

   D. 14

   E. 16

14. If T is 40% of 900, then $T =$

   A. 300

   B. 320

   C. 360

   D. 380

   E. 400

15. What is the maximum number of points of intersection between a rectangle and a circle if both lie on a plane?

   A. 1

   B. 2

   C. 4

   D. 6

   E. 8

16. {15, 13, 6, 15, 8, 3, 24, 12, 5}

   What is the median of the above set?

   A. 6

   B. 8

   C. 12

   D. 13

   E. 15

Questions 17–18 refer to the following graph.

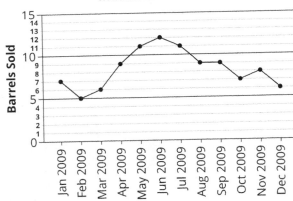

17. How many barrels of industrial solvent were sold in January 2009?

   A. 4

   B. 5

   C. 6

   D. 7

   E. 8

18. How many barrels of industrial solvent were sold in June and July of 2009 combined?

    A. 16

    B. 19

    C. 23

    D. 25

    E. 28

3

19. What is the area of the isosceles right triangle shown above?

    A. 3

    B. 3.5

    C. 4

    D. 4.5

    E. 6

20. If $J + 2 = \dfrac{K}{4}$, then $J =$

    A. $K - 2$

    B. $2K - 2$

    C. $\dfrac{K}{2} - 4$

    D. $\dfrac{K}{4} - 2$

    E. $4K - 4$

21. Of the following expressions, which is NOT equivalent to the others?

    A. $4 \times 48 \times 8$

    B. $4 \times 8 \times 48$

    C. $4^2 \times 12 \times 8$

    D. $4^3 \times 12 \times 2$

    E. $4^2 \times 3 \times 2$

22. A Ferris wheel has 12 cars that can seat up to 3 people each. If every car on the Ferris wheel is full except for 2 that contain 2 people and 1 that is empty, how many people are currently riding on the Ferris wheel?

    A. 30

    B. 31

    C. 32

    D. 36

    E. 40

23. If $= J - (K \times H)$, then
     $=$

24. The four shapes below are made up of identical equilateral triangles. Which of the four shapes, if any, has the *least* perimeter?

    A.

    B.

    C.

    D.

    E. All have the same perimeter.

25. Nine temperature readings are taken, one reading every four hours, with the first reading taken at noon. When will the final reading be taken?

    A. midnight

    B. 8:00 AM

    C. noon

    D. 4:00 PM

    E. 8:00 PM

26. Which of the figures below, if any, has a perimeter value in units that is the same as the value of its area in square units?

A.
3
3

B. 2
3

C. 4
4

D. 3
4

E. None has a perimeter equal to its area.

27. If the length, x, of a rectangle is doubled and its width, y, is divided by 3, then the area of the new rectangle is given by which formula?

A. xy

B. $2xy$

C. $\dfrac{2xy}{3}$

D. $3xy$

E. $6xy$

28. Apple pie is served only on every even-numbered day in February.

Ice cream is served only on days in February that are multiples of three.

If both statements above are true, and if there are 28 days in February, then it is valid to conclude that both apple pie and ice cream are served on how many days in February?

A. 2

B. 3

C. 4

D. 5

E. 6

29. What is the average (arithmetic mean) of $\dfrac{3}{5}$ and $\dfrac{9}{2}$?

A. $\dfrac{51}{10}$

B. $\dfrac{45}{10}$

C. $\dfrac{51}{20}$

D. $\dfrac{45}{20}$

E. $\dfrac{45}{40}$

30. Which of the following represents 89,213 written in scientific notation?

A. 8921.3×10

B. 892.13×10^2

C. 89.213×10^3

D. 8.9213×10^4

E. 0.89213×10^5

Mathematics Mixed Practice Answers and Explanations

1.   D

The probability of an event is equal to the number of favorable outcomes divided by the number of possible outcomes. In this case, the number of slips labeled with a planet name that does *not* start with the letter M will be the number of favorable outcomes. As two of the eight planets have names starting with M, six do not. The number of favorable outcomes divided by the number of possible outcomes is $\frac{6}{8}$, which can be simplified to $\frac{3}{4}$, choice (**D**).

2.   D

This problem requires you to determine a scale factor and to apply that to a given measurement. Because 2 scaled inches on the diagram equal 8 inches in reality, a scale factor of $8 \div 2 = 4$ is being used. Since the speakers measure 6 inches in the diagram, multiply this by the scale factor to find their height in reality: $6 \times 4 = 24$. Because the answer choices are in feet and inches, convert 24 inches to feet by dividing 24 inches by 12 inches per foot to calculate that the speakers have an actual height of $24 \div 12 = 2$ feet, choice (**D**).

3.   C

The pie chart provided with this problem does not give the fraction of expenditure represented by savings, but it does give the fraction of expenditure represented by everything else. If $\frac{1}{3}$ is spent on mortgage payments, $\frac{1}{6}$ is spent on groceries, $\frac{1}{6}$ is spent on loan repayments, and $\frac{1}{6}$ represents miscellaneous spending, then these fractions can be subtracted from the whole to find the fraction saved:

$$1 - \frac{1}{3} - \frac{1}{6} - \frac{1}{6} - \frac{1}{6} = 1 - \frac{5}{6} = \frac{1}{6} \text{ saved}$$

Because the Petersons' annual income was \$42,000 and $\frac{1}{6}$ of this was saved, $\$42,000 \div 6 = \$7,000$ in savings, choice (**C**).

4.   D

This question requires two steps, one working backward and one working forward. To find the perimeter of a polygon, you must know the length of each side. Here only one is marked. The opposite side is easy to determine because the figure is a rectangle; it is also 3. The other two sides will also be equal to each other but must be found using the other information given: the rectangle has an area of 15. This is where you must work backward. Because the area of a rectangle is determined as $A = lw$, you know that $15 = 3l$. Thus, $l = 5$. You now know that the rectangle has two sides of length 3 and two sides of length 5. To find the perimeter, add them together: $3 + 3 + 5 + 5 = 16$, choice (**D**).

5.   D

Begin by combining like terms:

$26 - y = 2x + 14 + y$

$26 - 14 = 2x + y + y$

$12 = 2x + 2y$

Now it is possible to divide both sides by the common factor of 2:

$$\frac{12}{2} = \frac{2x + 2y}{2}$$

$x + y = 6$, so choice (**D**) is correct.

6.   B

This question asks you to analyze the information in the graph to determine how many stores sold at least twice as many bottles of shampoo X as shampoo Z. Only Store 2 fits, with 19 bottles of shampoo X sold and only 8 of shampoo Z. Choice (**B**) is correct.

7.   A

To find bottles of shampoo Y as a fraction of the total number of shampoo bottles sold at Store 3, first find the total number of bottles sold and then find the number of bottles of shampoo Y sold. Store 3 sold 12 bottles of shampoo X, 10 bottles of shampoo Y, and 18 bottles of shampoo Z. Thus, the fraction is $\frac{10}{12 + 10 + 18} = \frac{10}{40} = \frac{1}{4}$. Choice (**A**) is correct.

8. D

This question can be solved by creating an equation using x to represent the unknown number of times that 0.15 is being multiplied:

$$525 = 0.15x$$

$$\frac{525}{0.15} = x$$

$$\frac{525 \times 100}{0.15 \times 100} = x$$

$$\frac{52,500}{15} = x$$

$$3,500 = x$$

Choice (**D**) is correct.

9. A

This problem can most easily be solved by process of elimination. You may notice almost immediately that figure I has an area of 6, which allows you to eliminate choice (C). From there, go ahead to figure II, since II and III appear the same number of times in the remaining answer choices. Because figure II has an area of $\frac{1}{2} \times 3.5 \times 4 = 7$, it does not work, and choices (B) and (E) can be eliminated. To choose between (A) and (D), try figure III next. It has an area of $\pi(2^2) = 4\pi$, so it does not work, and choice (**A**) must be correct.

10. A

If a number leaves a remainder of 5 when divided into 137, then two things must be true: the number must be greater than 5, and the number must divide evenly into (137 − 5), or 132. Only (**A**), 12, is greater than 5 and divides evenly into 132.

11. B

To compare values easily, put them in the same form. To solve this problem, convert all values into either decimals or percentages. (**B**) is correct because $\frac{3}{2}$, or 1.5, is greater than 1.25. (A) is 1.25, (C) is 0.125, (D) is 0.125, and (E) is $0.\overline{66}$.

12. C

This question asks you to identify the correct part-to-whole ratio from among the answer choices. In this

case, the fraction will have the number of seventh graders, 18, as the numerator and the total number of students on the bus, $15 + 18 + 12 = 45$, as the denominator. Because $\frac{18}{45}$ is not an answer choice, it must be simplified:

$$\frac{18}{45} = \frac{18 \div 9}{45 \div 9} = \frac{2}{5}$$

Choice (**C**) is correct.

13. C

This problem can be solved by translating the question into an algebraic equation, with x as the number of times by which 12 must be multiplied:

$$36 \times 4 = 12x$$

$$\frac{36 \times 4}{12} = \frac{12x}{12}$$

$$3 \times 4 = x$$

$$12 = x$$

Choice (**C**) is correct.

14. C

If T is 40% of 900, then

$$T = 900 \times 40\%$$

$$T = 900 \times \frac{4}{10}$$

$$T = \frac{900 \times 4}{10}$$

$$T = 90 \times 4$$

$$T = 360$$

Choice (**C**) is correct.

15. E

This question requires that you consider the different ways in which a rectangle and a circle lying on a plane could overlap and determine the maximum number of points of intersection. It might be helpful to sketch various possibilities. If the rectangle is placed so that one side is tangent to the circle, there will be one point of intersection. However, if the rectangle is placed so that each of the four corners overlaps the circumference of the circle, there will be eight points of intersection. It is impossible to sketch a scenario in which the figures share more than eight points of intersection, so choice (**E**) is correct.

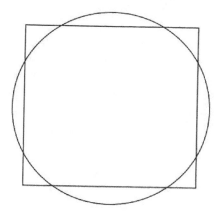

16. C

To find the median of a list of values, begin by ordering the values from least to greatest. Thus ordered, this list becomes {3, 5, 6, 8, 12, 13, 15, 15, 24}. Because there is an odd number of values in the list, the median is simply the middle value, which in this case is 12. Choice (**C**) is correct.

17. D

According to the graph, 7 barrels of solvent were sold in January 2009, choice (**D**).

18. C

Locate on the graph the number of barrels of solvent sold in June 2009, 12, and then locate the number of barrels sold in July 2009, 11. The combined number of barrels sold is $12 + 11 = 23$ barrels. Choice (**C**) is correct.

19. D

This question asks you to find the area of a given triangle, so you will need the area formula for a triangle: $A = \frac{1}{2} \times \text{Base} \times \text{Height}$. Because this is a right isosceles triangle, we know that the height is equal to the base, which measures 3, because they are opposite the congruent angles. Now plug the measurements of the base and height into the area formula:

$$A = \frac{1}{2} \times 3 \times 3 = 1.5 \times 3 = 4.5$$

Choice (**D**) is correct.

20. D

Solve the equation:

$$J + 2 = \frac{K}{4}$$

$$J = \frac{K}{4} - 2$$

Choice (**D**) is correct.

21. E

To determine which answer choice is not equivalent to the rest, first simplify the choices by dividing each by their common factor of 4:

    A. 48×8

    B. 8×48

    C. $4 \times 12 \times 8$, or 48×8

    D. $16 \times 12 \times 2 = 4 \times 4 \times 12 \times 2 = 48 \times 8$

    E. $16 \times 3 \times 2 = 4 \times 4 \times 3 \times 2 = 12 \times 8$

It is now clear that choice (**E**) is different.

22. B

The question states that each seat on the Ferris wheel can hold 3 people and that all but 3 of the 12 cars are full. Therefore, the 9 full cars containing 3 people each contain a total of 27 people. In addition, we are told that 1 car is empty and 2 cars contain 2 people each, adding 4 people to the 27 in the full cars for a total of 31 people on the Ferris wheel. Choice (**B**) is correct.

23. 12

This type of question involving symbols is a twist on a function problem, and boils down to substitution. Determine which numbers correspond to which letters and then plug them into the equation. Then, follow the order of operations and solve. In this case $H = -3$, $J = 6$, and $K = 2$. Plugging into the defining equation, you get $6 - [2 \times (-3)] = 6 - (-6) = 6 + 6 = 12$. Enter 12 in the box to receive credit for this question.

24. B

Because each figure is composed of identical equilateral triangles, we can call the length of any side of any triangle x. By counting the number of sides that form the perimeter of each figure, we can establish algebraic expressions for the perimeter of each figure.

   A.   has a perimeter of $6x$.

   B.   has a perimeter of $5x$.

   C.   has a perimeter of $6x$.

   D.   has a perimeter of $6x$.

Thus, choice (**B**) has the least perimeter.

25. E

The easiest way to solve this problem is to count in increments of four hours until the ninth reading, starting at 12:00 PM: 12:00 PM, 4:00 PM, 8:00 PM, 12:00 AM, 4:00 AM, 8:00 AM, 12:00 PM, 4:00 PM, 8:00 PM. Thus, the ninth reading will be taken at 8:00 PM. Choice (**E**) is correct.

26. C

Calculate the area and perimeter of each figure.

  (A)   Area $= 3 \times 3 = 9$ square units. Perimeter $= 4 \times 3 = 12$ units. Eliminate.

  (B)   Area $= 2 \times 3 = 6$ square units. Perimeter $= 2(2 + 3) = 10$ units. Eliminate.

  (C)   Area $= 4 \times 4 = 16$ square units. Perimeter $= 4 \times 4 = 16$ units. (**C**) is correct.

  (D)   Area $= \frac{1}{2} \times 3 \times 4 = 6$ square units. Perimeter must be greater than $3 + 4 = 7$ units. Therefore, perimeter cannot be equal to area for this figure. Eliminate.

27. C

When the length of a rectangle, x, is doubled, it becomes $2x$. When its width, y, is divided by 3, it becomes $\frac{y}{3}$. The area formula for a rectangle can now be applied to these new dimensions:

$$A = \text{Length} \times \text{Width} = 2x \times \frac{y}{3} = \frac{2xy}{3}, \text{ choice (C).}$$

28. C

By asking on how many days both apple pie and ice cream will be served in February, this question is asking how many days have numbers that satisfy both the first statement by being even and the second statement by being a multiple of three. To answer, simply count the number of dates in February that are even multiples of three, or multiples of $2 \times 3 = 6$: the 6th, the 12th, the 18th, and the 24th. Choice (**C**) is correct.

29. C

To find the average (arithmetic mean) of a set of values, divide the sum of the values by the number of values in the set. In this case, a common denominator must be found before $\frac{3}{5}$ and $\frac{9}{2}$ can be added; the lowest common denominator is 10:

$$\frac{3}{5} = \frac{6}{10} = \text{ and } \frac{9}{2} = \frac{45}{10}$$

The sum is

$$\frac{6}{10} + \frac{45}{10} = \frac{51}{10}$$

The average is

$$\frac{\frac{51}{10}}{2} = \frac{51}{10} \times \frac{1}{2} = \frac{51}{20}$$

That's choice (**C**).

30. D

Scientific notation is correctly represented by a value with digits only in the ones place and to the right of the decimal multiplied by a power of 10. The exponent that 10 is raised to represents the number of places the decimal has been moved in order to leave a value with only one digit to the left of the decimal. Only choice (**D**) is in proper scientific notation, so no calculations need to be made.

CHAPTER 3

PRAXIS CORE WRITING

LEARNING OBJECTIVES

By the end of this chapter, you will be able to do the following:

- Describe the structure and format of the Praxis Core Academic Skills for Educators: Writing test
- Outline and employ the Kaplan Method for Praxis Writing
- Apply Praxis Writing Strategies
- Refresh basic grammar and usage concepts and rules
- Outline and employ the Kaplan Method for Praxis Essay Writing
- Use the Praxis Core Writing practice test to assess your performance

---

Taking Your Core Writing Pre-Test

Before you begin studying and practicing Praxis Core Writing, take a pre-test to assess your initial strengths and areas of greatest opportunity on the test. With 25 multiple-choice questions to complete in 25 minutes and an essay outline to complete in 10 minutes, the pre-test is roughly one-third the length of the actual test. Find time to complete the pre-test in one sitting and time yourself strictly as you take it. Note: On the official Praxis Core Writing test, you will complete two essays in 60 minutes. For this pre-test, you will complete just the outline for one essay.

The purpose of the pre-test is self-assessment. Some test takers hesitate to take pre-tests because they haven't studied yet, or they want to try the questions without time restriction so that they can get them all correct. Those approaches, however, defeat the purpose of the pre-test, which is to get a clear-eyed look at your performance and skill level on all that the test entails.

Part of the test's challenge is its timing. Some of the questions may seem easy, and some may strike you as really difficult. When you encounter hard questions on the pre-test, don't be afraid to skip them or make your best guess. It's more valuable to get a broad view of your performance on different question types than to spend several minutes struggling to get one question right.

So, do your best, but don't get too excited or worried about your score on the pre-test. There's a lot of learning and practice to come, and your performance on the pre-test does not predict your official score. That will be the result of your study and effort.

Core Writing Pre-Test

35 Minutes: 25 Minutes—25 Questions; 10 Minutes—1 Essay Outline

Directions: You have 25 minutes to tackle questions 1–25. Read the instructions for each question type carefully and circle the correct answers in your book. You may use blank scratch paper to take notes.

Questions 1–11. Each of the sentences in this section of the test has four parts that are lettered and underlined. Read each sentence and decide whether any of the underlined portions contains an error in word use, an error in grammatical construction, or an error or omission in punctuation or capitalization, according the conventions of standard written English. If you find an error, note the letter printed beneath the underlined part and choose that as your answer. Try to answer every question.

If you do not find an error in any underlined part of the sentence, choose (E), "No error," which appears after the sentence. *No sentence has more than one error.*

1. <u>Children</u> <u>who</u> read books at home for pleasure
   A   B
   tend to utilize a larger vocabulary in <u>his or her</u>
   C
   daily speech <u>than</u> other children. <u>No error</u>
   D   E

2. The unique pine barrens ecosystem <u>support</u> only
   A
   small <u>pine</u> trees and shrubs, <u>but</u> the ecosystem
   B   C
   is also the <u>home to</u> rare species such as the
   D
   Karner blue butterfly. <u>No error</u>
   E

3. Edgar Allan Poe, the <u>great American</u> author,
   A   B
   composed hauntingly insightful tales that
   explore not only the dramatic range <u>of</u> human
   C
   emotions <u>but</u> the intricacies of the human
   D
   psyche. <u>No error</u>
   E

4. Carol had just <u>completed</u> her last final exam
   A
   when she received the news that her month-long
   trip <u>to Europe, which</u> was scheduled for next
   B   C
   semester, <u>had been cancelled</u>. <u>No error</u>
   D   E

5. Although <u>Senator Jones</u> expressed concern
   A
   about the <u>bill's</u> environmental impacts, the new
   B   C
   law was ultimately passed and <u>will have gone</u>
   D
   into effect next year. <u>No error</u>
   E

6. Animals <u>use</u> a variety of strategies for surviving
   A
   the bitter winter months, including <u>hibernation</u>
   B   C
   in sheltered locations, migrating <u>to</u> warmer
   D
   locales, and using the snow as insulation.

   <u>No error</u>
   E

7. <u>Although</u> she <u>is</u> an avid fan of opera, Dolores
   A   B
   hardly <u>never</u> attends the local opera house,
   C
   preferring <u>to watch</u> broadcasts of international
   D
   performances on the internet. <u>No error</u>
   E

8. After he <u>had traveled</u> extensively, in the then-
   A   B
   wilderness of the West, Albert Bierstadt <u>painted</u>
   C
   evocative landscapes that captured the
   adventurous <u>American spirit</u>. <u>No error</u>
   D   E

9. Compared <u>against</u> other defensive strategies,
            A
    playing a full-court press defense <u>is</u> an
                                        B
    exhausting and rarely employed, though

    potentially quite effective<u>,</u> strategy in the game
                                 C
    <u>of</u> basketball. <u>No error</u>
     D   E

10. The development of agriculture is often heralded

    <u>as</u> the historical tipping point in producing
     A
    civilization, <u>though</u> the consequential increase
                   B
    in concentrated <u>human</u> populations thousands
                     C
    of years ago also <u>results</u> in the spread of
                        D
    devastating diseases. <u>No error</u>
                           E

11. <u>Proponents'</u> of string theory <u>suggest</u> that the
     A   B
    universe <u>is</u> composed of one-dimensional
              C
    <u>strings,</u> while adherents to particle physics
     D
    propose particles. <u>No error</u>
                        E

Sentence Correction

Questions 12–18. In each of the following sentences, some part of the sentence or the entire sentence is underlined. Beneath each sentence you will find five ways of writing the underlined part. The first of these repeats the original, but the other four are all different. If you think the original sentence is better than any of the suggested changes, you should select the first answer choice; otherwise, you should select one of the other choices.

This is a test of correctness and effectiveness of expression. In choosing answers, follow the requirements of standard written English: pay attention to acceptable usage in grammar, diction (choice of words), sentence construction, and punctuation. Choose the answer that expresses most effectively what is presented in the original sentence; this answer should be clear and exact, without awkwardness, ambiguity, or redundancy.

Remember, try to answer every question.

12. Even after becoming blind, the poet John Milton's daughters took dictation of his epic poem *Paradise Lost*.

    A. the poet John Milton's daughters took dictation of his epic poem *Paradise Lost*

    B. the poet John Milton's daughters taking dictation, his epic poem Paradise Lost was written

    C. the epic poem *Paradise Lost* was dictated by the poet John Milton to his daughters

    D. the epic poem *Paradise Lost* was dictated to his daughters by the poet John Milton

    E. the poet John Milton dictated his epic poem *Paradise Lost* to his daughters

13. With his plays, George Bernard Shaw tested the limits of British censorship; the purpose being to make audiences aware of social inequities.

    A. censorship; the purpose being to

    B. censorship and the purpose was to

    C. censorship, with the purpose to

    D. censorship; so that he could

    E. censorship to

14. Even though the senators on the committee were reluctant to schedule a formal inquiry, they went on record as favoring one.

    A. were reluctant to schedule

    B. were reluctant as far as scheduling

    C. were reluctant in scheduling

    D. have been reluctant at scheduling

    E. have had reluctance to schedule

15. The Islandian government, under pressure to satisfy the needs of consumers, and loosening its control of the economy.

    A. and loosening its

    B. by loosening its

    C. is loosening their

    D. but loosening their

    E. is loosening its

16. Unusual numbers of playwrights and artists flourishing in the England of Shakespeare's time and the Italy of Michelangelo's day, when cultural conditions were particularly conducive to creativity.

    A. flourishing in the England of Shakespeare's time

    B. by flourishing in the England of Shakespeare's time

    C. while flourishing in Shakespeare's England

    D. flourished in the England of Shakespeare's time

    E. having flourished in Shakespeare's England

17. The politician is benefiting from behavioral <u>research, there are new techniques for them</u> to utilize and new broadcasting methods to experiment with.

    A. research, there are new techniques for them
    B. research; there are new techniques for they
    C. research; he has new techniques
    D. research, there are new techniques for him
    E. research; they have new techniques

18. <u>The young couple eventually returned to the grassy spot where they had left their sandwiches, strolling hand in hand.</u>

    A. The young couple eventually returned to the grassy spot where they had left their sandwiches, strolling hand in hand.

    B. Eventually, the young couple returned to the grassy spot where they had left their sandwiches, strolling hand in hand.

    C. Strolling hand in hand, the grassy spot where they had left their sandwiches was returned to by the young couple.

    D. The young couple, returning to the grassy spot where they had left their sandwiches, while strolling hand in hand.

    E. Strolling hand in hand, the young couple eventually returned to the grassy spot where they had left their sandwiches.

Revision in Context

Questions 19–22. This is an essay draft that requires some editing work. Choose the best versions of the sentences and/or paragraphs as examined in the questions. At times, you will not be able to improve the passage using the answer choices, and in those circumstances, you should indicate that the passage is correct as written. As you answer these questions, be sure to consider writing style; the author's tone and purpose; and standard English conventions of grammar, usage, punctuation, and capitalization.

Be sure to select an answer for each question.

Questions 19–22 refer to the following stimulus.

(1) Playwright José Rivera was born in San Juan, Puerto Rico, in 1955, but his family moved to New York when he was four years old. (2) <u>Yet</u> many of his relatives had already moved to the Bronx, a bustling neighborhood in New York, Rivera's father wanted to live in a place that felt more like a small town. (3) So they moved to a quarter acre of land on Long Island, New York, which at the time had dirt roads and woods.

(4) From an early age, <u>Rivera knew that he wanted to be a writer, as a kid he wrote comic strips, a novel about baseball, and composed essays in response to photographs, from *Life* magazine.</u> (5) When he was in middle school, he saw a play that inspired him to become a playwright. (6) He wrote several plays during high school and college.

(7) <u>Rivera, after graduating, returned to New York, from college, and was determined</u> to continue writing. (8) Eventually Rivera found an artistic home in a playwriting group called the Theater Matrix; the group met on Monday nights to share their work. (9) One of the plays that he wrote and produced, *The House of Iglesia*, received a good review in *The New York Times*. (10) The famous television producer Norman Lear read the review and immediately offered Rivera a job writing for Embassy Television in California.

(11) After many years of hard work and perseverance, Rivera has received recognition through countless productions of his plays and numerous awards. (12) Despite the challenges of show business, José Rivera <u>had become</u> an important playwright whose work has touched worldwide audiences.

19. In context, which of the following is the best version of the underlined portion of sentence 2 (reproduced below)?

<u>Yet</u> many of his relatives had already moved to the Bronx, a bustling neighborhood in New York, Rivera's father wanted to live in a place that felt more like a small town.

A. (As it is now)
B. Because
C. In addition,
D. Although
E. As a result

20. In context, which of the following is the best version of the underlined portion of sentence 4 (reproduced below)?

From an early age, <u>Rivera knew that he wanted to be a writer, as a kid he wrote comic strips, a novel about baseball, and composed essays in response to photographs, from *Life* magazine</u>.

A. (As it is now)

B. Rivera knew that he wanted to be a writer; as a kid he wrote comic strips, a novel about baseball, and essays in response to photographs from *Life* magazine

C. Rivera knew that he wanted to be a writer, as a kid he wrote comic strips, a novel about baseball, and essays in response to photographs, from *Life* magazine

D. having written comic strips, a novel about baseball, and composed essays in response to photographs from *Life* magazine, Rivera knew he wanted to be a writer

E. Rivera knew that he wanted to be a writer; as a kid he wrote comic strips, a novel about baseball, and composed essays in response to photographs, from *Life* magazine

21. In context, which of the following is the best version of the underlined portion of sentence 7 (reproduced below)?

<u>Rivera, after graduating, returned to New York, from college, and was determined</u> to continue writing.

A. (As it is now)

B. Rivera, being determined, returned to New York from college and decided

C. After graduating from college, Rivera returned to New York, determined

D. Rivera, returning to New York after graduating from college and being determined

E. Rivera, determined to return to New York after graduating from college

22. In context, which of the following is the best version of the underlined words from sentence 12 (reproduced below)?

Despite the challenges of show business, José Rivera <u>had become</u> an important playwright whose work has touched worldwide audiences.

A. (As it is now)

B. has become

C. will have become

D. would become

E. would have become

Research Skills

Questions 23–25. The following questions test your familiarity with basic research skills. For each question, choose the best answer.

Remember, try to answer every question.

> Eliot, T. S. "Tradition and the Individual Talent." *Selected Essays of T. S. Eliot*, Harcourt, Brace & World, 1950, pp. 3–11.

23. What type of work, publication, or record is cited above?

    A. A work in a collection

    B. A book

    C. A magazine article

    D. An article in a scholarly journal

    E. An interview

24. A historian is researching the effects of World War I on civilians in northern France. Which would NOT be a primary source for the historian's work?

    A. The memoir of a French civilian whose parents were killed during World War I when fighting reached their town in northern France

    B. The diary of a German soldier stationed in northern France describing how civilian prisoners were treated

    C. An article that appeared in *The New York Times* during World War I based on interviews with soldiers about the consequences of trench warfare for villages in northern France

    D. Official French government documents issued at the beginning of the war instructing French civilians to evacuate as the German army invaded northern France

    E. A letter from a farmer in northern France to a relative in Paris describing living conditions for civilians who had refused to evacuate as the German army invaded

25. A student is doing research for a paper on how well President Dwight D. Eisenhower and Congress worked together during Eisenhower's presidency. Which of the following pieces of information would NOT be directly relevant to the student's topic?

    A. Film footage of President Eisenhower criticizing Congress

    B. A contemporary news article describing tactics used by President Eisenhower to persuade members of Congress to vote for his proposals

    C. A historian's analysis of the balance of power between the president and Congress during the presidencies of Franklin Roosevelt, Harry Truman, and Dwight Eisenhower

    D. A list of bills passed by Congress that were vetoed by President Eisenhower and therefore prevented from becoming law

    E. A documentary film examining General Eisenhower's success in persuading British military leaders to accept his leadership during the last two years of World War II

Written Assignment

Essay (outline only). Read the following essay prompt and then create an outline that you would use in preparing to write an essay of about 300–600 words on the assigned topic. On test day, you will write a full essay, but for this pretest, just focus on making the outline. You have 10 minutes to analyze the prompt and outline an essay.

Finish writing your own outline before reading the sample outline and essay.

"America's students are too busy. Since students are always running around between extracurricular activities and after-school jobs, their education will inevitably suffer."

Do you believe that America's students are too busy and that, as a result, their education will inevitably suffer?

Core Writing Pre-Test Answers and Explanations

1. C

The pronoun's antecedent is the plural "Children," so the plural *their* is correct, rather than "his or her."

2. A

The singular subject "ecosystem" requires a singular verb: *supports*. Since it is accompanied by a comma, the conjunction "but" correctly joins the two independent clauses. The idiom "home to" is correct as written.

3. D

The correct wording of the idiomatic phrase is *not only... but also*. The appositive "the great American author" is correctly set off by commas and properly capitalized as written.

4. E

The sentence is correct as written. It properly uses the past perfect tense, "had just completed" and "had been cancelled," to signal actions that occurred before other past actions.

5. D

Since the bill will come into effect "next year" and has not begun yet, the simple future tense *will go* is required. "Senator Jones" is correctly capitalized, the singular possessive "bill's" is properly punctuated, and the comma correctly separates the introductory dependent clause.

6. C

As written, the list is not in parallel form. To match the last two items, the *-ing* form of *hibernating* is required. The plural verb "use" matches the plural subject "Animals," and the comma correctly sets off the modifying phrase in the second part of the sentence from the independent clause.

7. C

The sentence incorrectly uses the implicit double negative "hardly never;" the correct form is *hardly ever*.

8. B

The underlined comma unnecessarily separates the prepositional phrase from the rest of the introductory dependent clause. The sentence as written correctly uses the past perfect verb "had traveled" to signify an action that occurred before another past action and the simple past verb "painted" to signify an action that happened in the past.

9. A

The correct preposition in the idiom should be *compared with*. As written, the singular verb "is" agrees with the singular subject "playing," the commas correctly set off the modifying phrase, and the preposition "of" is used correctly.

10. D

Since the action happened "thousands of years ago," the simple past tense *resulted* is required. The idiom "heralded as" is correct. "Though" correctly makes the second clause dependent. The word "human" is an appropriate adjective to describe "populations."

11. A

Since it is not a possessive noun, no apostrophe is required at the end of "Proponents." The plural verb "suggest" agrees with the plural subject "Proponents." The present-tense singular verb "is" matches the subject "universe." The comma correctly joins the independent clause to the dependent clause that begins with "while."

12. E

"John Milton" has to be the subject of the sentence. The introductory phrase in this sentence can't modify anything else.

13. E

A semicolon can be used to join two independent clauses, but here the text after the semicolon is a sentence fragment that could not stand on its own. In fixing this error, seek concision: the preposition "to" conveys the meaning of "purpose" without extra words.

14. A

The original sentence is correct. It is more concise than the other options, and it correctly uses both the simple past tense and the idiom "reluctant to."

15. E

The original sentence doesn't have a verb, because an -*ing* word without a helping verb isn't a verb. Choices (C) and (E) supply verbs, but (C) introduces an incorrect pronoun. The pronoun must refer to "government," which is singular. So, the pronoun must be "its."

16. D

As written, the sentence lacks an independent clause. Only (**D**) corrects the problem by turning "flourishing" into "flourished"—a main verb in the past tense.

17. C

Choices (B), (C), and (E) all correctly use a semicolon to join the two independent clauses. Only (**C**), however, makes sense of the sentence by using the singular pronoun "he" to refer to the politician. (*She* would also be grammatically correct.)

18. E

"Strolling hand in hand" is a modifying phrase that describes the noun "couple." Only (**E**) places this modifying phrase next to "the young couple."

19. D

The relationship between where Rivera's relatives lived and where his father wanted to live is a *contrast*. "Yet" is used to show contrast, but the contrast would have to be between something in this sentence and something in the preceding sentence. That is not the case, so rule out choice (A). You can eliminate (E) for the same reason. Of the choices, only "Although" in (**D**) expresses a contrast and indicates that the contrast is between the two thoughts that follow it.

20. B

There are actually three errors in this sentence: two independent clauses are joined by only a comma, the list of the things that Rivera wrote is not parallel ("composed" should be deleted), and there is an unnecessary comma after "photographs." Choice (A) can be eliminated. Choice (C) drops "composed" but leaves the other two errors intact. (D) leaves "composed" but changes the syntax in a way that affects the sentence's meaning: Rivera didn't find that he wanted to become a writer *after* he wrote the comic strips, etc. (E) correctly inserts a semicolon after "writer," but it leaves in the other two errors. Only (**B**) correctly addresses all three issues.

21. C

As written, the sentence is awkward because the phrase "from college" modifies "graduating" and should be as close to that word as possible, but is placed some distance away. Eliminate choice (A). Choice (B) is incorrect because Rivera was "determined to continue writing," not just "determined." Both (D) and (E) create sentence fragments, so rule them out. That leaves (**C**), which logically and concisely presents the information.

22. B

The verb tense in this final paragraph is the present perfect—"has received"—so unless the author is moving into either the past or the future, she should be consistent with her verb tense. Choice (**B**), therefore, is correct. Choice (A), the past perfect, would apply only if the "becoming" had occurred before another event in the past. And neither the future nor the conditional tense applies here, so eliminate (C), (D), and (E).

23. A

Because the title of the work is in quotation marks, you know that it is short. You also know that it is part of something larger because its title is followed by the title of the collection or periodical in which it appeared. In this case, the title of the longer work indicates that it is a collection of essays. Also, no month or volume number is provided, further indicating this is not a periodical. (**A**) is correct.

24. C

Choices (A), (B), (D), and (E) all involve people who were directly involved in World War I and who had firsthand involvement in how civilians were affected by the war. Choice (C), though contemporary with the war, would have been written by a journalist, a source removed from the action. Though based on primary sources, it is not itself a primary source.

25. E

Choices (A), (B), (C), and (D) are all concerned with President Eisenhower's relationship with Congress. Although (C) also deals with presidents Roosevelt and Truman, it clearly involves President Eisenhower. While the information provided in (E) might shed some light on Eisenhower's leadership style and abilities, it is only indirectly related to the student's topic.

Written Assignment Sample Outline

Remember that your outline will not match the sample exactly, since you will choose your own relevant points. The following outline and sample essay provide one possible approach. Compare your outline to the sample and reflect on whether your outline provides a basis for writing an essay with a clear thesis, reasons and examples to support your claims, and clear paragraph-by-paragraph organization, as demonstrated by the example essay.

I. Introduction
    A. America is busy
    B. Appropriate amount of busyness good for teenagers' education

II. Body Paragraph 1: Extracurricular Activities
    A. Music: teach practice, math, concentration
    B. Sports: teach practice, teamwork
    C. Need for college applications

III. Body Paragraph 2: After-School Jobs
    A. Studies show benefit
    B. Teach real-world experience
    C. Example: high school friend

IV. Conclusion
    A. Avoid burnout
    B. Experience is part of complete education

High-Scoring Essay

A common view of life in America is that both children and adults fill their lives with so many activities that they are continually stressed and unable to really find fulfillment in anything. Indeed, moving to a tropical island or Mediterranean village with a more laid-back lifestyle is often viewed as the ultimate escape. While burnout in America is certainly a real possibility, I would argue that an appropriate amount of "busyness" is actually beneficial for American teenagers' education because it them enables to develop important life skills.

Students' various extracurricular activities, including music and sports, can build upon the skills they learn in the classroom, and thus are actually an integral part of their education. Both music lessons and sports participation require great commitment and practice, which are undeniably vital in the real world. Learning music skills also cultivates students' math-related abilities and concentration. The teamwork required by team sports develops people skills and the sense of shared achievement made possible by cooperation. These skills undeniably translate into other situations, both in the classroom and the future workplace. Indeed, college admissions personnel understand the value of developing these skills, as they consider involvement in extracurricular activities an important part of potential students' applications.

After-school jobs also benefit students, both academically and practically. In fact, studies have shown that students who work a reasonable amount of hours during a school week, perhaps fewer than 20, actually perform better in school than students who do not work at all. Like extracurriculars, jobs develop young people's sense of responsibility, commitment, and teamwork. The experience of working at a "real job" undeniably provides real-world preparation that cannot be duplicated in the classroom. For instance, my friend in high school worked in a restaurant most nights after school and also kept up very high grades. She was accepted into the best engineering schools in our region, most likely aided by her competitive application that demonstrated her work experience and glowing references from her employer.

Of course, it's easy to conceive of a student becoming burned-out from too many activities and hours working. However, when activities and work are reasonably balanced with students' school requirements, they actually add invaluable experiences and skills that could not otherwise be acquired in a classroom, thus, as acknowledged by their importance for college admissions, comprising an essential component of students' complete education.

Explanation

This high-scoring essay identifies and develops a well-thought-out thesis: extracurricular activities and jobs, in an "appropriate" quantity, constitute an important part of a well-rounded education. The author creates a well-organized essay with transition words (e.g., "In fact," "For instance"). The first paragraph introduces the topic and thesis, and it defines how the author will define *students* in the essay (i.e., as high school students). Each body paragraph discusses a potential type of "busyness"—extracurricular activities or jobs—and explains how it actually benefits students' education, using reasons and examples to support the claims made. The conclusion briefly acknowledges the other side of the argument and sums up the writer's claims. If the writer had had more time, he or she could have included a full paragraph discussing the drawbacks of the other side of the argument, or he or she could have proofread the essay to fix any grammatical mistakes, like reversing the order of "them enables" in the first paragraph when the writer clearly meant "enables them." The writer uses a variety of sophisticated sentence structures and appropriate word choices, and he or she avoids any distracting grammar/mechanics issues.

Introducing Praxis Core Writing

The Praxis Core Writing test consists of three sections that test two very different kinds of writing skills. The first section tests your ability to read sentences and to locate and correct grammatical errors. The second and third sections are essay sections, which will test your ability to write a clear, coherent essay in a limited amount of time.

Keep in mind that this test is not designed to discover the next Ernest Hemingway or Maya Angelou. Instead, this test assesses your ability to adhere to the basic rules of written English and to avoid common grammatical errors and traps.

Your approach to the Writing test should vary depending on the section. As with all other sections of the Praxis Core Writing test, strategic time management and understanding what the testmaker is looking for are the keys to success.

Know What to Expect

Test Format

The key to success on any test is knowing what you can expect. The Praxis Core Writing test is no exception. Here's what you'll be up against on the test.

PRAXIS CORE WRITING
Format: Computer-delivered
Number of Questions: 40 multiple-choice (called "selected-response" by the testmaker) and 2 essays
Time: 100 minutes (40 minutes for the multiple-choice section; 30 minutes for each essay section)
Essay Types: argumentative; source-based
Multiple-choice section may include questions that do not count toward your score
No penalty for incorrect answers
Scratch paper is available during the exam (it will be destroyed before you leave the testing center)

As you can see, there are three sections to the Praxis Core Writing test, and they require different approaches. Your score report will have separate reports for your selected-response questions and your essays. However, keep in mind that the same rules of standard written English are applicable to both the multiple-choice questions and the essay components of the Writing test. We'll cover the grammar rules that are tested most frequently and give you the proven Kaplan strategies for each question type you'll see on your test.

Core Writing: Selected-Response Questions

The selected-response (multiple-choice) section of the Praxis Core Writing test does not require you to do any writing. Also, you won't be tested on the names of grammatical terms; you won't need to identify nouns, pronouns, verbs, participles, or gerunds, and while a vague memory of how you may have diagrammed sentences back in the day may help a bit, it's not an essential skill for these questions.

The selected-response Writing questions test your ability to recognize the elements of good writing, including basic grammar, sentence structure, agreement, and word choice.

As you prepare for the test, read everything—and we mean everything—with an eye toward sentence structure. Look for fragments in advertisements. Find run-on sentences in emails from your friends. Ferret out misplaced modifiers in the newspaper. Develop "proofreader's eyes" as you read, read, read your way to success.

As you sharpen your vision and get ready to spot errors on the Praxis exam, be sure to fine-tune your hearing as well. Develop a more critical ear that notes errors and awkward constructions when you hear them. Listening to programs in which the speakers tend to use standard academic English is often helpful; examples include many public radio programs or podcasts. Frequently, you will have to trust your ear to identify errors and avoid trap answers on test day.

Introducing the Question Types

Because these question types may be new to you, begin by becoming familiar with the structure of the questions and the directions for each question type you will see on your test. Remember, you have only 40 minutes to answer 40 questions on the selected-response section of the Praxis Core Writing test. Getting familiar with the basics of each question type ahead of time will give you an edge when test day rolls around.

There are four main question types on the Core Writing exam: Usage, Sentence Correction, Revision in Context, and Research Skills. Within these four main categories, you may see some variation in the mode of delivery of the questions. The standard modes of delivery are shown below, but be prepared for some variation. Variations may include interactive questions that require some of the following:

- Selecting all of the answer choices that apply
- Constructing a short response in an entry box
- Entering more than one response in different places
- Checking off boxes (usually for all-that-apply questions)
- Selecting regions on a graph or other visual
- Choosing sentences in text
- Moving answer choices onto targets or into positions
- Choosing an answer from a drop-down menu

Each question type will be accompanied by clear directions for how to answer the question, so please read these carefully if you are not familiar with the question's mode of delivery. For additional practice and to build familiarity with the various modes of delivery, please refer to your online resources.

Usage Questions

Usage questions test a wide range of skills—including redundancy, singular versus plural nouns and verbs, pronoun reference, commas, verb tense, and capitalization. In these questions, you will always have four underlined portions of the sentence to choose from, as well as the option "No error." Your task is to choose which of the four underlined portions needs a revision, if any. You don't need to specify what the revision is, just the location of the error. If there is an error in the sentence, it will be in one of the four underlined portions.

The directions for Usage questions will look similar to this:

Directions: Each of the following sentence(s) will have four (4) underlined sections. After reading the sentence(s), decide which (if any) of the underlined portions contains an error of grammar, usage, punctuation, or capitalization. If there is an error, select the portion that has the error. Otherwise, select "No error." Each sentence contains at most one error.

Be sure to select an answer for each question.

Here's what a sample question might look like:

Even though he had to supervise a large staff, his salary was no greater than a clerk. No error
$\underset{A}{}$ $\underset{B}{}$ $\underset{C}{}$ $\underset{D}{}$ $\underset{E}{}$

The game you're playing with Usage questions is "Spot the Mistake!" You'll see a sentence like this one with words and phrases underlined. Look at each underlined part and decide which part is incorrect. Some sentences are correct as written, so do not be afraid to select "No error."

The testmaker puts Usage questions on the Writing test to test your ability to catch words or phrases that are frequently used incorrectly in student essays. If you can spot these types of errors, the testmaker assumes that you can use appropriate words and phrases in your own writing.

In the example above, the correct answer is (D). The current wording makes it sound as though the size of the subject's salary is being compared to the size of a clerk; in fact, the subject's salary should be compared to the size of a clerk's *salary*.

Keep in mind that you only have 40 minutes to answer 40 questions and that there is no penalty for incorrect answers. That means you need to move quickly through the Usage questions to allow for the more time-consuming questions. Aim to answer between 2 and 3 questions per minute.

To improve your efficiency with these questions, practice moving quickly through the practice sets we've provided. Also, learn to trust your ear on your first read of a question; always choose an answer on your first read through. If nothing sounds wrong, choose (E) and move on. Make a note on your scratch paper of any questions you are unsure of; then use the review screen to return to them if you have time. Never leave a question unanswered on the Core Writing test.

Sentence Correction Questions

Sentence Correction questions are similar to Usage questions, except that they have only one underlined portion for you to focus on. In this case, your task is to pick the best version of the underlined portion. Please note that the first answer will always be the same as the underlined portion of the question, so if there is an error, there is no need to consider the first choice.

The directions for Sentence Correction will look similar to this:

Directions: Each of the following sentences will have an underlined section and will be followed by five (5) versions of that section. The first is a reprint of the original sentence. After reading each sentence, decide whether the sentence is in its best form as written or could benefit from one of the four (4) proposed adjustments.

For this type of question, choose the answer that best expresses the essence of the sentence through correct grammar, usage, punctuation, or capitalization. Be sure to maintain the meaning of the sentence.

Be sure to select an answer for each question.

Here's what a sample question might look like.

The experts from the Fish and Wildlife Service could not decide which one of eight possible nesting sites along the Platte River <u>will provide the best habitat</u> into which to release the crane.

A. will provide the best habitat

B. would be providing the better habitat

C. would provide the better habitat

D. would provide the best habitat

E. is providing the best habitat

In the question above, **(D)** is correct. A quick scan of the answer choices reveals that this question tests verbs. The nonunderlined portion of the sentence speaks of a possibility and a decision about releasing the crane that has not yet been made, so the future tense "will provide," which applies to a definite future action, is incorrect. Choice (A) is out. Likewise, the continuous present tense in (E) is out, because the nesting site is not doing anything for the crane right now. Given that the experts are speculating (rather than making a factual statement) about the possible nesting sites, you need to use the subjunctive form of *will*, which is *would*. More scanning reveals another split, this one between *best* and *better*. *Better*/*best* is a frequently tested idiom: use *better* to compare two things and *best* to compare more than two. There are eight possible nesting sites, so the experts need to find the *best* one. Eliminate (B) and (C). **(D)** is correct because it is the only answer choice that uses "would" and "best." Quickly scanning your answer choices for differences such as these will help you identify what the question is testing and allow you to locate the correct answer efficiently.

Sentence Correction questions tend to take more time than Usage questions, and you should budget your time accordingly. Nonetheless, to perform well on the Writing section, you need to continue to move quickly and avoid getting stuck on any single question. Again, trust your ear and your instincts and press forward through the test. Getting one question wrong is not nearly as harmful as agonizing for five or six minutes on a question, regardless of whether you get it right. Always choose an answer on your first read through. If the sentence sounds good to begin with, choose (A) and move on. Don't waste time re-reading choice (A)—you already know what it says. As you move through the test, make a note on your scratch paper indicating the questions you are unsure of; then use the review screen to return to them if you have time.

You should spend no more than 1 to 1.5 minutes on each Sentence Correction question.

Revision in Context Questions

For Revision in Context questions, the testmaker will provide a short essay draft and ask you to choose the best version of a sentence or set of sentences, considering the essay's context. You may also be asked to remove sentences from or insert sentences into certain paragraphs or to adjust the sequence of the sentences in a given paragraph.

<u>Directions</u>: This is an essay draft that requires some editing work. Choose the best versions of the sentences and/or paragraphs as examined in the questions. At times, the passage cannot be improved using the answer choices, and in those circumstances, you should indicate that it is correct as written. As you answer these questions, be sure to consider writing style; the author's tone and purpose; and standard English conventions of grammar, usage, punctuation, and capitalization.

Be sure to select an answer for each question.

[The following is excerpted from a full-length essay.]

The oldest building still in use in California is the Mission at San Juan Capistrano, the seventh in the chain of California missions built by Spanish priests in the late eighteenth and early nineteenth centuries. The mission has gained fame as the <u>well-known summer residence</u> of the swallows of San Juan Capistrano.

A. NO CHANGE

B. seasonal residence for the summer

C. summer residence

D. residential summer home

E. famous summer mission home

The underlined selection may repeat something said elsewhere, so consider the underlined portion of the sentence in context before choosing an answer. This sentence already indicates that the mission has gained fame, so the adjective "well-known" is unnecessary. Eliminate (A). Choice (B) unnecessarily uses the adjective "seasonal" along with "summer"; summer is a season, so you can eliminate (B). Choice (D) describes the home as "residential," but a home is, by definition, residential. Choice (E) is doubly redundant; "famous" and "mission" are both repetitive. Choice **(C)** is the only choice that eliminates all redundant language.

Research Skills Questions

As the name suggests, Research Skills questions will test your basic understanding of acceptable research habits—including assessing the credibility of sources, recognizing different parts of a citation, recognizing different research strategies, and assessing the relevance of information to a research task.

<u>Directions</u>: Consider proper research techniques while answering these questions.

Be sure to select an answer for each question.

A student is writing a paper about the contributions of key people involved in the American Civil Rights Movement (1954–1968). Which of the following is the LEAST relevant to the paper?

A. During the Civil Rights Movement, Rev. Martin Luther King Jr. gave many inspirational speeches that moved large numbers of people to take action.

B. In 1955, Rosa Parks was arrested for refusing to give up her seat to a white person on a city bus—an event that sparked a boycott of buses.

C. During a period of incarceration, Malcolm X read extensively, gaining an education despite having left high school early.

D. In 1954, the Supreme Court ruled in favor of Oliver Brown, asserting in its decision that racial segregation in schools is unconstitutional.

E. In 1963, John F. Kennedy gave an address that argued that racial discrimination runs counter to American principles and urged Congress to enact legislation.

Choice **(C)** is correct because its only relation to the Civil Rights Movement is that it involves a leading figure of the movement. Choice (C) does not connect Malcolm X's self-education to the ideology he would contribute to the movement.

How to Approach Praxis Writing

Earlier in this chapter, you learned about the importance of developing an eye for mistakes and trusting your ear to help you locate and fix potential errors. You then read about the various question types you'll encounter on your test. Now we're going to show you how such search-and-repair tactics can help you succeed on real Core Writing questions. Start with these three simple steps.

The Kaplan Three-Step Method for Usage and Sentence Correction

> **THE KAPLAN METHOD FOR PRAXIS USAGE AND SENTENCE CORRECTION**
>
> **STEP 1** Read the sentence, listening for a mistake
>
> **STEP 2** Identify the error
>
> **STEP 3** Check the answer choices

This Method will serve you well for all types of Writing questions, although we'll show you how to refine it slightly to suit each question type.

Usage Questions

Usage is a great place for the Writing test to begin because you don't have to fix anything. You just have to point out what's wrong.

Try using Kaplan's Three-Step Method on the question below. First, read the sentence, *listening* for a mistake. Note: In preparation for test day, you should get used to reading silently and listening to the sentence in your head.

The <u>club members</u> are so busy <u>studying</u> for exams that attendance is <u>rare</u> more <u>than 50 percent</u>. <u>No</u>
     A   B   C   D
<u>error</u>
 E

Step 1. Read the sentence, listening for a mistake

When you read the sentence, did you hear an error? If so, you're all set. You don't need to figure out how you would fix the error. You just need to click on the right choice and move on.

Step 2. Identify the error

If you didn't hear the mistake, read the sentence again. There's no problem with the phrase *club members*. *Studying* is OK here. How about *rare*? There's the clunker.

Step 3. Check the answer choices

The correct construction would be "*rarely* more than 50 percent." This is a classic example of an adjective/adverb error. Choice (**C**) is correct.

Now, let's see the Kaplan Method applied to a Sentence Correction question.

Sentence Correction Questions

Sentence Correction questions test the same skills as Usage questions. You'll still be using your eyes and ears to spot errors and oddities in sentences. But here's the difference: you'll have to fix the mistakes you find. As you probably remember from earlier in this chapter, each Sentence Correction question has an underlined phrase. You need to decide whether the sentence is OK as is, in which case you should pick choice (A), or whether you need to replace the underlined portion with one of the other answer choices.

Take a look again at the Kaplan Three-Step Method for Writing. You'll see that the wording below is a little different, to help the Method work well for the Sentence Correction task.

> **STEP 1** Read the sentence, listening for a mistake
>
> **STEP 2** Predict a correction
>
> **STEP 3** Select the answer choice that matches your prediction and eliminate clearly wrong answer choices

Now apply the Three-Step Method to this Sentence Correction question.

Hoping to receive a promotion, <u>the letter he received instead informed Burt</u> that he had been fired.

A. the letter he received instead informed Burt

B. the letter having been received, instead informed Burt

C. Burt instead received a letter informing him

D. information from the received letter instead told Burt

E. Burt, instead informed by the letter he received

Step 1: Read the sentence, listening for a mistake

Something sounds wrong. Burt hoped to receive the promotion, but this makes it sound as if the letter hoped to receive the promotion.

Step 2. Predict a correction

You should predict that *Burt* will be at the beginning of the correct answer choice.

Step 3. Select the answer choice that matches your prediction and eliminate clearly wrong answer choices

Choices (C) and (E) both put Burt at the beginning of the phrase, but choice (E) does not contain a main verb and creates a fragment instead of a complete sentence. Choice (**C**) is correct.

Revision in Context Questions

Here is another variation on the Kaplan Method for Writing—one well suited to answering Revision in Context questions:

STEP 1	Read the passage and identify the issue
STEP 2	Eliminate answer choices that do not address the issue
STEP 3	Plug in the remaining answer choices and select the most correct, concise, and relevant one

Now let's apply the Method to this Revision in Context question.

I still remember the magic of walking home under the cold, brittle blue sky, watching the sun strike the glittering blanket laid down by that first snowfall. The world dripped with frosting, and everything was pure and silent. I breathed deeply, enjoying the sting of the icy air in my nostrils, and set off through the trees, listening to the muffled crunch of my footsteps and the chirps of the waking birds. Later, the cars and schoolchildren and mundane lives would turn the wonderland back into dingy slush; the hush would be interrupted by horns and shouts. <u>Indeed</u> for now, the sparkling, cloistered world was mine alone. I smiled, and for a moment, my mind was still.

A. Indeed

B. But

C. Consequently

D. In fact

E. After all

Step 1: Read the passage and identify the issue

The underlined word is a continuation transition showing emphasis. It is incorrect as written because the sentence preceding it discusses what will happen to the surroundings (they will be dirty and noisy), while this sentence discusses what the world is like now (beautiful and quiet). A contrast transition would be more appropriate in this context. Eliminate choice (A).

Step 2: Eliminate answer choices that do not address the issue

Eliminate (C), (D), and (E) because they are not contrast transitions.

Step 3: Plug in the remaining answer choices and select the most correct, concise, and relevant one

Choice (**B**) is all that remains. Plugging it into the passage confirms that it is correct.

Research Skills Questions

Kaplan Method for Research Skills Questions

STEP 1	Read the question, looking for clues
STEP 2	Make a prediction
STEP 3	Evaluate the answer choices and select the choice that best fits your prediction

Research Skills questions test a different skill than the rest of the multiple-choice questions in the Writing test. While the other questions test grammar and mechanics, Research Skills questions focus on the information-gathering and sharing phase of the writing process. These questions test a variety of concepts, including primary versus secondary sources, types of citations, and the relevance of information to the thesis. Let's take a look at Kaplan's Three-Step Method in action.

Dickens, Charles. *Great Expectations.* New York: Dodd, Mead, 1942. Print.

What type of citation is this?

A. Interview

B. Magazine article

C. Website

D. Book

E. Encyclopedia

Step 1: Read the question, looking for clues

This question provides a full citation, then asks what kind of citation it is. The key phrase is "type of citation," so you need to predict a source medium (painting, interview, article, book, website, etc.).

Step 2: Make a prediction

For this example, you can predict that the source is a book because the citation includes the publisher and the date of publication. An italicized title is generally given to a longer work, such as a book. The citation also states that the medium was print. Note that websites and articles will also include the date of publication (often a specific day), and online sources often include the date of access, as such content can change.

Step 3: Evaluate the answer choices and select the choice that best fits your prediction

Choice (**D**) matches the prediction and is correct.

Classic Errors in Praxis Writing Questions

It may seem as though there are many things to think about during the selected-response (multiple-choice) portion of the Writing test, but you can categorize many of the questions according to a few common types of errors. Familiarizing yourself with the most common error types, shown in the following pages, will help you sharpen your focus and achieve test day success.

Verb Tense Errors

As you know, the verb is the action part of the sentence. The verb's tense tells you when the action takes place. You won't need to identify verb tenses by name on the test, but you will need to recognize the difference between correct and incorrect verb tenses.

> When David was in Holland, he was seeing many windmills.

You don't need to know the rules about proper use of the past tense to know that something's wrong here. Your ear should tell you that the verbs don't sound right. Try this instead:

> When David was in Holland, he saw many windmills.

That sounds better, and it's correct. Now let's look at a test-like question that has a verb tense error.

> <u>Unsatisfied</u> with the ending, the director <u>considering</u> <u>reshooting</u> <u>the entire</u> film. <u>No error</u>
>   A   B   C   D   E

Did this sentence make sense to you? If not, where did the confusion come in? We don't know when the director's action took place because "considering" isn't a complete verb. You could substitute *is considering* or *was considering* or even *considered*. Because choice (**B**) contains the error in this sentence, it's the answer.

Subject-Verb Agreement Errors

Your grammar book tells you that the subject and the verb of a sentence must agree in number. Put simply, this means that a singular subject takes a singular verb and a plural subject takes a plural verb. Subject and verb also have to agree in person. This simply means that you need to use the right form of the verb depending on whether the subject is first person, second person, or third person.

You do this correctly a million times a day, and it's not as tricky as it sounds. Take a look at these sentences:

> The 4:05 train to Boston leave from the north platform.

> Henry's dog are brown with a white tail.

> The ballerinas practices for eight hours a day.

> You spends too much time thinking about subject-verb agreement.

Did you find the agreement errors? The sentences on the Core Writing test won't be quite this easy, but with a little practice, you'll be able to spot agreement errors in any sentence. You may have to learn to be on the lookout for the three classic subject-verb agreement traps. Let's take a look.

Trap 1: Collective Nouns

One very common way the testmaker tries to trap you into making errors is by using collective nouns.

Words such as *group*, *audience*, or *committee* require a singular verb.

> The group has decided to plan a trip to a chocolate factory.

> The audience was moved to throw rotten vegetables at the mime.

> The committee votes to clean up the waterfront every year.

All of these sentences are correct. Now try the following:

> That <u>particular</u> gang of pirates <u>were</u> often <u>referred to</u> as "The <u>Scourge of</u> the Seven Seas." <u>No error</u>
>   A   B   C   D   E

Even with advance warning, this one might be tricky. The correct answer here is (**B**) because the subject is the collective singular noun "gang." Making the error harder to spot in this case is the prepositional phrase "of pirates," which was thrown in between the subject and verb just to confuse you. This brings us to Trap 2.

Trap 2: Intervening Phrases

The testmaker will often try to confuse the issue of subject-verb agreement by inserting an intervening phrase between the subject and verb. Try this one.

Tax evasion, <u>a crime</u> that <u>has been documented</u> in many modern novels and films, <u>remain</u> a relatively
           A   B   C
<u>uncommon offense.</u> <u>No error</u>
     D   E

Did you pick choice (**C**)? You're right. The verb "remain" goes with "evasion," a singular word, which requires the verb form *remains*. Don't be fooled by the plural nouns "novels" and "films," which are part of the intervening phrase. Also, if you have trouble identifying the subject and verb, try ignoring all the extra adjectives, prepositional phrases, and subordinate clauses.

Trap 3: Subject After Verb

Another way that the testmaker tries to confuse you is by placing the subject after the verb. Take a look at this example:

<u>Although</u> nutritionists have <u>criticized pizza</u> for being too high in fat, there <u>is</u> many people <u>who</u> continue to
    A   B   C   D
enjoy it. <u>No error</u>
          E

"People" is the subject of the verb "is," and it requires a plural subject: ... *there are many people* ... Choice (**C**) is correct.

Pronoun Errors: Case and Number

You're sure to see at least a few questions on your Core Writing test that look at the use of pronouns. The key thing to remember about pronouns is that they must agree with their antecedents (the nouns they represent) in case and number.

> ### WHO IS *HE*? WHAT IS *IT*?
>
> Every pronoun must have an antecedent. The antecedent is the noun that corresponds to the pronoun in the sentence. Look at this sentence: *Beck is a great singer, and he is also a fine songwriter.* "Beck" is the antecedent, and "he" is the pronoun.

Case refers to the form in which the word appears in the sentence. If the pronoun refers to the subject, it has a different case than if it refers to an object.

Sally dances, and *she* also sings.

Bob praised Sally, and he also applauded *her*.

These sentences are correct.

The **number** of a pronoun is just what it sounds like: singular or plural.

Give this question a try:

> A part-time job <u>that</u> involves assisting Dr. Frankenstein <u>may include</u> more responsibilities than <u>their</u>
>   A   B   C
> description lists, including some <u>unusual</u> tasks. <u>No error</u>
>   D   E

Did you see the error here? The antecedent is "job," and the pronoun is "their." To make the pronoun agree with its singular antecedent, you would have to use *its*. Another option would be to repeat the noun: ... *include more responsibilities than the job's description lists ....*

Pronoun Errors: Ambiguous Reference

Another common pronoun problem you'll find on the Core Writing test is ambiguous reference. As you just read, every pronoun must have a clear antecedent.

Give this question a try:

> To expand the newspaper's <u>coverage</u> of local politics, <u>they</u> transferred a <u>popular</u> columnist <u>to</u> the
>   A   B   C   D
> city desk. <u>No error</u>
>   E

Who transferred the columnist? The sentence doesn't tell you. Therefore, choice (**B**), "they," is a pronoun without an antecedent and is the correct answer.

Questions like this one can be tricky because they read smoothly, with no bumpy parts to jar your ear. Keep an eye out for ambiguous references in sentences that seem too good to be true.

Idioms

The testmaker also occasionally likes to test whether students can recognize the proper use of idioms. This can be especially bad news for nonnative speakers of English because idioms are the hardest thing to learn in any foreign language. This is because idioms are simply word combinations that have become part of the language. They're correct, but there's no particular rhyme or reason to why they're correct. Most—although certainly not all—native speakers will know the proper idiom to use simply because their ears tell them what combination sounds correct.

Prepositions are the typically short words—such as *by, at, among,* and *before*—that link prepositional phrases to the rest of the sentence. Most preposition issues tested on the Praxis are idiomatic. This means that you'll be listening for word combinations that frequently go together. Use your ear to catch prepositions that just don't sound right.

Give the following question a try. Be sure to use the Kaplan Three-Step Method:

> Many people are <u>desensitized to</u> violence on TV shows, <u>but</u> this does not mean that they are not sensitive
>   A   B
> <u>of</u> the real-life violence around <u>them</u>. <u>No error</u>
> C   D   E

There are two idiomatic uses of prepositions in this sentence. Did you spot them? "Desensitized to" and "sensitive of" are choices (A) and (C), respectively. "Sensitive of" simply isn't idiomatic—it should be *sensitive to*—and choice (**C**) is correct. If you're not a native speaker of English or you don't have a good ear for idioms, you'll need to immerse yourself in idioms as you study for the test. Fortunately, they are everywhere in written and spoken English; they often involve combinations of two words—especially a verb form and a preposition—that are used together.

Comparison Errors

Another error that frequently shows up on the Core Writing test involves comparisons. This one can be a little sneaky because some of these sentences may sound OK to your ear. It's time to bring your brain into the picture!

When you compare two or more parts of speech, like nouns or verb phrases, the parts of speech must be in the same form. Take a look at this example:

> The producer agreed that casting a drama series is harder than comedy.

If you heard this sentence, you'd probably understand what it means, although it's not crystal-clear. "Casting a drama series" is harder than … what exactly? The sentence would be clearer if it were written as follows:

> The producer agreed that casting a drama series is harder than casting a comedy series.

Both parts of the comparison are in the same form, making the sentence easier to understand and grammatically correct.

See if you can spot the mistake in the next question:

> Even though <u>he</u> was a Nobel Laureate, <u>Elie Wiesel's name</u> is still <u>less well-known</u> than <u>last year's</u> Heisman
>   A   B   C   D
> Trophy winner. <u>No error</u>
>   E

This is a bit subtle. Did you spot the faulty comparison? The sentence compares "Elie Wiesel's name" with the "Heisman Trophy winner." If we changed choice (**B**) to read simply *Elie Wiesel*, the comparison would be parallel and easier to understand.

Adjective and Adverb Errors

You may not have thought about adjectives and adverbs since those junior high sentence diagrams. The good news is that you probably use adjectives and adverbs correctly all the time.

> That painting is beautiful.

> The artist painted it skillfully.

In the first sentence, "beautiful" is an adjective modifying "painting," a noun. In the second sentence, "skillfully" is an adverb modifying "painted," a verb form.

KNOW YOUR MODIFIERS

An adjective modifies a noun or pronoun. An adverb modifies a verb, an adjective, or another adverb. Most but not all adverbs end in -*ly*.

Now take a look at how adjectives and adverbs might be tested in the Usage section.

> <u>Since the onset</u> of <u>his</u> blindness, the artist <u>has sculpted</u> more <u>slow</u> than before. <u>No error</u>
>   A   B   C   D   E

Choice (**D**) is correct. The adverb *slowly* is required to modify the verb "has sculpted."

Double Negatives

In standard written English, the use of two negatives in a row can create ungrammatical or self-contradictory sentences. Just as in math, two negatives added together create a positive.

> I won't have none of that bureaucratic doublespeak!

This sentence, if you cancel the negatives, translates as follows:

> I'll have that bureaucratic doublespeak!

You'll find an occasional double negative question in the Usage section, although the sentences are a bit tougher than the one above. Give this one a try.

> The town hasn't <u>hardly any</u> money left in <u>its</u> budget <u>because of</u> the unexpected <u>costs</u> for snowplowing.
>   A   B   C   D
> <u>No error</u>
>   E

The words "hasn't" and "hardly any" cancel each other out, making it sound as if the town doesn't have money problems. We can figure out from the rest of the sentence that the author's trying to tell us that the town does have money problems because of the unexpected costs. Changing choice (**A**), "hardly any," to *much* would eliminate one of the negatives, clearing up the meaning of the sentence.

Sentence Fragments

Sentence fragments are incomplete sentences. To be complete, a sentence requires a main subject and a main verb. Some sentences are fragments because they lack the necessary elements to make logical sense or have an unnecessary connector like *that* or *because*.

Here are some fragments. How would you repair them?

> Stereo equipment on sale at the mall today!

> The busload of tourists that wandered curiously around the ancient ruins.

> Because Myrna likes the Adirondacks, frequently taking photos of them.

Did you get a feeling that something's missing when you read these fragments? Watch out for that feeling on test day, and you'll be able to spot the fragments.

Give this example a try, using the Kaplan Three-Step Method.

> Last of the world's leaders to do so, the prime minister admits that terrorist threats <u>credible enough to warrant</u> the imposition of stringent security measures.
>
> A. credible enough to warrant
>
> B. credible enough warrant
>
> C. are credible enough to warrant
>
> D. credible enough, warranting
>
> E. are credible enough to be warranted

That feeling that something's missing sits right in the middle of the sentence. The subject of the part of the sentence beginning with "that" is "terrorist threats," but where's the verb? "Credible" is the adjective modifying "terrorist threats," so adding *are*, as choices (C) and (E) do, repairs the fragment. Choice (E), however, introduces a new problem with the phrase "to be warranted," which is confusing when read back into the sentence. Choice (C) clearly fixes the fragment and is correct.

Run-On Sentences

A run-on sentence occurs when two complete sentences that should be separate are joined incorrectly. Here are some examples:

> Jane was the preeminent scientist in her class her experiments were discussed all over campus.

> Jane was the preeminent scientist in her class, her experiments were discussed all over campus.

You can tell that this is a run-on sentence because it sounds like it should be two separate sentences. There are four ways to fix a run-on sentence.

1. **Use a period.**

   Jane was the preeminent scientist in her class. Her experiments were discussed all over campus.

2. **Use a comma with a coordinating conjunction (*and, but, or, for, nor, yet,* and *so*).**

   Jane was the preeminent scientist in her class, and her experiments were discussed all over campus.

3. **Use a subordinating conjunction, making one sentence dependent.**

   Because Jane was the preeminent scientist in her class, her experiments were discussed all over campus.

4. **Use a semicolon.**

   Jane was the preeminent scientist in her class; her experiments were discussed all over campus.

Use the Kaplan Three-Step Method and the information you just learned to answer this question.

Jonas Salk was born in East Harlem, New York, the developer of the polio vaccine.

   A. Jonas Salk was born in East Harlem, New York, the developer of the polio vaccine.
   B. Jonas Salk being the developer of the polio vaccine and was born in East Harlem, New York.
   C. Being the developer of the polio vaccine, Jonas Salk was born in East Harlem, New York.
   D. Jonas Salk was the developer of the polio vaccine, having been born in East Harlem, New York.
   E. Jonas Salk, who was born in East Harlem, New York, was the developer of the polio vaccine.

Because the entire sentence is underlined, you know that either it's correct or there's a better rewrite among the choices. What's wrong with the sentence? Well, it's a run-on because there are two independent thoughts that aren't joined in any way. It's also a bit confusing because it sounds as if Salk was born the developer of the vaccine. (He probably had to grow up a bit and go to school for a while before he developed the vaccine.) Choice (E) fixes the problem by setting apart the facts about Salk's birthplace, thus clearing up the meaning and fixing the run-on problem.

Coordination and Subordination Errors

Sometimes a sentence won't make sense because it contains clauses that aren't logically joined. There are two types of errors involving the improper joining of clauses in a sentence: coordination and subordination errors.

DEFINITION ALERT

Clauses are groups of words that contain a subject and a verb. Dependent, or *subordinate*, clauses need to be linked to an independent clause by a conjunction—such as *because*, *although*, or *since*—in order for the sentence to express a complete thought.

Proper **coordination** expresses the logical relationship between two clauses. Misused conjunctions can bring about faulty coordination and make a sentence confusing or nonsensical.

> Because he was very thirsty, he refused to drink the water.

This sentence doesn't make much sense (unless we're dealing with a very stubborn or confused person, but let's not overrationalize things). What would be a better conjunction?

> Although he was very thirsty, he refused to drink the water.

This is better. We still don't know why he wouldn't drink the water, but the conjunction *although* sets up the contrast between the two clauses so the sentence makes sense.

Problems with **subordination** occur when a group of words contains two or more subordinate clauses (also known as dependent clauses) but no independent clause.

> Since the advent of inexpensive portable stereos, because there has been a boom in the manufacture of light, powerful headphones.

Connective words like *since, because, so that, if,* and *although* introduce subordinate clauses. As it stands, this sentence consists of two dependent clauses, with no independent clause. We can eliminate *because* in order to make this a grammatically correct sentence.

> Since the advent of inexpensive portable stereos, there has been a boom in the manufacture of light, powerful headphones.

Try the following two questions, using the Kaplan Three-Step Method.

> New restaurants appeared on the <u>waterfront, however merchants</u> were finally able to convince diners of the area's safety.

> A. waterfront, however merchants
>
> B. waterfront; merchants
>
> C. waterfront, yet merchants
>
> D. waterfront, because merchants
>
> E. waterfront, although merchants

"However" is a conjunction that indicates contrast. This sentence is about cause and effect. Choice (**D**) is correct because the conjunction "because" shows the relationship between the appearance of the new restaurants and the merchants' ability to convince diners that the area was safe.

Because Megan was unable to finish her tax forms before April 15, <u>so she filed</u> for an extension.

A. so she filed

B. but she was filing

C. she filed

D. and this led to her filing

E. and she filed

This question tests subordination. The sentence contains two dependent clauses, each beginning with a linking word. Choice (**C**) eliminates the linking word and fixes the problem by creating an independent clause.

Misplaced-Modifier Errors

Modifiers are phrases that provide information about nouns and verbs in a sentence. A modifier must appear next to the word or words that it's modifying. Otherwise, things can get a bit confusing (not to mention ungrammatical).

> **SPOT THE TROUBLE EARLY ON!**
>
> Most misplaced modifier errors on the Praxis occur in sentences that begin with a modifying phrase. When a short phrase followed by a comma begins a sentence, make sure that what follows the comma is what the phrase is supposed to modify.

Take a look at this example.

> Dripping on his shirt, Harvey was so eager to eat his hamburger that he didn't notice the ketchup.

As the sentence is written, it sounds as if Harvey was dripping on his shirt, which isn't a very pleasant image. In fact, it's the ketchup that's dripping on his shirt.

As long as you can spot them, misplaced modifiers are easy to fix.

> Harvey was so eager to eat his hamburger that he didn't notice the ketchup dripping on his shirt.

This clears up the confusion and is a logical sentence.

Now let's look at a test-like question that involves a misplaced modifier.

Flying for the first time, the roar of the jet engines intimidated the elderly man as the plane sped down the runway.

A. Flying for the first time, the roar of the jet engines intimidated the elderly man as the plane sped down the runway.

B. The roar of the jet engines intimidated the elderly man as the plane, flying for the first time, sped down the runway.

C. Flying for the first time, the elderly man was intimidated by the roar of the jet engines as the plane sped down the runway.

D. The plane sped down the runway as, flying for the first time, the roar of the jet engines intimidated the elderly man.

E. As the plane sped down the runway, flying for the first time, the elderly man was intimidated by the roar of the jet engines.

We need a choice that makes it clear that the elderly man, not the plane or the engines or the engines' roar, is flying for the first time. Choice (C) accomplishes this by placing the modifier "flying for the first time" next to "the elderly man." Note that choice (E) also places the two phrases next to each other, but the modifier is sandwiched between two phrases, making it unclear which phrase it is meant to modify. Choice (**C**) is correct.

Parallelism Errors

Parallelism is very much like comparison, which we covered earlier. Essentially, whenever you list items, they must be in the same form.

Take a look at this sentence:

On Saturday, Ingrid cleaned her apartment, bought her plane tickets for France, and was deciding to go out to dinner.

The first two verbs set us up to expect a parallel verb, but we get blindsided at the end with a nonparallel construction.

On Saturday, Ingrid cleaned her apartment, bought her plane tickets for France, and decided to go out to dinner.

In this corrected sentence, "cleaned," "bought," and "decided" are all in the same form, so the parallel structure is correct.

Try the following question and see how you do.

Changing over from a military to a peacetime economy means producing tractors rather than tanks, radios rather than rifles, and producing running shoes rather than combat boots.

A. producing running shoes rather than combat boots

B. the production of running shoes rather than combat boots

C. running shoes rather than combat boots

D. replacing combat boots with running shoes

E. running shoes instead of combat boots

Choice (**C**) does the trick by maintaining the parallel structure of the sentence: "tractors rather than tanks, radios rather than rifles, and running shoes rather than combat boots."

Praxis Essays

Essay writing evokes an immediate reaction from nearly everyone, and prospective teachers are no exception. Generally speaking, you either love to write or see it as a chore. Either way, the Praxis Core Writing test will require you to do a bit of it.

Keep in mind that even the strongest writers can have problems with the unique nature of the Praxis exam. You must respond directly to the topic, and you have to generate your essay in a short period of time. Overly ambitious or flamboyant essayists can run short on time or run too far afield from the topic at hand.

The testmaker requires you to perform a highly specialized type of writing. Creativity and improvisation are not your goals when writing a Praxis essay. Instead, keep in mind the definition of an essay: *a short literary composition on a single subject, usually presenting the personal view of the author.* That definition can take you a long way toward effective essay writing on the Praxis exam.

First, Praxis essays are meant to be *short*. For each essay, you have only 30 minutes to read and digest the essay prompt, compose the essay, and proof it for errors and clarity. That's not a lot of time. The testmaker is looking for brief, clear essays.

Second, Praxis essays are meant to be on a *single subject*. Although tangents, allusions, and digressions make for good fiction, they'll send you into dangerous territory on the Praxis exam. Be sure that whatever you include in your essays pertains to the subject at hand. Keep your essays on point. If a sentence or idea does not relate directly to the topic of your essay, omit it.

Finally, Praxis essays assess how well you respond *to the prompt provided*. One of the essays, the Argumentative essay, will ask you to express your views on a topic. But you must do more than just that. You will also be expected to provide illustrations, examples, and generalizations that support the views you express.

The other essay, the Informative/Explanatory or Source-Based essay, will ask you to evaluate two source texts and identify the main points of the issue as illustrated by the texts. A strong essay of this type addresses both texts with proper in-text citations. It does not take a stance on the issue provided; rather, it assesses the important points related to the topic.

The topics of Praxis essays are such that any educated person should be able to draw from experience to answer the questions. No specialized knowledge is required.

Keeping all of the preceding points above in mind as you pull together your essay will put you well on your way to success on the Praxis Core Writing test. Of course, the key to effective preparation is knowing what you're up against.

Know What to Expect

You have only 30 minutes to write each essay, so effective time management is key. Be sure to complete each essay in the time allotted. Even a well-crafted essay that abruptly ends without a conclusion will lose valuable points.

Speaking of points, the essay section is scored differently than are the other sections of the Praxis exam. Instead of receiving a score based on the number of questions you answered correctly, your essay is scored holistically on a scale of 0 to 6, meaning that a single score represents the overall quality of the essay. A score of 6 indicates "a high degree of competence in response to the assignment." An essay that scores a 4 or 5 also demonstrates competence, but to a lesser degree. A score of 3 or lower is given to an essay that may show some competence but also demonstrates organizational flaws, poor mechanics, or other significant errors.

Your essays are graded by two experienced teachers who have been trained in the scoring of Praxis essays, or one veteran teacher and a validated computer grading program. If your graders' scores differ by more than one point, a third reader will be brought in to decide where your mark should fall.

How to Approach the Praxis Essays

Even though you have only 30 minutes to complete each essay, you should take time to organize your thoughts before writing about a topic. You should also leave time to proof your essays after writing them.

Writing an essay for the Praxis exam is a two-stage process. First, you decide what you want to say about a topic. Second, you figure out how to say it. If your writing style isn't clear, your ideas won't come across no matter how brilliant they are. Good Praxis English is not only grammatical, but also clear and concise. By using some basic principles, you'll be able to express your ideas clearly and effectively in your essays.

Four Principles of Good Essay Writing

1. **Your Control of Language Is Important**

   Writing that is grammatical, concise, direct, and persuasive displays the "superior control of language" that earns top scores. This involves using the same good grammar that is tested in the selected-response (multiple-choice) questions. It also involves good word choice or diction and sentence structure.

2. **It's Better to Keep Things Simple**

   Perhaps the single most important thing to bear in mind when writing a Praxis essay is to keep everything simple. Because you are aiming to pass this test and get it out of your life, there is no reason to be overly wordy or complex as you write your essay. Simplicity is essential whether you are talking about word choice, sentence structure, or organization. Complicated sentences are more likely to contain errors. An essay with a complicated organizational structure is more likely to wander off topic. Keep in mind that *simple* doesn't mean *simplistic*. A clear, straightforward approach can convey perceptive insights on a topic.

3. **Minor Grammatical Flaws Won't Kill You**

   You are bound to make small mistakes when working under the kind of pressure you'll face on this exam. So don't panic. Essay readers expect minor errors, even in the best essays. That doesn't mean you should include an error or two to keep them happy. It means you should be aware of the kinds of errors you tend to make. If you have trouble with parallelism, double-check how you listed groups of things. Knowing your strengths and weaknesses should help you proof your essay before completing it.

4. **Keep Sight of Your Goal**

   Remember, your goal isn't to become a prizewinning stylist. Write a solid essay and move on. Write well enough to address the topic and demonstrate that you can write. Remember, essay graders aren't looking for rhetorical flourishes. They're looking for effective expression. Express your ideas clearly and simply, and you'll be well on your way to success.

The Kaplan Five-Step Method for Praxis Essays

THE KAPLAN METHOD FOR PRAXIS READING

STEP 1   Digest the issue or source texts and the prompt

STEP 2   Select the points you will make

STEP 3   Organize

STEP 4   Write

STEP 5   Proofread

By now, you should know what you're up against on the essay portion of the Praxis Core Writing test. You need to demonstrate that you can think quickly and organize an essay under time pressure. The essay you write is supposed to be logical in organization and clear and concise in its use of written English. Praxis essay writing is not about bells and whistles; it's about bread and butter. Nothing fancy—just answer the question in clear language.

The real challenge is to write an effective essay in a short time. With that goal in mind, we've developed a proven Five-Step Method that will help you make the most of your 30 minutes.

Step 1. Digest the Issue or Source Texts and the Prompt (1–3 minutes)

- Read the prompt and get a sense of the scope of the issue
- Note any ambiguous terms that need defining
- Crystallize the issue

Step 2. Select the Points You Will Make (4 minutes)

- Think of arguments for both sides of the issue and decide which side you will support
- Assess the specifics of the prompt
- Brainstorm about both source texts and select the elements of each that you plan to quote

Step 3. Organize (2 minutes)

- Outline your essay
- Lead with your best arguments
- Think about how the essay will flow as a whole

Step 4. Write (20 minutes)

- Be direct
- Use paragraph breaks to make your essay easy to read
- Make transitions, linking related ideas
- Finish strongly

Step 5. Proofread (1–3 minutes)

- Save enough time for one final read through the entire essay
- Have a sense of the errors you are likely to make and seek to find and correct them

Now that we've quickly outlined the five steps to effective Praxis essay writing, it's time to see these steps in action.

Applying the Kaplan Five-Step Method to the Argumentative Essay

Let's use the Kaplan Five-Step Method on a sample topic:

The drawbacks to the use of nuclear power mean that it is not a long-term solution to the problem of meeting ever-increasing energy needs.

Step 1. Digest the Issue

It's simple enough. The person who wrote this believes that nuclear power is not a suitable replacement for other forms of energy.

Step 2. Select the Points You Will Make

Your job, as stated in the directions, is to decide whether or not you agree and to explain your decision. Some would argue that the use of nuclear power is too dangerous, whereas others would say that we can't afford not to use it. So, which side do you take? Remember, this isn't about showing the admissions people what your deep-seated beliefs about the environment are—it's about showing that you can formulate an argument and write it down. Quickly think through the pros and cons of each side. Then choose the side for which you have the most relevant things to say. For this topic, that process might go something like this:

Arguments for the use of nuclear power:

- Inexpensive compared to other forms of energy
- Fossil fuels will eventually be depleted
- Other sources, like solar power, still too problematic and expensive

Arguments against the use of nuclear power:

- Radioactive hyperproducts are deadly
- Safer alternatives like nuclear fusion may be viable in the future
- Other sources, like solar power, already in use

Again, it doesn't matter which side you take. Let's say that in this case, you decide to argue against nuclear power. Remember, the question is asking you to argue *why* the cons of nuclear power outweigh the pros—the inadequacy of this power source is the end you're arguing toward, so don't list it as supporting evidence for your argument.

Step 3. Organize

You've already begun to think out your arguments—that's why you picked the side you did in the first place. Now is the time to write them all out, including ones that weaken the opposing side.

Nuclear power is not a viable alternative to other sources of energy because:

- Radioactive, spent fuel has leaked from storage sites (too dangerous)
- Reactor accidents can be catastrophic—Three Mile Island, Chernobyl, Fukushima (too dangerous)
- More research into solar power will bring down its cost (weakens opposing argument)
- Solar-powered homes and cars running on biofuel already exist (alternatives proven viable)
- No serious effort to research other alternatives like nuclear fusion (better alternatives lie undiscovered)
- Energy companies don't spend money on alternatives; no vested interest (better alternatives lie undiscovered)

Step 4. Write

Remember, open your essay with a general statement and then assert your position. From there, get down your main points. Your essay for this assignment might look like this one.

Sample Essay 1

At first glance, nuclear energy may seem to be the power source for the future. It's relatively inexpensive, it doesn't produce smoke, and its fuel supply is virtually inexhaustible. However, a close examination of the issue reveals that nuclear energy is more problematic and dangerous than other forms of energy production.

A main reason that nuclear energy is undesirable is the problem of radioactive-waste storage. Highly toxic fuel left over from nuclear fission remains toxic for thousands of years, and the spills and leaks from existing storage sites are hazardous and costly to clean up. Even more appalling is the prospect of accidents at the reactor itself: incidents at the Three Mile Island, Chernobyl, and Fukushima power plants have proven that the consequences of a nuclear melt-down can be catastrophic and have consequences that are felt worldwide.

Environmental and health problems aside, the bottom line for the production of energy is profit. Nuclear power is a business just like any other, and the large companies that produce this country's electricity and gas claim they can't make alternatives like solar power affordable. Yet—largely because of incentives from the federal government—there exist today homes that are heated by solar power, and cars that are fueled by corn have already hit the streets. If the limited resources that have been devoted to energy alternatives have already produced working models, a more intensive effort is likely to make those alternatives less expensive and more reliable.

Options like solar power, hydroelectric power, and nuclear fusion are far better in the long run in terms of cost and safety. The only money required for these alternatives is for the materials required to harvest them: sunlight, water, and the power of the atom are free. They also don't produce any toxic by-products for which long-term storage—a hidden cost of nuclear power—must be found. Also, with the temporary exception of nuclear fusion, these sources of energy are already being harnessed today.

Whereas there are arguments to be made for both sides, it is clear that the drawbacks to the use of nuclear power are too great. If other alternatives are explored more seriously than they have been in the past, safer and less expensive sources of power will undoubtedly prove better alternatives.

Step 5. Proofread

Take the last couple of minutes to catch any glaring errors. Be sure not to skimp on this step!

Tip: If you only have 30 seconds for this part, focus on your last paragraph to leave a good impression on your reader.

Source-Based Essay

Now it's your turn to use the Kaplan Method for Praxis Essays, this time on the Source-Based essay. This essay is meant to assess your ability to establish the key points raised by both of the sources. Be sure to take notes from the sources as you read through them. Then write about the concerns that the two pieces raise, on your own scratch paper. On test day, you'll take your notes on your scratch paper and type your essay response on the computer. Don't worry: we've provided the framework for your planning stage below, and some sample essays follow so you can see how your work compares.

Sample Prompt

Directions: In the following section, you will have 30 minutes to read two short passages on a topic and then plan and write an essay on that topic. The essay will be an informative essay based on the two source passages.

Read the topic and sources carefully. You will probably find it best to spend a little time considering the topic and organizing your thoughts before you begin writing. DO NOT WRITE ON A TOPIC OTHER THAN THE ONE SPECIFIED. Essays on topics of your own choice will not be acceptable. In order for your test to be scored, your responses must be in English.

The essay questions are included in this test to give you an opportunity to demonstrate how well you can write. You should, therefore, take care to write clearly and effectively, using specific examples where appropriate. Remember that how well you write is much more important than how much you write, but to cover the topics adequately, you will probably need to write more than one paragraph.

Assignment:

Solar power is a clean energy source that individuals are using as an alternative to fossil fuels. The following sources discuss the impacts, both positive and negative, of switching to solar power. Read the two passages carefully and then write an essay in which you identify the most important concerns regarding the issue and explain why they are important. Your essay must draw on information from BOTH of the sources. In addition, you may draw on your own experiences, observations, or reading. Be sure to CITE the sources, whether you are paraphrasing or directly quoting.

Passage 1: Solar Energy Council ("SEC"). *The Topaz Solar Project and Beyond.* **New York: Fleming Press. 2015. Print.**

The largest solar farm in the world, known as Topaz, opened in late 2014. The plant, which cost $2.5 billion to build, generates a whopping 550 megawatts of power. To put this number into perspective, this amount of power will be used to supply 160,000 homes. This switch from fossil fuels to solar power will save the environment exposure to approximately 377,000 tons of carbon dioxide emissions per year, which is equivalent to retiring 73,000 cars.

The benefits of constructing such a large-scale solar farm are not only environmental. There are also significant economic benefits. Over 400 construction jobs were added to the area during the construction phase, and $192 million in income was pumped into the local economy as a result. Economic benefits haven't stopped since the plant opened. Local energy suppliers are now able to enjoy $52 million in economic output.

Located in San Luis Obispo County in California, Topaz was built on part of California's Carrizo Plain. The plain is an area of native grassland northwest of Los Angeles. The land on which the plant sits was used as farmland in the past. Because of this, no new land disturbance was required in order to complete this large project. The land was no longer suitable for farming due to irrigation practices that had stripped the soil of its nutrients. The 4,700 private acres provided the perfect setting for a solar plant, meeting the developer's standards for low-impact development, which was a priority considering the site's proximity to the Carrizo Plain National Monument, a protected area that is home to native species and plants.

The plant's setup includes 460 panels mounted on steel support posts. The sunlight taken in by these panels is fed to power conversion stations. Each panel has its own conversion station. Made up of two inverters and a transformer each, the conversion stations are needed to make the power usable. The power is then sent to a substation that transforms it from 35.5 kilovolts to the standard 230 kilovolts. The Pacific Gas and Electric Company (PG&E) built a new switching station next to the solar farm. It is here that the power is looped into the grid that supplies neighboring areas.

Topaz will only remain the world's largest solar farm for a short period of time. The plant's owner, First Solar, is currently developing an even larger plant, also in California.

Passage 2: Everly, Gwen. *The Other Side of Solar.* San Francisco: Goldstar. 2016. Print.

With more and more large-scale solar farms being developed in the sunny southwestern United States, researchers and conservationists alike are beginning to notice surprising environmental effects. While solar energy is known for its positive environmental impacts, officials at the National Fish and Wildlife Forensics Laboratory have come to recognize one of its significant downsides: some species of birds that live in close proximity to large solar plants are dying off, including endangered birds.

A recent federal investigation recovered 233 birds that had been killed as a direct result of solar plants. Researchers believe that some of the affected birds have mistaken the large, reflective areas of the solar panels for bodies of water. This is a phenomenon referred to by scientists as "lake effect." The birds are drawn to what they assume to be water. They home in on the area and slam into the panels with great force. It is thought that the insects that birds eat fall victim to "lake effect" as well, leading the birds into the panels.

Researchers estimate that between 1,000 and 28,000 birds are killed each year as a result of harvesting solar energy. The number of birds affected by wind farming is much greater, ranging from 140,000 to 328,000 annually. Coal-fired electricity has the largest negative effect on birds, killing nearly 8 million a year. These numbers make solar farming seem like the best option. However, conservationists are quick to point out that the areas where solar is expected to boom between 2015 and 2020 are home to some of the rarest birds in the United States. This could put specific bird species at risk of extinction.

There exists a state mandate in California that 20 percent of all electricity sold must be renewable by the year 2017. This has been one driving force behind the rapid development of huge solar farms. The industry, which is expecting to boom as a result of this shift to renewable energy, is facing newly filed lawsuits by conservationist groups, citing the negative impact on wildlife. These lawsuits could prolong the approval process for the planned solar developments across the Southwest.

Apply The Kaplan Method

Step 1: Digest the issue or source texts and the prompt (3 minutes)

Topic of texts:

_____

_____

_____

_____

For what is the prompt asking?

_____

_____

Step 2: Select the points you will make (3 minutes)

Main points from text 1:

_____

_____

Main points from text 2:

_____

_____

Step 3: Organize (2 minutes)

Go back to Step 2 and star the points you want to put into your essay.

Step 4: Write (20 minutes)

On test day, you'll compose your essay directly on the computer. However, the word-processing software is basic, including only "Cut," "Paste," and "Undo" commands; there are no spell-check or grammar-check features. So, for the most realistic essay-writing practice, use a similarly basic word-processing software to type your practice essays.

Step 5: Proofread (2 minutes)

Congratulations on writing your first Praxis essay! Please review your work against the essays below. Of course, your essay will not exactly match any of the sample essays, but reading these examples will give you an idea of what kind of work gets a high or low score from the graders.

High-Scoring Response

With the issue of global warming growing increasingly alarming, many individuals have turned away from fossil fuels to alternative power sources in an attempt to lessen the environmental damage caused by power generation. Despite the many benefits of cleaner energy production, however, its universal adoption is not without debate.

A recent example of the implementation of a large-scale clean energy project is the solar plant Topaz (in southern California). The purpose of this project was to "save the environment exposure to approximately 377,000 tons of carbon dioxide emissions per year," which will greatly decrease the greenhouse gas levels in the atmosphere (Solar Energy Council ("SEC") 2016). As a result of this decrease, the overall air quality will improve, and the depletion of the ozone layer will slow down. The SEC also tells us that the field on which Topaz stands was claimed for this purpose specifically because the field was already existing but was no longer fertile, and thus not useful as farmland. These facts presented in Passage 1 show that Topaz was meant to be an entirely positive environmental project, as it was constructed with the goal of creating clean energy without the need to clear-cut a forest, which is one of the main concerns with other solar plants.

Unfortunately, these positive effects of the construction of Topaz also come with negative effects, which are laid out by Everly in Passage 2. "The Other Side of Solar" describes a phenomenon that birds experience called the "lake effect," in which birds effectively misidentify the solar panels as bodies of water. This poses a problem when they attempt to land in the "water," as they instead crash into the solid glass surface, resulting in their demise. According to Everly, this is especially problematic in Southern California, where Topaz is, because a number of endangered species of birds call that region home. The author of Passage 2 does concede momentarily that "the number of birds affected by wind farming is much greater" and that "coal-fired electricty has the largest negative effect on birds," but this hardly dampens the author's argument against solar power, as the death of "between 1,000 and 28,000 birds" is hardly a negligible figure (Everly 2016).

Ultimately, the decision to use or scrap solar power as a means of clean energy production is still up for debate. According to both sources, it would appear that solar power has the fewest negative impacts on the environment as compared to coal-fired or wind power. Solar power is not without its flaws, though, with negative effects ranging from using a field that could have other more beneficial uses to creating the "lake effect" that leads to a decrease in key bird populations.

Medium-Scoring Response

Both of these passages talk about solar power. The author of Passage 1 is for solar power because it can power 160,000 homes, and will "save the environment exposure to approximately 377,000 tons of carbon dioxide emissions per year, which is the equivalent of retiring 73,000 cars" (SEC 2015). Also, building the Topaz plant put "$192 million" into the economy and it made lots of jobs when it was being built (SEC 2015). It also has "$52 million in economic output" (SEC 2015) which is really good for the economy because it pushes money into the area around Topaz.

The author of Passage 2 is against solar power because birds "slam into the panels with great force" (Everly 2016). There is also the issue of lawsuits from environmental groups because of the dead birds, so it's important that we not use solar power to avoid these lawsuits. Passage 2 makes a better argument, because it talks about other types of power and compares solar power to them based on the numbers of birds killed.

In conclusion, there are lots of things we need to think about when we consider whether or not we should use solar power. No solution is ever perfect, and we have to make trade-offs that lead to the best results possible in the real world.

Low-Scoring Response

I think solar power is the best source of power because it usually hurts zero birds, which is not as many as coal-fired power or wind farming. Solar power also creates jobs for people, and makes money for people.

Honestly if people are so worried about birds then they should just use wave power, which doesn't hurt any animals and is the best power there is. It's a lot better than solar power.

Praxis Writing Practice

Now it's time to practice some Praxis Writing questions. Make sure to use Kaplan's Three-Step Method when working through this quiz.

1. The first woman aviator <u>to cross</u> the English
   _A
   Channel, Harriet Quimby, <u>flown</u> <u>by monoplane</u>
   _B   _C
   from Dover, England, to Hardelot, France, <u>in</u>
   _D
   1912. <u>No error</u>
   _E

2. The reproductive behavior of sea horses
   <u>is notable</u> <u>in respect of</u> the male, <u>who,</u> <u>instead of</u>
   _A   _B   _C   _D
   the female, carries the fertilized eggs. <u>No error</u>
   _E

3. Early <u>experience</u> of racial discrimination <u>made</u> an
   _A   _B
   <u>indelible</u> <u>impression for</u> the late Supreme Court
   _C   _D
   Justice Thurgood Marshall. <u>No error</u>
   _E

4. More journalists <u>as</u> you would suspect are
   _A
   <u>secretly</u> writing plays or novels, <u>which</u> they hope
   _B   _C
   someday <u>to have published.</u> <u>No error</u>
   _D   _E

5. <u>As long ago as</u> the twelfth century, before the
   _A
   division of alchemy into modern chemistry and
   a more metaphysical pursuit, French alchemists
   <u>have</u> perfected techniques <u>for refining</u> precious
   _B   _C
   metals <u>from</u> other ores. <u>No error</u>
   _D   _E

6. Galileo begged Rome's indulgence for his
   <u>support of</u> a Copernican system <u>in which</u> earth
   _A   _B
   circled the sun <u>instead of</u> <u>occupied</u> a central
   _C   _D
   position in the universe. <u>No error</u>
   _E

7. Arthur Rubinstein was long ranked <u>among</u>
   _A
   the world's finest pianists, <u>although</u> he was
   _B
   sometimes known <u>as playing</u> several wrong
   _C
   notes <u>in a single</u> performance. <u>No error</u>
   _D   _E

8. The new office complex is beautiful, but <u>nearly</u>
   _A
   two hundred longtime residents <u>were forced</u> to
   _B
   move when <u>they</u> <u>tore down</u> the old apartment
   _C   _D
   buildings. <u>No error</u>
   _E

9. Neither the singers <u>on stage</u> <u>or</u> the announcer in
   _A   _B
   the wings <u>could be heard</u> <u>over</u> the noise of the
   _C   _D
   crowd. <u>No error</u>
   _E

10. I loved my <u>college-level</u> math class <u>as well as</u>
    _A   _B
    my biology class; <u>but</u> I could have worked
    _C
    <u>harder and</u> gotten better grades. <u>No error</u>
    _D   _E

11. None of this injury <u>to life</u> and damage to
    _A
    property <u>wouldn't have</u> happened if the amateur
    _B
    pilot <u>had only</u> heeded the weather forecasts and
    _C
    <u>stayed</u> on the ground. <u>No error</u>
    _D   _E

12. The doctor recommended that young athletes
    <u>with a history</u> of severe asthma <u>take</u> <u>particular</u>
    _A   _B   _C
    care <u>not to exercise</u> alone. <u>No error</u>
    _D   _E

13. <u>Amelia Earhart was born in Kansas the first person to fly from Hawaii to California.</u>

    A. Amelia Earhart was born in Kansas the first person to fly from Hawaii to California.

    B. Amelia Earhart being the first person to fly from Hawaii to California and was born in Kansas.

    C. Being the first person to fly from Hawaii to California, Amelia Earhart was born in Kansas.

    D. Amelia Earhart was the first person to fly from Hawaii to California and was born in Kansas.

    E. Amelia Earhart, who was born in Kansas, was the first person to fly from Hawaii to California.

14. Beethoven bridged two musical eras; <u>his earlier works are essentially Classical, while his later ones are Romantic.</u>

    A. his earlier works are essentially Classical, while his later ones are Romantic

    B. his earlier works are essentially Classical, nevertheless, his later ones are Romantic

    C. his earlier works being essentially Classical and his later ones being Romantic

    D. whereas essentially his earlier works are Classical and his later ones were Romantic

    E. despite his earlier works' being essentially Classical, his later are Romantic

Smith, Mary. Interview with Steven Jones. *Pottery Quarterly*, vol. 20, no. 4, 1999, pp. 73–74.

15. In the citation above, what does the format of the citation indicate about the source?

    A. The source was an unpublished personal interview of Steven Jones conducted by the author of the document, whose name was Mary Smith.

    B. The source was an online interview of Steven Jones by Mary Smith.

    C. The source was a published print or broadcast interview of Steven Jones by Mary Smith.

    D. The source was a periodical article entitled "Interview with Steven Jones" by Mary Smith.

    E. The source was a lecture by Mary Smith about her interview with Steven Jones.

16. A student is writing an informative essay about the 20th-century painter Jackson Pollock and his process. Which of the following would be the most credible source for the student's essay?

    A. A documentary produced by film students at a local community college about persistent themes in Pollock's work

    B. A defense of the value of Pollock's work from a leading art history expert

    C. A Wikipedia article about Pollock's life and works

    D. A series of photographs of Pollock working on a painting published in a leading art periodical in 1950

    E. A best-selling biography focusing on Pollock's tumultuous private life

17. In a research paper, which one of the following elements contains a brief summary of the paper's contents?

    A. Glossary

    B. Findings

    C. Abstract

    D. Bibliography

    E. Appendix

Questions 18–20

(1) Born in Everett, Massachusetts, the American Sculptor Hermon Atkins MacNeil (1866–1947) studied at the Massachusetts Normal Art School, now the Massachusetts College of Art and Design, before training further in Paris and Rome. **(2)** After becoming a National Academician, he created *Fountain of Liberty* for the Louisiana Purchase Exposition, as well as a sculpture of President William McKinley in Columbus, Ohio. **(3)** He sculpted *Justice, the Guardian of Liberty*, which can be seen on the east pediment of the United States Supreme Court Building. **(4)** His most _____ work, though, is probably the Standing Liberty Quarter, minted from 1916 to 1930.

18. A student is writing a paper about the behavioral tendencies of domestic dogs.

    Which of the following would best serve as a primary source for this student?

    A. A blog in which dog lovers post photographs of their dogs in costumes

    B. An encyclopedia of the history and behavior of dog breeds worldwide

    C. A blog in which dog trainers share tips for training dogs

    D. An article written by an animal control agent about the problem of stray dogs in Chicago

    E. A magazine article based on interviews with experts that highlights the pros and cons of owning various breeds of dogs

19. Where would the following sentence best be inserted?

    The first works to gain him some measure of prominence were a number of portrayals of North American Indians.

    A. Before the first sentence

    B. After the first sentence

    C. After the second sentence

    D. After the third sentence

    E. After the fourth sentence

20. Which is the best word to fill in the blank in sentence 4 (reproduced below)?

    His most _____ work, though, is probably the Standing Liberty Quarter, minted from 1916 to 1930.

    A. familiar

    B. mysterious

    C. obscure

    D. conventional

    E. recent

Praxis Writing Practice Answers and Explanations

1. B

The use of the word "flown" isn't right. *Flown,* the past participle form of *fly,* can't be used as a main verb without a form of the verb *have.* What's needed here is the simple past form of *fly,* which is *flew.*

2. B

"In respect of" is not the correct phrasing. The phrase *with respect to* would be correct.

3. D

Does something make an "impression for" someone? No, it makes an *impression on* someone.

4. A

The correct comparative form is *more … than,* not "more … as."

5. B

This sentence describes an event that took place before another past event. The present perfect "have perfected" suggests that the improvement of these techniques is still going on. Instead, the sentence should use the simple past *perfected,* or the past perfect tense *had perfected* if the first past event ended before the second past event started.

6. D

"Instead of" takes a participle: "occupied" should be corrected to *occupying.*

7. C

The idiomatically correct sentence would read *known to play . . . .*

8. C

Who tore down the old buildings? Surely not the "long-time residents." The pronoun "they" requires a logical antecedent—some group such as *landlords* or *developers.*

9. B

"Neither" calls for *nor. Either* is used with *or.*

10. C

It is not correct to use a semicolon with the coordinating conjunction "but" joining two independent clauses. Substituting a conjunctive adverb such as *however* would correct the sentence.

11. B

To see the double negative more easily, remove the intervening words: "none of this … wouldn't have happened." The correct phrase would be *would have.*

12. A

In this sentence, the plural noun "athletes" is modified by the prepositional phrase "with a history of severe asthma." But the athletes don't have a collective medical history; each athlete has his or her own. The sentence should read either *young athletes with histories of severe asthma* or *a young athlete with a history of severe asthma.* Because the prepositional phrase is the part of the sentence that is underlined, it must be changed.

13. E

The original sentence is a run-on. Choice (**E**) provides a fix by tucking the less important information about where Earhart was born into a subordinate clause. (D) also fixes the run-on, but it awkwardly gives the two unrelated facts equal prominence.

14. A

The original sentence is correct. A semicolon is used to join two sentences with closely related ideas. (B) turns the sentence into a run-on because "nevertheless" is not a conjunction and cannot be used to join two ideas. (C) would be weak but correct if the semicolon were a comma. However, as written, it contains a fragment prior to the semicolon. (D) is incorrect because the conjunctive adverb "likewise" contradicts the implied contrast between the two musical eras. (E) begins with a connecting word ("despite") that turns the clause before the semicolon into a fragment.

15. C

The italicized name, the volume and edition numbers, and the page number citations all indicate that a periodical was the source for the material cited here, as described in **(C)**. Personal interviews, as in (A), would not include the name of the publication, as this citation does. Online interview citations, as in (B), would include the web address of the source, which this citation does not. Titles of articles, as indicated in (D), must always be in quotation marks, which are missing from this citation. Citations of lectures, as described in (E), always include a venue name and location, which this citation does not have.

16. D

The most credible sources are factual evidence from the time period being studied and sources written by unbiased and professional experts. The authors of the sources in (A), (C), and (E) are unlikely to be professional experts in the field; in addition, the scope of each source is unlikely to provide logical evidence for the essay's thesis. Choice (B) is incorrect because although the author is a respected expert, the article is likely biased in favor of the artist. Choice **(D)** is a highly credible source, as it is a primary source of factual information on Pollock's artistic process.

17. C

An abstract, **(C)**, is a brief summary of the contents of a research paper. Choice (A), the glossary, defines specialized terms used in the paper. (B), the findings, is a section of the paper in which the researcher summarizes the results of the research or testing on which the paper is based. (D), the bibliography, provides the citations for all outside work consulted in the writing of the paper. (E), an appendix, is an optional part of the paper used to present related information inappropriate for the body of the paper or additional supporting documentation that may be of interest to the reader.

18. C

Choice (C) is correct, as this document is written by experts in the field of dog behavior. Choices (A) and (D) are primary sources, but they are not on the topic of dogs' "behavioral tendencies." Encyclopedia articles, (B), are often summaries of primary research by people other than the articles' authors and so are not primary sources. The magazine article in (E) could also be reporting on various experts' opinions, rather than the author's observations.

19. B

The new sentence would fit best after the first sentence. It mentions the first works of MacNeil's to gain him some fame, so it must precede mention of the more prominent works in the list.

20. A

The word "though" contrasts this coin with MacNeil's work on a prominent public building, with the implication that the Standing Liberty Quarter is even more well-known. Therefore, "familiar," **(A)**, is correct. His design for the quarter is not obscure, and there's nothing mysterious about it, so (C) and (B) are incorrect. There is no support for "conventional," (D), and although the work is the last listed, there is no information about whether or not he completed other works later, so (E) is also unsupported.

Practice: Argumentative Essay

Directions for the Written Assignment

This section of the test consists of a written assignment. It asks you to prepare a written response of about 300–600 words on the assigned topic. *The assignment is below.* You should use your time to plan, write, review, and edit your work on the assignment.

Read the assignment carefully before you begin to write. Think about how you will organize what you plan to write. Your response to the written assignment will be evaluated based on your demonstrated ability to do the following:

- State or imply a clear position or thesis
- Present a well-reasoned and well-organized argument that connects ideas in a thoughtful and logical way
- Use support and evidence to develop and bolster your ideas and account for the views of others
- Display competent use of language through well-constructed sentences of varying lengths and structures
- Express yourself without distractions caused by inattention to sentence and paragraph structure, choice and use of words, and mechanics (i.e., spelling, punctuation, and capitalization)

Your response will also be evaluated based on your demonstrated ability to express and support opinions, not on the nature or content of the opinions you express. The final version of your response should conform to the conventions of edited American English. It should be your original work, in your own words—do not copy or paraphrase other people's work.

Be sure to write about the assigned topic and use multiple paragraphs. Please write legibly. You may not use any reference materials during the test. Remember to review what you have written and make any changes you think will improve your response.

Written Assignment

With more violent acts occurring in our schools, there is a call for more obvious security measures—such as installing metal detectors, posting security guards in the hallway, banning backpacks, and requiring students to wear uniforms.

Do you believe implementing these or other security measures is a good idea or bad idea?

Write an essay to support your position.

Written Assignment Sample Response

The following is an example of a strong response to the written assignment:

I believe that some security measures in a school are important. If the idea of the security is actually to keep children safe while at school, it is a very good thing. If the measures have no safety value but infringe on the rights of the students, I would not be in favor of them. Let me explain my position with examples.

Security guards in the school, and even a local police precinct located in a school, can be very beneficial for all involved. In this way, students and police generally get to know each other on a more personal basis and can begin to trust and respect each other. If a police officer knew the students on a personal, informal basis, it might help him or her not to jump to conclusions based on a student's appearance or perceived behavior. It also might afford the students the opportunity to talk to the police when they thought trouble might be coming.

Since it is easy to hide a weapon in a backpack, another safeguard that might be helpful is not allowing students to carry backpacks to class. The backpacks can be kept in the lockers and only books carried to class. Schools might need to adjust the time allowed for changing between classes so students have the time to go to their lockers to exchange their books. This would be a minor modification and could mean a big difference in the safety of all the students.

On the other hand, I do not believe that all proposed changes would lead to greater student safety. For example, requiring students to wear uniforms would not have much impact on improving safety. Granted, in some schools, certain dress may have the appearance of gang clothing, but I think this is a limited argument. Dress, as long as it does not contain obscene material and sufficiently covers the student, is a matter of personal style. I do not believe it is the school's job to try to make everyone alike. Schools attempt to create individuals who can think critically and take a stand on an issue. By making everyone look alike, they tend to send the message that everyone should think alike. I do not believe that this is the job of school.

In summary, I believe that there are measures that can be taken to improve safety in schools. They should be well thought out and not unduly infringe on the rights of students in the school. In other words, the measures taken should have the sole purpose of improving safety of everyone in the school.

CHAPTER 4

PRAXIS CORE PRACTICE TESTS

Taking Your Practice Tests

Now that you're more familiar with the format and content of the Praxis Core tests, it's time for full-length practice. Your official Praxis Core tests will be administered on computer, and you have additional practice tests to take in your online resources (more on those shortly). For your convenience, Kaplan has included three full-length Core Practice Tests—one each for Reading, Math, and Writing—in this chapter.

The best practice is to take these tests under timed, test-like conditions. On the official exam, you won't be allowed to have a cell phone or any other electronic items with you. So, during your in-book practice tests, turn off your phone and computer or tablet. Find a quiet environment in which you will not be interrupted while taking the test. Time yourself using a watch or kitchen timer. To get used to the test day experience, take any notes on plain scratch paper.

When you're done, review the entire exam, question by question, using the Kaplan explanations. While it's important to build up your concentration and stamina by taking full-length tests, reviewing the explanations is where much of your learning and improvement actually takes place. Review even the questions you got right. The explanations often point out patterns and strategies you can use to tackle the questions efficiently and confidently on your official exam.

In your online resources, you have the following additional practice materials:

- Two full-length Praxis Core Reading Practice Tests with complete answers and explanations
- Two full-length Praxis Core Math Practice Tests with complete answers and explanations
- Two full-length Praxis Core Writing Practice Tests with complete answers and explanations

GO ONLINE

kaptest.com/login

Keep in mind the exhortations above about creating a test-like environment for your full-length practice. The same goes whether you're testing from your book or online.

Core Reading Practice Test 1

85 Minutes—56 Questions

Directions: You have 85 minutes to complete the Reading Test. In this section of the test, each statement or passage is followed by one or more questions based on its content. After reading a statement or passage, select the best answer to each question from among the five choices below it. Base your answer to each question on what the statement or passage actually says. You will not need to have any prior knowledge of the topics in the statements and passages in order to answer the questions.

Try to answer every question and mark all of your answers so you can check your work later.

When Babe Ruth was traded from the Boston Red Sox to the New York Yankees in 1920 for $100,000, most thought it was a bad trade. Few could have predicted that the Yankees, who had never before won a World Series title, would go on to become the most successful franchise in sports history or that, inversely, the Red Sox, who had won the World Series five times before the Ruth trade, would not again win a World Series title until 2004, and then again in 2007, 2013, and 2018.

1. According to the statements above, the Red Sox have won how many World Series titles?

   A. Nine

   B. Six

   C. Five

   D. One

   E. None

America had remained neutral in World War I before the sinking of the passenger ship *Lusitania* by the Germans on May 7, 1915. Until that time, America was offering only financial and tactical support for Britain and France against Germany and Austria-Hungary. However, the sinking of the huge passenger ship altered public opinion about U.S. involvement and subsequently led to military escalation, truly making the war a matter for the whole world.

2. The main idea of the passage is that

   A. the Germans sank the *Lusitania* in response to America's financial and tactical support for Britain and France

   B. Austria-Hungary and Germany were allies in World War I

   C. American involvement in World War I was minimal

   D. the sinking of the *Lusitania* prompted increased American involvement in World War I

   E. the German government was justified in sinking the *Lusitania*

Louis "Satchmo" Armstrong was born in New Orleans in 1901. In his childhood, he worked on a junk wagon, cleaned graves, and sold coal—anything to make ends meet. As a self-taught cornet player entertaining on the streets of New Orleans, Armstrong caught the eye of Joe "King" Oliver, an established trumpet player in Kid Ory's band. Soon after he began to study with Oliver, Armstrong found a place in Ory's band and continued as a professional performer for the rest of his life. He popularized jazz and scat singing and influenced numerous musicians who came after him.

3. According to the statement above, Armstrong was first noticed by an established musician while

   A. selling coal as a youngster

   B. scat singing in Kid Ory's band

   C. playing the cornet on street corners

   D. studying with Joe "King" Oliver

   E. popularizing jazz with Joe "King" Oliver

Questions 4–6

Cats were first domesticated 4,000 years ago by the ancient Egyptians, who revered them as household gods. By the third century BCE, the domestic cat was widely distributed across Europe, thanks to seafaring Greek merchants and colonizers who associated cats with the goddess Artemis and used them to protect their grain supplies.

After millions of the creatures were slaughtered alongside the hundreds of thousands of pagans, heretics, and Jews with whom they were associated during the Middle Ages, cats may have gotten their revenge. The absence of cats in Europe probably contributed to the spread and the severity of the bubonic plague that devastated the continent in the 14th century.

4. Which of the following would be an appropriate title for the passage?

   A. Ancient Egyptian Deities

   B. From Gods to Outcasts: The Early History of the Domestic Cat

   C. Cats and the Bubonic Plague

   D. Cats and Dogs from Antiquity Through the Middle Ages

   E. The Goddess Artemis and the Domestic House Cat

5. It can be inferred from the passage that

   A. after cats were slaughtered in the Middle Ages, the rodent population in Europe increased

   B. cats are a vengeful species

   C. Greek merchants sold domestic cats for large sums of money

   D. the bubonic plague could be spread through cats

   E. cats were especially popular house pets among pagans, heretics, and Jews

6. Which of the following best describes the relationship between the two paragraphs in the passage?

   A. The first paragraph describes a time period when the subject matter was generally viewed positively, and the second paragraph describes a time period with the subject matter was generally viewed negatively.

   B. The first paragraph introduces a claim about the subject matter, and the second paragraph refutes the evidence for this claim.

   C. The first paragraph presents one theory about the subject matter, and the second paragraph presents an alternative theory about the subject matter.

   D. The first paragraph introduces a topic, and the second paragraph introduces a new topic.

   E. The first paragraph conveys the author's positive viewpoint about the subject matter, while the second paragraph conveys the author's reservations about the subject matter.

Questions 7–11

     Alchemy is the name given to the attempt to change lead, copper, and other metals into silver or gold. Today, alchemy is regarded as a pseudoscience. Its associations with astrology
(5) and the occult suggest primitive superstition to the modern mind, and the alchemist is generally portrayed as a charlatan obsessed with dreams of impossible wealth. However, for many centuries, alchemy was a highly respected art.
(10) In the search for the elusive secret to making gold, alchemists helped to develop many of the apparatuses and procedures that are used in laboratories today. Moreover, the results of their experiments laid the basic conceptual framework
(15) for the modern science of chemistry.

     The philosophy underlying the practice of alchemy emerged in similar forms in ancient China, India, and Greece. They regarded gold as the "purest" and "noblest" of all metals and
(20) believed that "base" metals such as copper and lead were only imperfectly developed forms of gold. With purification, the alchemists believed that base metals attained a state of perfection, just as human souls attained a perfect state in
(25) heaven.

     In the 12th century, translations of Arabic works on alchemy started to become available in Europe, generating a new wave of European interest in the art. Ultimately, the possibility of
(30) making gold was conclusively disproved in the 19th century. Yet, this belief provided the basis for some of the most fascinating chapters in the history of science.

7. According to the passage, why are alchemists not favorably regarded today?

  A. Their secret techniques have mostly been forgotten.

  B. The results of all of their experiments were disproved.

  C. Europeans were not interested in Middle Eastern art forms.

  D. Their connection with astrology seems superstitious to scientists.

  E. Many of their apparatuses and procedures are out-of-date.

8. What does the passage imply about the process of "purifying" metals?

  A. It was perfected by the Europeans.

  B. It was distorted in translations of Arabic works.

  C. The alchemists regarded it as similar to a spiritual experience.

  D. It was discovered in the 12th century.

  E. Few people realized its commercial value.

9. The author would most likely agree with which of the following statements about alchemy?

  A. Belief in alchemy delayed scientific progress for centuries.

  B. The principles of alchemy are still valid today.

  C. Modern chemistry owes nothing to the achievements of the alchemists.

  D. Though not a science, alchemy is an important part of scientific history.

  E. Most alchemists wanted to produce gold only for their own financial benefit.

10. Which of the following could be substituted for the phrase "a pseudoscience" in lines 3–4 with the least change in meaning?

    A. A fanciful belief

    B. A phony discipline

    C. A technical field

    D. An antiquated practice

    E. An experimental topic

11. Which of the following best describes the organization of the first paragraph?

    A. It explains a problem, offers a modern solution, and then identifies an alternative solution.

    B. It contrasts a historical practice with a modern practice, then describes the drawbacks of each.

    C. It describes a historical phenomenon chronologically.

    D. It identifies a theory, then proves the theory with examples.

    E. It identifies why a topic is often viewed negatively, then explains the basis of an opposing view of the topic.

Questions 12–14

A human body can survive without water for several days and without food for as long as several weeks. However, if breathing stops for as little as three to six minutes, death is likely. All animals require a constant supply of oxygen to the body tissues and especially to the heart or brain. In the human body, the respiratory and circulatory systems perform this function by delivering oxygen to the blood, which then transports it to tissues throughout the body. Once there, the oxygen aids in the conversion of nutrients to usable energy. Respiration in large animals, however, involves more than just breathing in oxygen. It is a complex process that delivers oxygen while eliminating carbon dioxide produced by cells.

12. According to the passage, which bodily function is least essential to the immediate survival of the average human being?

    A. Eating

    B. Drinking

    C. Breathing

    D. Blood circulation

    E. Sleeping

13. The function of the first sentence in the passage is to

    A. provide scientific facts that are essential to understanding the rest of the passage

    B. argue that food is relatively unimportant for human survival

    C. highlight the importance of breathing for human survival, as described in the next sentence

    D. supply examples that will be explained in the remainder of the passage

    E. criticize popular misconceptions about the importance of nutrition for human survival

14. According to the passage, which of the following best describes the relationship between human body tissues and the human brain?

    A. Both require sufficient amounts of oxygen, but the brain requires a more steady supply.

    B. Both require sufficient amounts of oxygen, but the body tissues require a more steady supply.

    C. The brain requires sufficient amounts of oxygen, while the body tissues do not.

    D. Both require sufficient amounts of oxygen, but only the brain requires the removal of carbon dioxide.

    E. The cells of both would die after three minutes without oxygen.

The number of chronically hungry people in the world is expected to decrease by nearly one half by 2030, according to recent computer models. Whereas this estimate is encouraging, it falls short of previous estimates that anticipated world hunger to be halved by 2015. The model concludes that global grain production will need to increase by 1.2 percent every year to meet demands for food and feed.

15. The tone of the statement above is best described as

    A. pessimistic

    B. discouraged

    C. critical

    D. passionate

    E. guardedly optimistic

Scientists are able to predict the occurrence of earthquakes with a reasonable degree of accuracy using a device called a seismograph. In 1990, scientists used a seismograph to predict that City *X* would experience a major earthquake in 1994. However, no major earthquake actually occurred.

16. Based only on the information above, which of the following statements is a valid conclusion?

    A. City *X* will probably experience a major earthquake in the next few years.

    B. Natural disasters are impossible for scientists to predict.

    C. Scientists are currently researching other ways of predicting earthquakes.

    D. Seismographic predictions are not always reliable.

    E. City *X* actually experienced a minor earthquake in 1994.

The media is really out of control. When the press gets a story, it seems that within minutes, they have produced flashy moving graphics and sound effects to entice viewers and garner ratings. Real facts and unbiased coverage of an issue are totally abandoned in exchange for an overly sentimental or one-sided story that too often distorts the truth. Viewers need to learn to recognize real reporting from the junk on nearly every television channel these days.

17. The author would most likely agree with which of the following statements?

    A. Newspapers should have more editorials.

    B. Flashy graphics add substance to television news reporting.

    C. Objective news reporting is a dying art.

    D. Television news anchors are valuable sources of information.

    E. Television news needs more human interest stories.

Questions 18–20

In computer design, the effectiveness of a program generally depends on the ability of the programmer. Still, remarkable progress has been made in the development of artificial intelligence. (5) In light of this progress, scientists wonder whether it will eventually be possible to develop a computer capable of intelligent thought. When a computer defeated Garry Kasparov, considered by many the greatest chess player of all time, it (10) was taken to be a vindication of the claims of the strongest supporters of artificial intelligence. Despite this accomplishment, others argue that whereas computers may imitate the human mind, they will never possess the capacity for (15) true intelligence.

18. The main idea of this passage is that

    A. computers can never learn to think

    B. chess is a game in which computers are superior

    C. great strides have been made in artificial intelligence

    D. artificial intelligence is a scientific miracle

    E. Garry Kasparov is a great chess player

19. The author mentions "Garry Kasparov" (line 8) most likely in order to

    A. provide an example of a computer performing the equivalent of human thought

    B. argue that the quality of a computer program depends on how well it was programmed

    C. prove that Kasparov is not the world's greatest chess player

    D. refute the claim that computers will be capable of intelligent thought

    E. identify evidence used by those who think computers will someday be able to think intelligently

20. As used in line 11, "strongest" most nearly means

    A. most vocal

    B. most muscular

    C. firmest

    D. most powerful

    E. brawniest

Questions 21–24

It is the use of language that sets humans apart from animals. Language is what enables us to reveal our conscious selves, to transmit knowledge to each other and to succeeding
(5) generations, to discuss and debate ideas, and to build and maintain the framework of civilization.

Is a human born with the innate capacity for language, or is language a complex form of behavior that one learns as a child? Although
(10) this question is still unanswered, it is clear from the work of neuroscientists that once a human possesses language, certain structures and areas of the brain do control its use.

Nineteenth-century scientist Pierre Paul Broca,
(15) for example, discovered the specific region of the brain that controls the flow of words from brain to mouth: he did the autopsy of a brain-damaged patient who had been incapable of speaking for over 20 years and found the lesion in the brain
(20) tissue that had caused the problem. The area of the brain that enables us to comprehend speech was located by Broca's contemporary Carl Wernicke in a similar way.

21. The author's claim about what "language" entails (lines 2–6) is made primarily by using

    A. quotations

    B. scientific data

    C. generalizations

    D. analogies

    E. inferences

22. The function of the question in the second paragraph (lines 7–9) is to

    A. present a scientific dilemma that has been resolved

    B. suggest that there are some questions that scientists are not addressing

    C. summarize an issue that is the subject of continued debate

    D. outline the position of the author

    E. introduce a topic that will be discussed for the rest of the passage

23. The author discusses the work of Broca and Wernicke in the third paragraph to illustrate

    A. the method by which early discoveries were made about the brain and language

    B. the imprecision of the techniques of 19th-century scientists

    C. some parts of the brain involved in language use

    D. the study of language processing in the brain of normal patients

    E. the range of neuroscientific ideas about where language is processed in the brain

24. As used in line 7, "innate" most nearly means

    A. infantile

    B. essential

    C. acquired

    D. inborn

    E. objective

Questions 25–27

Desert plants have evolved very special adaptations for living in extremely dry conditions. Most have small, thick leaves, an adaptation that limits water loss by reducing surface area
(5) relative to volume. During the driest months, some desert plants shed their leaves. Others, such as cacti, subsist on water the plant stores in its fleshy stems during the rainy season. Some send out long, deep taproots in order to
(10) reach underlying water. Others have developed shallow, widespread root systems, which allow them to take advantage of very occasional but heavy rainfalls. Some plants have ways of actively protecting their water supplies. The creosote
(15) bush, for instance, produces a powerful poison that discourages the growth of competing root systems.

25. The passage is primarily concerned with

    A. the discovery of stomates

    B. the process of photosynthesis

    C. how desert plants adapt to survive

    D. competition between plants in the desert

    E. the shortage of water in the desert

26. Based on the information provided, which of the following weather conditions would most benefit plants with wide, shallow root systems?

    A. A prolonged drought

    B. A windstorm

    C. A light spring rain

    D. A winter snowfall

    E. A flash flood

27. The author most likely mentions the "desert plants" that "shed their leaves" (line 6) in order to

    A. provide an example of a way some plants have adapted to dry conditions

    B. highlight an interesting desert plant

    C. provide an example of a way some plants protect their water supplies in dry conditions

    D. argue that some adaptations to dry conditions are better than others

    E. contrast such plants with those that have "small, thick leaves"

The actor who played the Tin Man in the movie *The Wizard of Oz* was not the first choice to play that role. Another actor was cast for the role but had to be replaced because he was allergic to the makeup for the role.

28. According to the statements above, which of the following must be true?

    A. The originally cast actor was generally considered a better actor than his replacement.

    B. Actors can be allergic to the makeup used in films.

    C. It is very unusual for actors to be allergic to makeup.

    D. The originally cast actor had to give up his acting career because of his unusual illness.

    E. The actor originally cast as the Tin Man would have become rich and famous if he had played that role.

Local elementary schools have changed considerably over the past 50 years. Where we once had schools in every small town, now students bus for miles to attend larger, more advanced schools. Whereas most parents see this as a positive step for progress and education, some worry about their children losing touch with the simple things around them. A few have even decided to homeschool their children instead of sending them to school in nearby towns.

29. The author's attitude toward the changes to elementary schools in the past 50 years can best be described as

    A. embittered

    B. objective

    C. biased

    D. ambivalent

    E. accusatory

Questions 30–32

Most life is fundamentally dependent on photosynthetic organisms that store radiant energy from the sun. The existence of organisms that are not dependent on the sun's light has long
(5) been established, but until recently, they were regarded as anomalies. However, over the last 20 years, research in deep-sea areas has revealed the existence of entire ecosystems in which the primary energy producers are bacteria that are
(10) dependent on energy from within the earth itself. Larger organisms that cannot produce their own energy consume these bacteria, creating a cycle of energy production and consumption that supports an entire deep-sea ecosystem. Indeed,
(15) growing evidence suggests that these unique chemosynthetic ecosystems model the way in which life first came about on this planet.

30. The passage suggests that most life is ultimately dependent on what?

    A. Deep-sea hot springs

    B. The world's oceans

    C. Bacterial microorganisms

    D. Light from the sun

    E. Chemosynthesis

31. Why does the passage describe this ecosystem as "unique" (line 15)?

    A. It has no need for an environmental source of energy.

    B. It thrives in the absence of sunlight.

    C. It exists in airless, waterless surroundings.

    D. It is infested with dangerous octopods.

    E. It is the only ecosystem found in deep ocean water.

32. The author mentions "research in deep-sea areas" (line 7) most likely in order to

    A. give evidence that chemosynthetic organisms are unusual

    B. demonstrate the superiority of chemosynthetic ecosystems over other types of ecosystems

    C. argue that the first life on earth used energy from sources other than the sun

    D. show a contrast with chemosynthetic ecosystems

    E. provide evidence that there is more life that is not dependent on energy from sunlight than originally thought

Questions 33–38

Passage 1

Although it still isn't exactly mainstream, many people practice meditation. Mindfulness meditation, in particular, has become more popular in recent years. The practice involves
(5) sitting comfortably, focusing on one's breathing, and bringing the mind's attention to the present. Releasing all concerns, an individual can picture worries popping like a bubble or flitting away like a butterfly.

(10) Practitioners of mindfulness enjoy a better quality of experience, deeper engagement, and greater measure of fulfillment. Additionally, the emotional benefits include reduced negative emotions, increased self-awareness, and stress
(15) management skills. Dr. Robert Schneider, director of the Institute for Natural Medicine and Prevention, says, "I have been researching effects of meditation on health for thirty years and have found it has compelling benefits."

Passage 2

(20) Every week, Representative Tim Ryan, a Democrat from Ohio, hosts a mindfulness meditation session for his staff and any other members of Congress who want to join. Ryan believes that the benefits of meditation ought
(25) to appeal to members of both parties and is an advocate for the benefits of meditation on health, performance, and social awareness.

Word seems to be spreading around Capitol Hill. "I've had members of Congress approach
(30) me and say, 'I want to learn more about this,'" Ryan says. "Between the fundraising, being away from family, [and] the environment of hyperpartisanship, Washington is really stressing people out." Ryan supports legislation
(35) that puts meditation to good use for everyone. Among other bills, he has sponsored one to increase the holistic-medicine offerings of the Department of Veterans Affairs.

33. Both passages support which generalization about mindfulness meditation?

    A. It can be embraced by adherents of any political philosophy.

    B. It is making inroads into U.S. culture.

    C. It should be utilized in public institutions.

    D. It will soon be embraced by the American public.

    E. It promotes spiritual well-being.

34. Which best categorizes how the author of Passage 1 feels about mindfulness meditation?

    A. Passionate

    B. Skeptical

    C. Critical

    D. Neutral

    E. Supportive

35. Both authors do which of the following?

    A. Include testimonies of actual practitioners of mindfulness meditation

    B. Provide the history of mindfulness meditation

    C. Use quotes from others to support their claims

    D. Argue against the detractors of mindfulness meditation

    E. Use statements from health experts to provide evidence for their views

36. Which best describes the relationship between Passage 1 and Passage 2?

    A. Passage 1 explains a practice and its benefits, and Passage 2 describes why and how a practitioner supports the practice.

    B. Passage 1 provides an example of a health practice, and Passage 2 explains why the practice is beneficial.

    C. Passage 1 presents a theory about a health practice, and Passage 2 provides evidence against the theory.

    D. Passage 1 describes a widespread cultural phenomenon, and Passage 2 gives a real-life example of a practitioner of the phenomenon.

    E. Passage 1 provides an expert's view of a health practice, and Passage 2 provides an alternative expert view of the practice.

37. Which of the following, if true, would most weaken the argument in Passage 1 regarding mindfulness meditation?

    A. Many health insurance plans do not currently cover mindfulness meditation sessions.

    B. Other forms of meditation have positive results similar to those of mindfulness meditation.

    C. Dr. Robert Schneider does not actually practice mindfulness meditation.

    D. Many practitioners of mindfulness meditation report increased anxiety after meditation sessions.

    E. A small number of mindfulness meditation practitioners experience a deep sense of well-being after meditation sessions.

38. As used in line 19, "compelling" most nearly means

    A. creative

    B. judicial

    C. persuasive

    D. urgent

    E. interesting

According to a recent school survey, the number of students who regularly play after-school sports has increased by 50 percent in the last 10 years. It must be the increased interest in health and physical fitness among the students in our school that has massively reduced the amount of pizza purchased in the cafeteria.

39. Which of the following, if true, would most weaken the argument above?

   A. Most of the students who now play after-school sports do so only for social reasons.

   B. School health teachers have time and again spoken about the importance of a low-fat diet.

   C. Fifteen years ago, the school switched from requiring physical education to making it an optional program.

   D. Not all students responded to the survey.

   E. Pizza was never very popular in the cafeteria.

It was without a sense of humor that the foreign ambassador responded to allegations that his driver had over 2,000 unpaid parking tickets. For a moment, it seemed as if he would perhaps go item by item to discount the allegation. Not only did he demand an apology for the way the story had been handled by the press, but he also insinuated that the incident might actually affect the two countries' relations in the future. One thing that was never addressed was the fact that the tickets have still not been paid.

40. It can be inferred from the passage that the foreign ambassador would be most likely to

   A. support a resolution to grant diplomats immunity from parking tickets

   B. support a call for more police on the beat

   C. admit involvement in parking scams around the city

   D. return to his country if the tickets were paid

   E. use mass transit instead of his car

Whereas Major League Baseball players' salaries skyrocket because of owners' willingness to overpay for top players, NBA salaries follow a system of paying players based on experience. This system rewards veterans and keeps players happy. The most recent infusion of international talent into the NBA has only broadened the league's marketability overseas. Previously untapped markets in places as far away as China, Japan, Russia, and Australia are now opening up to the NBA, thus giving players even more leverage at the bargaining table.

41. According to the statement above, the NBA's marketability will increase because

   A. players are getting more money from owners

   B. Major League Baseball is losing fans

   C. international markets are opening up to the game

   D. its system rewards veteran players

   E. basketball owners do not overpay their top players

Questions 42–46

All telescopes use curved lenses to focus the light from distant objects, such as stars. Generally, the larger a telescope is, the greater its magnifying power. Telescopes can use two
(5) different kinds of lenses. The first telescopes, made during the 16th century, were refractors. However, their perfectly round lenses did not focus light sharply. Lenses made of a single piece of glass also bent light of different colors
(10) differently, producing color distortions.

Meanwhile, the problems of refractors led some telescope makers to experiment with reflectors. They used mirrors that were not perfectly round and that therefore sharply
(15) focused the light. Moreover, mirrors did not produce color distortions. But these early reflectors had other problems. They were made of polished metal, which did not reflect light well. Also, metal mirrors often cracked as they cooled
(20) after being cast.

For two hundred years, opticians worked to perfect both kinds of telescopes. Finally, in 1851, two Englishmen, Varnish and Mellish, found a way to cover glass with a very thin sheet of (25) silver. This made it possible to build reflecting telescopes using a large curved mirror made of silver-covered glass. These telescopes reflected much more light than earlier reflectors and did not crack so easily. Today, nearly all large optical (30) telescopes are built on this basic design.

42. The passage is primarily concerned with

    A. the design of modern telescopes

    B. how the telescope was developed

    C. the problems of early telescopes

    D. the experiments of Varnish and Mellish

    E. how lenses are made

43. The passage suggests that there is usually a relationship between the size of a telescope and its

    A. ability to reflect light

    B. magnifying power

    C. resistance to cracking

    D. accuracy in focusing light

    E. ability to bend light of different colors equally

44. Some early telescope makers experimented with reflecting telescopes because

    A. refractors had not yet been invented

    B. they did not need telescopes with great magnifying power

    C. opticians had stopped working to build better refractors

    D. early refractors produced distorted images

    E. opticians had found a way to coat glass with silver

45. The passage suggests that telescope makers most likely want to construct larger telescopes in order to

    A. avoid the blurred images produced by small telescopes

    B. be able to view a wider range of colors

    C. enlarge the focused image for easier viewing

    D. create a more polished metal surface

    E. reduce the need to use silver-coated glass for lenses

46. Which of the following best describes the organization of the passage?

    A. The problems of two different types of telescopes are explained, and then a solution is described.

    B. The debate about two different types of telescopes is explained, and then the author concludes that one is superior.

    C. A complete history of the development of the telescope is provided.

    D. The basic mechanics of telescopes are explained, and then examples of telescopes are described.

    E. The drawbacks of different types of telescopes are explained, and then the author rejects the usage of one type.

Questions 47–49

In order to better predict how much inventory to order next summer, the manager at the concession stand at Brunswick Beach kept a record of how many items of each available type (ice cream cones, soft drinks, and pizza slices) were sold each month of last summer's operating season. The manager also noted the average temperature for each month: May: 74°, June: 83°, July: 87°, and August: 88°. Below is a graph of the data collected.

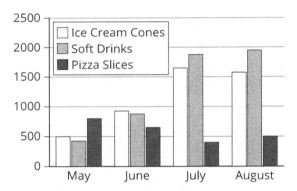

Concession Items Sold at Brunswick Beach

47. Which month had the lowest total concession sales by number of items sold?

    A. May

    B. June

    C. July

    D. August

    E. The answer cannot be determined from the given information.

48. Which of the following statements is supported by the information provided?

    Select <u>all</u> that apply.

    A. For the whole summer, the concession stand made the least amount of profit on pizza sales compared to either ice cream cone or soft drink sales.

    B. As the temperature increased from month to month over the summer, sales of soft drinks also increased.

    C. The product with the highest total number of items sold for the entire summer was ice cream cones.

49. Based on the information provided, which of the following is the best explanation for the differences between concession item sales in May and sales in August?

    A. Most visitors to the beach in warmer months avoid purchasing from the concession stand and spend all their time in the water instead.

    B. The sole supplier of the concession items could only supply 500 pizza slices in August.

    C. There are fewer visitors to the beach in cooler months, so sales of each item are at their lowest then.

    D. Visitors to the beach prefer to purchase hot food when the outside temperature is higher and prefer cold food and drinks when the outside temperature is lower.

    E. Visitors to the beach prefer hot food when the outside temperature is lower and prefer cold food and drinks when the outside temperature is higher.

Questions 50–53

The dancer and choreographer Martha Graham is regarded as one of the outstanding innovators in the history of dance. Trained in a variety of international dance styles, she set
(5) out in the mid-1920s to break away from the rigid traditions of classical ballet. She wanted to create new dance forms and movements that would reflect the changed atmosphere of the post–World War One period. Her early dances
(10) reflect this spirit. For instance, discouragement and isolation are themes in her dances, reflecting events like the Great Depression. She avoided decorative sets and costumes and used an all-female dance troupe. In fact, Graham's early work
(15) was so stark and severe that it was described by one critic as "uncompromisingly ugly."

As the decades passed, Graham's work found wider acceptance. By the 1940s, it had already become the tradition against which a new avant-
(20) garde was rebelling; this is a fate common to all artistic revolutions. Even in the face of this later resistance, Graham's influence on dance was profound. She is considered by many today as the forerunner of modern dance. Her dance principle
(25) referred to as "Contraction and Release" mirrors the breathing cycle and also emphasizes the spiraling movement of the torso. This technique is considered foundational to modern dance; Graham's legacy lives on in the expressive moves
(30) of countless dancers today.

50. According to the passage, Martha Graham introduced new dance techniques in order to

    A. attract attention to her all-female troupe

    B. visually dramatize the ugliness of life

    C. express the changed mood of her time

    D. strike a blow against the traditions of classical ballet

    E. emphasize the rigidity of conventional dance movement

51. It can be inferred from the passage that classical ballet of the early 20th century generally

    A. was loose and formless

    B. was initially disliked by critics and the public

    C. sought to dramatize ugliness

    D. reflected the changing times

    E. employed elaborate sets and costumes

52. Which of the following best illustrates the "fate common to all artistic revolutions" (lines 20–21) that the passage describes?

    A. A revolutionary method of painting that is eventually accepted but later rejected by innovative artists

    B. A style of musical composition that ignores the rules of harmony and emphasizes dissonance and ugly sounds

    C. A movement in fiction that focuses on the gritty aspects of everyday life, rather than its beautiful aspects

    D. A new trend in theatrical performance that never achieves widespread popularity and is eventually forgotten

    E. A technical innovation in cinematography that makes moviemaking much less expensive

53. The function of the quoted phrase "uncompromisingly ugly" (line 16) is to

    A. refute the argument that Graham's early work was terrible

    B. provide an example of how Graham's early work was viewed

    C. supply evidence for the author's opinion about Graham's early work

    D. argue that Graham's work would never be accepted in her lifetime

    E. criticize Graham's early work as extremely displeasing to viewers

Despite a steady stream of pessimistic forecasts, our economy continues to grow and prosper. Over the last 15 years, the service sector of our economy has greatly expanded. Last year alone, 500,000 Americans found employment in the service sector. In the face of evidence such as this, one cannot argue that our economy is wilting.

54. Which of the following, if true, would most seriously undermine the conclusion drawn in the statements above?

   A. Many Americans who took jobs in the service sector last year were also offered jobs in other sectors of the economy.

   B. Most of the job growth in the service sector can be attributed to people being forced out of the declining manufacturing sector.

   C. American society has developed many programs that greatly offset the consequences of a sluggish economy.

   D. Forty years ago, the American economy experienced a period of prosperity far greater than that of today.

   E. The importance of the service sector in determining the well-being of the overall American economy has decreased slightly in the past 10 years.

The jaguarundi is a species of cat native to Central and South America. Jaguarundis are most often found in lowland habitats with good cover. They are solitary hunters who tend to roam the floor of the rainforest, using the features of their habitat to their advantage. There has been some debate as to when the jaguarundis hunt. Although the bulk of data points to a diurnal, or daytime, hunting schedule, there is evidence that some jaguarundis adopt a crepuscular hunting schedule. These jaguarundis emerge to hunt in the twilight of dusk and dawn.

55. Which of the following can be inferred from the passage?

   A. Jaguarundis hunt only during dusk and dawn.

   B. The vegetation on the floor of the rainforest aids jaguarundis in hunting.

   C. All jaguarundis live in Central and South America.

   D. Most jaguarundis are diurnal hunters who hunt at night.

   E. Some jaguarundis are herbivorous.

You can change your car's oil safely and fairly easily by following these steps. First, make sure the car is stationary and on a level surface, with the emergency brake engaged. Next, locate the drain plug for the oil under the engine. Remember to place the oil pan under the plug before you start. Remove the plug and let the oil drain out. When it has drained fully, wipe off the drain plug and the plug opening, and then replace the drain plug. Next, simply place your funnel in the engine and pour in new oil, replacing the oil cap when you're done. Finally, run the engine for a minute, and then check the dipstick to see if you need to add more oil.

56. According to the passage, immediately after draining the old oil from the engine, one should

   A. replace the oil cap

   B. run the engine for a moment and check the dipstick

   C. wipe off and replace the drain plug

   D. engage the emergency brake

   E. make sure the car is stationary and on a level surface

IF YOU FINISH BEFORE TIME IS CALLED, YOU MAY CHECK YOUR WORK ON THIS SECTION ONLY. DO NOT TURN TO ANY OTHER SECTION IN THE TEST. **STOP**

222

Core Reading Practice Test 1 Answers and Explanations

1. A

Detail. This is a Detail question that demonstrates the efficacy of reading the question before the passage on statement questions. Much of the information is irrelevant: skim to the end to find only the facts you need. The passage states that before the Ruth trade, the Red Sox had won the series five times; they then went through a title drought but have won it four times this century. So as of the writing of this article, the Red Sox had won a total of nine World Series titles, meaning (**A**) is correct.

2. D

Global. This is a Global question, so reading the passage for details is not necessary. Rather, note that all the details in the passage describe the idea that the sinking of the *Lusitania* prompted increased American involvement in World War I. Choice (**D**) is a paraphrase of this main idea. (A) is out because it distorts a detail found in the passage—implying a causal link between America's support for Britain and France and Germany's sinking of the *Lusitania* that is not supported by the passage. (B) refers to a minor detail in the passage, and (C) is simply not true according to the passage, particularly after the sinking of the *Lusitania*. The passage never discusses whether the German government was "justified" in sinking the *Lusitania*, so (E) is out as well.

3. C

Detail. Be sure to read the question stem first so you can zero in on the specific information you need. According to the passage, Armstrong caught the eye of Joe "King" Oliver while playing the cornet on the streets of New Orleans, so (**C**) is correct. Whereas he did sell coal as a youngster, (A), no established musician took note of him doing so. He joined Kid Ory's band and began studying with Oliver after he was noticed, so (B) and (D) are out. (E) is out because it was Oliver who noticed Armstrong. By the time Armstrong was playing with Oliver, he had already been noticed.

4. B

Global. The passage briefly touches on the history of domestic cats, from ancient Egypt (when they were viewed as household gods) through the Middle Ages (when they were slaughtered by superstitious Christians). Thus, the title "From Gods to Outcasts: The Early History of the Domestic Cat" covers all of these areas, and (**B**) is correct. If the answer does not jump out at you, you can always eliminate incorrect choices, which will either include ideas outside the scope of the passage or be too narrow to represent the passage as a whole. (A) is wrong because the passage is about domestic cats, not "ancient Egyptian deities." (C) is too narrow, given that it refers only to the latter part of the passage. (D) is out because the author never mentions "dogs." Finally, (E) is out because Artemis is only briefly mentioned in the passage.

5. A

Inference. You are told that after cats were slaughtered in the Middle Ages, the absence of cats probably "contributed to the spread and the severity of the bubonic plague that devastated the continent." Why would this be the case? The logical inference is that animals typically hunted by cats must have helped spread the bubonic plague, meaning (**A**) is correct.

You also could have eliminated incorrect choices. (B) is a distortion of the information in the passage; whatever revenge cats wrought was not deliberate on their part. There's nothing in the passage to indicate that Greek merchants sold domestic cats "for large sums of money," (C), and it doesn't follow that the bubonic plague could be "spread through cats" given that their absence, not their presence, precipitated the plague. Finally, just because cats were slaughtered along with "pagans, heretics, and Jews" does not necessarily mean that they were "especially popular house pets" with these groups, as (E) states.

6. A

Function/Organization. Review your notes for the passage and paraphrase each paragraph before looking at the answer choices; since the answer choices for Function questions often mention arguments, also consider whether the author expresses an opinion. The entire passage chronologically describes the history of the cat's relationship with humans; the first paragraph describes a time when the cat was revered, while the second paragraph moves to a time when it was despised. The author does not express a particular claim or opinion in the passage, except for the Emphasis Keywords "slaughtered" and "revenge" in the second paragraph, suggesting the author thinks these actions were extreme. These predictions match choice (**A**). (B) and (C) are incorrect because this informative passage does not present *claims*, *evidence*, or *theories*. Although the first paragraph could be said to introduce the *topic* of humans' relationship with the cat, the second paragraph does not introduce a *new* topic (D); it just continues the same topic. (E) incorrectly equates the descriptions of how the cat was viewed historically with the author's own viewpoints about the cat.

"Alchemy" Passage Map

Main Idea: A review of the history of alchemy shows this pseudoscience of trying to turn base metals to gold contributed to modern science.

¶1: Considered silly today, but contributed to modern science

¶2: Philosophy of alchemy

¶3: Disproved, but significant

7. D

Detail. Lines 3–8 describe the reputation of alchemists today—they tell you alchemy's associations with astrology suggest "primitive superstition" to the modern mind, meaning choice (**D**) is correct. (A) contradicts the gist of the passage, which suggests overall that historians know a lot about alchemy. (B) reflects a detail from paragraph 3, which tells you that the alchemists' idea of making gold was "disproved." However, the passage does not identify this refutation as the reason for alchemists' reputation today; in fact, the passage suggests at the end

of the first paragraph that alchemists' results contributed to chemistry. (C) is contradicted in paragraph 3. (E) distorts paragraph 1, which states that alchemists helped develop modern "apparatuses and procedures."

8. C

Inference. Toward the end of the second paragraph, the passage says, "metals attained a state of perfection, just as human souls attained a perfect state in heaven." You can infer from this that the alchemists regarded the process as a kind of "spiritual experience"—making (**C**) correct. The passage does not mention Europeans in connection with purification, nor does the author suggest that the process was ever perfected, since the possibility of transforming metals into gold was eventually disproved; eliminate (A). The passage does not state or imply any distortion of Arabic works, (B). Paragraph 3 identifies the 12th century as the time when many Europeans became interested in alchemy again after reading Arabic works on the subject, so presumably the purification process was first attempted earlier, and (D) can be eliminated. (E) is a distortion—alchemists were clearly aware that they were trying to make gold, the most valuable of metals.

9. D

Logical Reasoning. Keep in mind the author's main idea as you evaluate the answer choices. The author sums up her point of view on alchemy at the end of the passage— although not practiced today, alchemy "provided the basis for some of the most fascinating chapters in the history of science," making (**D**) correct. (A) and (C) are incorrect because the passage argues that alchemy did contribute to the development of science. (B) is a distortion; although alchemy left some legacies for modern science, its principles have been conclusively disproved. (E) is a also a distortion; although alchemy's goal was to produce gold, the author never identifies financial benefit as alchemists' primary motivation but rather asserts that alchemy was considered "a highly respected art."

10. B

Vocabulary-in-Context. Consider the surrounding context to determine the intended meaning of the phrase "a pseudoscience." The passage states that alchemy is regarded in this manner at present, and it goes on to state alchemy is associated with "primitive superstition" and that an alchemist would today be considered "a charlatan." Predict the phrase must mean a *bogus* or *fake* science, meaning **(B)** is correct. Choice (A) miscategorizes the term "pseudoscience" in context: "fanciful" and "belief" carry connotations of the imagination, rather than of a scientific field that was later disproved. (C) and (E) both lend more authenticity to alchemy than is warranted for a practice associated with "superstition." (D) also misses the mark; although alchemy was practiced only in the past, making it "antiquated," the phrase in question is not addressing alchemy's age but rather whether it is a valid science.

11. E

Function/Organization. It can be easy to get lost in the abstract language of the answer choices on an Organization question, so be sure to paraphrase the paragraph's organization in your own words before looking at the choices. The first paragraph defines alchemy and then explains why it is viewed as a "pseudoscience" today (line 4). Then the Structural Keyword "however" (line 8) signals a contrasting view: its historical respectability and contributions to modern science. Though more abstract in its wording, choice **(E)** matches this prediction. You can eliminate (A) because the passage does not describe problems and solutions. The paragraph does not contrast alchemy with any "modern practice," nor does it offer the "drawbacks" of any modern practices; eliminate (B). (C) could be tempting, as the passage does provide historical background about alchemy, but this information is found mostly in later paragraphs. Further, (C) does not address the contributions of alchemy to modern science, which is the subject of the second half of the paragraph. Likewise, (D) may be tricky; perhaps alchemy itself, its classification as a "pseudoscience," or alchemy's value might be considered a "theory." However, the choice is incorrect because the remainder of the paragraph does not prove either of the first two possible theories, and if alchemy's value is the theory, the answer choice disregards the first half of the paragraph.

12. A

Detail. The first two sentences discuss what the human body needs to survive. Because the body can survive without food longer than it can survive without "drinking," (B), or "breathing," (C), choice **(A)**, "eating," is the least essential to survival. (D) is incorrect because "blood circulation" is mentioned in regard to breathing, which is more essential to survival than eating. (E) is incorrect because "sleeping" is never mentioned in the passage. Always answer questions based entirely on information given in the passage; never rely on outside knowledge to answer a question.

13. C

Function. Paraphrase the function of the portion of the passage in your own words. The entire passage explains that breathing is vital for human survival and describes the basics of the process. The first sentence does not mention breathing, but it introduces the topic by stating that water and food are important for human survival; the Structural Keyword "However" in the next sentence signals that breathing is dramatically more vital. This matches choice **(C)**. Choice (A) is incorrect because although the sentence does contain "scientific facts," these facts are not related to breathing and thus are not strictly necessary to "understanding the rest of the passage." Similarly, (D) incorrectly states that the information in the first sentence will be "explained" by the rest of the passage. You can eliminate (B) and (E) because the passage is informational in tone; the author does not "argue" or "criticize" anything—he certainly does not argue that food is "unimportant," (B), and doesn't even mention "nutrition," (E).

14. A

Connecting Ideas/Connections. Research the text to make a prediction before looking at the answer choices. Both "body tissues" and the "brain" are mentioned in the third sentence. Since "all animals require a constant supply of oxygen to the body tissues and especially to the heart or brain," predict that oxygen is necessary for both and that the brain must need oxygen even more. This matches choice **(A)**. (B) describes the opposite. (C) incorrectly states that the body tissues do not need oxygen at all. (D) distorts the passage; the last sentence explains that large animals require not only the delivery of oxygen to cells but also the removal of carbon dioxide. Nowhere does the passage suggest that body tissues are excluded from this process. (E) is also a distortion; the second sentence claims "death is likely" for the whole organism after "three to six minutes" without breathing, but the passage does not state whether three minutes without oxygen is sufficient to kill the particular cells of the brain and body tissues.

15. E

Writer's View. Since there is only one question, be sure to read the question stem first. You only need to determine the author's tone, so skim the passage for keywords that indicate the author's view. These clues are especially apparent in the sentence that begins with the Structural Keyword "whereas": the expected decrease in hunger is encouraging, but it falls short. Also, the author concludes in the next sentence that global grain production will have to continue to increase over the years. Therefore, the tone of this passage is guardedly optimistic, or **(E)**. Passages on the Praxis tend to avoid an overly negative or positive tone, so practice looking for keywords that indicate subtler viewpoints. Since the author expresses some encouragement, the negative answers of (A), (B), and (C) are incorrect. Neither does the author display a strong viewpoint in this relatively informational passage, so "passionate," (D), is incorrect as well.

16. D

Logical Reasoning. Remember to read the question stem first: you need to determine a valid conclusion that logically follows from the facts in the passage. Notice the keywords about seismographic predictions: they entail "a reasonable degree of accuracy." Then the passage describes an inaccurate prediction. Therefore, choice **(D)** is a valid conclusion. There is no reason to think, at least as far as you know from the passage, that the earthquake is still coming, (A), or that there was a "minor earthquake" instead of the predicted major one, (E), although both are of course possible. (B) is too harsh an indictment of scientists based on the failure of one prediction, and there is no evidence to support (C).

17. C

Logical Reasoning. You know the correct answer will be a statement the author would agree with, so keep in mind the author's viewpoint as you read. The author considers the media and its methods "out of control." Eliminate the answers that do not follow from the passage. (B) clearly contradicts the author's claim that flashy images are used to entice viewers. The author is not likely to agree that "news anchors are valuable sources of information," choice (D), since she differentiates real reporting from junk. Likewise, the author claims news is

overly sentimental, so it is unlikely she thinks the news needs more "human interest stories," (E). (A) is about *newspapers* and therefore goes beyond the scope of the passage. The correct answer will be something that must be true based on what's given in the passage; since the author thinks television news is junk that has abandoned "real facts and unbiased coverage," **(C)** is correct.

18. C

Global. The correct choice for a Main Idea question will express what the author believes and capture the scope of the entire passage. The passage states that "remarkable progress" has been made in artificial intelligence, so choice **(C)** is correct. Whereas the author discusses the difference of opinion between those who believe that there will eventually be a computer capable of intelligent thought and those who do not, he does not assert the truth of either statement, so choice (A) is incorrect. Be wary of answers such as (D) that use extreme language, such as "miracle"; they will be correct only if the passage also contains such extreme language, and this passage does not. Chess is not the main focus of the passage, so (B) and (E) are incorrect.

19. E

Function. Before looking at the answer choices, carefully consider the author's viewpoint and purpose for this passage. This is especially important when the passage presents various opinions. The author believes "remarkable progress" has been made in artificial intelligence and goes on to identify two contrasting viewpoints on the subject. However, the author does not take either side. So why does the author mention Kasparov? He does so in conjunction with the first view, identifying Kasparov's defeat as being interpreted as "a vindication of the claims of the strongest supporters of artificial intelligence" (lines 10–11). Notice that the author does not say the defeat was a vindication, but that it was viewed by the *strongest supporters* of artificial intelligence as a vindication. Therefore, choice **(E)** is correct. Choice (A) may be tempting, but remember that the author never claims that computers are already capable of intelligent thought, only that "remarkable progress" has been made. Choice (B) reflects the first sentence of the passage, but it is not related to Kasparov. (C) is incorrect because the author does not mention Kasparov to make any claims about his chess ability, but rather to serve the discussion of the possibility of artificial intelligence. Finally, the author never "refutes" any claims, so (D) cannot be correct; additionally, the author uses the example of Kasparov with the argument that artificial intelligence is possible, not impossible.

20. C

Vocabulary-in-Context. Consider the context and predict a word that could substitute for "strongest." The sentence describes how the "strongest supporters of artificial intelligence" considered the chess player's defeat by a computer a "vindication" of their views. So predict that "strongest" refers to those who believed in artificial intelligence the most. Since *firm* can mean "lacking uncertainty" or "resolved," this matches (C). (B) and (E) refer to physical strength, which does not fit the context. And although these supporters are wholly convinced of their view, they are not necessarily the "most vocal" about their view or the "most powerful."

21. C

Function. Re-read the sentence in question: what device does the author employ? She uses a list of statements beginning with *to* and a verb that describes how humans use language. It's easy to see that the author here is not using "quotations," (A), or "scientific data," (B). Nor is the author using "analogies," (D), or "inferences," (E). Phrases such as "to discuss and debate ideas" are "generalizations," (C).

22. C

Function. The question that begins paragraph 2 serves to introduce and summarize the debate about language origin. The next sentence says the question is "still unanswered" (line 10), so it is logical to assume debate is continuing—making choice (C) correct. Scientists have not "resolved," as in (A), or failed to address, (B), the issue. The author never takes a position on the issue, so (D) is incorrect. Finally, (E) is incorrect because the topic shifts in the middle of the paragraph from the debate about language origin to the involvement of the brain; the latter, not the former, is the topic of the rest of the passage.

23. C

Function. Scan for the reference to Broca and Wernicke in the third paragraph, and re-read this portion to figure out its relevance to the passage. Notice the keywords "for example" in regard to Broca's work, and then read back to find what Broca's work is an example of: that "certain structures and areas of the brain do control [language's] use" (lines 12–13). This matches choice (C). Although the paragraph does describe the way these discoveries were made, (A), the author includes these scientists' work as examples of how the brain controls language; not primarily as examples to help readers understand the research processes. The author never mentions any "imprecision," (B), or "range of neuroscientific ideas," (E), in relation to early neuroscience work. And the scientists' work was on patients with brain injuries, not "normal patients," (D).

24. D

Vocabulary-in-Context. Search the context for clues before predicting a word that could substitute for "innate." The sentence contrasts (Structural Keyword "or") learning language as a child with being "born with the innate capacity for language." Therefore, predict "innate" means the opposite of something learned: *born with*. This matches choice (D). Beware of alternate definitions of "innate," such as (B), that do not fit the context. Choice (A) is incorrect because you do not need a word that means "like an infant" but rather one that means "something you are naturally born with." Choice (C) is the opposite, as it corresponds with learning language as a child. "Objective," (E), whether meaning "free from bias" or "experience based," does not fit the context of something one is *born with*.

25. C

Global. Resist the urge to get bogged down in the details of this science passage. The first sentence provides the main idea: desert plants have "special adaptations" for living in extremely dry conditions, which corresponds to choice (C). A quick skim of the remainder of the passage reveals that it just lists examples. (A) and (B) are topics pertaining to plants that are not mentioned in the passage. "Competition," (D), is only one aspect of how plants survive, and "shortage of water in the desert," (E), is only discussed in reference to desert plants.

26. E

Inference. Search the passage for the reference to "wide, shallow root systems" and make a prediction. It says that wide, shallow root systems help plants adjust to "occasional, but heavy rainfalls" (lines 12–13). No answer choice matches this exactly, so make an inference: choice (E), "a flash flood," fits the description, since it also constitutes a large amount of water.

27. A

Function. Reviewing the particular structure of this passage should help you determine why the author mentions these particular plants. The first sentence states that desert plants have "special adaptations," and the rest of the paragraph lists examples of plants with these adaptations. Therefore, mentioning these plants serves the purpose of providing an example, making choice (A) correct. The author does not mention them because they are "interesting" (B), but because they are examples of plants that evolved adaptations. Later in the passage, the author lists the "creosote bush" (lines 14–15), not the plant that sheds its leaves, as an example of a plant that *protects* its water supply, (C). The author never makes an argument, so (D) is incorrect. Finally, the author does not mention the plants in question for the purpose of *contrasting* them with any other plants, (E), but rather to provide examples.

28. B

Logical Reasoning. Let's review the facts. The original Tin Man couldn't play the part because he was allergic to the makeup, so he was replaced by another actor. The only conclusion you can draw from this is that it is possible for an actor to be allergic to the makeup used in films, (B). You don't know which actor was "better," (A); how "unusual" this allergy is, (C); what subsequently happened to the original actor, (D); or what would have happened had he played the role, (E), so none of the other choices has to be true.

29. B

Writer's View. After reading the question stem first, you know you only need to determine the author's attitude, so don't focus on the details. There are no strong keywords that signal the author's opinion, so she is likely rather neutral. Rather, Structural Keywords such as "whereas"

and "some" indicate that the author is just relating the differing views of others. Therefore, choice (B) is correct because the passage merely conveys relevant facts about an issue. Whereas the author does describe two opposing reactions that parents have had to the changes in elementary schools, no preference is implied. Therefore, choices (A), (C), and (E) are incorrect. Be cautious with choices such as these that use extreme language. The author never expresses mixed feelings about the subject matter (D); rather, she just does not take a side.

30. D

Inference. Lines 1–3 provide the answer here; they say, "Most life is fundamentally dependent on photosynthetic organisms that store radiant energy from the sun." The question stem asks for what most life is "ultimately" dependent upon—so, it's "light from the sun," (D), not "bacterial microorganisms," (C), that powers most life on earth. The other answer choices refer more to the opposite: the rare chemosynthetic ecosystems that rely on energy from the earth.

31. B

Detail. Research the line reference; the author refers to chemosynthetic ecosystems as "unique." The reason they are unique does not appear in the same sentence, but the Structural Keyword "indeed" highlights that these ecosystems are, according to the previous sentence, "dependent on energy from within the earth itself," in contrast to the photosynthetic ecosystems that depend on sunlight. Therefore, (B) is correct. (A) distorts the passage—it's not that chemosynthetic ecosystems have "no need" for a source of energy. (C) is illogical—these deep-sea ecosystems are plainly not "waterless." (D) is never mentioned, and you're not told if these are the "only" ecosystems found at these depths, (E).

32. E

Function. Think about the function this reference to "research" serves before looking at the answer choices. The entire passage explains that although most life on earth is dependent on energy from the sun, there is some life that gets energy from the earth. In the sentence in question, the Structural Keyword "however" signals a contrast: the previous sentence states that organisms not dependent upon the sun were considered "anomalies" (lines 5–6), but recent studies have found "entire ecosystems" of this type. This reflects choice (**E**). (A) is the opposite—the research shows such organisms are more abundant than originally thought. (B) and (C) misrepresent the author's informative tone, since he never *argues* or claims that anything is *superior*. (D) is entirely incorrect, as the research actually describes chemosynthetic ecosystems.

"Meditation" Passage Map: Passage 1

Main Idea: Mindfulness meditation (MM) has several benefits.

¶1: MM popularity and description

¶2: MM benefits, doctor quote

"Meditation" Passage Map: Passage 2

Main Idea: A politician promotes MM practice.

¶1: Ryan hosts MM for Congress, benefits

¶2: Interest and why

¶3: Ryan supports bills

33. B

Connecting Ideas/Paired Passages. Look for an answer that fits with the purposes of both passages. Both passages discuss the increasingly positive attitudes regarding mindfulness meditation: Passage 1 states it is becoming "more popular" (lines 3–4), while Passage 2 describes the impact of a politician who is successfully promoting meditation in Washington. Only (**B**) reflects this. Avoid choices that are suggested by only one of the passages: (A) and (C) reflect only Passage 2. Furthermore, Passage 2 does not claim mindfulness "should" be in public institutions; it only cites an example of it. (D) is an extreme choice; although it is becoming more popular, neither author claims mindfulness "will soon be embraced." Finally, (E) is not mentioned directly in either passage.

34. E

Connecting Ideas/Paired Passages. Be careful to only consider the viewpoint of the author of Passage 1. Do any keywords hint at the author's opinion? The passage seems fairly objective overall, but notice that the author certainly

endorses mindfulness meditation. In the second paragraph, especially, the author reports on all the potential benefits of the practice as definite results: "practitioners . . . enjoy a better quality of experience" (lines 10–11), and "the emotional benefits include" (lines 12–13). This aligns with "supportive," choice (**E**). Although the view presented is subtle, the author is not entirely "neutral" (D), nor can you go so far as to say the author is "passionate," (A), about the practice. Certainly, the author does not have a negative view (B and C) of mindfulness.

35. C

Connecting Ideas/Paired Passages. Be careful to pinpoint a strategy that *both* authors employ. Beware of choice (A): both passages include quotes from relevant individuals, but Dr. Schneider in Passage 1 *studies* mindfulness meditation—you do not know that he necessarily *practices* it. Neither passage provides the "history of mindfulness," so choice (B) is out. Choice (**C**) is correct: both authors include "quotes from others" (specifically, a doctor and a practitioner) to add to their claims. While both seem to support mindfulness, neither author argues against its "detractors," (D). Finally, only the author of Passage 1 references the words of a "health expert," (E).

36. A

Connecting Ideas/Paired Passages. Think about the purpose of each passage individually before you dive into the answer choices. Passage 1 describes mindfulness meditation and then lists its benefits, using a quote from an expert. Passage 2 describes a prominent public figure who practices meditation and explains how the practice is spreading in Washington. This best matches choice (**A**). (B) is incorrect because Passage 1 does more than give an "example" of a health practice (mindfulness meditation), and Passage 2 only briefly describes its "benefits." Passage 2 certainly does not argue against mindfulness (C). (D) is incorrect because although Passage 1 describes meditation as growing in popularity, a practice that "isn't exactly mainstream" (line 1) cannot be considered a "widespread cultural phenomenon." (E) is incorrect on several counts: although Passage 1 includes an "expert's" statement, there is more to Passage 1 than that, and Passage 2 provides no "expert views" and certainly not an "alternative" viewpoint.

37. D

Connecting Ideas/Paired Passages. Before looking at the answer choices, review Passage 1's argument and consider what type of evidence would weaken it. The author of Passage 1 claims that mindfulness meditation has various experiential and emotional benefits, so a statement that calls into question mindfulness meditation's effectiveness at bringing about these results would undermine the argument. That makes choice **(D)** correct. Whether or not mindfulness meditation is covered by "insurance," (A), is irrelevant to whether it has benefits, as is whether other kinds of mediation have similar results, (B). (C) is incorrect because the quoted doctor is identified as *researching* meditation rather than *practicing* it, so whether or not he practices it does not impact his statement about the results of his research. (E) certainly does not weaken the argument that mindfulness meditation is beneficial; even if *some*, not *all*, practitioners experience "deep . . . well-being," it can still be the case that all practitioners benefit in some way.

38. C

Connecting Ideas/Paired Passages. Predict a word that could substitute for "compelling" in context. Since the author is quoting a health expert who will vouch that mindfulness meditation has health advantages, the context suggests that it has *obvious* or *convincing* benefits. Therefore, **(C)** is correct. Choice (B) is not a meaning of *compelling*, and the other answer choices are alternative meanings of *compelling* that do not fit the context.

39. A

Logical Reasoning. Read the question stem first: you will be reading an argument and will need to determine what type of information would weaken it. Two assumptions hold this argument together. First, the author decides that the survey results mean the student body has become more interested in physical fitness. Then, she decides that this is what has reduced pizza purchases in the cafeteria. So, look for a choice that suggests that either increased participation in after-school sports or reduced purchasing of pizza could be attributed to other factors. You get the former in **(A)**. If most students join intramural sports for "social reasons," then this majority isn't playing sports

because of increased interest in physical fitness—and this destroys one of the author's primary assumptions. (B) would strengthen the author's argument because it could address both assumptions. If the students had really become more interested in physical fitness due to their health teachers' influence, the author would be justified in asserting that such interest was a factor in the decrease in pizza sales. Choice (C) is irrelevant, as a change made to the PE program 15 years ago is not shown in this argument to have had an impact on either of the two assumptions: increased interest in fitness in the past 10 years or a decrease in pizza sales. (D) tries to attack the author's evidence, positing that not all students responded to the survey, but a survey only needs a sufficient representative sample. As for choice (E), it is irrelevant how popular pizza was in the past; all you know is that pizza sales have dropped dramatically.

40. A

Inference. This question asks you to infer what the foreign ambassador might do in a given situation. From the details given, you can infer that the ambassador is someone who expects certain favors and protests "without a sense of humor" when those favors are not granted. Thus, of the choices given, **(A)** makes the most sense, because the ambassador clearly does not feel parking tickets should apply to diplomats. Given his expectation of immunity from paying for parking violations, it is unlikely the ambassador would support more policing and therefore presumably more tickets, choice (B); admit wrongdoing in regard to parking, (C); or prefer to use public transportation, (E). Although the ambassador suggests the incident could impact international relations, he never implies he will leave the country, (D).

41. C

Detail. Read the question first so you can look for just the information you need. The text states, "The most recent infusion of international talent has . . . broadened the league's marketability overseas." Choice **(C)** paraphrases this. Whereas the passage mentions (A), (D), and (E), it does not list them as reasons for the NBA's increasing marketability. (B) is not mentioned at all.

42. B

Global. The passage describes several stages in the development of the modern telescope. So really, the passage is about how the telescope was developed—choice (**B**). (A) and (D) describe paragraph 3 only. (C) describes paragraphs 1 and 2 only. How lenses are produced, (E), isn't really discussed anywhere in the passage.

43. B

Inference. Your notes should indicate the first paragraph describes how telescopes work. The second sentence states that "the larger a telescope is, the greater its magnifying power," so there must be a relationship between telescope size and magnifying power, (**B**). Lines 25–29 suggest that both a telescope's "ability to reflect light," (A), and its "resistance to cracking," (C), are related to the construction of its mirror, not the mirror's size. Lines 13–15 show that telescopes achieved "accuracy in focusing light," (D), regardless of their size, by using "mirrors that were not perfectly round." Lines 8–10 state that color distortions—bending different colors of light differently as in (E)—were caused by single layers of glass, not the telescope's size.

44. D

Connecting Ideas/Connections. This question asks about a cause-and-effect relationship. Your notes should indicate that the second paragraph discusses reflectors. Lines 7–10 describe why scientists moved on to experimenting with reflectors: there were too many problems with refractors. Check the paragraph about refractors to determine the problem: refractors produced "distorted images," as choice (**D**) suggests. (A) is wrong because refractors had already been invented—their issues led to work on reflectors. Lack of "magnifying power," (B), is not mentioned as a problem. (C) is contradicted in lines 21–22, as scientists "worked to perfect both kinds of telescopes." Finally, silver coating, (E), wasn't invented until later, in 1851 (lines 22–25).

45. C

Inference. Lines 3–4 indicate the advantages of building large telescopes: "Generally, the larger a telescope is, the greater its magnifying power." You can infer from this that telescope makers produce larger telescopes to enlarge the focused image for easier viewing. This makes choice (**C**) correct. The passage relates round lens shape (lines 7–8) not to telescope size but to image clarity, (A). The qualities of refractor lenses (lines 8–10), not telescope size, are associated with color distortions, (B). Finally, metal surfaces, (D), and silver-coated lenses, (E), are physical components of reflecting telescopes that have nothing to do with the telescopes' size.

46. A

Function/Organization. Use your notes to paraphrase the paragraph-by-paragraph passage organization before reading the answer choices. The first paragraph introduces telescopes and the benefits and drawbacks of refractors, the second paragraph describes the benefits and drawbacks of reflectors, and the last paragraph explains how opticians optimized reflector telescopes. This best answer mirrors (pun intended) choice (**A**). The development of telescopes is not presented as a "debate," as in (B), nor does the author claim one type is "superior"; rather, he explains that scientists finally perfected one type. The passage provides historical information about telescope lenses, but it certainly does not relate a *full* account of telescope development throughout history, (C). Choice (D) lacks mention of the drawbacks of the telescope types and the eventual development of an ideal model. (E) begins adequately, but the author doesn't *reject* one model; he just describes how one was optimized.

47. A

Connecting Ideas/Infographic. This question requires simply reading data from the graph: just be sure you understand exactly what information is needed. The month with the lowest sales will have the lowest combined bars for the three item types. Clearly, July (C) and August (D) had high sales, so you can eliminate them. Rather than calculating total item sales for each month, compare the bars for May and June to determine if you can estimate which is lower. While sales of pizza were a bit higher in May, ice cream and drinks sales were considerably higher in June, so you can confidently choose (**A**) as lowest. You can determine the answer from the graph, so (E) is incorrect.

48. B

Connecting Ideas/Infographic. Keep in mind overall trends—such as increasing sales for ice cream and soft drinks, and decreasing sales for pizza—over the course of the summer. Then carefully evaluate each answer choice, remembering that more than one may be correct. Be careful about what information you are given and not given; (A) is incorrect, since no information on profits is given. Although the fewest pizza slices were sold in total, you cannot make determine the amount of profit: perhaps, as an exaggerated example, the stand makes $100 in profit per pizza slice sold and 1¢ in profit on each cone and drink. Now evaluate (B). A quick survey of the graph shows that soft drink sales increased each month; check the information in the paragraph to confirm that the temperature also increased each month. **(B)** is correct. Evaluate (C) as well. No need for exact calculations; just estimate. Ice cream had small leads over drinks in May and June, but drinks had large leads in July and August, so soft drinks must have the highest total sales. Only **(B)** is correct.

49. E

Connecting Ideas/Infographic. Before looking at the answer choices, review the relevant information from the graph and paragraph to make a general prediction of what could account for the differences. With the exception of pizza, sales for items were considerably higher in August than in May; you also know the temperatures were higher in August, according to the introductory paragraph. Differences in temperature could be a factor here, but be open to other logical possibilities as well. It's possible that (A) could be true: if there were an exceptionally high number of visitors in August, only some could have purchased from the stand, and the total sales could still have been at their highest for the summer. But this fact does not by itself account for the differences in sales between May and August. (B) could also be true, but this fact about pizza sales does not explain the overall differences in sales for the two months. Based on the given information, (C) is untrue: pizza sales were at their highest in May. The remaining answers are opposites of each other, so determine which describes the situation. **(E)** is correct; it accounts for the relatively high pizza sales in the coldest month of May and the relatively

high ice cream and drinks sales in August. Although not asked about in the question, the trends of temperature and sales displayed in June and July further support this explanation.

50. C

Detail. Paragraph 1 puts Graham's approach in context—lines 6–9 tell you that she wanted to create "new dance forms and movements that would reflect the changed atmosphere of the post–World War One period," for instance, the feelings created by the Great Depression. **(C)** fits the bill here. (A) and (B) touch on minor elements of Graham's style, but they do not capture her overall motivation for creating new techniques. Choices (D) and (E) exaggerate Graham's reaction against classical ballet; Graham was disenchanted with classical ballet, so she decided to invent a new dance form that she felt was more appropriate for the period—but she didn't set out to destroy the ballet tradition, (D), or even parody it by emphasizing one of its features, (E).

51. E

Inference. Use the clues in the passage to determine what it is implying about classical ballet. The first paragraph states that Graham wanted to "break away from the rigid traditions of classical ballet." So you can infer that classical ballet is *rigid*. You can also assume that Graham's style must reflect the *opposite* of classical ballet: ballet must use "decorative sets and costumes" and mixed-sex troupes, both of which she avoided (lines 12–14). Classical ballet must also not reflect a "stark and severe" style (line 15). Therefore, choice **(E)** must be correct. Choices (A) through (D) all describe Graham's style and how it was received.

52. A

Connecting Ideas/Application. The line "the tradition against which a new avant-garde was rebelling" (lines 19–20) is the "fate" the author is describing. In other words, whereas Graham's work was revolutionary in the twenties, it had become quite acceptable by the forties, with the result that younger dancers and choreographers were rebelling against it. So you need an answer that reflects a new technique eventually being accepted and then being rejected. Choice **(A)** describes this chain of events. Choice (D) describes an alternate series of events. Choices (B), (C), and (E) each refer to only possible aspects of a new style or technique, rather than the fate of acceptance and rejection experienced by revolutionary movements.

53. B

Function. Review the context of the quotation to determine why the author included it. The surrounding paragraph describes Graham's early work as a departure from tradition, an expression of her time, and as "stark and severe" (line 15). Notice that the quotation is not from the author but is attributed to a *critic* of Graham's work. The author does not necessarily agree with this assessment, but she includes it as a description of how Graham's work was viewed at the time—making choice **(B)** correct. The author never mentions any argument that Graham's work was considered "terrible," (A); if anything, the quotation would bolster rather than refute that argument. The quote does not express the author's views on Graham's work but those of a critic, so (C) is incorrect. The author never makes a *criticism*, (E), or *argument*, (D), expect perhaps to claim that Graham was influential in her field. So the last two choices are incorrect as well.

54. B

Logical Reasoning. As identified in the first and last sentences, the conclusion here is that the U.S. economy continues to "grow and prosper." As evidence, the author cites the expansion over the last 15 years of the service sector, where last year alone, 500,000 Americans found employment. The author assumes that this growth correlates with growth in the overall economy. But what if declines in other sectors offset the growth in the service sector? If, as choice (B) states, growth in the service sector can be at least partly attributed to a decline in the manufacturing sector, then growth in the service sector can't be a reliable indicator of growth in the overall economy; therefore, **(B)** would undermine the statement's conclusion. (A) tends to support the conclusion—job offers imply economic health, and since the offers were in fields other than the service sector, the statement implies greater overall economic growth. (C) doesn't do much to affect the author's conclusion. Just because

the consequences of a sluggish economy may have been lessened, that doesn't mean the economy is growing and prospering. (D) can be eliminated because the level of economic prosperity in the past does not equate with prosperity (or lack thereof) in the present. Finally, (E) weakens the argument a bit, suggesting that the evidence for the claim of overall economic growth based on the strength of the service sector isn't as strong as the author believes. But even though the service sector's performance isn't as good an indicator of the overall economy's performance as it was in the past, it might still be a very good indicator of overall performance.

55. B

Inference. You can't make a definite prediction for this Inference question, so evaluate each answer choice against the passage. (A) is a distortion. There is evidence that some jaguarundis hunt during the "dusk and dawn," but the passage also states that the majority of data suggest that they hunt during the day. The passage states that jaguarundis are hunters who use the cover provided by the rainforest to hunt. Therefore, it is a logical inference that "the vegetation on the floor of the rainforest" helps the animals hunt, **(B)**. Although the passage states the animals are native to Central and South America, this does not necessarily mean that all jaguarundis today live in these locations, (C); consider that some at least may reside in zoos outside this geographic area. (D) contradicts the passage, which defines *diurnal* as hunting during the day. (E) is far afield. There is no mention of jaguarundis eating plants, and they are only described as hunters in the passage.

56. C

Detail. Reading the question stem first will save you valuable time on short-statement Detail questions. Just skim to find what to do after draining the old oil: wipe and then replace the drain plug, choice **(C)**. The steps in the other answer choices are stated in the passage, but the do not occur immediately after draining the old oil.

Core Mathematics Practice Test 1

90 Minutes—56 Questions

Directions: You have 90 minutes to complete the Mathematics test. Most of the questions on this test are followed by five answer choices. Unless otherwise stated, select the best answer for each question. If a question asks you to "Select all that apply," then more than one answer could be right and you should select all of the choices you believe are correct. If a question is followed by a box instead of answer choices, write your response directly into the box.

Note: The figures accompanying problems in this test are intended to provide information useful in solving the problems. The figures are drawn as accurately as possible unless the problem indicates that the figure is not drawn to scale. You can assume that figures lie in a plane unless the problem states otherwise. You can also assume that lines shown as straight are straight, and that points are positioned in the order shown. A right angle is denoted by the symbol ⌐.

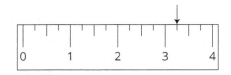

1. What measurement is the arrow pointing to on the ruler?

    A. $2\frac{1}{4}$

    B. $2\frac{1}{2}$

    C. $3\frac{1}{4}$

    D. $3\frac{1}{2}$

    E. $4\frac{1}{4}$

2. Which of the following scatter plots gives the strongest indication that the relationship between x and y could be a linear relationship described by $y = ax + b$, where a is positive?

    A.
    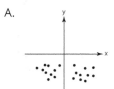

    B.
    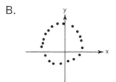

    C.

    D.
    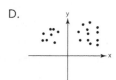

    E.
    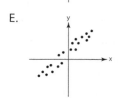

3. Which of the following lists has the numbers arranged in order from the largest to the smallest?

    A. $8, -4, -5, -\frac{1}{3}, -\frac{1}{7}$

    B. $8, -\frac{1}{3}, -\frac{1}{7}, -5, -4$

    C. $8, -5, -\frac{1}{3}, -\frac{1}{7}, -4$

    D. $8, -\frac{1}{7}, -\frac{1}{3}, -5, -4$

    E. $8, -\frac{1}{7}, -\frac{1}{3}, -4, -5$

4. In an auditorium, the number of seniors is 56 more than the number of juniors. The ratio of the number of juniors to the number of seniors is 5 to 12. What is the total number of juniors and seniors in the auditorium?

    A. 49

    B. 84

    C. 120

    D. 136

    E. 168

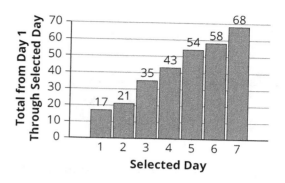

5. Store X was open from 10 AM through 10 PM during each of 7 consecutive days. The vertical axis shows how many brand Y widgets were sold from the beginning of day 1 through the conclusion of a selected day. For example, the total number of brand Y widgets sold on days 1, 2, 3, 4, and 5 was 54. What was the total number of brand Y widgets sold on day 4, day 5, day 6, and day 7?

    A. 14

    B. 25

    C. 33

    D. 41

    E. 47

6. A measuring cup contains $1\frac{2}{3}$ cups of water.

    It needs to be filled to the $3\frac{3}{4}$ cup mark. Approximately how much water must be added?

    A. A little less than 1 cup

    B. A little more than 1 cup

    C. A little less than 2 cups

    D. A little more than 2 cups

    E. A little less than 3 cups

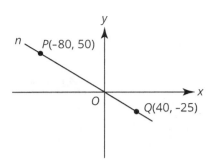

7. In the xy-plane above, line n goes through the points P (−80, 50) and Q (40, −25). The point R (v, 155) is a point on line n. What is the value of v?

A. −312

B. −280

C. −264

D. −248

E. −224

4.3, 7.5, 3.1, 5.6, 4.8, 7.4, 1.8, 7.3, 4.6, 5.1

8. The volumes, in cubic feet, of 10 different containers are shown above. What is the range of the volumes of these containers, in cubic feet?

A. 4.1

B. 4.3

C. 5.6

D. 5.7

E. 7.4

9. A jar contains 3 chocolate chip cookies, 2 snickerdoodles, and 8 raisin cookies. Which of the following is greater than the probability of getting either a snickerdoodle or a chocolate chip cookie by drawing a random cookie from the jar?

Select all that apply.

A. $\frac{2}{13}$

B. $\frac{3}{13}$

C. $\frac{5}{13}$

D. $\frac{8}{13}$

E. $\frac{10}{13}$

10. The integers x and y are positive. Inside a drawer, there are 5 brand A hats, x brand B hats, 12 brand C hats, and y brand D hats. There is nothing else in the drawer. If one hat is randomly chosen from the drawer, what is the probability that the hat chosen is a brand C hat or a brand D hat?

A. $\frac{y + 12}{x + y + 17}$

B. $\frac{y + 5}{x + y + 12}$

C. $\frac{x + 5}{x + y + 17}$

D. $\frac{y}{17 + x + y}$

E. $\frac{y + 17}{x + y + 17}$

a	*b*
$\frac{41}{70}$	$\frac{1}{3}$
$\frac{401}{700}$	$\frac{2}{9}$
$\frac{4,001}{7,000}$	$\frac{3}{27}$
$\frac{40,001}{70,000}$	$\frac{4}{81}$
$\frac{400,001}{700,000}$	$\frac{5}{243}$

11. Which of the following is true about the data shown above?

    A. As *a* decreases, *b* decreases.

    B. As *a* decreases, *b* increases.

    C. As *a* decreases, *b* does not change.

    D. As *a* increases, *b* does not change.

    E. As *a* increases, *b* decreases.

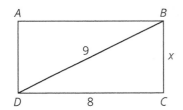

12. The figure above is a rectangle where the length of side *DC* is 8, the length of side *BC* is *x*, and the length of diagonal *BD* is 9. What is the approximate value of *x*?

    A. 3.3

    B. 4.1

    C. 5.2

    D. 6.1

    E. 7.4

13. A carmaker wants five people to evaluate its brand *X* cars. Which of the following groups would be most likely to give the carmaker the most accurate evaluation of its brand *X* cars?

    A. Five people who have heard of brand *X* cars

    B. Five people who have driven a car

    C. Five people who have friends who have bought a brand *X* car

    D. Five people who have considered buying a brand *X* car

    E. Five people who are experts on the manufacture and operation of brand *X* cars

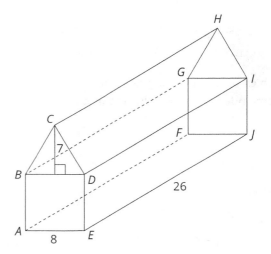

The figure shown above is a solid. Squares *ABDE* and *FGIJ* are identical. Triangles *BCD* and *GHI* are identical. Rectangles *BGID* and *AFJE* are identical. Rectangles *BGFA* and *DIJE* are identical. The length of line segment *JE* is 26. The length of the altitude drawn from point *C* to side *BD* in triangle *BCD* is 7. The length of side *AE* of square *ABDE* is 8.

14. What is the volume of the entire solid?

    A. 2,184

    B. 2,392

    C. 2,496

    D. 2,600

    E. 2,912

List *L*: 7.3, 3.5, 4.1, 8.5, 6.4, 3.7, 10.4

15. In list *L* above, what is the median?

   A. 6.4

   B. 7.3

   C. 7.4

   D. 8.5

   E. 10.4

16. Which of the following numbers is greatest?

   A. 72.563

   B. 73.526

   C. 73.652

   D. 72.536

   E. 73.625

17. Which of the following does not have a remainder of 7 when divided into 163?

   A. 6

   B. 12

   C. 13

   D. 26

   E. 52

18. Which of the following lists of 15 numbers, which are represented by dot plots, has a median of 1 and a range of 12?

   A.
   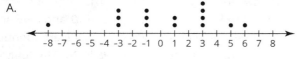

   B.
   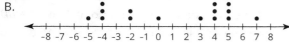

   C.

   D.
   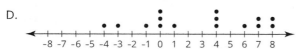

   E.
   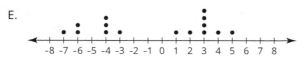

Number Sold

Brand *W*	♦♦♦♦♦♦♦♦♦
Brand *X*	♦♦♦♦
Brand *Y*	♦♦♦♦♦♦♦♦
Brand *Z*	♦♦♦♦♦♦♦♦

Each ♦ represents 25 widgets

19. The table above shows the numbers of brand *W*, brand *X*, brand *Y*, and brand *Z* widgets a store sold in a certain week. The store sold no other widgets that week. The gross sales revenue from widgets that week was $3,150. The price of each brand *W* widget sold was $3, the price of each brand *X* widget sold was $7, the price of each brand *Y* widget sold was *p* dollars, and the price of each brand *Z* widget sold was *q* dollars. What is the value of $p + q$?

   A. $7.25

   B. $7.70

   C. $8.50

   D. $8.75

   E. $10.00

The only contents of a container are 10 identically shaped disks, and each disk is labeled with a different integer from 1 to 10. A person drew one disk at random from the container and replaced it, then drew a second at random and replaced it, and continued drawing random disks and replacing them one at a time. The numbers on the first seven randomly drawn disks were 3, 5, 4, 7, 5, 8, and 1.

20. What is the probability that the eighth randomly drawn disk will bear the number 4?

   A. $\frac{1}{20}$

   B. $\frac{1}{15}$

   C. $\frac{1}{10}$

   D. $\frac{1}{8}$

   E. $\frac{1}{5}$

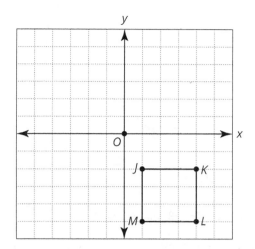

21. Square *JKLM* is shown in the *xy*-plane above, and point *K* is located at (4, −2). After square *JKLM* is translated 5 units to the left and 8 units up, what will the coordinates of point *M* be?

    A. (−4, 3)

    B. (−4, 5)

    C. (−3, −4)

    D. (−1, 3)

    E. (1, 6)

22. At 3:00 AM yesterday, the volume of water in a tank was 210 gallons. From 3:00 AM to 8:00 PM yesterday, water was added to the tank at a constant rate. If the volume of water in the tank at 7:00 AM yesterday was 370 gallons, what was the volume of water in the tank in gallons at 5:00 PM yesterday?

    A. 400

    B. 540

    C. 580

    D. 650

    E. 770

23. Ebony and Luis each rented a booth at a craft fair to sell their hand-painted mugs. At the fair, Ebony sold *m* mugs and paid $24 for booth rental. Luis sold $\frac{2}{3}$ as many mugs as Ebony but paid $4 less to rent a booth. Both Ebony and Luis sold their mugs for $5 each. Which of the following represents how many dollars Luis earned after paying for his booth?

    A. $\frac{2m}{3} - 4$

    B. $\frac{2m}{3} + 4$

    C. $\frac{10m}{3} - 20$

    D. $\frac{10m}{3} - 4$

    E. $5m - 24$

24. Which of the following is greater than $\frac{13}{20}$?

    A. 0.655

    B. $\frac{5}{8}$

    C. $\frac{3}{5}$

    D. 58%

    E. 0.074

25. Which of the following questions are statistical questions?

Select <u>all</u> that apply.

A. How much did Edward pay for the hat he is now wearing?

B. How many minutes are there in an hour?

C. What is the height of a randomly selected red-wood tree in the United States?

D. How many inches of rain fall in London in April?

26. Miguel cleaned $\frac{1}{4}$ of his room Saturday morning and $\frac{1}{6}$ of his room on Sunday. What is the ratio of the amount of the room he has cleaned to the amount that he has not cleaned?

A. 5:12

B. 7:12

C. 5:7

D. 7:5

E. 12:5

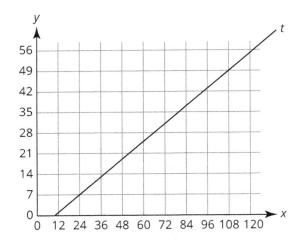

27. In the *xy*-plane above, line *t* is graphed. Which of the following tables of values contains only correct values for *y* for each given value of *x*?

A.

x	y
24	14
60	25
84	37
108	42

B.

x	y
10	0
24	7
84	37
108	49

C.

x	y
24	21
60	25
84	37
108	49

D.

x	y
60	25
84	43
108	42
120	55

E.

x	y
24	7
72	35
84	37
108	56

28. One-fourth of the 1,600 sales representatives employed by a company work in its corporate headquarters. Of these, 62.5 percent met or exceeded their sales goals last year. Which computation shows the number of sales representatives working at the corporate office who failed to meet their sales goals last year?

    A. 375×400

    B. 37.5×400

    C. 3.75×400

    D. 0.375×400

    E. 0.0375×400

Questions 29 and 30 refer to the graph below.

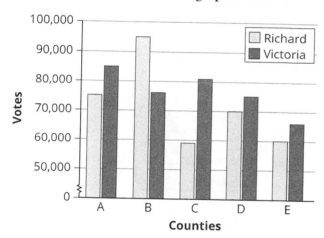

29. The graph above shows voting results by county for two candidates: Richard and Victoria. Based on the graph, what is the ratio of counties Victoria won to the counties that Richard won?

    A. 1:4

    B. 4:5

    C. 17:20

    D. 20:17

    E. 4:1

30. Which two counties had the smallest difference in the number of votes cast for Richard and Victoria?

    A. A and D

    B. A and E

    C. D and E

    D. C and D

    E. A and C

31. In 2014, 70 percent of a department store's total sales came from clothing. Which of the following circle graphs has the shaded area representing 70 percent of the total sales?

    A.

    B.

    C.

    D.

    E.

32. The only items in a container are 9 red, x white, and 36 blue marbles. If the probability of randomly drawing a white marble is $\frac{2}{7}$, how many marbles are in the container?

    A. 18

    B. 45

    C. 54

    D. 63

    E. 90

33. A map is drawn to scale. A square region on this map has an area of $25x^2$ square inches, where $x > 0$. The scale of this map is y inches $= 4$ miles, where $y > 0$. What is the length of a side of the actual square region, in miles, in terms of x and y?

    A. $20xy$

    B. $\frac{5y}{x}$

    C. $\frac{5x}{y}$

    D. $\frac{20y}{x}$

    E. $\frac{20x}{y}$

34. The integers x and y are positive. Each type A item weighs 5 ounces, and each type B item weighs 7 ounces. What fraction of the total weight of y type B items is the total weight of x type A items, in terms of x and y?

    A. $\frac{7y}{5x}$

    B. $\frac{5y}{7x}$

    C. $\frac{7}{5xy}$

    D. $\frac{5x}{7y}$

    E. $\frac{5x}{5x + 7y}$

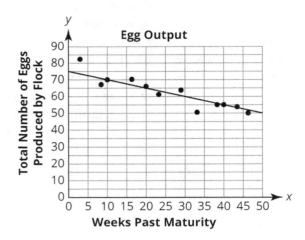

35. In the scatterplot above, how many times do the data points differ from the line of best fit by at least 5 eggs?

    A. 1

    B. 2

    C. 3

    D. 4

    E. 5

36. If $y = 70$, then what is the value of x?

37. 1,400 divided by 70 is the same as 2 times z. What is the value of z?

    A. 1

    B. 10

    C. 100

    D. 1,000

    E. 10,000

38. What is the value of x if $\frac{x}{12} + 3 = 10$?

    A. 84

    B. 96

    C. 108

    D. 112

    E. 120

39. For a finite interval of positive values of Quantity *H*, Quantity *T* decreases when Quantity *H* increases. Which of the following graphs shows this relationship between Quantity *H* and Quantity *T* for the entire interval of values of Quantity *H*?

A.

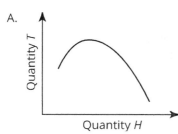

B.

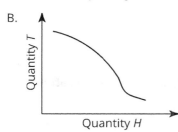

C.

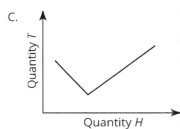

D.

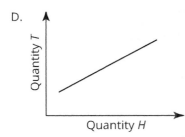

E.

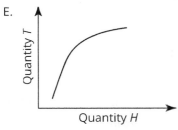

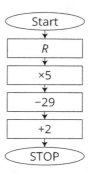

40. What is the result of the computation outlined in the chart above if *R* = 5?

   A. −4

   B. −2

   C. 0

   D. 2

   E. 4

41. Which of the following is LEAST?

   A. $\frac{5}{8}$

   B. $\frac{9}{16}$

   C. $\frac{17}{32}$

   D. $\frac{33}{64}$

   E. $\frac{65}{128}$

42. Each of seven runners on a relay team must run a distance of exactly 1.27 kilometers. Rounded to the nearest kilometer, what is the total combined number of kilometers the team runs in the race?

   A. 10

   B. 9

   C. 8

   D. 7

   E. 6

43. What is the range of all integers greater than 14 and less than 63 that are multiples of 7?

    A. 35

    B. 37

    C. 42

    D. 45

    E. 49

44. The expression $18y - 47$ is equal to which of the following expressions for all y?

    A. $3(8y - 16) - 6y - 1$

    B. $4(7y - 3) - 10y + 59$

    C. $23 - 5(3y + 14) + 31y$

    D. $21y + 35 - 3(y + 4)$

    E. $5(7y - 16) - 17y + 33$

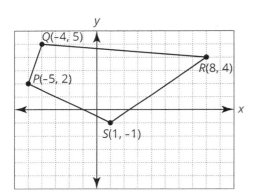

45. Quadrilateral $PQRS$ is shown in the xy-plane above. After quadrilateral $PQRS$ is moved in the xy-plane 12 units to the right and 10 units down, what will the coordinates of point Q be?

    A. $(5, -10)$

    B. $(5, -5)$

    C. $(6, -5)$

    D. $(8, -7)$

    E. $(8, -5)$

46. The average (arithmetic mean) of the scores of a team in its 8 most recent games was 7.5. If the scores of the team in these 8 most recent games are 9, 3, 4, 12, 6, 1, 8, and x, what is the value of x?

47. What is the value of $(w - x)(y + z)$ if $4w = 4x + 20$ and $7y = -7z + 56$?

    A. 28

    B. 35

    C. 40

    D. 42

    E. 48

Average Monthly Temperature	
May 2019	65°F
Jun 2019	61°F
Jul 2019	57°F
Aug 2019	52°F
Sep 2019	54°F
Oct 2019	58°F
Nov 2019	65°F
Dec 2019	71°F
Jan 2020	73°F
Feb 2020	70°F
Mar 2020	68°F
Apr 2020	64°F

48. The chart above shows the average temperatures in a city from May 2019 to April 2020. Which of the following is true of the average temperature in this city between May 2019 and December 2019?

    A. The temperature increased continually.

    B. The temperature increased and then decreased.

    C. The temperature remained constant.

    D. The temperature decreased and then increased.

    E. The temperature decreased continually.

49. If $-8(x - 3) = 4(3x + 7) - 16$, then what is the value of x?

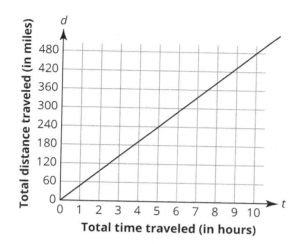

Total time traveled (in hours)

50. The graph above plots both the distance that a train traveled and its travel time. The distance d from the starting point is in miles, and the time t is in hours. What was the speed of the train, in miles per hour?

   A. 42

   B. 48

   C. 60

   D. 72

   E. 78

51. Which of the following numbers, if any, are the same?

   I. 0.76×10^5

   II. $7,600 \times 10^{-4}$

   III. 7.6×10^2

   A. None of them

   B. I and II only

   C. II and III only

   D. I and III only

   E. I, II, and III

52. What is x if $\frac{2x}{3} - 1 = 11$?

   A. 17

   B. 18

   C. 19

   D. 20

   E. 21

53. Eighty percent of G is 352. What is G?

   A. 44

   B. 281.6

   C. 428

   D. 440

   E. 633.6

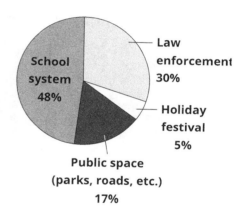

54. The pie chart above shows the budget for the town of Magnolia this year. If the town spends $5,400 on law enforcement, what is the total budget?

   A. $11,000

   B. $16,000

   C. $18,000

   D. $30,000

   E. $108,000

55. The numbers x, y, and z are the three scores of a team in three consecutive games. List L is the list of numbers x, y, z where $50 < x < y < z$. List M is the list of numbers $x - 7$, y, $z + 7$. Which of the following statements about the lists L and M is true?

    A. The median of the numbers in list L is less than the median of the numbers in list M.

    B. The median of the numbers in list L is greater than the median of the numbers in list M.

    C. The range of the numbers in list L is equal to the range of the numbers in list M.

    D. The range of the numbers in list L is less than the range of the numbers in list M.

    E. The average (arithmetic mean) of the numbers in list L does not equal the average of the numbers in list M.

56. Each week, an employee is paid $170 plus x percent commission on all the employee's sales. If, during a certain week, the employee had total sales of $4,000 and was paid a total of $810, what is the value of x?

Core Mathematics Practice Test 1 Answers and Explanations

1. C

The ruler is divided into fourths—that is, every tick mark indicates $\frac{1}{4}$ of an inch. Start by finding a clear measurement, like 3 inches. From there, count how many more tick marks it takes to get to the arrow. In this case, it is only one tick mark away from 3, so add on $\frac{1}{4}$ of an inch: $3 + \frac{1}{4} = 3\frac{1}{4}$.

2. E

The question is asking for a linear relationship with a positive slope.

(A): There is no suggestion of a linear relationship. Discard.

(B): There is no suggestion of a linear relationship. Discard.

(C): There is a linear relationship, but the slope is negative. Discard.

(D): There is no suggestion of a linear relationship. Discard.

(E): There is a linear relationship, and the slope is positive.

3. E

Consider a sample number line:

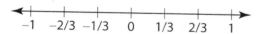

From largest to smallest, there are

- positive numbers greater than 1
- positive fractions less than 1
- 0
- negative fractions greater than -1
- negative numbers less than -1

The answer that follows this trend is **(E)**.

4. D

Since the ratio of the number of juniors to the number of seniors is 5 to 12, and there are 56 more seniors than there are juniors, use a variable for the number of juniors (here, j) and solve for it. $\frac{5}{12} = \frac{j}{j + 56}$. To solve this ratio for j, cross-multiply $5(j + 56)$ and $12(j)$: $5j + 280 = 12j$. Then subtract $5j$ from both sides so $280 = 7j$. Next, $j = \frac{280}{7} = 40$. Since there are 56 more seniors than juniors, add 56 to get 96 seniors. (To confirm, $\frac{40}{96}$ simplified is the $\frac{5}{12}$ ratio). Since the question asks for the total number of juniors and seniors in the auditorium, add both together: $40 + 96 = 136$.

5. C

The day 7 total of 68 shows that 68 total widgets were sold day 1 through day 7. The question asks for the total sold on days 4 through 7, so you must subtract the total for days 1 through 3 (35 on the graph) from 68: $68 - 35 = 33$.

6. D

The question asks for "approximately" how much water to add, and the answer choices are themselves approximate amounts. This is therefore an estimation question. You need to compare the relative values of the two amounts. If the amounts were simply 1 cup and 3 cups, the answer would clearly be 2 cups. But here you also have to determine the relationship between $\frac{2}{3}$ and $\frac{3}{4}$. Because $\frac{3}{4}$ is a little more than $\frac{2}{3}$, a little more than 2 cups must be added to go from $1\frac{2}{3}$ to $3\frac{3}{4}$. You could also arrive at the answer by converting both fractions to a common denominator: $\frac{2}{3} = \frac{8}{12}$ and $\frac{3}{4} = \frac{9}{12}$. Again, $\frac{2}{3}$ is slightly less than $\frac{3}{4}$, so a little more than 2 cups of water are needed. Choice **(D)** is correct.

7.   D

The graph goes through the origin, which is the point O (0, 0). To find the slope of the line, choose two points: O (0, 0) and Q (40, −25). The slope m of a line is given by the formula $m = \dfrac{y_2 - y_1}{x_2 - x_1}$.

So the slope of the line is $m = \dfrac{-25 - 0}{40 - 0} = \dfrac{-25}{40} \dfrac{-5}{8}$.

The equation of the line is $y = -\dfrac{5}{8}x + 0$.

Substitute the point in the problem:

$$155 = -\frac{5}{8}v + 0$$
$$1240 = -5v$$
$$v = -248$$

8.   D

The range of a list of numbers is the largest number minus the smallest number. The largest number on this list is 7.5. You can confirm this by comparing 7.5 with each other number on the list—it is greater than each of them. The smallest number on the list is 1.8. Confirm this by comparing 1.8 with each other number on the list—it is less than each of them. The range of the volumes is therefore $7.5 - 1.8 = 5.7$.

9.   D, E

There are 13 total cookies. The probability of getting either a snickerdoodle (2 of these cookies) or a chocolate chip cookie (3 of these cookies) is $\dfrac{2 + 3}{13} = \dfrac{5}{13}$. Since the question asks for values greater than this, **(D)** and **(E)** are correct.

10.   A

The probability formula is

$$\text{Probability} = \frac{\text{Number of desired outcomes}}{\text{Number of possible outcomes}}.$$

Since there are 12 brand C hats and y brand D hats, the number of desired outcomes is $12 + y$ (or $y + 12$). The number of possible outcomes is the number of hats in the drawer, which is $5 + x + 12 + y = 17 + x + y$ (or $x + y + 17$). The probability that a brand C hat or a brand D hat is drawn is $\dfrac{y + 12}{x + y + 17}$.

11.   A

The answer choices deal with whether a and b are increasing, decreasing, or staying the same. Going from top to bottom, compare the fractions in a's column to determine the trend. Use common denominators to compare just the first two fractions, since the whole set follows the same pattern throughout. To compare $\dfrac{41}{70}$ to $\dfrac{401}{700}$, use a common denominator of 700: $\dfrac{410}{700}$ is larger than $\dfrac{401}{700}$, so comparing the other consecutive pairs of fractions, it must be that a is decreasing as it goes down the chart. Now, evaluate b's column from top to bottom. To compare $\dfrac{1}{3}$ to $\dfrac{2}{9}$, use a common denominator of 9: $\dfrac{3}{9}$ is larger than $\dfrac{2}{9}$, so the fractions in b's column are also decreasing from top to bottom. So **(A)** is correct, because as a decreases, b decreases. Notice, though, that the question does not specify going from top to bottom. If you went from bottom to top, you would find that as a increases, b increases. This would also be correct, but it is not among the answer choices.

12.   B

All four interior angles of a rectangle have a measure of 90 degrees, so triangle BCD is a right triangle. Use the Pythagorean theorem to find the value of x. The Pythagorean theorem says that in a right triangle, the square of the hypotenuse is equal to the sum of the squares of the legs. Here, since triangle BCD is a right triangle, $(BD)^2 = (BC)^2 + (CD)^2$ So:

$$9^2 = x^2 + 8^2$$
$$81 = x^2 + 64$$
$$17 = x^2$$

Thus, $x^2 = 17$, and $x = \sqrt{17}$. It is most efficient to use estimation to arrive at the answer. The number 17 is just slightly larger than 16, whose square root is 4, so the square root of 17 must be just slightly greater than 4. This means **(B)** is correct. Alternatively, if you have access to an onscreen or physical calculator during your test, you can use it to find the square root of 17.

13. E

Choice (A): Five people who have heard of the brand X car may not have ever driven one. Choice (A) is not likely to provide an accurate evaluation.

Choice (B): Five people who have driven a car may have driven a car other than a brand X car. Eliminate (B).

Choice (C): Five people who have friends who have bought a brand X car may themselves know little or nothing about brand X cars. Eliminate (C).

Choice (D): Five people who have considered buying a brand X car may not be very knowledgeable about brand X cars. Eliminate (D).

Choice **(E)**: Five people who are experts on the manufacture and operation of brand X cars would probably give an accurate evaluation of brand X cars.

14. B

The volume of rectangular and triangular prisms can be expressed as: Volume = Cross-sectional Area × Length.

For the rectangular prism described by $ABDE$:

- Area $= 8 \times 8 = 64$
- Length $= 26$
- Volume $= 64 \times 26 = 1{,}664$

For the triangular prism described by BCD:

- Area $= \frac{1}{2}(\text{Base})(\text{Height}) = \frac{1}{2} \times 7 \times 8 = \frac{1}{2} \times 56 = 28$
- Length $= 26$
- Volume $= 28 \times 26 = 728$

Total volume $= 1{,}664 + 728 = 2{,}392$

15. A

To find the median of a list of numbers, arrange the numbers in increasing order. If there is an odd number of elements in the list, such as in list L, the median is the middle number. (If there were an even number of elements, the median would be the average of the two middle numbers.)

List L in increasing order reads:

3.5, 3.7, 4.1, 6.4, 7.3, 8.5, 10.4

The middle number is the fourth number: 6.4.

16. C

Compare the values in each choice, digit by digit, moving from left to right. In the tens place, all choices have 7s. In the ones place, (A) and (D) have 2s, whereas the rest have 3s, so eliminate (A) and (D). In the tenths place, (B) has a value of 5, whereas (C) and (E) have 6s, so eliminate (B). Finally, the hundredths place value of (C) is 5, whereas that of (E) is 2, so eliminate (E). **(C)** is correct.

17. A

One helpful way to solve remainder problems is to first subtract the remainder from the larger number. For this question, subtract 7 from 163, leaving 156. Then test each answer choice to see which one does not go evenly into 156. In this case, however, every answer choice goes into 156 evenly. Note, though, that 6 could not leave a remainder of 7, because 7 is larger than 6. Six goes into 163 twenty-seven times and leaves a remainder of 1. Choice **(A)** is correct.

18. E

Range is easier to calculate than median, so start by eliminating the sets that do not have a range of 12. Find the range by subtracting the maximum from the minimum:

(A): $6 - (-8) = 14$

(B): $7 - (-5) = 12$

(C): $8 - (-7) = 15$

(D): $8 - (-4) = 12$

(E): $5 - (-7) = 12$

Eliminate (A) and (C). Now calculate the medians of the remaining answers. For a set containing an odd amount of numbers n, find the middle number (median) by dividing n by 2 and rounding up. For example, these sets contain 15 numbers:

$$15 \div 2 = 7.5$$

So the eighth number of each set will be the median. For each set, count the dots one at a time, from left to right, until you reach the eighth dot.

(B): median is 3

(D): median is 4

(E): median is 1

19. C

Look at the horizontal row of the table for each brand. Each diamond symbol represents 25 widgets. For brand W, there are 10 diamond symbols. So the number of brand W widgets sold that week was $25(10) = 250$. Since each brand W widget had a price of \$3, the gross sales revenue from the 250 brand W widgets was $(\$3)(250) = \$750$.

Do the same for the other brands. For brand X, there are 4 diamond symbols: $25(4) = 100$. Since each brand X widget had a price of \$7, the gross sales revenue from the 100 brand X widgets was $(\$7)(100) = \$700$. For brand Y, there are 8 diamonds: $25(8) = 200$. Since each brand Y widget's price is unknown, use variable $\$p$ to represent price. The gross sales revenue from the 200 brand Y widgets was $(\$p)(200) = \$200p$. Brand Z is similar. There are 8 diamonds, so $25(8) = 200$. Again, each brand Z widget has an unknown price, so use variable $\$q$. The gross sales revenue from the 200 brand Z widgets was $(\$q)(200) = \$200q$.

Since the gross sales revenue from the four brands of widgets was \$3,150, write the equation $750 + 700 + 200p + 200q = 3{,}150$ and solve for $p + q$.

Add the numbers on the left side: $1{,}450 + 200p + 200q = 3{,}150$.

Subtract 1,450 from both sides: $200p + 200q = 1{,}700$.

Factor 200 out of the left side: $200(p + q) = 1{,}700$.

Divide both sides by 200: $p + q = \dfrac{1{,}700}{200} = \dfrac{17}{2} = 8.5$.

The value of $p + q$ is \$8.50.

20. C

$\text{Probability} = \dfrac{\text{Number of desired outcomes}}{\text{Number of possible outcomes}}$. When the eighth disk is drawn, there is one desired outcome: 4. There are 10 possible outcomes: 1 through 10. So the probability that the eighth disk will be numbered 4 is $\dfrac{1}{10}$. Note that because the first seven disks were replaced each time, the results of the first seven draws do not affect the probability that the eighth disk will be numbered 4.

21. A

Point M is located at $(1, -5)$. A left shift of 5 will subtract 5 from the x value. An up shift of 8 will add 8 to the y value.

$$1 - 5 = -4$$
$$-5 + 8 = 3$$

So the coordinates of point M will be $(-4, 3)$.

22. E

Since the volume of water in the tank at 3:00 AM was 210 gallons and the volume of water in the tank at 7:00 AM was 370 gallons, in the four hours from 3:00 AM to 7:00 AM, the amount of water added to the tank was $370 - 210 = 160$ gallons. Since 160 gallons were added to the tank at a constant rate over those four hours, $\dfrac{160 \text{ gallons}}{4 \text{ hours}} = 40$ gallons per hour.

The time difference between 3:00 AM and 5:00 PM is 14 hours. Multiply the constant rate of water increase by the time elapsed: 40 gallons $\times$ 14 hours $=$ 560 gallons of water. Also keep in mind that there were already 210 gallons of water in the tank at 3:00 AM. Add $210 + 560 = 770$ gallons of water.

23. C

The question provides information about Ebony's earnings but asks about Luis's earnings. The money Ebony received from sales of mugs is the price per mug, \$5, times the number of mugs she sold, m. This is $5m$. Luis sold $\dfrac{2}{3}$ as many mugs, which is $\left(\dfrac{2}{3}\right)(5m) = \dfrac{10m}{3}$. Each person paid out money to rent a booth, so that amount is subtracted from the sales revenue. Ebony paid \$24 and Luis paid \$4 less than Ebony, or $\$24 - \$4 = \$20$. So, Luis earned $\dfrac{10m}{3} - 20$.

24. A

This question requires you to compare a few numbers in different formats, so first convert them to the same format. For instance, $\dfrac{13}{20}$ as a decimal is 0.65. The only choice that's bigger is (**A**), 0.655.

25. C, D

A statistical question involves estimation of a value that cannot be directly observed, such as for a future event or a generalization over all events.

(A): No estimation is needed, as there is a specific answer to this question. Eliminate (A).

(B): Again, there is a specific answer to this question. Eliminate (B).

(C): Since the height of redwood trees varies, this is a statistical question.

(D): Since the number of inches of rain in London can vary from April of one year to April of another year, this is a statistical question.

26. C

To determine the ratio of the amount cleaned to the amount not cleaned, you must first determine the amount cleaned. Miguel cleaned $\frac{1}{4}$ and then $\frac{1}{6}$ of his room, so find a common denominator and add those fractions: $\frac{3}{12} + \frac{2}{12} = \frac{5}{12}$. Since he has cleaned $\frac{5}{12}$, that leaves $\frac{7}{12}$ not clean. So the ratio of clean to not clean is $\frac{5}{12}$ to $\frac{7}{12}$. Since the denominators are the same, ignore them and simplify to 5:7.

27. B

For each table, go through each given (x, y) coordinate until you can prove that table wrong and eliminate it. Try to use obvious points instead of points that are difficult to discern.

(A): (24, 14) is wrong.

(B): No obviously wrong points; do not spend time on the points that are difficult to tell.

(C): (24, 21) is wrong.

(D): (84, 43) is wrong.

(E): (72, 35) is wrong.

After eliminating the rest, you can assume that (B) is correct.

28. D

Translate the information in this word problem one step at a time. First, there are $1,600 \div 4 = 400$ sales representatives at the company's corporate headquarters. Because 62.5 percent of these met or exceeded their sales goals last year, 100 percent − 62.5 percent = 37.5 percent failed to meet their goals. Convert 37.5 percent into a decimal by dividing by 100: $37.5 \div 100 = 0.375$. You can thus find the number of sales representatives at headquarters who failed to meet their sales goals last year by multiplying 0.375 by 400, making (D) correct.

29. E

Victoria won four counties, whereas Richard only won County B. The ratio is therefore 4:1, as in (E). Remember, the question is not asking for the ratio of votes, nor is it asking for the ratio of counties Victoria won to total counties.

30. C

For each county, compare the relative heights of the two bars and find the two with the smallest difference. The two counties with the least difference in votes between Richard and Victoria are D and E, which is choice (C).

31. C

Remember that 70% would be slightly less than 75%, which is $\frac{75}{100}$, simplified to $\frac{3}{4}$. Keeping this in mind, make an educated estimate as to which of the answer choices looks like just less than $\frac{3}{4}$ of the total. Choice (C) is the winner. All of the other responses either portray a shaded area that is significantly less or more than this amount.

32. D

The probability formula is Probability = $\frac{\text{Number of desired outcomes}}{\text{Number of total outcomes}}$. There are x white marbles and $9 + x + 36$ total marbles. The probability of drawing a white marble is $\frac{2}{7}$, so $\frac{2}{7} = \frac{x}{9 + x + 36} = \frac{x}{45 + x}$. Cross-multiply to get $7x = 2(45 + x)$. This simplifies to $7x = 90 + 2x$. Subtract 2x from each side of the equation to get $5x = 90$. Divide both sides by 5 to see that $x = 18$. The question asks for the total number of marbles, which is $9 + 18 + 36 = 63$.

33. E

The question asks for a length of one of the sides of the square, so start by simplifying the given area of $25x^2$. The square root of $25x^2$ equals $5x$, so the square on the map is $5x$ inches on all sides.

Next, simplify the conversion between inches and miles:

y inches $= 4$ miles

1 inch $= \dfrac{4}{y}$ miles

The question asks for how many miles the $5x$-inch side will be, so multiply the conversion by $5x$ on both sides:

$5x$ inches $= \dfrac{4(5x)}{y}$ miles

Simplify: $5x$ inches $= \dfrac{20x}{y}$ miles

34. D

Since each type A item weighs 5 ounces, you can calculate the total weight of x type A items as follows:

(5 ounces per type A item) $\times$ (x type A items) $= 5x$ ounces

Since each type B item weighs 7 ounces, you can calculate the total weight of y type B items as follows:

(7 ounces per type B item) $\times$ (y type B items) $= 7y$ ounces

Thus, the total weight of x type A items is $5x$ ounces, and the total weight of y type B items is $7y$ ounces.

Since this question asks for the fraction *of* the total weight of y type B items . . . ," that value, $7y$, should be the denominator of the fraction. So $\dfrac{5x \text{ ounces}}{7y \text{ ounces}} = \dfrac{5x}{7y}$.

35. B

This scatterplot question asks how many data points are different from the line of best fit by at least 5 eggs. Note that eggs are depicted on the y-axis and that one "grid mark" up or down equals 5 eggs. There are two points that are that far away: one at $x = 3$ and one at $x = 33$. The answer is (**B**).

36. 10

There is a clear point with a y-value of 70 that intersects the line of best fit at $(10, 70)$, so the answer is **10**. Be careful not to use $x = 70$ and answer with the corresponding value of y.

37. B

Translate words into math: $\dfrac{1,400}{70} = 2z$. Now solve for z by dividing both sides by 2: $\dfrac{1,400}{2 \times 70} = z$ or $\dfrac{1,400}{140} = z$. Because 1,400 is just 140 with a zero added to the end, 1,400 divided by 140 is 10, and $z = 10$.

38. A

Solve this equation for x. First, subtract 3 from both sides. Then multiply both sides by 12 to isolate x.

$$\frac{x}{12} + 3 = 10$$

$$\frac{x}{12} = 7$$

$$x = 84$$

39. B

The question is looking for the graph where Quantity T decreases whenever Quantity H increases.

(**B**): For the entire interval of possible values of Quantity H (x-axis), the graph is a curve where Quantity T decreases when Quantity H increases.

All other choices show Quantity T increasing at some point, which is incorrect.

40. B

Perform the operations in the chart in order after substituting 5 for R.

R is 5

$5 \times 5 = 25$

$25 - 29 = -4$

$-4 + 2 = -2$

The answer is -2.

41. E

This question requires you to compare fractions whose denominators are different and determine which one is least. Compare the fractions one by one, using a common denominator. For instance, to compare $\frac{5}{8}$ to $\frac{9}{16}$, use the common denominator of 16. Thus, compare $\frac{10}{16}$ to $\frac{9}{16}$ and determine that (B) is smaller. Then, compare (B) to (C), $\frac{9}{16}$ to $\frac{17}{32}$, or $\frac{18}{32}$ to $\frac{17}{32}$. So (C) is smaller. (D) $\frac{33}{64}$ is less than (C) $\frac{34}{64}$. Finally, (E) $\frac{65}{128}$ is less than (D) $\frac{66}{128}$. Choice (**E**) is correct.

42. B

If each of 7 runners runs 1.27 kilometers, then the total distance run by the 7 runners is 8.89 kilometers (1.27×7). This is closest to 9, choice (**B**).

43. A

The list of integers greater than 14 and less than 63 that are multiples of 7 is 21, 28, 35, 42, 49, and 56. The range of the list is the difference between the largest value on the list and the smallest: $21 - 56$, or 35. (**A**) is correct. (C) would be the value if the range were calculated by including either 14 or 63. (E) would be the value if the range were calculated by using 14 and 63.

44. E

Simplify each expression until you find the one that is equal to $18y - 47$.

(A): $3(8y - 16) - 6y - 1 = 24y - 48 - 6y - 1 = 18y - 49$. Eliminate.

(B): $4(7y - 3) - 10y + 59 = 28y - 12 - 10y + 59 = 18y + 47$. Eliminate.

(C): $23 - 5(3y + 14) + 31y = 23 - 15y - 70 + 31y = 16y - 47$. Eliminate.

(D): $21y + 35 - 3(y + 4) = 21y + 35 - 3y - 12 = 18y + 23$. Eliminate.

(**E**): $5(7y - 16) - 17y + 33 = 35y - 80 - 17y + 33 = 18y - 47$. This is correct.

45. E

Left and right shifts change the x-coordinate. Up and down shifts affect the y-coordinate. The original point is $(-4, 5)$.

$-4 + 12 = 8$ for the new x-coordinate.

$5 - 10 = -5$ for the new y-coordinate.

So, the coordinates of the new point are $(8, -5)$.

46. 17

The average formula is Average $= \frac{\text{Sum of the terms}}{\text{Number of terms}}$. The average is $\frac{9 + 3 + 4 + 12 + 6 + 1 + 8 + x}{8} = \frac{43 + x}{8}$. The average also equals 7.5, so you can write the equation $\frac{43 + x}{8} = 7.5$. Multiply both sides by 8: $43 + x = 60$. Subtract 43 from both sides: $x = 17$.

47. C

Work with the equations $4w = 4x + 20$ and $7y = -7z + 56$.

Since the equation $4w = 4x + 20$ contains the variables w and x, solve this equation for $w - x$, which is one of the factors in the expression $(w - x)(y + z)$.

$$4w = 4x + 20$$
$$4w - 4x = 20$$
$$w - x = 5$$

Similarly:

$$7y = -7z + 56$$
$$7y + 7z = 56$$
$$y + z = 8$$

Now that you have the value of each factor in the expression, use substitution:

$$(w - x)(y + z) = (5)(8) = 40.$$

48. D

The temperature given for May 2019 in the graph is 65°F. Because the temperature is recorded as 52°F in August 2019 and 71°F in December 2019, choice (**D**) is correct.

49. $\dfrac{3}{5}$

Solve the equation for x and simplify:

$$-8(x - 3) = 4(3x + 7) - 16$$
$$-8x - 8(-3) = 4(3x) + 4(7) - 16$$
$$-8x + 24 = 12x + 28 - 16$$
$$-8x + 24 = 12$$
$$-20x + 24 = 12$$
$$-20x = -12$$
$$x = \frac{-12}{-20} = \frac{12}{20} = \frac{12 \div 4}{20 \div 4} = \frac{3}{5}$$

50. B

The formula for average speed is Average speed = $\dfrac{\text{Total distance}}{\text{Total time}}$. Since the graph is a straight line, the speed was constant throughout the time interval. Plug in a pair of numbers for distance and time into the formula to obtain the average speed. It is easy to divide by 10, so use the distance 480 miles and divide by the corresponding time of 10 hrs: $480 \div 10 = 48$ miles/hour. This makes (**B**) correct. Because the graph is a straight line, you can check other points on the line using this formula to confirm your answer (e.g., $240 \div 5$ also equals 48).

51. A

When multiplying by powers of 10, move the decimal point the number of places indicated in the exponent of 10. Move the decimal point to the left if the exponent is negative and to the right if the exponent is positive. Convert the three given values this way:

I. $0.76 \times 10^5 = 76{,}000$

II. $7{,}600 \times 10^{-4} = 0.76$

III. $7.6 \times 10^2 = 760$

Because none of the values are the same, (**A**) is correct.

52. B

Your task in this algebra problem is to isolate the variable. The first step is to add 1 to each side. This operation yields $\dfrac{2x}{3} = 12$. Next, multiply both sides by 3 to get $2x = 36$. Finally, divide both sides by 2: $x = 18$.

53. D

Set up a part-to-whole proportion: $\dfrac{80}{100} = \dfrac{352}{G}$.

Cross-multiply and solve for G: $\dfrac{80}{100} = \dfrac{352}{G} \rightarrow \dfrac{4}{5} = \dfrac{352}{G}$, $4G = 5 \times 352$, $4G = 1{,}760$, and $G = 440$. Alternatively, use the fact that $\dfrac{1}{8}$ of 80% is 10%. So $\dfrac{1}{8}$ of 352, which is 44, is 10% of G. Multiply 44 by 10 to determine that G is 440. Choice (**D**) is correct.

54. C

This pie chart shows part-to-whole relationships by percent. The budget for law enforcement is 30% of the whole budget. Therefore, $5,400 is 30% of the whole budget. Set up the proportion $\dfrac{30}{100} = \dfrac{\$5{,}400}{x}$.

Cross-multiply and solve for the whole budget: $30x = 100 \times 5{,}400$; $30x = 540{,}000$; $x = \$18{,}000$.

55. D

Though you can analyze these lists using variables, Picking Numbers can easily show you what is happening to the median, average, and range.

List L: 51, 52, 53

median = 52; average = 52; range = 2

List M: 44, 52, 60

median = 52; average = 52; range = 16

Comparing the two lists, both have the same median (52), but the range of List M (16) is larger than the range of List L (2). Choice (**D**) is correct.

56. 16

The employee had total sales of $4,000. The commission earned, in dollars, on this $4,000 was x percent of 4,000 dollars, which is $\dfrac{x}{100}(4{,}000 \text{ dollars}) = 40x$ dollars. So the employee earned a total of 170 dollars plus $40x$ dollars, which is $(170 + 40x)$ dollars. Since the employee earned a total of 810 dollars, write the equation $170 + 40x = 810$ and solve this equation for x. Subtract 170 from both sides of the equation $170 + 40x = 810$ to get $40x = 640$. Divide both sides by 40 and simplify:

$$x = \frac{640}{40} = \frac{64}{4} = 16$$

The value of x is **16** percent.

Core Writing Practice Test 1

100 Minutes: 40 Minutes—40 Questions; 60 Minutes—2 Essays

Directions: You have 40 minutes to answer questions 1–40, and you have 30 minutes each for the two essays.

Questions 1–40. Each of the sentences in this section of the test has four parts that are lettered and underlined. Read each sentence and decide whether any of the underlined portions contains an error in word use, an error in grammatical construction, or an error or omission in punctuation or capitalization, according the conventions of standard written English. If you find an error, note the letter printed beneath the underlined part and choose that as your answer. Try to answer every question.

If you do not find an error in any underlined part of the sentence, choose (E), "No error," which appears after the sentence. *No sentence has more than one error.*

1. Before <u>the advent of</u> modern surgical techniques,
   A
   <u>bleeding patients</u> with leeches <u>were considered</u>
   B   C
   therapeutically <u>effective</u>. <u>No error</u>
                    D   E

2. The recent establishment of "Crime Busters,"
   officially sanctioned neighborhood block-
   watching groups<u>,</u> <u>has</u> <u>dramatic</u> improved
                    A   B   C
   relations <u>between</u> citizens and police. <u>No error</u>
              D   E

3. The masterpiece auctioned so <u>successfully</u>
                                   A
   today<u>,</u> depicts a biblical scene in <u>which</u> the king
        B   C
   is on his throne <u>with</u> his counselors respectfully
                     D
   standing below. <u>No error</u>
                    E

4. <u>During</u> the election campaign, the major political
   A
   parties <u>have agreement</u> that minorities must
            B
   <u>be given</u> the opportunity <u>to advance</u> in society.
    C   D
   <u>No error</u>
    E

5. Most of the delegates <u>which</u> attended the
                           A
   convention <u>felt</u> the resolution was <u>too strongly</u>
               B   C
   worded, and the majority voted <u>against</u> it.
                                    D
   <u>No error</u>
    E

6. <u>Lost in the forest</u> on a cold night, <u>the hunters built</u>
    A   B
   a fire <u>to keep themselves</u> warm and
          C
   <u>to frighten away</u> the wolves. <u>No error</u>
    D   E

7. The effort to <u>create appropriate</u> theatrical
                   A
   effects <u>often result</u> in settings that cannot be
            B
   <u>effective</u> without an imaginative <u>lighting</u> crew.
    C   D
   <u>No error</u>
    E

8. Every one of the shops in the town <u>were closed</u>
                                        A
   on Thursday <u>because</u> of the <u>ten-inch</u> rainfall that
                B   C
   <u>had fallen</u> during the day. <u>No error</u>
    D   E

9. <u>According to</u> the directions on the package, the
   A
   contents <u>are</u> intended for external use <u>only</u> and
   B   C
   <u>should not hardly</u> be swallowed, even in small
   D
   quantities. <u>No error</u>
   E

10. Mr. Webster's paper is <u>highly imaginary</u> and
    A
    <u>very creative</u> <u>but</u> seems to be <u>lacking in</u> cogency.
    B   C   D
    <u>No error</u>
    E

11. The thirtieth <u>presidents'</u> numerous memoirs now
    A
    <u>about to be</u> published <u>promise</u> to be of special
    B   C
    <u>historical</u> interest. <u>No error</u>
    D   E

12. The point <u>on issue</u> was whether the dock
    A
    workers, <u>who</u> were <u>an extremely</u> vocal group,
    B   C
    <u>would decide to</u> return to work. <u>No error</u>
    D   E

13. <u>Raising</u> living costs, <u>together</u> with escalating
    A   B
    taxes, <u>have</u> proved to be a burden for <u>everyone</u>.
    C   D
    <u>No error</u>
    E

14. A number of <u>harried</u> department store
    A
    employees <u>were congregating</u> <u>around</u> the water
    B   C
    cooler <u>to compare and discuss</u> their grievances.
    D
    <u>No error</u>
    E

15. The deep-sea diver <u>considered herself</u> not only
    A
    a competent barnacle scraper <u>but</u> an amateur
    B
    scientist <u>capable of</u> collecting <u>interesting</u>
    C   D
    specimens of seashells. <u>No error</u>
    E

16. A *round robin* is a competition <u>in which</u> each
    A
    team <u>will have to</u> compete <u>against</u> every <u>other</u>
    B   C   D
    team. <u>No error</u>
    E

17. The voters were <u>dismayed</u> at <u>him retiring</u> from
    A   B
    <u>elected</u> office at such an early age, seemingly
    C
    <u>at the outset of</u> a brilliant career. <u>No error</u>
    D   E

18. <u>Having</u> a reasonable amount of intelligence and
    A
    steady persistence <u>assure</u> <u>one</u> of acquitting
    B   C
    oneself <u>creditably</u> in any undertaking. <u>No error</u>
    D   E

19. "Elementary, my dear Watson" <u>is</u> <u>frequently</u>,
    A   B
    though erroneously, said to be an observation
    of the <u>distinguished Detective</u> Sherlock Holmes.
    C   D
    <u>No error</u>
    E

Sentence Correction

Directions: In each of the following sentences, some part of the sentence or the entire sentence is underlined. Beneath each sentence, you will find five ways of writing the underlined part. The first of these repeats the original, but the other four are all different. If you think the original sentence is better than any of the suggested changes, you should select the first answer choice; otherwise, you should select one of the other choices.

This is a test of correctness and effectiveness of expression. In choosing answers, follow the requirements of standard written English: pay attention to acceptable usage in grammar, diction (choice of words), sentence construction, and punctuation. Choose the answer that most effectively expresses what the original sentence presents; this answer should be clear and exact, without awkwardness, ambiguity, or redundancy.

Remember, try to answer every question.

20. In *War and Peace*, Tolstoy presented his theories on history and illustrated them with a slanted account of actual historical events.

    A. illustrated them
    B. also illustrating them
    C. he also was illustrating these ideas
    D. then illustrated the theories also
    E. then he went about illustrating them

21. The variety of healthcare services offered to residents of Scandinavian countries at reduced cost far exceeds low-cost health programs available in the United States.

    A. far exceeds low-cost health programs
    B. far exceeds the number of low-cost health programs
    C. tends to be greater than low-cost health programs
    D. far exceed the number of low-cost health programs
    E. are greater than comparable low-cost health programs

22. Developed by a scientific team at his university, the president informed the reporters that the new process would facilitate the diagnosis of certain congenital diseases.

    A. Developed by a scientific team at his university
    B. Having been developed by a scientific team at his university
    C. Speaking of the discovery made by a scientific team at his university
    D. Describing the development of a scientific team at his university
    E. As it had been developed by a scientific team at his university

23. One ecological rule of thumb states that there is opportunity for the accumulation of underground water reservoirs but in regions where vegetation remains undisturbed.

    A. but in regions where vegetation remains undisturbed
    B. unless vegetation being left undisturbed in some regions
    C. only where undisturbed vegetation is in regions
    D. only in regions where vegetation remains undisturbed
    E. except for vegetation remaining undisturbed in some regions

24. The Equal Rights Amendment to Islandia's constitution is dying a lingering political death, <u>many dedicated groups and individuals have attempted</u> to prevent its demise.

    A. many dedicated groups and individuals have attempted

    B. although many dedicated groups and individuals have attempted

    C. many dedicated groups and persons has attempted

    D. despite many dedications of groups and individuals to attempt

    E. also, many dedicated groups and individuals have attempted

25. Economists should become proficient in <u>data mining, exploring the massive databases available today yield</u> insights that may overturn long-accepted thinking.

    A. data mining, exploring the massive databases available today yield

    B. data mining; the massive databases available today being explored to yield

    C. data mining, because exploring the massive databases available today yields

    D. data mining, because of exploring the massive databases available today to yield

    E. data mining; today they explore the massive databases that are available and yield

26. Developing a suitable environment for houseplants <u>is in many ways like when you are managing</u> soil fertilization for city parks.

    A. is in many ways like when you are managing

    B. is in many ways similar to when you are managing

    C. in many ways is on a par with managing your

    D. is in many ways similar to the managing of

    E. is in many ways like managing

27. Most students would get better grades if <u>writing were to be studied by them</u>.

    A. writing were to be studied by them

    B. they studied writing

    C. writing was studied by them

    D. they would have studied writing

    E. they were to have studied writing

28. <u>If they do not go into bankruptcy</u>, the company will probably survive its recent setbacks.

    A. If they do not go into bankruptcy

    B. Unless bankruptcy cannot be avoided

    C. If they can avoid bankruptcy

    D. If bankruptcy will be avoided

    E. Unless it goes bankrupt

29. Now that I have read the works of both Henry and William James, I am convinced that Henry is <u>the best psychologist and William the best writer</u>.

    A. the best psychologist and William the best writer

    B. a better psychologist, William is the best writer

    C. the best as a psychologist, William the best as a writer

    D. the best psychologist, William the better writer

    E. the better psychologist and William the better writer

30. When he arrived at the hospital, the doctor found that <u>several emergency cases had been admitted before</u> he went on duty.

    A. several emergency cases had been admitted before

    B. there were several emergency cases admitted prior to

    C. two emergency cases were being admitted before

    D. a couple of emergency cases were admitted before

    E. several emergency cases was admitted before

Revision in Context

Directions: This is an essay draft that requires some editing work. Choose the best versions of the sentences and/or paragraphs as examined in the questions. At times, the passage cannot be improved using the answer choices, and in those circumstances, you should indicate that it is correct as written. As you answer these questions, be sure to consider writing style; the author's tone and purpose; and standard English conventions of grammar, usage, punctuation, and capitalization.

Be sure to select an answer for each question.

Questions 31–36 refer to the following stimulus.

(1) If you are young and love football, it is advantageous to live near a large sporting-goods store that carries a wide variety of paraphernalia from different teams. (2) My daughter and I visit our local store at least once a year to buy another football jersey for yet another team. (3) <u>Whenever</u> my daughter is a fan of our city's professional team, she frequently changes her jersey to match that of her favorite player no matter what team he joins.

(4) A free agent is a professional football player who is no longer under contract with a team, which means he can choose the team with which he wants to play. (5) In the NFL today, players can become free agents easily. (6) Things were much different when I was growing up. (7) <u>My favorite player was on the same team, for his entire career I had one jersey</u>. (8) My daughter has bought over eight team jerseys in the past six years! (9) At seventy-five dollars a shirt, this is not a sustainable trend.

(10) There are many disadvantages <u>to free agency</u>. (11) <u>When my daughter and I</u> went to pre-season training practice to get a preview of this year's team, we constantly consulted the team roster to figure out the new team line-up, because there were so many new players. (12) At one point, a number of fans even started to cheer for a <u>player, who was no longer with the team</u>, because they did not realize someone new was wearing his number. (13) A second disadvantage of free agency <u>is having some camaraderie and cohesion</u>. (14) Football is the ultimate team sport, in which players must depend upon each other to win. (15) A team trains, strategizes, and plays together for months. (16) The players learn each other's strengths and weaknesses. (17) Eleven players are on the field at one time, and their goal is to stop the other team from progressing down the field. (18) If any one of those players leaves the team, it disrupts the dynamics and cohesion that the entire team has worked together to build. (19) <u>The quarterback is usually the player who is most important in maintaining a team's cohesion</u>.

31. In context, which of the following is the best version of the underlined portion of sentence 3 (reproduced below)?

    <u>Whenever</u> my daughter is a fan of our city's professional football team, she frequently changes her jersey to match that of her favorite player.

    A. (As it is now)
    B. Because
    C. In addition
    D. Although
    E. As a result

32. In context, which of the following is the best version of sentence 7 (reproduced below)?

    <u>My favorite player was on the same team, for his entire career I had only one jersey.</u>

    A. (As it is now)
    B. My favorite player was on the same team; for his entire career I had one jersey.
    C. As a result of my favorite player having been on the same team, for his entire career I had one jersey.
    D. My favorite player was on the same team for his entire career, I had one jersey.
    E. My favorite player was on the same team for his entire career, so I had one jersey.

33. In context, which of the following is the best version of the underlined portion of sentences 10 and 11 (reproduced below)?

    There are many disadvantages <u>to free agency. When my daughter and I</u> went to pre-season training practice to get a preview of this year's team, we constantly consulted the team roster to figure out the new team lineup, because there were so many new players.

    A. (As it is now)
    B. to free agency: for when my daughter and I
    C. to free agency, for when my daughter and I
    D. to free agency for when my daughter and I
    E. to free agency, because when my daughter and I

34. In context, which of the following is the best version of the underlined portion of sentence 12 (reproduced below)?

    At one point, a number of fans even started to cheer for a <u>player who, was no longer with the team</u>, because they did not realize someone new was wearing his number.

    A. (As it is now)
    B. player who, was no longer with the team,
    C. player who was no longer with the team,
    D. player who was no longer, with the team,
    E. player, who was no longer with the team,

35. In context, which of the following is the best version of the underlined portion of sentence 13 (reproduced below)?

    A second disadvantage of free agency <u>is having some camaraderie and cohesion.</u>

    A. (As it is now)
    B. would be to have some camaraderie and cohesion
    C. is total camaraderie and cohesion
    D. is the loss of camaraderie and cohesion
    E. is having camaraderie and cohesion become less important to the game

36. The writer is trying to decide whether to end the paragraph with sentence 19 (reproduced below):

    <u>The quarterback is usually the player who is most important in maintaining a team's cohesion.</u>

    The writer should:

    A. keep it because it adds a point of further interest on the subject
    B. keep it because it is an example of how free agency can be a problem for a team
    C. omit it because quarterbacks have no more effect on a team's cohesion than other players
    D. keep it because it demonstrates how important a player can be to a team's cohesion
    E. omit it because the paragraph is about free agency in general, and a comment about one position on a team is off topic

Research Skills

Directions: The following questions test your familiarity with basic research skills. For each question, choose the best answer.

Remember, try to answer every question.

37. A student is writing a paper on climate change. Which of the following could be a primary source for the paper?

    A. A book discussing the possible causes of fluctuations in Earth's climate and atmospheric levels of carbon dioxide over the past 500 million years

    B. A report by *Inside Climate News* stating that in the 1970s, scientists at a major oil company had identified global warming caused by fossil fuel consumption as a strong probability

    C. An international scientific group's publication of measurements of temperature and atmospheric carbon dioxide levels at various locations on earth over the past 25 years

    D. A report by a congressional committee presenting several conflicting analyses of climate data gathered over the past 25 years

    E. A passage from a science textbook reporting how much carbon dioxide is emitted as a result of fossil fuel consumption and explaining the degree to which increased levels of atmospheric carbon dioxide can cause changes in climate

38. A student is writing a paper on U.S. foreign policy during the presidency of Bill Clinton (1993–2001). Which of the following is NOT directly related to the student's paper?

    A. Statistical information about changes in U.S. consumer prices between 1995 and 2000

    B. Information concerning the number of American soldiers stationed in Europe during the 1990s

    C. A summary of negotiations between Israel and the Palestinian Liberation Organization (PLO) that were mediated by the United States

    D. A description of trade sanctions implemented against Iran in 1995

    E. Negotiations between the United States and North Korea concerning North Korea's plans to build nuclear weapons

39. Which of the following would be a secondary source on President Franklin Roosevelt?

 A. President Roosevelt's notes on a conversation between him and British Prime Minister Winston Churchill

 B. A description of President Roosevelt's physical condition by a person who visited the White House in 1944

 C. A historian's analysis of the manner in which President Roosevelt exercised leadership during World War II

 D. Excerpts from the portion of President Roosevelt's diary written at the beginning of World War II

 E. An interview with President Roosevelt by a *New York Times* reporter after the 1944 presidential election

Harris, Lloyd. "Finding a New Basis for Chinese-American Cooperation." *Essays on Contemporary American Foreign Policy*, edited by Sanders Fisher, Doubleworth & Company, 2013, pp. 59–94.

40. What kind of written work is cited above?

 A. A book

 B. An essay in an edited collection of essays

 C. A magazine article

 D. An article in a professional journal

 E. An essay posted on a website

Directions for the Written Assignment

This section of the test consists of a written assignment. It asks you to prepare a written response of about 300–600 words on the assigned topic. *The assignment is on the next page.* You should use your time to plan, write, review, and edit your response to the assignment.

Read the assignment carefully before you begin to write. Think about how you will organize what you plan to write. Your response to the written assignment will be evaluated based on your demonstrated ability to do the following:

- State or imply a clear position or thesis
- Present a well-reasoned and well-organized argument that connects ideas in a thoughtful and logical way
- Use support and evidence to develop and bolster your ideas and account for the views of others
- Display competent use of language through well-constructed sentences of varying lengths and structures
- Express yourself without distractions caused by inattention to sentence and paragraph structure, choice and use of words, and mechanics (i.e., spelling, punctuation, and capitalization)

Your response will be evaluated based on your demonstrated ability to express and support opinions, not on the nature or content of the opinions you express. The final version of your response should conform to the conventions of edited American English. It should be your original work, in your own words—do not copy or paraphrase other people's work.

Be sure to write about the assigned topic and use multiple paragraphs. Please write legibly. You may not use any reference materials during the test. Remember to review what you have written and make any changes you think will improve your response.

Written Assignment

41. "Schools are not providing an equal education for students of all genders. Among other things, it has been shown that teachers call on boys more often, allow boys to call out answers while requiring girls to raise their hands, allow boys more time to respond to questions, and give boys more feedback. Since the attitudes that lead to these unequal practices are deeply embedded, there is little that can be done to change this unequal education for students of different genders."

    Do you believe that schools are not providing equal education for students of different genders, and if so, do you agree that little can be done to address such inequalities?

    Write an essay to support your position.

Directions for the Written Assignment

In the following section, you will have 30 minutes to read two short passages on a topic and then plan and write an essay on that topic. The essay will be an informative essay based on the two sources provided.

Read the topic and sources carefully. You will probably find it best to spend a little time considering the topic and organizing your thoughts before you begin writing. DO NOT WRITE ON A TOPIC OTHER THAN THE ONE SPECIFIED. Essays on topics of your own choice will not be acceptable. In order for your test to be scored, your responses must be in English.

The essay questions are included in this test to give you an opportunity to demonstrate how well you can write. You should, therefore, take care to write clearly and effectively, using specific examples where appropriate. Remember that how well you write is much more important than how much you write, but to cover the topics adequately, you will probably need to write more than one paragraph.

Written Assignment

42. Modern scientific research provides historically unprecedented insight into ways for society to combat diseases, create reliable infrastructure, and understand the biology and mechanics of our universe. The mass media also makes it possible for the general public to access the growing corpus of literature on research findings. Both of the following sources address the significance of how the public responds to the results of scientific research.

Read the two passages carefully and then write an essay in which you identify the most important concerns regarding the issue and explain why they are important. Your essay must draw on information from BOTH of the sources. In addition, you may draw on your own experiences, observations, or reading. Be sure to CITE the sources, whether you are paraphrasing or directly quoting.

Source 1

Adapted from:

Jones, Virginia. *Knowing It All: Public Knowledge in the Digital Age*. New York: Worldwide Books, 2015. 37–38. Web. 11 Jan. 2017.

The way that people in present-day industrial societies think about science in the modern world actually tends to cultivate the very unscientific perception that science supplies us with unquestionable facts. However, if there is one unquestionable fact about science, it is that science is inherently uncertain. Every research study, every experiment, and every survey incorporates an extensive statistical analysis that is meant to qualify the probability that the results are actually consistent and reproducible. Yet policy makers, public relations interests, and so-called experts in the popular media continue to treat the results of every latest study as if they were surefire truths. Yet statistics are complicated, and in our need to feel that we live in a universe of predictable certainties, it is tempting to place our faith in the oversimplified generalities of headlines and sound bites rather than the rigorous application of probabilities.

Science serves an important practical function; predictability and reproducibility are vital to making sure that our bridges remain standing, our nuclear power plants run smoothly, and our cars start in the morning so we can drive to work. When these practicalities become everyday occurrences, they tend to encourage a complacent faith in the reliability and consistency of science. Yet faced with so many simple conveniences, it is important to remember that we depend on the advance of science for our very survival. And as technological advances engage increasingly complex moral questions within fields such as pharmaceutical developments, indefinite extension of life, and the potential for inconceivably potent weapons, an understanding of the limitations of science becomes just as important as an understanding of its strengths.

Source 2

Adapted from:

Greyson, Clark. "The Science of Doubt." *Albany Public Journal.* 17.1 (2016): 44–47. Web. 11 Jan. 2017.

While it is important that scientific knowledge be taken into consideration in significant matters of public interest, such consideration must be tempered with critical rigor. Who performs a research study, what kind of study it is, what kinds of scrutiny it comes under, and what interests support it are every bit as important as a study's conclusions.

Studies of mass media and public policy reveal that, all too often, scientific findings presented to the public as objective and conclusive are actually funded at two or three degrees of removal by corporate or political interests with a specific agenda related to the outcome of those findings. For example, some critics question the issue of whether a study of the effectiveness of a new drug is more likely to produce favorable results when the study is funded by the pharmaceutical company that owns the drug patent. In cases where such findings conflict with the interests of the funding parties, analysts sometimes wonder if information was repressed, altered, or given a favorable public relations slant in order to de-emphasize dangerous side effects. Some critics of company-funded studies argue that the level of misrepresentation included in such studies borders on immoral.

Part of the problem grows from the public's willingness to place blind faith in the authority of science without an awareness of the interests that lie behind the research. Public officials then, in turn, may sometimes be too willing to bend to public or private political pressure, rather than pursuing the best interests of their constituents. It is the duty of active citizens in a free society to educate themselves and to resist passive acceptance of every "scientific" finding.

Core Writing Practice Test 1 Answers and Explanations

1. C

"Bleeding," the gerund, is the subject of the verb "were considered" (the bleeding, not the patients, was therapeutically effective), so the sentence should read *bleeding . . . was considered.*

2. C

The verb "improved" needs to be modified by an adverb. You would change "dramatic" to *dramatically.*

3. B

The comma after *today* is unnecessary: never separate the subject (*masterpiece*) from its verb (*depicts*) with a comma.

4. B

The phrase "have agreement" is unidiomatic. People can *reach agreement* or *agree to do something* or *agree on something* or *agree that something is a certain way*, but agreement is not something one has. If editing this, you could change "have agreement" to *have agreed.*

5. A

Did you ever hear "people aren't whiches" in your English class? That old grammar saying applies here: the delegates are people, so the sentence requires *who* instead of "which."

6. E

This sentence contains no error.

7. B

"The effort" is the subject of the verb "result," and because "effort" is singular, the verb should be changed to *results.*

8. A

"Every one" is the subject of the verb "were closed." "Every one" takes the singular form of the verb, so the sentence should read *was closed.*

9. D

"Should not hardly" probably just sounds wrong to you. There's no need for the word "hardly," which creates an implicit double negative, so it should be omitted.

10. A

This question focuses on word choice. "Imaginary" refers to something that is not real, and the paper in question is surely real. *Imaginative* would be a better choice here.

11. A

The words "the thirtieth" indicate the sentence refers to the memoirs of only one president, so the singular possessive *president's*, rather than the plural possessive, is required.

12. A

"The point on issue" is an example of an idiomatic expression in which the wrong preposition has been used. The correct idiom is *point at issue.*

13. A

"Raising" is a form of the active verb *to raise*. Because no one is raising the cost of living, the passive verb *to rise* should be used. The correct phrasing would be *rising living costs.*

14. E

This sentence contains no error.

15. B

The sentence incorrectly uses the idiomatic phrase *not only . . . but also*. The word *also* must be added to the second part of the phrase.

16. B

There's no need for the future tense in this sentence, which describes how a round robin works. *Has to* or *must* would be good replacements for "will have to."

17. B

The sentence is incorrect because the pronoun "him" should be changed to the possessive *his* before the gerund (*-ing* verb form).

18. B

The gerund "Having" is the subject of the verb "assure." This subject is singular, so *Having . . . assures* would be correct.

19. D

There is no reason for *Detective* to be capitalized.

20. A

The original sentence is correct (**A**). It involves a past-tense compound verb ("presented . . . and illustrated") that maintains a parallel structure and conciseness. The verb form in choice (B) is wrong. Choice (C) creates a compound sentence with neither proper punctuation nor parallel structure. (D) and (E) are not grammatically incorrect, but both are too wordy.

21. B

There are two issues in this question. First, the subject of the sentence is "variety," which is singular. That means a singular verb form is needed and choices (D) and (E) are out. The sentence also involves a comparison, and only like things can be compared—in this case, numbers of programs. Both (A) and (C) result in a comparison between "a variety" and "programs," unlike things that cannot be compared. Only (**B**) corrects the subject-verb agreement issue and presents a comparison between like things.

22. C

The modifying phrase at the beginning of the sentence needs to modify the noun or pronoun that immediately follows—in this case, the president. As it stands, the sentence tells you that the president himself was developed by a scientific team (a scary thought!). Neither (B) nor (E) corrects this problem. Choice (D) suggests that the team was developed at the university. Only (**C**) corrects the problem.

23. D

The second part of the sentence describes regions that have certain characteristics. "Only" is the correct linking word to set those regions apart. Choice (C) doesn't make sense, so (**D**) is correct.

24. B

Choice (**B**) most clearly shows the contrast between the lingering political death and the efforts of groups and individuals to prevent this death. Choice (D) also shows a contrast, but "dedications of groups" doesn't make sense. Choices (A), (C), and (E) all create run-ons by combining two independent clauses with only a comma.

25. C

As written, this sentence incorrectly joins two independent clauses with a comma. (B) and (E) replace the comma with a semicolon. However, (B) changes the text after the comma to a fragment, and (E) is wordy and subtly changes the meaning of the sentence. (C) and (D) retain the comma. While (D) is passive and wordy (with "because of" and "to yield"), (**C**) correctly uses "because" to introduce a dependent clause that clearly states the reason economists should learn data mining.

26. E

(**E**) is the most clear and concise choice, omitting needless words and retaining a parallel structure: "developing . . . managing."

27. B

Choices (A) and (C) use the passive voice, which is awkward and wordy. (D) and (E) are incorrect forms of the conditional. (**B**) is correct, clear, and concise.

28. E

"The company" is singular, so the use of the plural pronoun "they" in choices (A) and (C) is incorrect. (B) and (D) awkwardly use the passive voice. Choice (E) correctly uses "it" to refer to "The company" and is clear and concise.

29. E

When comparing two of anything, use *better* instead of *best*. Only choice (**E**) does this correctly.

30. A

The original sentence, (**A**), is correct because it uses the past and past perfect tenses correctly. The doctor's actions occur in the past tense ("arrived" and "found"), and admission of the emergency cases had occurred earlier than that, making the past perfect ("had been admitted") correct.

31. D

Neither (C) nor (E) makes sense in context. Choice (A) is wrong because even if the daughter is only periodically a fan of the local team, she would not need to change her jersey whenever this occurred. Finally, (B) is out because her being a fan of the local professional team would not cause her to change her jersey to match that of her favorite player. Only (**D**) conveys the contrast between being a fan of the local team and frequently changing her jersey to match that of her favorite player.

32. E

Choices (A) and (D) join two independent clauses with a comma, so both are out. Choice (C) uses an incorrect verb form ("having been"), and its comma is in the wrong place. (He wasn't just "on the same team"; he was on the same team "for his entire career.") (B), although it correctly joins two independent clauses with a semicolon, also divides the sentence in the wrong place. Only (**E**) clearly and succinctly conveys the cause-and-effect relationship between the favorite player's being on one team for his entire career and the narrator's having just one jersey.

33. A

Make sure that independent clauses are properly separated. These two sentences are correctly separated with a period because they express two separate, independent thoughts—making choice (**A**) correct. Choice (B) is incorrect because, while the colon draws the reader's attention to a specific point directly related to what precedes it, the words *for when* make the sentence structure awkward. Furthermore, the first sentence says there are many disadvantages to free agency, but the information in the second sentence expresses only one disadvantage. (C) is incorrect because it joins two independent clauses with a comma, creating a run-on, and (D), with no punctuation, is also a run-on. (E) makes no sense because the narrator and his daughter do not cause disadvantages to free agency.

34. C

When a word, phrase, or clause is set off from the rest of the sentences with commas, the sentence must make sense without it. In this case, a comma incorrectly separates "who was" from the remainder of the sentence. Choice (B) makes a similar error. The placement of the comma in choice (D) breaks the sentence up incorrectly. (E) would be correct if the clause "who was no longer on the team" were not necessary to the meaning of the sentence, but it is necessary and the commas are wrong. (**C**) correctly removes the comma, recognizing that this clause is necessary.

35. D

The context suggests that free agency leads to instability on a team's roster, which in turn results in less cohesion. Choices (A), (B), and (C) suggest that free agency results in more cohesion, so they can all be ruled out. (E) does relate free agency to camaraderie and cohesion, but it also states that free agency makes camaraderie and cohesion less important, which is not what the context indicates. Only (**D**) is consistent with the context in observing that free agency causes less camaraderie and cohesion on a team.

36. E

The paragraph is about how free agency damages a team's camaraderie and cohesion. A closing statement about the importance of one position on a team introduces a new topic and therefore should be omitted from this paragraph. This means choice (**E**) is correct. Choice (C) gives the wrong reason for omitting this sentence because the paragraph is not concerned with the relative importance of the positions on a team.

37. C

For this kind of paper, a primary source would be one that supplies actual data, (**C**), as opposed to interpretations of data. Choices (A), (D), and (E) all present analysis/interpretation of data. Choice (B) is concerned with behavior related to the discovery of climate change, but it also involves secondhand reporting.

38. A

The subject of the paper is U.S. foreign policy under President Clinton. Choices (B), (C), (D), and (E) all directly involve relations between the United States and other nations. Only choice (**A**) is concerned with the internal affairs of the United States. Any relationship between U.S. consumer prices and its foreign policy could only be indirect.

39. C

A secondary source is one not written by people directly involved in the situation or events being studied. In this case, choices (A), (B), (D), and (E) all involve firsthand witnesses or participants in the events. Only choice (**C**) is not a firsthand account.

40. B

Because the first title in the citation is in quotation marks, it cannot be a full-length work—so eliminate choice (A). (C) and (D) both involve periodicals, but no volume or issue number is provided—only the title of a full-length work, the name of a publisher, and the year of publication. That rules out (E) also. Choice (**B**) is correct. This is a shorter work (essay) contained in a full-length edited book that was published in 2013.

Written Assignment Sample Response

The following is an example of a strong response to the written assignment.

In my 16 years as a student in the public schools, I have witnessed teacher practices that at times favored boys, but in other instances favored girls. I have experienced examples of unequal treatment by gender at all grade levels: elementary, high school, and post-secondary. When I have witnessed unequal treatment, I believe teachers have been at least partially responsible; I think that teachers could address these inequities and create more equitable educational experiences for all students.

I first witnessed gender-related differences in teaching practices when I was an elementary school student. In these grade levels, teachers divided us into reading groups. The high group was always mostly girls. Once you were put into a group (high, medium, or low), you were almost never moved, so it was difficult for boys to achieve the high group. Boys were often more active in elementary school, so they would get into trouble for being loud or getting out of their seats. The teachers' perhaps unconscious attitudes impacted their expectations, and therefore their teaching practices, for students of different sexes in the classroom. These preconceptions about girls' reading ability and boys' rambunctiousness would obviously have an impact on how students, both male and female, would perceive themselves academically: girls are good with words, while boys are too physical for academic success.

The gender differences I observed at the elementary level changed, but did not disappear, in my high school years. Once again, the teachers' attitude about each sex's abilities would impact how both were treated academically. I went to a school where girls were encouraged to take math and science courses, although there were more boys in chemistry, physics, and pre-calculus. When we did group work, the girls talked a lot but didn't usually get into trouble. The teacher probably thought they were talking about the project. Boys got into trouble for talking, because they often yelled across the room. Sometimes the girls didn't get to participate as much in class because boys called out answers, and the teachers accepted them. If a girl tried to just call out an answer, she was usually told to hush and raise her hand.

Even at the college level, I see what appear to be traces of gender difference. I am majoring in elementary education, and there are very few males in the program. It is hard to say if this is unequal. Were they discouraged from going into elementary education because their previous teachers instilled the idea, consciously or not, that the little kids are for women and the high school content areas are for men? It is difficult for me to say if this is true, but it seems likely.

Fortunately, educators can address some of these gender-based inequities found in the public education system. Elementary schools need more male teachers so the reading groups even out and the boisterous boys don't lose their playfulness. It might even help some girls find their inner playfulness. At the high school level, schools can continue to encourage girls to participate in math and science courses. Female teachers in math and science might serve as role models for girls, showing them that they can succeed and even pursue careers in these subject areas. Perhaps most importantly, teachers should be educated about their possible gender biases and the likely impact so that they can monitor these attitudes and practices in the classroom. In these ways, the unequal treatment and resulting imbalance in educational opportunities afforded boys and girls might be remedied.

Explanation

This high-scoring essay identifies and develops a well-thought-out thesis: the writer agrees that unequal education occurs, but disagrees that it always plays out as described in the quote. Most importantly, the author disagrees that the problem is unsolvable. The author creates a well-organized essay with transition words (e.g., "Fortunately"), includes introductory and concluding paragraphs, and discusses the inequalities that occur at each education level in separate body paragraphs. The author fully explains examples from his or her own experience that illustrate gender inequality in school, using these as support for his or her claims about how teachers' attitudes impact their actions in the classroom. The author effectively concludes by providing examples of how teachers could address inequality, based on points the author previously described. The author uses a variety of sentence structures and appropriate word choices, and he or she only makes a few errors in grammar and mechanics (e.g., the unclear/incorrect sentence structures in the clauses that begin *girls are good with . . .* and *Boys got into trouble for talking . . .*).

Written Assignment Sample Response

The following is an example of a strong response to the written assignment.

Both authors address the problems with the publics' generally easy acceptance of scientific study results. Virginia Jones claims that the publics' tendency to view science as "unquestionable facts" rather than as "inherently uncertain" can have significant consequences ("Knowing it All"). She uses examples of the mostly reliable infrastructure we encounter every day, such as bridges and cars, to show that we tend to take science for granted; however, she claims science's "advance" will be necessary "for our very survival" (Jones) Jones implies that another consequence of the public's oversimplification of study results is that by ignoring the complexities of statistical analysis, the media reports on studies misleadingly and policy makers might make misinformed decisions. Finally, this over-simplification could hinder the careful consideration of the "increasingly complex moral questions" we face about the application of new scientific achievements (Jones).

Clark Greyson also calls the blind acceptance of scientific research into question, but provides a different reason than Jones. Greyson claims that the background of any study is "every bit as important as a study's conclusions" ("The Science of Doubt"). Citing other studies, Greyson points out that much research, pharmaceutical studies, for instance, are ultimately funded by groups that have financial interest in the research's outcome, which may result in skewed findings, perhaps even to the extant of being "immoral" (Greyson). Implying these misleading studies could put their health at risk, Greyson encourages the public to learn about possible conflicts of interest. Like Jones, Greyson mentions the impact of policy makers' response to findings, specifically calling on them to resist pressures and make decisions that will benefit those they represent.

Thus, both sources discuss the negative consequences of the public's willingness to accept all scientific findings as facts without questioning. In both allowing questionable practices to go unchecked as described by Greyson, and oversimplifying scientific results as described by Jones, this acceptance can result in the enacting of practices and public policy that are not necessarily in the best interests of society.

Explanation

This high-scoring essay explains the primary issue identified by both authors: the public's "generally easy acceptance of scientific study results." The writer uses details and examples from both sources to fully describe the main issues that each author identifies concerning this practice. The writer expertly links the two sources by identifying their common general idea (the public's too-easy acceptance of scientific studies), discussing points of agreement (such as how this practice impacts policy decisions), and describing differing points (distinctive reasons/consequences for this practice). The writer cites the sources consistently. The writer employs effective organization, describing one author per paragraph and summarizing in a concluding paragraph. The essay displays sentence variety and effective word choice, and has a relatively small number of errors (e.g., the improper use of the apostrophe in *publics'*, the incorrect word choice "extant").

Go Online for More Practice

Congratulations! By finishing up the Practice Tests, you've completed your work in the book for the Praxis Core Tests.

Now, continue your prep by moving on to your online resources. If you haven't yet registered your book to access your online practice, do so now using these simple steps:

1. Go to **kaptest.com/moreonline**.
2. Follow the on-screen directions. Have your copy of this book available.

GO ONLINE

kaptest.com/login

Please note that access to the online portal is limited to the original owner of this book.

Once you've registered your book, go to **kaptest.com/login** anytime to log in with your email and password.

For the Praxis Core tests, your online resources include the following:

- Kaplan's Math Foundations. This is a course designed specially for adult learners who need to reacquaint themselves with the foundations of arithmetic, algebra, and geometry. It has 5 hours of video lessons and 225 practice questions designed to restore your skill level and confidence in these areas of math.
- Two full-length Praxis Core Reading practice tests with complete answers and explanations
- Two full-length Praxis Core Math practice tests with complete answers and explanations
- Two full-length Praxis Core Writing practice tests with complete answers and explanations

Use your performance on the in-book practice and test material to assess your strengths and areas of opportunity among the Praxis Core tests you'll be required to take. Then, find time in your study calendar for additional learning and practice. Account for the length of each practice test you want to take and block out the time required to complete it.

Take each online practice test under test-like conditions to the greatest extent possible. Turn off your phone and close all other programs and apps while you are testing. Part of becoming an expert Praxis Core test taker is honing your concentration and building the stamina for 1 hour 20 minute to 1 hour 40 minute tests.

When you finish, review your results thoroughly, question by question, using the Kaplan explanations. Review is where your greatest learning and improvement will occur. Go over even those questions you got right. The explanations will help you identify patterns you can spot to more quickly and confidently handle similar questions on your official exam.

Thank you for your decision to become an educator—and thank you, too, for studying with Kaplan. We wish you all the best in your educational and professional endeavors.

PART TWO

PRAXIS: PRINCIPLES OF LEARNING AND TEACHING

INTRODUCING THE PRAXIS PRINCIPLES OF LEARNING AND TEACHING (PLT) TESTS

This section of the book is dedicated to the Praxis Principles of Learning and Teaching (PLT) tests. You should refer to the requirements for the state in which you plan on teaching to determine which of these tests you will need to take. See your book's online resources for a list of links to state licensing requirements websites and other contact information for state teacher certification offices.

What is the PLT?

The Praxis PLT tests focus on the basic principles of learning and teaching that are essential for running a classroom. These principles are built on theoretical foundations provided by key educational theorists and developmental psychologists.

Chapter 5 provides a review of the main names and theories that appear on the PLT tests. Although the PLT tests are divided up according to grade levels, the review here is designed to address universal concerns and theories relevant to learning and teaching. These same principles are tested in each of the four PLT tests. Consequently, Chapter 5 applies to you if you are required to take any of the following exams (each test's code appears in parentheses after the test's name): PLT: Early Childhood (5621), Grades K–6 (5622), Grades 5–9 (5623), or Grades 7–12 (5624). Note: This material is also relevant to the Praxis Elementary Education: Curriculum, Instruction, and Assessment test (5017).

Please note that all four of the Praxis PLT tests reference the same PLT concepts and vary only slightly from each other. In this book, we have provided three sets of practice questions, one each for PLT: Grades K–6, PLT: Grades 5–9, and PLT: Grades 7–12. Because there is so much overlap, you may find it useful to practice with sets designed for grade levels other than the one for which you will test. Just keep in mind that each set will ask you to apply the common principles to the grade levels covered by the specific test.

In Chapter 6, you'll find two full-length PLT practice tests, one each for grades K–6 and grades 7–12 (the two most popular PLTs for test takers nationwide). In your online resources, you'll find four more full-length PLT practice tests—one for grades K–6, two for grades 5–9, and one for grades 7–12.

If you are taking any of the PLT tests (or the Elementary Education: Curriculum, Instruction, and Assessment test), begin by taking your PLT pre-test at the start of Chapter 5. Then, work through the review in Chapter 5. Continue your preparation with the sample PLT practice questions and explanations. Finally, wrap up by taking and thoroughly reviewing the full-length PLT tests in this book and in your online resources.

Taking the PLT

The four Praxis PLT tests share the same format. Each is two hours long and consists of 70 multiple-choice questions and two case studies accompanied by four short essay questions. The testmaker suggests spending approximately 1 minute on each multiple-choice question, leaving 50 minutes to read, evaluate, and answer the case study questions.

We agree with those timing guidelines. However, it's important to note that you need not take the sections of this test in order—in fact, Kaplan recommends against taking this test front to back.

Ideally, you should spend a little less than an hour on your first pass through the multiple-choice section. If you've spent enough time reviewing the content in this chapter, you'll have a framework to answer the majority of questions. But even the most prepared test takers may find that a few questions on this test are outside their areas of expertise. Don't spend too much time when this happens; if you run into a stumper, "mark" the question using the computer interface and move on.

Once you've wrapped up your case study answers, head back to the questions you marked earlier. Some of them might be easier to answer when you take a second look. Others may take a little longer. At this stage, you've done enough that you can afford to spend some extra time on the last few problems. Make sure to keep your eye on the clock, though. There is no wrong-answer penalty on the PLT, so you should never leave a question blank. Use your last two minutes to randomly pick answer choices for any unanswered questions.

CHAPTER 5

PRINCIPLES OF LEARNING AND TEACHING

LEARNING OBJECTIVES

By the end of this chapter, you will be able to do the following:

- Describe the structure and format of the Praxis PLT test
- Outline the four major content areas covered on the PLT test
- Apply strategic analysis to evaluate and answer PLT case study questions
- Use the Praxis PLT practice test to assess your performance

Taking Your Core PLT Pre-Test

Before you begin studying and practicing Praxis Principles of Learning and Teaching, take a pre-test to assess your initial strengths and areas of greatest opportunity on the test. With 35 multiple-choice questions and one case study with two questions to complete in 60 minutes, the pre-test is half the length of the official exam. Find time to complete the pre-test in one sitting, and time yourself strictly as you take it.

The purpose of the pre-test is self-assessment. Some test takers hesitate to take pre-tests because they haven't studied yet, or they want to try the questions without time restriction so that they can get them all correct. Those approaches, however, defeat the purpose of the pre-test, which is to get a clear-eyed look at your performance and skill level on all that the test entails.

Part of the test's challenge is its timing. Some of the questions may seem easy, and some may strike you as really difficult. When you encounter hard questions on the pre-test, don't be afraid to skip them or make your best guess. It's more valuable to get a broad view of your performance on different question types than to spend several minutes struggling to get one question right.

So, do your best, but don't get too excited or worried about your score on the pre-test. There's a lot of learning and practice to come, and your performance on the pre-test does not predict your official score. That will be the result of your study and effort.

PLT Pre-Test

60 Minutes—37 Questions

Directions: You have 35 minutes to answer questions 1–35. Read each question carefully and circle the correct answer(s) in your book. You may take notes on blank scratch paper during the pre-test.

1. During a lesson on slope-intercept form of linear equations, a student blurts out that his family owns a car repair shop. He explains that the shop charges $35 per hour for labor plus a $75 diagnostic fee. Which of the following is the most appropriate teacher response to the interruption?

    A. Discussing how to represent the family business's pricing model with an equation in slope-intercept form.

    B. Ignoring the student and continuing the lesson on slope-intercept form.

    C. Asking the student to write that thought down and discuss it with the teacher another time.

    D. Assigning the student extra work as punishment for interrupting the class.

2. A student in Mr. Smythe's science class has joined the Big Sisters/Big Brothers mentoring program in the local community. The student's mentor calls Mr. Smythe, requesting information regarding the student's attendance, grades, and behavior in school. The mentor is planning to help the student do better in school and would like to discuss the information with the student at their next meeting. Mr. Smythe is unable to provide the requested information to the mentor according to which of the following federal mandates?

    A. Individuals with Disabilities Education Act of 1997

    B. No Child Left Behind Act of 2001

    C. Family Educational Rights and Privacy Act of 1974

    D. Title IX of the Education Amendments of 1972

3. Which of the following are appropriate to include in anecdotal records?

    Select all that apply.

    A. The date and time when the teacher is taking the notes.

    B. What the teacher taking the notes thinks about the student's progress.

    C. A description of what the student is saying.

    D. Details about the actions the student is taking.

4. Ms. Hayes is interested in purchasing a new math manipulatives kit to use with her students. She has no experience with such kits and wants to make sure she is making the best purchase for her classroom. Which of the following would be the best source of information for Ms. Hayes to consult before purchasing the new materials?

    A. An article describing the role of manipulatives in the classroom

    B. A review published by the National Council of Teachers of Mathematics, comparing this kit to similar ones

    C. A blog review from a teacher who is sponsored by the company that makes the kit

    D. A brief description of the kit in a periodical dedicated to education trends

5. Which of the following are examples of the formal operational stage?

   Select all that apply.

   A. Students in a 9th-grade biology class are able to develop a hypothesis before beginning a lab.

   B. Students in a 6th-grade math class are able to properly place data points on a graph in descending order.

   C. Students in a 4th-grade class are able to determine that two different-shaped lumps of clay contain approximately the same amount.

   D. Students in a 7th-grade civics class are able to logically discuss the consequences of segregation.

6. A local military facility has expressed an interest in partnering with the school district to enhance the schools' JROTC program. Which of the following actions would help strengthen the partnership between the school district and the local military establishment?

   A. Sending home a newsletter to parents of JROTC students announcing the new partnership with the local military establishment.

   B. Inviting military personnel to visit the school and participate in upcoming JROTC events at the school.

   C. Posting a list of JROTC students on the district website.

   D. Inviting students to watch a live broadcast of a military ceremony occurring on the local base.

7. Which of these is NOT an example of helping students develop their executive function?

   A. Having students write down their assignments in a daily planner

   B. Listing the steps to solve a math problem

   C. Having students predict the next plot twist in a story

   D. Having students organize themselves into groups for a project

8. Ms. Hidenrite gives her math class a pre-assessment prior to the start of a new unit. She asks her students to reflect on the knowledge they already have regarding the upcoming unit. At the end of the unit, she gives her students a post-test. She asks her students to reflect on post-test data to identify their strengths, weaknesses, and misconceptions about the concepts covered in the unit. In which of the following complex cognitive processes is Ms. Hidenrite developing her students' abilities?

   A. Metacognition

   B. Transfer

   C. Problem solving

   D. Critical thinking

9. The most powerful use of self-assessment in the classroom is

   A. as an introductory activity to obtain data on student proficiency in lab activities

   B. as a point of reflection and adjustment midway through a project with clear criteria

   C. as a diagnostic assessment of student math skills at the beginning of the school year

   D. as an end-of-the-year essay on how students think their work habits impacted their learning

10. Which of the following scenarios complies with the fair-use provisions of copyright law?

   A. A music clip is used in a multimedia presentation. Copyright and attribution are provided for the clip.

   B. The teacher provides students with photocopies of the next three chapters of the novel they are reading together in class.

   C. Multiple, rented versions of a movie are being shown throughout the school during a reward activity.

   D. A math teacher runs copies of a practice worksheet from a workbook to give to her students during class.

11. Joel is a new student at Monroe High School. He has a speech and language disability that requires him to use alternative communication. What are some ways in which Joel's teachers can facilitate his class participation?

    Select all that apply.

    A. Encourage partner and group work where Joel can work with a peer to contribute ideas.

    B. Give Joel alternative work so he does not have to participate in class discussion.

    C. Modify Joel's written assignments so he has less work to complete.

    D. Allow Joel to use a computer voice program for his oral presentations.

12. Which of the following terms describes the quality of a test or assessment repeatedly reproducing the same results?

    A. Criterion

    B. Validity

    C. Reliability

    D. Norm

13. Which of the following are part of a constructivist approach to learning?

    Select all that apply.

    A. Students read a science text related to a concept in class.

    B. Students write a paragraph discussing their ideas and experiences regarding a concept in class.

    C. Students talk about their ideas and experiences regarding a concept in class.

    D. Students listen carefully as the science teacher provides information regarding a concept in class.

14. Which educational theorist formulated the idea that an environmental stimulus leads to a mediational process before there is an output of behavior?

    A. Bandura

    B. Bruner

    C. Piaget

    D. Bloom

15. Which behavioral theorist developed the idea that trust versus mistrust is a developmental stage?

    A. Watson

    B. Maslow

    C. Erikson

    D. Skinner

16. Which of the following is a limitation of using selected-response as a method to assess student understanding of a mathematical concept?

    A. A selected-response assessment can be time consuming to grade.

    B. Selected-response questions make it difficult to determine the source of student error.

    C. The format of selected-response questions is often confusing for students.

    D. A selected-response assessment is likely to result in a subjective evaluation of student performance.

17. Ms. Hudson and Ms. Emerson recently attended a math training workshop where they learned about and received new methods and materials for teaching equations to students. Both teachers believe these new methods and materials would benefit the students in their classrooms. The two teachers agree to implement the strategies; collect student data daily while using the new strategies; and meet twice a week to discuss student data, student learning results, and the effectiveness of the new strategies. Which of the following terms best describes the research methodology the two teachers are using?

    A. Action research

    B. Descriptive research

    C. Correlation study

    D. Experimental research

18. Which of the following statements regarding wait time is supported by research?

    Select <u>all</u> that apply.

    A. Increased wait time deepens student understanding of the topic.

    B. Increased wait time causes more off-topic disruptions in class discussions.

    C. Increased wait time generates more student questions.

    D. Increased wait time results in longer/more detailed student responses.

19. Mr. Trujillo's third-grade class structure involves peer interactions designed to promote social skills and learning opportunities. He feels his students see greater academic growth as they utilize their social skills. Mr. Trujillo's structure best aligns with the philosophies of which educational theorist?

    A. Piaget

    B. Vygotsky

    C. Kohlberg

    D. Bloom

20. Jalissa is a gifted student who requires enrichment beyond the regularly assigned classroom tasks. Which of the following best provides enrichment for Jalissa within the regular classroom setting?

    A. Asking Jalissa to complete 10 extra math problems from the same section of the book from which all students are working

    B. Asking Jalissa to rotate around the math classroom as a "student leader" to assist struggling students with the problems she has already completed

    C. Encouraging Jalissa to read ahead and attempt to answer problems in the next section

    D. Inviting Jalissa to participate in an extra activity after she finishes the regularly assigned math problems, allowing her to explore the math concepts covered in class in more depth

21. On the annual statewide assessment, Ms. Wohl's students receive a scaled score in mathematics. Ms. Wohl is thinking through how to explain this score to her students' parents. Which of the following best uses parent-friendly language to describe why Ms. Wohl uses a scaled score?

    A. A scaled score lets you compare scores across tests with slight variations in the test content.

    B. Scaled scores are calculated by statistically adjusting a student's raw points onto a common scale.

    C. A scaled score compares student performance to that of all other test takers.

    D. A scaled score shows how many questions your child was able to answer correctly.

22. The Law of Effect states that positive consequences will result in more desired behavior and negative consequences will serve to stop unwanted behavior. Which behavioral theorist formulated this law?

    A. Erikson

    B. Maslow

    C. Thorndike

    D. Watson

23. Which of the following science learning objectives focuses on the highest level of Bloom's taxonomy?

    A. Students will be able to design an experiment to further explore a concept learned in class.

    B. Students will be able to identify an acid and a base.

    C. Students will be able to describe a chemical reaction.

    D. Students will be able to predict a value based on a given data set.

24. Which of the following is an example of an appropriate use of a formative assessment?

    A. Dr. Taba administers an assessment of all prerequisite skills at the beginning of every semester.

    B. Mr. Noram always gives an end-of-year test to see how much of the year's content his students have mastered.

    C. Ms. Elton has conferences with all new kindergarten students to evaluate their language and counting skills.

    D. Ms. Kyla uses student performance on morning math work to form her small groups for the afternoon.

25. Mr. Johnson has been working on classroom management skills with his 6th-grade class. He has been trying to model cause-and-effect relationships for his students to help them increase their positive choices. Which motivational theory forms the foundation of Mr. Johnson's approach?

    A. Self-determination

    B. Cognitive dissonance

    C. Intrinsic motivation

    D. Attribution

26. Which of the following describes a primary goal of a professional learning community (PLC)?

    Select all that apply.

    A. To examine and select new, effective teaching practices

    B. To collaborate with other teachers to advocate for higher salaries

    C. To track student performance and analyze student results

    D. To arrange individual classroom space

27. Ms. Collins is interested in having her honors social studies class research a significant figure in history and then create a multimedia presentation about the chosen historical figure. Which of the following school personnel can best support Ms. Collins and her social studies students with this project?

    A. District technology coordinator

    B. Instructional coach

    C. Library media specialist

    D. Technology education teacher

28. Dr. Price wants to evaluate her students' writing throughout the unit. She also wants her students to select which pieces of their writing best reflect their mastery of the unit content. Which of the following assessment types best supports her objectives?

    A. Conference

    B. Selected-response

    C. Portfolio

    D. Self-assessment

29. Teachers at Leestown Middle School are required to complete two 15-minute walk-through observations during their planning time each school year. Teachers choose a partner and complete the walk-through process with this partner. The two teachers are required to pre-conference, complete a 15-minute observation, and post-conference. They also complete and discuss an observation template for each observation. Observation results remain confidential between the two teachers. The results are not used as a formal evaluation. Which of the following best describes the process described above?

    A. Peer coaching

    B. Mentoring

    C. Evaluating

    D. Observing

30. Which of the following best identifies an observable and measurable learning objective for a unit of study on genetics?

    A. Students will recognize the influence of genetics on the theory of evolution.

    B. Students will use a Punnett square to calculate genotype and phenotype ratios and to make predictions about the offspring formed in a genetic cross.

    C. Students will learn the significance of Gregor Mendel's work with pea plants.

    D. Students will understand the influence of technology on modern-day genetics.

31. Mr. Carmen brought in a variety of models and other visual aids for the science lesson today. What is the primary purpose of the materials Mr. Carmen brought?

    A. To capture students' attention so there will be fewer behavioral issues during the lesson.

    B. To reduce the amount of time Mr. Carmen will need to explain the material during the lesson.

    C. To make the information appear more interesting during the lesson.

    D. To help clarify the information Mr. Carmen will teach during the lesson.

32. Which of the following represents effective use of modeling in the classroom?

    Select all that apply.

    A. Running a role-playing session between two teachers to demonstrate an appropriate academic conversation during collaborative group work

    B. Providing examples of completed projects from the previous year for students to examine

    C. Providing step-by-step instructions for completing a task in class

    D. Demonstrating the use of a math strategy when solving a problem on the board in front of the entire class

33. Cooperative learning exercises are designed to pair up lower-performing students with higher-performing students. The idea is that the peer assistance will help with skills acquisition. This is an example of:

    A. schema

    B. self-efficacy

    C. self-regulation

    D. zone of proximal development

34. Which of the following is a characteristic of many intellectually gifted students?

   A. High level of curiosity, often expressed in a diverse range of interests

   B. Prolonged periods of low energy

   C. Ability to challenge themselves

   D. Ability to perform better when moved up in grade level to be with their intellectual peers

35. Ms. Seacat provides her students with a list of vocabulary words for their upcoming unit on fractions. She asks each student to collaborate with a partner to create a concept map using the words she provided. Which of the following is Ms. Seacat's primary purpose for this activity?

   A. Determining students' prior knowledge of fractions

   B. Determining students' motivation for learning

   C. Offering an opportunity for collaborative work

   D. Measuring students' progress with fractions

Case Study

Directions: You have 25 minutes to complete this case study. Read each question carefully and note the correct answer(s). You may take notes on blank scratch paper during the pre-test.

The case history below is followed by two short-answer questions. On the actual test, your responses to the questions will be evaluated with respect to professionally accepted principles and practices in teaching and learning. Be sure to answer all parts of the question.

Scenario

Mr. Bappin is a second-year 4th-grade teacher at a suburban elementary school near Detroit. His class has been working on identifying and modeling fractions. His third-period class has been making slower progress than his other sections, and he is concerned that classroom disruptions by one student in that class are the cause of its slower progress. He has asked his team leader, Ms. Morrow, to help him figure out how to improve the situation in the classroom.

Document 1

Mr. Bappin's Lesson Plan:

Objective: Students will:

1. Be able to create models for fractions with varying denominators
2. Be able to use models to compare fractions with like and unlike denominators

Procedure:

1. Students will receive a set of fraction tiles that they will use to make models of the fractions assigned by the teacher.
2. Students will work with a partner. Each pair will create a set of fractions with models and compare the size of the models to determine which fraction is larger.

Assessments:

1. The teacher will walk around and visually confirm that students can successfully create models of fractions.
2. Students will receive a grade on the worksheet containing all 10 sets of fractions to be compared.

Document 2

Excerpt from a transcript of audio recorded during Mr. Bappin's third-period class:

Mr. Bappin: OK, guys, go ahead and work through the 10 sets of fractions with your partner. You can each make a model of one of the fractions and then compare them together. Be sure to record your answer on the sheet that you will each turn in at the end of this period! Darnell, Julia, Fred, and Willa—please come work at the group table in the back.

*About 5 minutes pass with the class working on the assignment.

Aric: I cannot work with Sarah, Mr. B. She is not making the fractions that are on the sheet.

Mr. Bappin: Sarah, you must work on the assignment. I know you can do this work, and your partner is depending on you.

Sarah: I AM WORKING!! Aric is just mad because he's bad at fractions.

Mr. Bappin: That's fine. Let's all just get back to work.

*4 minutes pass while the class works and Mr. Bappin works with the group at the table.

Reggie: Sarah! Go back to your table!

Mr. Bappin: Sarah ...

Sarah: I know, I'm going back. I just wanted a partner that had a clue.

Mr. Bappin: Sarah, you may not speak about your classmates that way. Please apologize to Aric.

Sarah: No way! He was trying to get me in trouble in the beginning, and he doesn't know what's going on, and I am out of here!!

*Sarah gets her bag and storms out of class. The other students start talking and laughing.

Document 3

Excerpt from a conversation between Ms. Morrow and Mr. Bappin:

Ms. Morrow: How did today's lesson compare with the normal course of things in your classroom?

Mr. Bappin: It's like that pretty often. The lesson part usually goes OK, but when it's time for independent or group work, Sarah not only doesn't do the work, but also distracts other students to the point where no one gets anything done at all. She always has some issue with something or someone in the classroom, and she ends up storming out of class 80 percent of the time. Honestly, it takes a while for the other kids to calm down once she leaves, but the class gets more accomplished when she's gone. I just don't know what to do.

Constructed-Response Questions

Question 1

Review Mr. Bappin's lesson plan.

- Identify TWO ways in which Mr. Bappin could improve the effectiveness of his lesson plan.
- Explain how EACH of your two improvements would address the issues with the lesson plan. Base your response on your knowledge of the principles of effective instructional strategies.

Question 2

- Identify TWO strategies or techniques Mr. Bappin could use to manage Sarah's behavior during the group activity.
- Explain how EACH strategy or technique you identify would improve Sarah's behavior and the classroom environment. Base your responses on your knowledge of the strategies and principles of classroom management.

PLT Pre-Test Answers and Explanations

1. A

The student's blurted-out observation is actually a teachable moment. The teacher can show the class how the pricing model described by the student fits perfectly into a slope-intercept equation involving the rate of change and a one-time fee. Choice (**A**) is correct.

2. C

The Family Educational Rights and Privacy Act of 1974 (FERPA) is a federal law that provides protection and rights for the family in regard to educational records. Choice (**C**) is correct.

3. A, C, D

Teachers use anecdotal records to collect data about students in an observational format. Teachers should record the date and time, making choice (**A**) correct. They should also record details about what the student is saying and doing, making choices (**C**) and (**D**) correct. Anecdotal records should be objective, so teachers should not include their opinions, making (B) incorrect.

4. B

A review is an evaluation that rates an item based on its content and quality. A review written by an unbiased but knowledgeable professional would be more useful than one written by someone sponsored by the company, as in choice (C). Choices (A) and (D) do not address the specific question of the suitability of this specific kit for Ms. Hayes's classroom. Choice (**B**) is correct.

5. A, D

Students do not enter the formal operational stage until around age 11. Therefore, choice (C) would be incorrect. In addition, the formal operational stage marks the start of more abstract ways of thinking; (B) is incorrect because it describes a concrete skill. Choices (**A**) and (**D**) are correct.

6. B

Inviting military personnel to the schools will provide an opportunity for the soldiers to be directly involved with the current JROTC program. The military personnel can also discuss their future roles with the school programs and other opportunities for supporting the school programs while they are visiting and participating in the current program. Choice (**B**) is therefore correct.

7. C

"Executive function" refers to mental control and self-regulation. This includes paying attention, staying organized, remembering key information, and navigating social situations. In other words, executive function covers the classroom skills and behavior that lay the foundation for learning. Choice (**C**) is about reading comprehension and thus is the only choice that is *not* an example of executive function.

8. A

Metacognition is the intellectual process that enables an individual to think about/reflect on his own learning/thinking. (**A**) is the correct choice.

9. B

When students have clear goals and are asked to complete a self-evaluation, they are better able to improve their product or adjust their learning habits accordingly. However, students need to be taught how to evaluate their work and can benefit from strategies like teacher modeling. Therefore, using student self-assessment in diagnosing skill levels at the beginning of the year is not appropriate, making choices (A) and (C) incorrect. Self-assessment is most powerful as a strategy when students are able to use their self-assessment to make improvements, such as in (**B**). Choice (D) is incorrect because it would not provide the student with opportunities to apply what she had gained from the self-reflection.

10. A

Choice (**A**) is correct. Including copyright and attribution to the creator of the clip are within the provisions of fair use in copyright law. Choices (B), (C), and (D) are not in compliance with the fair-use provisions of copyright law.

11. A, D

Joel's teachers serve him best in the classroom by including him in as many class participation activities as possible, making choice (B) incorrect. Choice (C) is incorrect because Joel is not described as having cognitive issues, so reducing his workload is not an appropriate accommodation. Choices (**A**) and (**D**) are correct.

12. C

Reliability is a measure of how consistent an evaluation is, making choice (**C**) correct. Validity describes the degree to which a test is an accurate determination of what it is seeking to measure, making (B) incorrect. A test can have high reliability without having high validity.

13. B, C

Jean Piaget stated that students must be able to incorporate information into their schema. Experiences, discussions, and writing help students assimilate what they learn. Choices (**B**) and (**C**) are therefore correct. (A) and (D) are too passive, so they are incorrect.

14. A

Bandura added to behaviorist learning theories a belief that there is a cognitive link from an environmental stimulus that leads to the behavioral output. He called this a mediational process. Choice (**A**) is correct.

15. C

Trust versus mistrust is the first stage of Erikson's psychosocial development. Choice (**C**) is correct.

16. B

Selected-response, sometimes referred to as multiple-choice, is useful in that it is quick and easy to grade. This makes choice (A) incorrect. Selected-response is straightforward in format and always includes the right answer, making (C) and (D) incorrect. However, when a student makes an error on a selected-response question, the source of the student's error will not be as evident as it might be in other assessment formats. Choice (**B**) is therefore correct.

17. A

Action research is a study conducted by a teacher or a group of teachers to improve instruction by working through a series of reflective stages. The teachers in this scenario are reflecting often throughout the implementation of new strategies and materials. They are evaluating student learning and the effectiveness of the new strategies and materials in an effort to improve classroom instruction. Choice (**A**) is therefore correct.

18. A, C, D

Research does not support (B). Choices (**A**), (**C**), and (**D**) are supported by research and are correct.

19. B

The idea of increased social interaction to promote cognitive learning is a key component of Vygotsky's theories. Choice (**B**) is therefore correct.

20. D

Choice (**D**) is correct. This is a differentiated activity at an appropriate level that allows Jalissa and other advanced students to find greater enrichment.

21. A

A scaled score is adjusted so that the same score is comparable across tests that may vary in difficulty level, making choices (C) and (D) incorrect. While both (A) and (B) convey correct information, choice (**A**) better explains the reasons for using a scaled score and what it means for parents and students.

22. C

Thorndike is well-known for laying the foundation of the effects of consequences on behavior. He preceded Skinner in this by studying animal behavior, which led him to formulate the Law of Effect. Choice (**C**) is correct.

23. A

Designing an experiment focuses on level V (synthesis) of Bloom's taxonomy. Students must originate, integrate, and combine ideas into a product, plan, or proposal that is new to them. Choice (**A**) is correct.

24. D

A formative assessment is part of the learning process and allows teachers to adjust instruction accordingly, making choice (**D**) correct. Dr. Taba and Ms. Elton are both conducting diagnostic assessments, while Mr. Noram is administering a summative assessment.

25. D

Attribution theory is based on the observer's ability to use information to arrive at conclusions, or cause-and effect-relationships. Choice (**D**) is correct.

26. A, C

Choices (**A**) and (**C**) are correct. The primary goal of a professional learning community (PLC) is to help teachers collaborate in an effort to improve classroom practice and increase student achievement. (B) and (D) do not fit with this goal.

27. C

Library media specialists have been trained to serve as resources for teachers who are incorporating information technology into the curriculum. Choice (**C**) is correct.

28. C

While students will be doing some level of self-assessment by determining which of their own written pieces to submit for evaluation, Dr. Price would benefit the most from facilitating student portfolios, making choice (**C**) correct. She can provide her students with clear criteria at the beginning of the unit and help them choose pieces that reflect their progress and achievement.

29. A

Peer coaching is a confidential process by which two or more professional colleagues work together to reflect on current practices, share ideas, and observe new teaching skills and strategies. Choice (**A**) is correct.

30. B

Choice (**B**) is correct. This learning objective is observable and measurable because it focuses directly on what the student should know and be able to do by the end of the lesson.

31. D

Visual aids clarify information and help students understand it better. Choice (**D**) is correct.

32. A, B, D

Choices (**A**), (**B**), and (**D**) are correct. Modeling is a process by which people learn by observing others. Choice (C) does not provide an opportunity for students to observe behavior, strategies, or examples of expected outcomes.

33. D

The zone of proximal development is the area in which students can perform a task with assistance. In this case, the higher-performing students will serve as guides and help to scaffold the information in ways that will help the lower-performing students understand and acquire skills. Choice (**D**) is correct.

34. A

Gifted students require unique adaptations to the curriculum to satisfy their drive to learn. Without this, they can become bored and slip in academic performance. They are not able to bring in their own challenges to the curriculum and therefore need challenges from the teacher. They also need to be with age-level peers to develop social skills. Choice (**A**) is correct.

35. A

Concept maps are graphic representations of students' knowledge. Using them can be a useful strategy for assessing the knowledge students have coming into a unit or course of study. Ms. Seacat used this activity prior to the unit to assess prior knowledge. Choice (**A**) is therefore correct.

Sample Response to Question 1

36.

The teacher does not teach how to compare the models of the fractions. The assessment at the end of the class involves creating two models and comparing them, and the teacher has not explained or demonstrated how to determine which model is larger. The teacher could include an activity where the class compares models with a partner, or the class could compare models on an overhead or on their worksheet.

Additionally, the objective addresses like and unlike denominators in the fractions being compared, but the lesson plan does not indicate whether the fractions being compared have like or unlike denominators. It is essential that the lesson should address all the skills in the objective and create scaffolding for the students to be successful in the ultimate task. In this case, the teacher must ascertain that the students can create models of fractions, compare models of fractions with like denominators, and compare models of fractions with unlike denominators.

Sample Response to Question 2

37.

Mr. Bappin should begin by making sure Sarah isn't having outbursts based on her ability to do the work. He should make sure she is able to understand the topics he is teaching her and the assignments he is giving her.

The teacher could try to get Sarah invested in completing her work. He could offer some incentives, such as extra computer time, or a reward program, such as a checkbook system where she can earn "money" for positive behavior. She could use the money to buy prizes of any sort.

Additionally, Mr. Bappin could try to move Sarah's seat and grouping. There may be a student that Sarah would work well with or a spot in the room that would allow her the freedom to do her work in her own space. If she has trouble working independently and in groups, he could have her work with the group that he is teaching in the back. In that case, she could earn the privilege of working independently by completing assignments with him.

Test Structure and Format

The following table shows you what to expect from the Principles of Learning and Teaching test.

PRAXIS PRINCIPLES OF LEARNING AND TEACHING
Format: Computer-delivered
Number of Questions: 70 multiple-choice (called "selected-response" by the testmaker); 4 constructed response
Time: 120 minutes (all questions; the constructed-response questions are not timed separately)
Test may include questions that do not count toward your score
No penalty for incorrect answers
Scratch paper is available during the exam (it will be destroyed before you leave the testing center)
Content covered: Students as Learners: approximately 21 questions, 22.5 percent of the test Instructional Process: approximately 21 questions, 22.5 percent of the test Assessment: approximately 14 questions, 15 percent of the test Professional Development, Leadership, and Community: approximately 14 questions, 15 percent of the test Analysis of Instructional Scenarios: approximately 4 constructed-response questions, 25 percent of the test

Multiple-choice (the testmaker calls these "selected-response") questions that test your understanding of the principles of learning and teaching make up 75 percent of the Praxis PLT test. These questions cover the following four content areas:

- Students as Learners
- Instructional Process
- Assessment
- Professional Development, Leadership, and Community

The other 25 percent of the test consists of four essays (the testmaker calls these "constructed-response" questions) for two case histories. These questions test your ability to apply your knowledge of the principles of learning and teaching to extended instructional scenarios.

The first four sections of this chapter cover the basics of the four content areas on the PLT. The final section of this chapter offers strategies for analyzing case histories and writing effective answers to constructed-response questions.

Students as Learners

Human Development

The Praxis exam requires you to have foundational knowledge of human development as it relates to learning. It is important to understand the stages of human development and how various theorists have applied them. All children will reach developmental milestones at various times, so the ranges given by theorists are guidelines and not hard standards for measurement.

Knowledge is acquired in stages, and mastery of one stage becomes the foundation for building up to the next stage. Since the methods by which children learn vary, it is imperative to be able to apply a broad range of educational theories to encompass a wide variety of learning styles.

Skills acquisition is based on physical, emotional, and cognitive abilities. If a child has not met the minimum needs to acquire a new skill, there will be a delay until the child's abilities have caught up. This means that the developmental needs of a class will fall into a wide range of possibilities. It is important to understand the possible ranges for each class level and the techniques required to meet those needs.

Theories of Development

To create an effective lesson plan, you must have knowledge of the major theorists' basic views of developmental stages, ways of learning, social development, and moral and reasoning development. What follows is a discussion of some of the most prominent theorists and their theories, which describe widely acknowledged stages of development.

Piaget

Jean Piaget was a theorist who worked on the development of thinking. He observed infants and found that as they explored the objects in their environment, they gained knowledge of the world around them. Piaget called these skills **schemas**. When an infant used the schemas to observe a new object, Piaget called this **assimilation**, or interpreting an experience in terms of current ways of understanding. When an infant tried the old schema on a new object and molded it to fit the new object and to recategorize it, Piaget called this **accommodation**, or a change in cognitive structures that produces a corresponding behavioral change.

Piaget developed four stages of cognitive development:

- **Sensorimotor Level:** Children from birth to age 2 base their thoughts primarily on their senses and motor abilities.
- **Preoperational Stage:** Children ages 2–7 think mainly in symbolic terms—manipulating symbols used in creative play in the absence of the actual objects involved.
- **Concrete Operational Stage:** Children ages 7–11 think in logical terms. They are not very abstract. At this stage, children need hands-on, concrete experiences to manipulate symbols logically. They must perform these operations within the context of concrete situations.
- **Formal Operational Stage:** Children ages 11–15 develop abstract and hypothetical thinking. They use logical operations in the abstract rather than in the concrete. Children at this stage are capable of **metacognition**, or "thinking about thinking." Piaget noted that not all children move successfully to the formal operational stage.

Piaget believed in cognitive **constructivism**, which is the idea that students construct their own knowledge when they interact in social ways. Learning involves risk taking and mistakes, but over time, students develop greater moral and intellectual capacities.

Piaget, as well as Vygotsky and Dewey (see below), defined learning as the creation of meaning that occurs when an individual links new knowledge within the context of existing knowledge.

Kohlberg

Lawrence Kohlberg expanded Piaget's work and presented six stages of **moral development**, based on **cognitive reasoning**. Everyone begins at Stage 1 and progresses through the stages in an unvarying and irreversible order. According to Kohlberg, few people reach Stages 5 and 6. Stages 1 and 2 in the **preconventional level** involve an "egocentric point of view" and a "concrete individualistic perspective." Children from ages 4 to 10 respond mainly to reward and punishment. Stages 3 and 4 of the **conventional level** involve the maintenance of positive relations and the rules of society. Children conform to the rules and wishes of society to preserve the social order. Stages 5 and 6 of the **postconventional level** involve reasoning from an abstract point of view and possessing ideals that take precedence over particular societal laws. Individuals act according to an enlightened conscience at this level.

Montessori

Maria Montessori believed that childhood is divided into four stages: birth to age 2, ages 2–5, ages 5–6, and ages 7–12. Adolescence is divided into two levels: ages 12–15 and ages 16–18. Age ranges are approximate and refer to stages of the cognitive and emotional development common to most children. The process of learning is divided into three stages: (1) introduction to a concept by means of a lesson, something read in a book, or some other outside source; (2) processing the information and developing an understanding of the concept through work, experimentation, and creation; and (3) knowing the information or possessing an understanding of it, as demonstrated by the ability to pass a test with confidence, teach another, or express information with ease. Children learn directly from the environment and from other children more than from the teacher. The teacher prepares the environment and facilitates learning. The environment should nurture **multiple intelligences** and all **styles of learning**. Teaching movement and character comes before education of the mind. Children learn to take care of themselves, their environment, and each other, and they learn to speak politely, be considerate, and be helpful. The learning experiences that teachers design for children's absorbent-mind years promote cognitive and emotional development.

Dewey

John Dewey established the progressive education practice that fosters individuality, free activity, and learning through experience. **Cooperative learning** among peers; the individual needs of the students; and the introduction of art, music, dancing, etc. in education were all cornerstones of Dewey's educational approach. He believed that school should prepare the child for active participation in the life of the community. He thought that education should break down, rather than reinforce, the gap between the experience of schooling and the needs of a truly participatory democracy. He felt that school was primarily a social institution, and education was a social process and a process of living, not a preparation for future living. His *Pedagogic Creed*, published in 1897, explained his views on education and was a guide for teaching.

Bruner

Jerome Bruner considered learning to be an active process in which learners construct new ideas or concepts based on their current and past knowledge. Within this **constructivist** theory, the learner selects and transforms information, constructs hypotheses, and makes decisions, relying on a cognitive structure to do so. This process allows students to go beyond the information given to them and encourages them to discover principles by themselves, or participate in **discovery learning**. Teachers and students should engage in an active dialogue. The curriculum should be organized in a spiral manner so that students continually build upon what they have already learned. This is known as **inquiry teaching**, in which the students are active partners in the search for knowledge.

Vygotsky

Lev Semenovich Vygotsky's social development theory is based on the principle that social interaction plays a fundamental role in the development of cognition. Every function in the child's cultural development appears twice: first, on the social level, and second, on the individual level. The potential for cognitive development is limited to a certain time span called the **zone of proximal development**, in which full development depends on full social interaction—either with teacher guidance or peer collaboration, as in **cooperative learning**. Cognitive development is limited to a certain range at any given age. The development of thought and language and their interrelationships led Vygotsky to explain consciousness as the end product of socialization. The learning of language begins with thought, undergoes changes, and turns into speech. Children's learning development is affected by their culture, including the culture of the family environment in which they are enmeshed. The language used by adults transmits to the child. Children's language serves as their primary tool of intellectual adaptation. Eventually, children can use their internal language to direct their own behavior in a process known as **self-regulation**.

Vygotsky also introduced an instructional technique called **scaffolding**, in which the teacher breaks a complex task into smaller tasks, models the desired learning strategy or task, provides support as students learn to do the task, and then gradually shifts responsibility to the students. In this manner, a teacher enables students to accomplish as much of a task as possible without adult assistance. The skills, in essence, are gradually transferred to the learner.

You should know the above theorists' views on students' learning and have a basic grasp of each theory's key terms and proposed stages of development. Understanding each theory's implications for children and what, as a result, you will need to know and do in planning, assessment, motivation, and management will enhance your teaching.

Diversity

You should have an understanding of the diversity of your students and the factors that may affect how they learn—including dialect, immigrant status, socioeconomic background, ethnicity, race, creed/religion, language, culture, gender, social styles, learning or thinking styles, scholastic abilities, challenges, and lifestyles. You will need to understand how the influences of students' culture, language, and experiences are related to students' success in the classroom.

Regarding bilingual education, understand the differences between English immersion instruction, English-as-a-second-language instruction, transitional bilingual education, and two-way bilingual education.

- **English immersion instruction** is entirely in English. Teachers deliver lessons in simplified English so that students learn both English and academic subjects.
- **English-as-a-second-language instruction** may be the same as immersion but also may have some support for individuals using their native languages. Students may have a special class each day to work strictly on their English skills.
- **Transitional bilingual education instruction** is in the students' native language, but there is also instruction each day in developing English skills.
- **Two-way bilingual education instruction** is given to students in two languages. The goal of this instruction is to have students become proficient in both languages. In this case, teachers team-teach. This approach is sometimes called *dual-immersion* or *dual-language instruction*.

When working with students who are English language learners (ELLs), it is especially important to include collaborative (small-group) activities in class. Teachers should aim to include examples relevant to the students' cultural backgrounds, along with visual representations of content whenever possible.

Learning Styles

Learning styles are different approaches or ways of learning. The four learning styles are **visual learning**, **auditory learning**, **tactile learning**, and **kinesthetic learning**.

- Visual learners learn through seeing. These students watch the teacher's body language and facial expressions to understand the content of the lessons. They learn best from visual displays, diagrams, illustrated books, overhead transparencies, videos, flip charts, and handouts. Visual learners take detailed notes to absorb information.

- Auditory learners learn through listening. Attending verbal lectures, participating in class discussions, and listening to what others have to say is how they learn best. Written information may have less meaning for auditory learners unless it is read aloud. Auditory learners learn well by listening to a tape recorder or audio program on a computer.

- Tactile learners learn through touching. They have to actively explore the physical world around them. These students learn best through a hands-on approach.

- Kinesthetic learners learn through moving and doing. These students find it difficult to sit still for long periods of time and need activity and exploration.

Another approach comes from David Kolb's theory of learning styles, which includes **concrete experiences** (being involved in a new experience), **reflective observation** (watching others or developing observations about one's own experiences), **abstract conceptualization** (creating theories to explain one's observations), and **active experimentation** (using theories to solve problems and make decisions). Each of these learning styles requires teachers to offer different methods for students to learn the lessons.

The concrete experiencer learns well through activities such as field trips, lab work, or interactive computer programs. Writing in journals or learning logs is an effective means of helping reflective observers learn, because it forces them to concentrate on the content of the lesson. Students who learn through abstract conceptualization will work well with lectures, papers, and text. Simulations, case studies, and active homework are the most helpful activities for students who are active experimenters.

Multiple Intelligences

Dr. Howard Gardner developed the theory of **multiple intelligences** in 1983. Rather than accept the traditional and limited idea of intelligence, based on IQ testing of mathematics and reading skills, Dr. Gardner proposed eight areas of intelligence. These are as follows:

- *Verbal/linguistic intelligence* or *word smarts*: Students who are word smart demonstrate highly developed auditory skills and sensitivity to the meaning and order of words. They learn best by saying, hearing, and seeing words. Motivate them by talking with them, providing them with books and recordings, and giving them opportunities to use their writing abilities.

- *Logical-mathematical intelligence* or *number-reasoning smarts*: Students who are number-reasoning smart demonstrate the ability to handle chains of reasoning and recognize patterns and order. They are conceptual thinkers who explore relationships and patterns and like to experiment with things in an orderly and controlled manner. They typically compute arithmetic in their heads and reason out other problems. Provide them with time and concrete materials for their experiments, such as science kits, games like chess, brainteasers, and a computer.

- *Visual/spatial intelligence* or *picture smarts*: Students who are picture smart think in mental pictures and images. They have the ability to perceive the world accurately and to re-create or transform aspects of that world. These students learn visually. Teach them with images, pictures, and color. Films, videos, diagrams, maps, and charts motivate them. Provide them with cameras, telescopes, 3-D building supplies, and art supplies.

- *Bodily-kinesthetic intelligence* or *body smarts*: Students who are body smart are athletically gifted and pick up knowledge through bodily sensations. They communicate by using gestures and body language. They like to act out their thoughts and are clever mimics. Their learning comes with touching and moving. Motivate them through role-playing, dramatic improvisation, creative movement, and all kinds of physical activity. These students require hands-on activities for their learning opportunities.

- *Musical intelligence* or *music smarts*: Students who are music smart have sensitivity to pitch, melody, rhythm, and tones. They often sing, hum, or whistle melodies to themselves. They may play musical instruments or want to. They are also sensitive to nonverbal sounds that others overlook, such as chirping crickets or a singing bird. These students learn through rhythm and melody. They can memorize easily when they sing it out. They study effectively with music in the background. Motivate them with records, tapes, and musical instruments.

- *Interpersonal intelligence* or *people smarts*: Students who are people smart have the ability to understand people and relationships. They are "people people" who often become leaders in the classroom, on the playground, and around the neighborhood. These students know how to organize, communicate, mediate, and manipulate. They have many friends. Provide them with opportunities in peer group, school, and community activities that open doors to learning for them.

- *Intrapersonal intelligence* or *self smarts*: Students who are self smart have the ability to assess their own emotional life as a means to understanding themselves and others. They have a powerful sense of self and shy away from groups to work alone. Their inner life is rich and filled with dreams, intuition, feelings, and ideas. They write diaries. They learn best by themselves. Provide them with private space where they can work and spend time in quiet introspection. Respect their privacy and validate that it's all right to be independent.

- *Naturalist intelligence* or *nature smarts*: Students who are nature smart have the ability to observe nature and discern its patterns and trends. They recognize species of plants or animals in their environment. They learn the many characteristics of different birds. They are aware of changes in their local or global environment. They enjoy collecting and cataloging natural material. They learn best in the outdoors. Provide them with opportunities to explore the outdoors regularly and bring the outdoors indoors. Supply them with many books, visuals, and props related to the natural world. Have them create notebooks of their observations of natural phenomena. Have them draw or photograph natural objects. Provide them with binoculars, telescopes, or microscopes for their observational work.

According to Dr. Gardner, teachers should place equal attention on linguistic and logical-mathematical intelligence, along with incorporating strategies that include individuals who show gifts in the other intelligences. If teachers are trained to present their lessons in a wide variety of ways—using music, cooperative learning, art activities, role-playing, multimedia, field trips, and inner reflection, rather than lectures and worksheets—children will have an opportunity to learn in ways harmonious with their unique multiple intelligences.

By incorporating factors of the multiple-intelligence theory into instruction, teachers can facilitate learning. They will not have as much difficulty reaching students. Teachers do not have to teach all the lessons in all eight intelligences, but they should address multiple intelligences as appropriate for the lesson content.

Differences Between the Sexes

Boys and girls differ in their physical, emotional, and intellectual development. Numerous studies indicate several differences in the learning strategies typically adopted by boys and girls. Note that not all of these behaviors will manifest in any given individual, and there is overlap between the groups.

Girls tend to emphasize memorization. Boys learn more through elaboration strategies. Girls evaluate their own learning during the learning process. They use control strategies more often than boys. Boys may need more assistance in planning, organizing, and structuring their learning activities. Students who lack confidence in their own ability to learn are often exposed to failure. Self-concept plays an important part in studying reading and mathematics. Girls perform well in reading activities but often lack self-confidence in mathematics. The opposite is true for boys.

Teachers must be aware of motivation and self-esteem differences among boys and girls and use appropriate teaching strategies in instruction. Classroom variables to consider when viewing gender differences are the grouping of the students, management of the class, the use of time on tasks, assessment standards, and the expectations of the students.

Cultural Expectations

Teachers can better meet students' needs by gaining an understanding of how different students think about cultures other than their own. Having a clear understanding of the students, their families, and their communities will help you provide meaningful instruction and help enhance your teaching methods and strategies.

The expectations that a family places on a student—based on cultural influences such as tradition, religion, or hopes for future advancement—may differ from the expectations of the teacher. For example, a match between the cultural expectations for literacy and the teacher's expectations for literacy is vital to a student's successful acquisition of reading skills. Positive connections between life and culture at home and the school environment help to ensure the success of each student.

Having a diverse group of students means having students with numerous sets of expectations regarding teacher relationships and behaviors that most likely were set in their home countries, their former schools, or their families. Some students may expect more traditional teaching, and they may be offended or upset if their new teacher is more informal. These students may be used to a clear, ordered pattern of classroom activities. In certain cultures, students expect the teacher to be the only one to present knowledge. These students may be unfamiliar with working in groups and participating in cooperative learning activities. They may have difficulty respecting other students' ideas, and they may be uncomfortable in classroom situations that disagree with their cultural understanding of how to learn.

In schools with students from migrant populations, it is important to understand that frequent moves often affect students' learning, self-esteem, and behavior. Teachers must create an exceptional learning environment that enables all students to meet high academic standards and meets their other needs, such as health and nutrition. Problems such students have are often exacerbated as their families move around. In addition, many of these students lose quite a lot of schooling over the course of a year and can benefit from the careful guidance of their new teachers.

Accelerating the curriculum; using innovation in instruction; making positive use of time and other resources; and involving parents more centrally in planning, decision making, and instructional support roles will upgrade teachers' effectiveness and improve migrant students' academic achievement. Teachers need to create lessons that use such students' previous knowledge to help them make connections. Effective use of technology will help students learn in active ways. Teachers should try to create an accepting, comfortable climate in the classroom so that these students don't feel isolated.

Teachers must know the cultural and personal sensitivities of their students so that they can present appropriate topics for discussion and study in the classroom. In a high-achieving classroom environment, teachers can have students explore ideas and issues by drawing on their own and other students' cultures, experiences, and knowledge. At-risk students need classroom environments that provide them with authentic tasks, many opportunities, and many ways to learn and succeed.

Teachers must remember that their own cultural values may not be the same as those of their students. Different cultural values are formed by experiences in different social, historical, and economic environments. Cultural values are also formed through contact with other cultural groups.

Understanding age-appropriate knowledge and behavior, as well as working with the student culture at school, will help teachers differentiate instruction for different students. Knowing the family backgrounds, linguistic patterns and differences, cognitive patterns and differences, and social and emotional issues students bring with them to the classroom is also important for classroom instruction.

Students with Special Needs

Areas of exceptionality in students' learning vary when the students are eligible for special education. Regular classroom teachers must know how to accommodate the diversity of learning abilities in the classroom when special-education students are mainstreamed into the regular classroom. Special-education students can have visual and perceptual difficulties, special physical or sensory challenges, learning disabilities, attention deficit disorder (ADD), attention deficit hyperactivity disorder (ADHD), fetal alcohol syndrome, intellectual disability (ID), or giftedness.

Assuming responsibility for teaching each student in the classroom becomes challenging when the number of students with special needs increases. In this case, the teacher's task is to determine which strategies will help these students succeed not only in the classroom, but also in the environment in which they will live. Teachers must have an open mind, an understanding of what exceptionalities are, and a willingness to accept the challenge of teaching students who have them. Having an extensive repertoire of teaching methods and strategies, and knowing that there is no one-size-fits-all way to meet special education students' needs, will allow you to be creative in developing new strategies to help your students succeed. You should always try to use strategies that rely on your students' strengths.

Legislative Influences

Teachers must know the legislation concerning students with exceptionalities and understand how to apply the legislation in the classroom. You may encounter questions about the following laws and provisions on the PLT test.

The Americans with Disabilities Act (1990) (ADA) established a clear and comprehensive prohibition of discrimination on the basis of disability. It provides a national mandate for clear, strong, consistent, and enforceable standards addressing discrimination against individuals with disabilities. It ensures that the federal government plays a central role in enforcing the standards established in the Act. The Act further invokes the sweep of congressional authority, including the power to enforce the 14th Amendment and to regulate commerce so as to address major areas of discrimination faced by people with disabilities.

The Individuals with Disabilities Education Act (IDEA) became Public Law 105-17 in 1997. It ensures that children with disabilities and the families of such children have access to a free, appropriate public education. The Act further provides incentives for whole-school approaches and pre-referral interventions to reduce the need to label children as disabled to address their learning needs. It focuses resources on teaching and learning while reducing paperwork and requirements that do not assist in improving educational results. The federal government has a role in assisting state and local efforts to educate children with disabilities, to improve results for such children and ensure their equal protection under the law.

There are also specific regulations related to students' rights and teachers' responsibilities within your own state and school district. Understand these laws as they relate to confidentiality and privacy, appropriate treatment of students, and procedures for reporting situations related to possible child abuse. Check local resources for specific regulations within your school and school district.

The Individualized Education Plan (IEP), a provision of IDEA, describes the special-education and related services specifically designed to meet the unique educational needs of special-needs students. The IEP covers all deficit areas, related services, and needed accommodations in both general (regular and vocational) and special education. As a teacher, you will need to understand how to develop and use IEPs. The goals and short-term instructional objectives of an IEP must be stated in measurable, observable behaviors, and must fit the student's current level of functioning and probable growth rate. The IEP must indicate a sequence of skills and include a statement of related specific services, special education placement, and time and duration of services. The language of the IEP must be understandable to both parents/guardians and professionals. The IEP must represent a consensus among parents/guardians, the students, and school personnel. The law requires an annual meeting to review progress and goals, but many states now use "benchmarks" as often as four times a year to let parents/guardians know the progress a student is making. If the goals need to be adjusted, parents/guardians must attend an IEP update meeting. The IEP must also include a list of the individuals who are responsible for the IEP's implementation.

Students with disabilities may also receive **504 accommodations**. Similar to IEPs, 504 plans may require that students receive needed accommodations to help ensure their chances for academic success. In contrast, students with IEPs receive specialized instruction and services.

IDEA requires a "least-restrictive environment" to enable special-education students to function effectively. The least-restrictive environment provision stipulates that, when possible, students must not be taught in separate settings but be taught along with their age peers. When considering the special-education student for regular classroom activities, the IEP must specifically state exactly what the student needs to enable him or her to receive satisfactory benefits from an environment with typical students. This may include receiving assistance in other areas of the school, away from the regular classroom.

Motivation and Successful Learning

Motivation can be **intrinsic** (from within) or **extrinsic** (from without). Intrinsic motivation comes from self-determination—students are in control of their own destiny and can make choices. With intrinsic motivation, students themselves want to learn and do not need external incentives, such as stickers or candy. Motivation is what energizes, drives, and directs students' behaviors.

Motivational Theories

Skinner and other behavior theorists suggest that teachers first identify the behavior they are trying to change, then reward positive behavior and provide consequences for negative behavior. This approach controls students' behaviors with immediate, extrinsic rewards. Critics charge that this approach works to produce short-term behavioral changes but impairs learning and does not support long-term changes. To promote the development of intrinsic motivation in students, teachers can create celebrations of learning. Anything spontaneous that acknowledges students' accomplishments is more motivating over a longer period of time. Students are eager to learn when teachers provide a positive learning environment.

Using a mixture of teaching and learning methods, engaging emotions and natural curiosity, communicating high expectations, and showing students how to manage their own states of learning will spark intrinsic motivation. Teachers need to provide safe and optimal learning environments by ensuring the opportunity for intrinsic motivation—as opposed to extrinsic motivation, which is often considered manipulative and believed to promote negative learning outcomes.

By using appropriate grouping in the classroom and correct curriculum and assessment systems (while limiting distractions), teachers can influence students' motivation to learn. Teachers must consider students' learning strategies, because these activate motivational issues.

The **humanistic** approach to motivation uses **Maslow's hierarchy of needs**. Maslow introduced the term *self-actualization* to describe one of these needs. The underlying assumption of self-actualization is that people are basically good and have within themselves all they need to develop their full potential to be worthwhile individuals. Maslow's hierarchy of five motivational needs consists of security, social, esteem, physiological, and self-actualization. Following Maslow's approach, teachers must make sure students are safe and secure in their environment—for example, not hungry or uncomfortable—because students cannot focus on the learning task in the classroom until their need for security is met.

The **cognitive** approach is based on the learning-goal theory, self-monitoring and reflective behaviors, and self-evaluation.

The **attribution theory** approach is centered on the social-cognitive needs of students. This theory allows students to accept ownership of their own performance or nonperformance. Attributions can influence cognition and behavior, such as emotional reactions to success and failure and expectations for future successes and failures.

Increased learning can take place if teachers provide **positive reinforcement** (or **operant conditioning**) for the responses students make. This often leads to students repeating successful learning responses. Teachers can promote better learning motivation if they capitalize on students' interests and communicate the belief that all students can learn. Teachers can develop appropriate strategies to focus students on learning, rather than performance. They can allow students to fail and model how to respond constructively.

Instructional Process

Choosing Objectives, Writing Objectives, and Modifying Objectives

As a teacher, you will need to know how to develop effective instructional objectives. Objectives should answer the question "What are students supposed to know or be able to do once the lesson is completed?" They should not describe what the teacher does during the lesson. They should not be overly specific, involved, or complicated. The objectives need to address behaviors and knowledge so that teachers can determine whether they are met. They must be observable, detectable, and measurable/assessable. Objectives must incorporate appropriate district, state, and national standards.

Madeline Hunter developed a **direct instruction** model for effective instruction. Her outline of a lesson consists of the objectives, standards of performance and expectations, anticipatory set or advance organizer, the teaching (input, modeling and demonstration, direction giving, and checking for understanding), guided practice and monitoring, closure, and independent practice. This model is generally referred to as the Madeline Hunter Method.

David Ausubel proposed an instructional technique called the **advance organizer**. Advance organizers are introduced before the learning begins and presented at a higher level of abstraction. They are selected on the basis of their suitability for explaining, integrating, and interrelating the material to be presented to the class. These are not overviews or summaries, but rather act as bridges for the students between the new material they will learn and their previous knowledge. Making a semantic web with the students before the lesson or unit begins is an example of using an advance organizer.

You also will need to know how to use student-centered learning activities, such as collaborative learning, cooperative learning groups (CLGs), concept development, discovery learning, independent study, inquiry, interdisciplinary and integrated study, project-based learning, simulations, and units. When creating lessons and teaching strategies, you should incorporate some of the following concepts: creative thinking, concept mapping, higher-order thinking, induction, deductive reasoning, problem solving, and recall.

Taxonomy of Objectives

Benjamin Bloom created a taxonomy (or classification system) for categorizing the level of abstraction of various skills and abilities that learners can develop once they have acquired knowledge. With the help of others, he established a hierarchy of educational objectives, which is often known as **Bloom's taxonomy**. They identified three domains (or types) of learning of educational activities. The **cognitive domain** involves knowledge and development of intellectual attitudes and skills. The **affective domain** deals with growth in feelings or emotional areas and attitudes. The **psychomotor domain** deals with manual or physical skills. Teachers mainly use Bloom's taxonomy of educational objectives in the cognitive domain, to write lesson plan objectives, formulate questions, and use methods and teaching strategies from the simplest to the most complex. If the lesson requires manual or physical skills, teachers use the psychomotor domain to plan.

Bloom's Taxonomy of the Cognitive Domain

Here, we list educational objectives from lowest to highest, according to Bloom:

- **Knowledge:** Recall of specific facts and terms from the materials
- **Comprehension:** Ability to understand facts and principles and interpret the meaning of the material
- **Application:** Ability to use learned concepts and principles in new and concrete situations
- **Analysis:** Ability to break down material into its component parts so that the organizational structure may be understood
- **Synthesis:** Ability to put parts together to create a new whole, using creative behaviors to formulate new patterns and structure
- **Evaluation:** Ability to judge the value of the material for a given purpose, basing value judgments on either internal or external definite criteria

While this original version of Bloom's taxonomy is still often cited, some educators and educational researchers now refer to the revised version of Bloom's taxonomy, which emphasizes verbs instead of nouns: Remembering, Understanding, Applying, Analyzing, Evaluating, and Creating. Note that the placement of Evaluating and Creating (similar to Synthesis in the original version) have been switched.

Planning to Teach the Lesson

You should use techniques for planning instruction that will meet curriculum goals, including the incorporation of learning theory, subject matter, curriculum development, and student development. You should create effective bridges, such as advance organizers, between curriculum goals and students' experiences. You should include **modeling** and use **guided** and **independent practice**. Your lessons will be successful if you use **transitions**, activate students' **previous knowledge**, encourage exploration and **problem solving**, and help students build new skills.

Questions to Ask Yourself

1. **How will you group the students for instruction?** Be specific about why you have chosen a given grouping and how it will help to achieve the desired objectives. Will you use small groups, whole groups, cooperative learning groups, or independent learning? Will you use **heterogeneous** or **homogeneous** groupings?

2. **What teaching method(s) will you use for the lesson?** Is this lesson teacher directed only? Is there a holistic question/activity? Do the methods incorporate the learning styles, learning modalities, and multiple intelligences of your students?

3. **Have you considered all the instructional strategies you could use?** Cooperative learning? Direct instruction? Discovery learning? Whole-group discussion? Independent study? Interdisciplinary instruction? Concept mapping? Inquiry method? Will any of these help you attain your educational goals?

4. **What specific activities have you planned?** What will the students do to meet the lesson's learning objectives? Do these activities incorporate learning styles, modalities, and multiple intelligences? Have you allocated sufficient time for the activities?

5. **What instructional and curricular materials are you planning to use?** Include multimedia technology and websites. Other materials include textbooks, teacher guides, kits, models, visuals, and any other innovative ways to deliver the curriculum. Resources to use in instructional planning may also include local experts, field trips, and library research.

6. **Will you include accommodations for specific students in the lesson, and will they help you meet the objectives?** Can you provide instructional support for students who are exceptional, are gifted, have ADD or ADHD, are intellectually disabled, are learning disabled, have visual or perceptual challenges, are hearing impaired, have physical or sensory challenges, or are second-language learners?

7. **Do you have a plan for evaluation and assessment that takes into account each student's learning style?** How will you know whether students meet the objectives? Do you have a follow-up plan for after this lesson? Can you use the knowledge the students gain from this lesson in future lessons?

Adapting Instruction and Cultural and Linguistic Diversity

Teachers plan their teaching strategies and methods based on the needs of their students in the areas of cognition, physical activity, emotional growth, and social adjustment. You will need to know how to plan and implement **developmentally appropriate programs (DAPs)** based on knowledge of the individual development levels of the students.

You should amend or change instruction plans to meet the unique learning or social needs of students. Consider all aspects of individual differences—including cultural diversity, exceptionalities, and students' developmental levels—when planning instruction.

Managing the Instructional Environment

Classroom management begins before students arrive in the fall. You should communicate your expectations clearly and with an understanding of your students. Effective verbal and nonverbal communication is a part of teaching. You need to have methods of stimulating discussion and responses in your classroom. Always consider the effects of cultural and gender differences on communication in your classroom. By using various instructional methods, you will enable more students to have the opportunity to participate in the learning environment. Having some general knowledge of the impact of limited English proficiency on students and parents/guardians—and its implications for teachers in planning, teaching, assessing, motivating, managing, and communicating—will allow you to better serve your students. Know how to use both verbal and nonverbal communication, and understand the various questioning techniques.

Know the principles of effective classroom management and strategies to promote positive relationships, cooperation, and purposeful learning:

1. Establish daily procedures and routines.
2. Establish classroom rules, rewards, and consequences.
3. Give timely feedback.
4. Maintain accurate records.
5. Communicate with parents, guardians, and caregivers.
6. Use objective behavior descriptions.
7. Respond to student misbehavior.
8. Arrange the classroom physical environment.
9. Pace and structure the lessons.

Classroom Management

Classroom management and management of student behavior are skills that teachers acquire and perfect over time. Effective classroom management skills are central to teaching and require consistency, courage, common sense, and fairness.

The basics to keep in mind for effective classroom management are (1) know what you want and what you don't want; (2) show and tell your students what you want; (3) when you get what you want, acknowledge it—but don't overly praise it, as if the desired behavior were unexpected; and (4) when you get something else, act quickly and appropriately. By meeting each student at the door with a friendly greeting, you can handle many minor problems before they become public classroom confrontations.

For effective management, teachers should also do the following:

1. Maintain eye contact with students.
2. Move around the room; being near students can extinguish potential problems.
3. Establish a "quiet" signal (e.g., clapping your hands, ringing a bell, or making a hand signal).

4. Let the students take ownership of their work.

5. Use age-appropriate humor, smiles, choices, and positive reinforcement.

6. Remember that learning is a social activity. When appropriate, allow students to talk during their work time. A totally quiet classroom is not always a good learning environment.

Know the basics of the three classroom management styles: authoritarian, laissez-faire, and authoritative.

Authoritarian teachers establish rules and expect students to obey them. These teachers give rewards and administer punishments for following and breaking rules, respectively. The motto of the authoritarian teacher is, "Do as I say, because I say so!"

Laissez-faire teachers establish no rules, and students can do what they want. These teachers provide advice only when directly asked by a student. Their motto is "Do as I say because you like and respect my judgment."

Authoritative teachers provide rules and discuss the reasons for those rules with the students. They teach students how to meet goals, praise them for demonstrating self-control, and reward them with more self-governance as they demonstrate more responsibility. This approach to classroom management instills intrinsic motivation in students. The authoritative style of teaching is considered the most effective, and the motto of the authoritative teacher is, "Do what I say, because doing so will help you learn more."

You will also need to know the basics of conflict resolution and behavior modification, and how to use them in the classroom.

Conflict resolution is a constructive approach to interpersonal and intergroup conflicts that helps students with opposing positions work together to arrive at a mutually acceptable compromise. The main theme is active listening, by which each student can understand and verbally summarize the other's differences. Initially, teachers serve as facilitators and coaches and may use role-playing to model the mediation process to the students. Afterward, the teacher sets up an area in the classroom for students themselves to use for mediating their conflicts.

Behavior modification arose from Skinner's modern behavior modification techniques and Pavlov's classical conditioning techniques. Behavior modification is the application of the principles of conditioning and is used to promote desirable behaviors or discourage undesirable behaviors. Behavior modification is used to change observable and measurable behaviors. All behavior is maintained, changed, or shaped by the consequences of that behavior. Students function more effectively under the right set of consequences or reinforcers that strengthen good behavior and punishments that weaken bad behavior.

Steps a teacher can take to apply the behavior modification techniques are as follows: (1) identify the problem, (2) design a way to change the behavior, (3) identify an effective positive reinforcer and use it often when the behavior is positive, and (4) apply the reinforcer consistently to shape or change the behavior.

Assessment

Teachers must know how to select and use culturally unbiased, informal, and formal assessment strategies to plan and individualize curricula and teaching practices.

Knowing how to make **accommodations** for the various learning styles, multiple intelligences, and exceptionalities of your students will help you help your students be successful in your classroom. This does not mean that you should lower your expectations of student learning, but it does mean students will learn and express their knowledge in different ways. Making reasonable accommodations for your students gives them a better chance of academic success, better motivation, and greater confidence. One common accommodation is letting students take an untimed test and providing a tape of the test.

You should be able to provide **alternative** or **authentic assessment** options that let students choose how to perform a task or answer a question. For example, you could let them prepare demonstrations, exhibits, portfolios, oral presentations, or essays. Authentic assessments allow students to really show what they can do, and they will make schoolwork more meaningful to students as well. This will give you a better sense of your students' level of success or failure.

A different kind of test, the paper-and-pencil objective test, is called **traditional assessment**. Traditional assessment is a means of securing information about what students know by way of responses to a list of multiple-choice, true-or-false, or matching questions. Traditional assessments of students' learning can help you formulate lesson plans and decide what to communicate to students and their parents/guardians.

Standardized tests are assessments administered and scored in exactly the same manner for all students. Traditional standardized tests are typically mass-produced and machine scored. They are designed to measure skills and knowledge taught to all students according to state standards. Standardized tests can be **norm referenced**, such that the performance results of the students who take the test are compared with the performance results of other students taking the test. Alternatively, standardized tests that are **criterion referenced** compare students' knowledge and achievement in an academic area to the objectives of the curriculum established by state standards. Criterion referencing does not compare students to each other; instead, the test results show a student's level of mastery of particular content areas.

Performance assessments can also be standardized if they are administered and scored in the same way for all students. This is accomplished with systematic and direct observation of student performance or examples of student performance. These assessments are ranked according to pre-established performance criteria or guidelines that are listed on **rubrics**.

As an active participant on the school team in the development and implementation of Individual Education Plan goals, you will need to know how to communicate assessment results and integrate them for others. As noted above, IEPs are made for specific students based on their individual abilities.

You will also need to know how to develop and use formative and summative program evaluations to ensure the comprehensive quality of the total environment for children. **Formative assessment** is intended to aid learning by providing feedback to students about what they have learned so far and what they still need to learn. An example would be a quiz covering the material addressed by a particular lesson or homework assignment. Students and teachers can use this type of assessment as a diagnostic tool to identify and improve areas of weakness, and as a means of practicing a skill.

Summative assessment is a measure of the students' achievement at the completion of a block of work. It summarizes the students' learning at a specific point in time. Examples include an end-of-the-chapter test or a unit test.

Informal assessments are supplemental to the standardized testing formats. Teachers use them to improve their understanding of students' learning strengths and weaknesses. These assessments show the teacher the *why* and *how* of their students' learning. Such assessments include learning logs, journals, observations, checklists, teacher-made classroom tests, and anecdotal records of student work and behavior. Teachers use **holistic scoring**, in which a paper or project is given a single score, to assess the overall quality of the student's work. Here, feedback is usually provided in paragraph form. This is in contrast to **analytic scoring**, in which separate scores are recorded for each predetermined element of the student's work, and the overall grade is determined by the total or average of the scores on those elements. In this case, feedback is usually quantitative, not qualitative. Teachers can create detailed rubrics to use in holistic scoring of students' work. Students receive these rubrics beforehand so that they know the quality expectations for the work they must do.

Professional Development, Leadership, and Community

Dewey suggested that teachers understand the factors in their students' environments outside of school that may influence their lives and learning (family circumstances, community environment, health, and economics). You must be aware of ways to involve members of the community in the school setting. Develop ways to include parents and guardians in classroom lessons, and treat them as partners in the educational process. Develop basic strategies for involving community leaders in the educational process. Remember that teachers and schools are resources for the entire community.

You should have knowledge of professional literature and associations within your field of education. In addition, know the current views of specific professional associations and how they relate to best teaching practices in your area. Understand the purpose of the professional development requirements of your state and local agencies. Know what types of resources are available for professional development and learning in your field. Seek out opportunities to grow professionally.

You should know the value of reflection as it pertains to you in the teaching profession. Understand that being a **reflective practitioner** is critical. Truly effective teachers are those who evaluate their teaching strategies at all times to become the most effective educators possible. Teachers must reflect on their methods and strategies continually to ensure that they are reaching all students. Continually evaluating the effects of one's choices and actions on students, parents, and other professionals in the learning community is part of the reflective process.

Effective teachers use reflective statements that include clear descriptions of the information sources they have used to evaluate their teaching and students' learning. These teachers use self-evaluation methods and problem-solving strategies to reflect on their practice and make changes in their teaching, respectively. They also describe how they have used specific resources, such as readings and professional relationships with colleagues and others, to learn and grow as teachers.

You should also be aware of the support personnel available to assist you, your students, and their families. These include paraeducators, guidance counselors, special education teachers, IEP team members, therapists, teachers of the gifted and talented, and library media specialists.

Analysis of Instructional Scenarios

The PLT requires that you not only answer multiple-choice questions, but also write your own short-answer responses to case histories of classroom scenarios. You will see two case histories on the day of your test, each with two associated questions. These four responses make up a total of 25 percent of your overall score, so it's important to be prepared. Also keep in mind that on test day, you will type your responses directly on the computer—so for the most realistic practice, you should type your practice responses directly into a basic word-processing program.

Case Histories

The case histories are all approximately the same length: 800–850 words. They come in a variety of forms. Some are narrative, featuring a teacher's self-reflection and evaluation; others are document based, providing between three and five student responses, lesson plans, report cards, and/or similar documents. Some focus on issues relating to one or more students; others are primarily concerned with the practices of a single teacher. Don't be overly concerned with these distinctions. Few case histories fall purely within a single category, and the strategy for success is the same for all of them.

Below is an example of a document-based, teacher-focused case history. Like all case histories, it begins with a brief scenario providing basic background information. The documents are clearly labeled.

Scenario

Mr. Hallet is a ninth-grade English teacher beginning the second semester of his first year of teaching. His district encompasses mostly middle-class families on the outskirts of a major metropolis. However, about 15 percent of the students in the district are from the poorer inner city and often face academic hardship. Mr. Hallet is successfully managing his three regular classes and one advanced class. He also has a remedial ELA class, which is giving him trouble. He has requested the guidance of his department head, Ms. Erdogan, in managing the situation. Ms. Erdogan has agreed to observe a class and is recording it on audio for reference.

Document 1

Mr. Hallet's "connotation vs. denotation" lesson plan

Objectives: Students will:

1. Understand the difference between the denotation and connotation of words.
2. Be able to identify the tone of a piece of writing based on the connotation of the words chosen by the author.
3. Be able to alter the tone of a piece of writing by replacing words with synonyms that have different connotations.

Assignments:

Students will receive a list of 10 words. In pairs, students should label 5 of them as "good" and 5 of them as "bad." Then, students should identify 5 pairs of words that have similar meanings.

Students will receive a review of a restaurant. Individually, they will circle all the words with strong connotations and identify those words as having a positive or negative connotation.

Students will rewrite the review. They will preserve the denotation of the review (e.g., whether the restaurant was hot or cold, whether the food was spicy or mild, whether the location was busy or quiet) but reverse the connotation (e.g., from "delicate" flavors to "bland" flavors, or from a "lively" restaurant to a "noisy" restaurant).

Assessments:

Students will have an opportunity to share their answers from the initial assignment with the 10 words.

Students will receive a grade out of 20 points for their writing.

Document 2

Transcript of Mr. Hallet's class, 10:42 AM

Mr. Hallet: What can I do for you, Darred, Mike?

Darred: We don't know what "sweltering" means.

Mike: Dude, who cares? I don't even get the point of this anyway.

Darred: Shut up, Mike. If I fail this class, my parents are gonna ground me!

Mr. Hallet: Well, think about the word. Have you heard it anywhere before?

Mike: Sounds like "shelter" or "sweater."

Mr. Hallet: Good! "Sweater" is exactly right, the word means "hot." And how does the word sound?

Darred: I dunno, if "sweltering" is like "sweating," then it's kinda gross or something?

Mr. Hallet: Exactly! It's an unpleasant word, very negative, that means "hot." Good guessing!

Document 3

Transcript of Mr. Hallet's class, 11:04 AM

(The class is very noisy. A few students mention things relating to the assignment. Most of the chatter is off-topic.)

Mr. Hallet (loudly): Students, this is quiet writing time.

(The conversations continue, albeit quieter.)

Mr. Hallet (walking up to a student): Rod, you're not writing anything.

Rod: I don't get what I'm supposed to do. How can I keep the writing the same *and* make it the opposite?

Mr. Hallet: You did very well on the worksheet—you know how to do this! Remember how "sweltering" meant hot and was bad, while "toasty" also meant hot but was good? (Mr. Hallet pauses. Rod nods.) Do you see anything here like that?

Rod: Tanya did most of that work. I didn't really get it. Like, is "truffle" a good or bad word?

Mr. Hallet: No, a truffle is a type of mushroom. It's not good or bad.

Mike (from across the room): See, I *told* you this assignment was dumb!

(The class laughs.)

Mr. Hallet: Mike! That attitude is inappropriate. Everyone, get back to your work. We'll talk about the assignment in more detail once we're done. For now, do your best.

(Several students make comments under their breath. Most stare at their papers; few go back to work.)

Document 4

Conversation between Mr. Hallet and Ms. Erdogan, two days later

Mr. Hallet: . . . and in the end, I couldn't give a single assignment a score higher than a 10 out of 20.

Ms. Erdogan: What about Tanya's? She seemed surprisingly engaged, at least toward the beginning.

Mr. Hallet: I know. It was so disappointing. She wrote a completely original review. She made great use of negatively charged words, but she wasn't actually following instructions for the assignment—even though

I went over the instructions *and* handed them out in writing. So 10 was the best I could give her under the circumstances.

Ms. Erdogan: And how did she take that grade?

Mr. Hallet: Poorly. I had to write her up; she skipped my class yesterday and today.

Ms. Erdogan: That's unfortunate.

Mr. Hallet: It's the worst possible outcome. I had her interest in learning, but then I lost it. But I'm not sure what I could have done differently.

Ms. Erdogan: Well, let's talk about it.

Case History Questions

The questions associated with the case histories can test a variety of subjects. You will always have at least one question from the content category of "Students as Learners" and at least one from "Instructional Process." You may also see up to one question each on the topics of "Assessment" and "Professional Development, Leadership, and Community."

Although questions may differ in terms of subject matter, their formatting is formulaic. First, they present a summary of part of the case or a direction to review a particular section or document. Next, they ask you to identify two specific things, such as two behaviors that are typical of an age group or two modifications to a failed activity. Finally, they instruct you to justify your examples on the basis of various educational principles.

Make sure to read each question thoroughly. Generic or tangential explanations that do not directly address the assignment will not receive full credit, regardless of their quality.

Below are the two questions that accompany the previous case history.

Constructed-Response Questions

Question 1

Review Mr. Hallet's lesson plan in Document 1.

- Identify TWO shortcomings in Mr. Hallet's lesson plan.
- Explain how addressing EACH shortcoming could have improved the effectiveness of Mr. Hallet's lesson. Base your response on principles of effective instructional strategies.

Question 2

Throughout the case history, Mr. Hallet's students display behaviors typical of students who struggle academically.

- Identify TWO such instances of the typical behavior of struggling students.
- For EACH example you identify, indicate what characteristic of the behavior is typical of the behavior of struggling students. Base your response on the principles of remedial education.

Case History Answers

Short answers, technically known as constructed responses, aren't scored as right or wrong in the same way that multiple-choice questions are. Instead, each response is assigned a score of 0, 1, or 2 by a team of professional educators. Multiple graders will review your answers, and their grading habits will in turn be statistically reviewed by a computer to ensure consistency. If you're interested in precisely how these results are generated, ETS's official study materials explain the inner workings of the process in detail. But for our purposes, it's enough to know that you don't have to worry about "the luck of the draw" assigning you a strict reviewer. Your writing will consistently and accurately receive the score that is merited.

As we've already explained, you can expect questions on a variety of educational themes. However, all responses are graded on the same basic rubric:

2 A 2 is the highest score possible. It represents an excellent and thoughtful answer—though not necessarily a perfect one, as the graders understand that you are working under time constraints! To earn a 2, you must produce a response that:

- demonstrates clear and thorough understanding of pedagogy, methodology, and theory
- demonstrates clear and thorough understanding of the specifics of the case
- responds to all parts of the question
- supports its reasoning with evidence or examples, when required

1 A response that earns a 1 falls short. It still answers the question, but it fails to do so as accurately or as comprehensively as a response that earns a 2. Your response may earn a 1 if it:

- demonstrates only basic understanding of pedagogy, methodology, and theory
- demonstrates only basic understanding of the specifics of the case
- does not fully respond to all parts of the question
- provides weak or insufficient evidence for its points, where required

0 A response that earns a 0 makes one or more critical errors. It's likely that such an answer:

- demonstrates little or no understanding of pedagogy, methodology, and theory
- demonstrates little or no understanding of the case
- does not respond to the question at all, perhaps by giving an off-topic answer or attacking the basis of the question (e.g., when asked to modify a lesson, arguing that the lesson requires no modification)
- completely lacks requisite support or evidence

It's important to note what is *not* in these guidelines. For one thing, they do not mention grammar and structure. ETS has gone out of its way to select multiple formats among the sample 2-scoring answers it provides. Single narrative paragraphs, pairs of unconnected paragraphs, and even bulleted lists can get a perfect score as long as they directly address the prompt and clearly display your knowledge.

Here are some effective responses to the two questions above. Each of these would earn a 2.

Sample Response to CR 1:

Mr. Hallet's plan doesn't scaffold effectively. He transitions too quickly from a very explicit and clear assignment in groups to a very challenging assignment that students must complete alone. An intermediate step could have helped Rod connect his success on the first assignment to the skills required on the second.

Mr. Hallet's objectives are very content focused. Mike repeatedly commented that the assignment was "stupid." If Mr. Hallet had included an objective related to applying the new concept, such as "Students will understand the effect word choice has on listeners and readers," and included things in the lesson designed to illustrate that concept, Mike and other students might have understood why they were studying the topic and thus been more engaged.

Sample Response to CR 2:

Mike and Darred reach for answers rather than admit they don't understand. Despite Mr. Hallet's praise, the connection they draw between "swelter" and "sweater" is pure coincidence. In a practice typical of many struggling students, Darred fired off several answers, more concerned with getting a positive response from the teacher than with actually understanding or learning.

Rod gives up on his assignment without asking for help. Remedial students are often resigned to academic failure, especially if they are struggling in multiple subjects. Also, many struggling students believe that teachers cannot be relied on or even trusted, and they may avoid asking questions on challenging assignments for that reason. Either or both of those common attitudes could explain Rod's silence.

Case History Strategies

Read the questions first. Before you begin analyzing the case, take a look at the questions. Doing so can help focus your reading. If you look at the text first and are then surprised by an unusual question prompt, you may have to re-read part or even all of the case history, looking for information you didn't think was relevant the first time through. If you know what you need, you can use that knowledge to go through the case history efficiently.

Make a "map" of the case history. It's important that you take notes, either by circling or underlining parts of your test booklet or by jotting down the locations of key details on your scratch paper. Your goal here is not to summarize or copy information—you can and should review pertinent details directly from the text itself. However, misplacing or forgetting about those details can cost you time. When you need that information, you want to be able to locate it instantly. We refer to these notes as "maps" because they are meant to help you find your way!

Brainstorm. Don't just write the first two ideas that come into your head. Spend a few minutes thinking of three or four possible responses. Then pick the two you are most comfortable with. Your final response will be much stronger this way. More importantly, you're less likely to find yourself halfway through composing an answer before realizing you can't justify your argument and need to start over from scratch.

Refer to the case. It may seem as though you can answer some case history questions, especially those related to pedagogical practice, in purely theoretical terms. However, such an answer would never score higher than a 1. The question will always ask you to relate your suggestions to the students or teachers in the case history in some way. Follow this instruction.

Keep it simple. Don't overcomplicate. One good piece of supporting evidence is sufficient to demonstrate deep understanding. However, one weak example can undercut your answer, even if you present it alongside other, more compelling points.

Use one idea per paragraph. As mentioned before, scores of 2 are awarded regardless of formatting. However, many lower-scoring answer samples take the form of a single paragraph that goes into depth about only one part of the prompt or that loses sight of the goal and meanders off-topic. You should write one paragraph for each of the two parts of your answer so you can more easily check your work and ensure that you've completed your task.

Proofread. Always double-check your work. Once you've written both responses to one case, re-read each question and answer. Make sure you've answered the question thoroughly, and though you won't be graded on grammar, make sure your work is at least intelligible.

PLT Constructed-Response Practice

PLT Case Histories

Directions: Each case history in this section is followed by two short-answer questions. Your responses to the questions will be evaluated with respect to professionally accepted principles and practices of learning and teaching. Be sure to answer all parts of the questions.

Constructed-Response Questions: Case History #1

Case History #1: Early Childhood

Scenario

Ms. Jackson is a second-grade teacher at the East Hill Elementary School, a well-run suburban school with a sizable low-income community. This is Ms. Jackson's first year of teaching. She meets regularly with her mentor, Ms. Evenson, to discuss her experiences as a new teacher.

Document 1

Ms. Jackson's self-reflection notes

My college adviser described East Hill as a place where I could "make the mistakes of a beginning teacher and come out a better teacher on the other end." I'm starting to wonder what I'm doing here, though. For the most part, I've been focused on classroom management and on creating a structured and disciplined academic environment. In my classroom, I tolerate no excuses for behavior that disrupts others' learning or falls short on effort—and that goes for every student. But with all of my efforts to gain authority, I feel like I'm missing out on the mentoring role of teaching.

Document 2

Excerpt from Ms. Evenson's observation of Ms. Jackson's class—November

During my observation, Ms. Jackson tried to conduct a reading group with the eight slowest readers in the class, including a boy named William Baker. I was informed that last year's standardized test placed William at the lowest level in reading. He had been absent for 35 days last year and had spent a good number of his school days in the principal's office, many times missing the reading lessons in his first-grade classroom. When the eight members of the reading group met, the rest of the class worked on workbook assignments at their desks.

Several times, I noticed that William would start an argument, and most of the children at their desks would snap to attention to watch the scene William was making. Ms. Jackson harshly censured William each time, telling him that his behavior was unacceptable and rude, and sometimes loudly telling him to sit down and pay attention or she would call his parents. In one instance, when William openly defied her, Ms. Jackson directed William to sit in the time-out chair. When he refused, she sent him to the principal's office. Even in William's absence, the chemistry in the classroom seemed strained, with a lot of bickering among the children.

Ms. Jackson seems genuinely invested in helping her students progress. Whenever a child who was reading aloud hesitated with a word, Ms. Jackson pronounced the complete word two or three times, then had the child repeat what she had said. When Ms. Jackson asked the students to summarize the story they had read, most of the members of the small reading group were lost and could not paraphrase the key events of the plot. Similarly, when she repeated a sentence from the story and asked students to tell her what the sentence meant, the children were hesitant to reply and often gave incorrect answers.

Document 3

Excerpt from transcript of post-observation conversation between Ms. Jackson and Ms. Evenson

Ms. Evenson: I noticed that William Baker created quite a stir in your classroom today.

Ms. Jackson: That young man has really tested my resolve this year. How frustrating and embarrassing to be drawn into a battle of wills with a second-grader!

Ms. Evenson: Can you expand on "battle of wills"? Beyond what I saw today, what kind of stuff is William doing in class?

Ms. Jackson: Throwing pencils and wadded paper at other students. Refusing to stay at his desk. Stepping out of line when we walk to lunch or to recess. Interrupting other students. You name it, really.

Ms. Evenson: That's got to be so frustrating. What strategies have you used for helping minimize the effect of William's disruptive behavior on others?

Ms. Jackson: I tell the others to ignore him—that their attention is only encouraging him. I've taken William out into the hall and told him to straighten up. Sometimes, I tell him right in the classroom that he needs to clean up his act—but nothing seems to embarrass him or get through to him. He just doesn't have any respect for others, and his little performances frequently derail the other students' progress in their workbook assignments.

1. Ms. Jackson knows that the progress of the class in reading is being slowed down by external disturbances.

   - Identify TWO instructional strategies that she could use in teaching reading to the class to minimize the effect of distractions and improve progress.

   - Explain how EACH of the two strategies would improve the environment in her classroom and assist in her students' development as readers. Base your response on the principles of effective instructional strategies.

2. There are a number of measures Ms. Jackson could take regarding William's conduct and behavior in the reading group.

   - Identify TWO teaching strategies or behavior management techniques she could use with William in particular.

   - Discuss how EACH strategy or technique would improve William's classroom behavior and make the classroom more conducive to his learning. Base your response on the principles and strategies of classroom management.

Constructed-Response Questions: Case History #2

Case History #2: Grades K–6

Scenario

Ms. Carter is a fourth-grade teacher at the Hudson Elementary K–6 school. Approximately 430 of the 750 students at Hudson are ELL children. There are 10 languages represented in the school, plus many dialects of each language. Ms. Carter, now in her second year of teaching, meets regularly with her mentor, Mr. Guo, to discuss problems and to share teaching and classroom management strategies.

Document 1

Ms. Carter's journal notes

I'm worried that two of my special education students, Tuyet and Luis, are going to have trouble passing the upcoming state-administered reading test. I'm also slightly concerned that their behavior is making it harder for the other students to get ready for the test.

Tuyet is 10 years old and a first-generation immigrant from Vietnam. Her parents, whom I met at a beginning-of-the-school-year open house, seem open to a wide range of ideas when it comes to Tuyet's education. They're learning English themselves and are therefore keenly aware of the challenges Tuyet faces as a nonnative speaker in school.

Although Tuyet's English is limited, she can read at a third-grade level. However, she was recently diagnosed with ADHD. Although Tuyet is receiving medication, she has trouble concentrating and is extremely hyperactive.

Luis, on the other hand, doesn't speak any English and is not yet literate in Spanish, his native language. Until this year, he'd apparently had little in the way of formal schooling. He seems unhappy here at Hudson and often creates disruptions during my lessons.

Document 2

Mr. Guo's notes following observation of Ms. Carter's class

Ms. Carter has 18 ELL students in her class of 35 fourth graders. These ELL students speak Arabic, Farsi, Spanish, Vietnamese, Lao, and Mandarin Chinese. Ms. Carter is bilingual, but her second language, Russian, is not spoken by any of the students in the class.

During my observation, non-English-speaking students spent some time individually with Ms. Carter or her paraprofessionals, and occasionally, they left the classroom altogether to work with ELL teachers in the school's resource room. Now and then, one of the paraprofessionals chatted with several of the students in Spanish.

While Ms. Carter was speaking before the entire class, she shared some of her knowledge of Russian with curious students in the class. The students then took turns teaching her some phrases from their own languages. Ms. Carter asked them open-ended questions, praising them for their responses.

One student, however—a girl named Tuyet—had trouble staying on task, often failing to answer direct questions or playing private games instead of following along with the class's conversation. Ms. Carter, at one point, let one of her paraprofessionals take over primary instruction so that she could work with Tuyet one-on-one.

Another student, Luis, repeatedly got up from his seat and walked around the room, talking to himself and disturbing the rest of the class. The paraprofessional in Ms. Carter's room escorted him out, finally, and took him down to the ELL resource room, where there was someone who spoke his language. The paraprofessional told me that this happens quite often with Luis.

After the observation, Ms. Carter and I agreed that it would be productive to schedule a conference with the parents of each child. Ms. Carter will recommend that Tuyet be allowed to take her reading test separately from the other students, but she is concerned that this special treatment might make the other children jealous. She isn't sure what changes are appropriate for Luis.

Document 3

Excerpt from transcript of Luis's conference

Ms. Carter [through translator]: Luis's behavior is disruptive to some of the other children, but that's not what I'm really concerned about. I'm concerned that his acting out is a symptom of his need for an educational program better tailored to his specific challenges. And I'd love to listen to your thoughts about what those needs are and how I can help to meet them.

Luis's father [through translator]: Well, he shouldn't be misbehaving. I'll talk to him about that. On the other hand—if he can't understand what the teacher is saying, it makes sense that he would get bored, right?

Luis's mother [through translator]: Without disrespect—because I'm sure you're an excellent teacher—Luis has told us that he prefers to be in the ELL room with Ms. Martinez and Mr. Glass. He says that he learns more from those teachers than he does in your classroom—probably because he can't understand the words you use.

Ms. Carter [through translator]: I understand. But it's important for Luis to spend time with the other children at the school as well, including English-speaking students. And I need to work with him to make sure that he's ready for the state reading test.

Luis's mother [through translator]: The test—why is Luis taking it to begin with? What's the point of making him take a test he can't even read? Just let him spend his time in the ELL room. He learns a lot there.

3. Ms. Carter's students have a wide range of special needs related, in some cases, to their relative inexperience with the English language.

   • Identify TWO effective instructional strategies that Ms. Carter and the paraprofessionals, resource teachers, and administrators at Hudson Elementary are currently using in order to better meet the needs of the ELL students in Ms. Carter's class.

   • Describe how EACH strategy you identify helps Ms. Carter's ELL students progress in their learning. Base your response on the principles of planning for students as diverse learners.

4. Some of the ELL students in Ms. Carter's diverse classroom are not as engaged in the lessons as they should be.

   • Identify TWO strategies Ms. Carter could use to improve student engagement and foster greater progress in the students' learning. Include one general strategy and one strategy that applies specifically to Luis and/or Tuyet.

   • Describe how EACH strategy you identify would help Ms. Carter improve her ELL students' progress in English. Base your response on the principles of student motivation and learning theory and the principles of planning for students as diverse learners.

Constructed-Response Questions: Case History #3

Case History #3: Grades 5–9

Scenario

Thomas Williams is a sixth-grade student in a relatively affluent suburban school district. His teachers describe him as quiet and shy; they comment that his work is inconsistent but is not a major cause for concern. He is heavily overweight and has been since early childhood.

Ms. Ross is Thomas's third-period science teacher. It is Ms. Ross's second year, but she already has a reputation as a popular and exciting teacher. Her mentor, Mr. Perry, has just observed her teaching Thomas's class.

Document 1

Ms. Ross's self-reflection—third-period science, Tuesday

Today's class went well. Most of the class was excited by the water cycle. The discussion of last year's blizzard was a great last-minute addition that let the students establish a personal connection to the weather. Carlos, Zhou, and Jenny all asked very insightful questions that let me reteach challenging parts of the lesson. I also tried to use my mentor's suggestions about handling off-topic questions, and I think I was able to turn Sasha's questions about acid rain into a teachable moment.

Document 2

Excerpt from Ms. Ross's post-observation meeting with her mentor, Mr. Perry

Mr. Perry: And did your students meet all the learning objectives for your lesson?

Ms. Ross: Absolutely. When I asked review questions after the first 10 minutes of the lesson, the students answered quickly and accurately. And when I opened the floor for questions at the half-hour mark, the responses I got were surprisingly sophisticated and thoughtful. It's a good thing I knew enough about acid rain to answer them.

Mr. Perry: What about the quieter students? The reason I ask is that from the back of the room, I saw that Thomas gave incomplete answers to most of the study questions on his worksheet.

Ms. Ross: He did? Well, that's disappointing. After the lesson, he had several opportunities to ask questions if he was having trouble.

Mr. Perry: Is it possible he just doesn't feel comfortable asking questions in front of his peers?

Ms. Ross: It could be. He has a few friends in class, but he isn't very popular and does get teased about his weight. I'll check with his guidance counselor to see what I can do for him.

Document 3

Thomas's answers to Ms. Ross's study questions:

What are the steps of the water cycle? _____ → _____ → _____ → _____ → _____
(Hint: the last step is the same as the first.)

Thomas's answer: Consation → Rain?? → Running water → _____ → Consation

How do plants play a role in the water cycle?

Thomas's answer: Roots in the ground are part of the water cycle.

Why is the water cycle important to the environment?

Thomas's answer: Acid rain can kill trees and fish.

Document 4

Guidance counselor's note to Ms. Ross

Saw your message about Thomas. I've spoken to him several times recently about teasing from peers. According to Thomas, it's worse than it was in elementary school, but he "can put up with it." However, it wouldn't surprise me if he were trying to keep a low profile in class.

One other thing: He's made a few comments about teachers "playing favorites." He didn't specify how or why, but he may have gotten an impression that some teachers value other students' contributions more highly than his own.

Document 5

Excerpt from Ms. Ross's third-period science class, Thursday.

(The bell rings. Students are mostly in their seats, talking among themselves.)

Ms. Ross: Hello, class!

(The class replies "Hello, Ms. Ross!" Several conversations continue, while other students wait silently.)

Ms. Ross: All right, settle down. Today, we're going to talk about different types of clouds and start work on your terrariums. But first, I wanted to talk about something important.

(The class settles down. A few students still whisper.)

Ms. Ross: In Tuesday's class, I got some really great questions. Carlos's questions about condensation were very helpful because they let me know what parts of the lesson were hard to understand, and Sasha's question about acid rain was a great learning opportunity for all of us.

(Sasha beams. Carlos laughs but is embarrassed.)

Ms. Ross: So I want everyone to know that questions are very important to learning. All of you should be okay asking questions about things you don't understand. It doesn't matter whether the person who asks is a boy or a girl, if they're good at science or having trouble, if they're a jock or overweight. This should be a safe environment. *(A student raises his hand.)* Arthur, do you have a question?

Arthur *(joking)*: What if they're really *really* overweight like Tom Tub?

(The class laughs. Thomas glares, then puts his head on his desk.)

Ms. Ross *(angry)*: Arthur, that's completely out of line. Go to the office. Now!

Arthur: But Carlos and Zhou call him that all the time. Why am I getting in trouble?

Ms. Ross: Don't argue with me, young man. Go to the office.

(Ms. Ross starts her lecture. The class is subdued for the whole period, and Thomas doesn't pay any attention to the lesson at all.)

5. Ms. Ross helped students take notes by having them complete a study sheet while she lectured. Review Thomas's notes on his study sheet in document 3.

   - Suggest TWO modifications to the study sheet activity that could have helped Thomas better understand Ms. Ross's lecture.

   - Explain how EACH modification would have helped Thomas produce more accurate and complete responses. Base your responses on the principles of planning instruction.

6. Ms. Ross's attempt to encourage a safe environment for students to participate in class was not successful, in part because she inadvertently singled Thomas out in front of his peers.

   - Propose TWO ways that Ms. Ross could make students like Thomas feel more comfortable participating in her classes.

   - Explain how EACH method you propose would encourage Thomas to participate more in classroom discussions. Base your responses on the principles of effective classroom management.

Constructed-Response Questions: Case History #4

Case History #4: Grades 7–12

Scenario

Mr. Fayerwether is a math teacher in the only high school in a small suburb. Of the 24 students in his fourth-period Algebra II class, 21 are 10th-grade students. At the beginning of the second month of school, Mr. Fayerwether is collecting documents to prepare a self-evaluation, focusing in particular on the one freshman and two juniors in his class.

Document 1

Mr. Fayerwether's first impression of the three students

Johnny is a bright, positive student one-on-one. However, as the only 9th grader in the class, he often seems uncomfortable interacting with students who are older than he is. On Johnny's first day, he was teased for his high-pitched voice; though the perpetrator was disciplined and the teasing has not recurred, I think the incident left a negative impression on him. Johnny has nevertheless proved to be one of the highest-performing students in the class despite his youth—he finishes most in-class assignments well before his classmates.

Lucy is a popular girl. She is comfortable speaking out in class, but she makes as many off-topic jokes as she makes legitimate contributions. Math has consistently been a struggle for her. She failed Algebra I as a freshman and only passed her second time through with a C–. She is clearly a capable student, as demonstrated by her As in English and social studies and Bs in science. But it's hard to tell how dedicated she is to her math studies. She is determined to follow in the footsteps of her mother, a traveling art dealer, and has repeatedly made comments such as "I suck at algebra, but who cares? I know what I want to do and don't need math to do it!"

Karl is struggling to recover after a car accident caused him to miss a significant part of his sophomore year. He has an aide to help him carry his belongings (as he is still on crutches) and, more importantly, to help him read; neurological damage makes it hard for him to focus his eyes on small text. Unfortunately, Karl often refuses to let his aide help him. His weekly quiz grades have been much lower than his B average from last year, and I am convinced that he would have done better if he had accepted assistance. Karl's parents are both very concerned with his recovery, academic and physical, but they do not live together and the information I get from them is sometimes contradictory. When I asked Karl about it, he told me his parents "are both full of it."

Document 2

Lesson plan for class to be observed by Mr. Fayerwether's supervisor

Goals:

- Students will refresh knowledge of inequalities from earlier grades.
- Students will apply the tools for solving systems of equations to solve systems involving both equations and inequalities.
- Students will understand how real-world problems can translate to systems of equations and inequalities.

Students will work on a review sheet to start off the class. I offered Karl a large-print version of the review sheet, but he unsurprisingly refused. The small-group work that I used for this lesson last year was pure math. Lucy's grades in English suggest she is a verbal thinker, so I've replaced a few equations with word problems; I hope this will engage her. I have not made any modifications to the lesson for Johnny, as his performance suggests he does not need them.

Document 3

Supervisor's notes on Mr. Fayerwether's class

Mr. Fayerwether begins by handing out a review sheet with symbols, terms, and images. He asks for an explanation of each term from a particular student. When students shout out an answer out of turn, Mr. Fayerwether politely but firmly tells them it's not their turn. Next, he lectures on applying concepts from the previous week's class. He pauses regularly to write equations, steps, and rules on the overhead projector. The class ends with a group-work activity. Each group of students is given 12 problems. Each student is instructed to do a third of the problems, then check his or her partners' work on the other problems.

Document 4

Mr. Fayerwether's post-observation self-evaluation

Today's results were disappointing. My original plan had been to ask Lucy easy questions early in the review and to save the hard questions for high-performing students like Johnny. However, Lucy responded by making jokes about how I expected her to remember things from sixth grade. By the time I got an answer out of her, Johnny had already finished the entire review and stopped paying attention. Karl was one of several students who shouted out his answers, and he held a grudge; he refused to answer when it was actually his turn. And even Johnny stumbled when it was his turn to answer a question. He had finished and was no longer paying attention, and several students laughed out loud.

The second half didn't go much better. Karl was frustrated because he misread the problem numbers on his worksheet and ended up doing three of the same problems as his partners before his aide spotted the error. Lucy and her partners spent most of the period talking rather than doing math, and Johnny finished 10 of 12 problems before his partners were done with their 8. In retrospect, these were predictable outcomes given these students' recurring behavior, but I'm still frustrated.

7. Mr. Fayerwether ends his self-evaluation by commenting that Johnny and Lucy's behavior during group work was part of a recurring pattern. Suppose that you are Mr. Fayerwether's supervisor.

   - For each of these two students, suggest ONE guiding question to ask Mr. Fayerwether about a specific aspect of that student's pattern of behavior.

   - For EACH question, explain how different answers would suggest different approaches for Mr. Fayerwether to improve his students' behavior. Base your answer on the principles of modifying instruction for diverse learners.

8. Throughout the study, Karl refuses direct offers of assistance for coping with his disability.

   - Suggest TWO modifications Mr. Fayerwether could make to his teaching style that would indirectly help Karl.

   - Explain how EACH modification would aid Karl while still being indirect enough that he would not refuse. Base your answers on the principles of educating students with disabilities.

PLT Constructed-Response Practice Answers and Explanations

1. One strategy Ms. Jackson could use would be to teach reading using the phonetics approach and basal readers. The students in her class are attempting to learn in a volatile environment, and breaking down the reading lessons to form a narrow learning path will help her to gauge the success of individual students and the lessons better than if the class were trying to absorb a broader curriculum. While Ms. Jackson intends to be helpful, interrupting a student who is struggling with a word, then supplying the complete pronunciation for the student, is actually ineffective: it further distracts from the learning environment and contributes to classroom outbursts. When Ms. Jackson pronounces the word to the student, the student may become embarrassed, and others may laugh at the struggling student when they see the teacher intervene with such a harsh method of teaching the word. This frustration could further create an unpleasant learning environment, thereby undoing any progress made with the instructional strategies. An alternative approach, such as the use of phonics, would give students limited guidance when needed, while letting them find their way to the correct pronunciation.

   Ms. Jackson could also use writing as a strategy to enhance her students' focus and reading levels. Writing assignments based on reading passages that focus on correct spelling and grammar forces the students to understand the individual words, rather than attempting to decipher the meaning of an entire passage. If the students are busy working on these assignments, it is less likely that they will be so easily distracted by William's behavior.

2. Ms. Jackson should sit down and have a personal conversation with William, in which she discusses his behaviors that must change. She can provide him with a list of positive and negative reinforcements that will come with certain types of behavior. For instance, if he continues to disrupt the class, he will have to accept the consequences of that action. The list must be specific so that William's negative behavior will be shaped into a positive state. A contract designed by William and Ms. Jackson together, to actually set goals—not only for completed work, but also for practiced behavior—would also be useful. There should be an incentive for reaching these goals.

   In a conference with William's parents or guardians, Ms. Jackson can discuss the areas in which William shows strengths, along with her concerns about William's weaknesses in his performance in class. She needs to share with William's parents/guardians the positive growth and development William is making and how much more progress he can make. Ms. Jackson should find out in which room William completes his reading at home. For example: if William reads at the kitchen table, then is it free of distractions, such as physical objects on the table and other people in the room talking or eating? If William reads in his bedroom, is he supervised to make sure he remains on task? After asking about these rooms, Ms. Jackson can suggest how William's parents can help him succeed, such as by having a clean area on the table where William can work, or having an older sibling also do work in William's room to make sure William remains on task. Ms. Jackson can share the reinforcement guidelines she is using to help with behavior modification in the classroom and ask the parents/guardians to do similar things at home so that William's behavior modification will be consistent. Finally, as a reward, Ms. Jackson could give William time in the school library to select a book from his favorite genre. This would reward his good behavior and further encourage his reading skills.

3. Ms. Carter's class includes ELL students in an inclusion classroom. Hudson's administrators and staff are correct to consider ethnic diversity when placing non-English-speaking students new to this country in regular classrooms. In fact, the Individuals with Disabilities Education Act requires children with special needs to be placed in the "least restrictive environment" that is appropriate for their education. Immersion of ELL students in an English-speaking classroom fosters multiculturalism and can help ELL students learn English from their peers and from their teacher. Ms. Carter increases the benefits of immersion by including her ELL students in general discussions and by treating them as equal participants in the learning process. Also, she asks students open-ended questions without "correct" or "incorrect" answers and praises them for their responses. This technique is appropriate, for it provides the children with the confidence they need to creatively use a new language.

Ms. Carter provides individual resources for students needing additional help. ELL students will learn effectively when placed in an environment that fosters diversity but also has resources catering to differentiating the instruction. In Ms. Carter's classroom, ELL students benefit from specialized, one-on-one attention during the regular classroom activities, plus the support of a dedicated resource room where ELL resource teachers tailor instruction to each child's needs.

4. To ensure that non-English-speaking students do not feel different, left out, or unequal, and to thereby increase their engagement, Ms. Carter could structure her lesson plan to include activities for the entire class that incorporate the ELL teachers and paraprofessionals. She could, for instance, have a class discussion on culture using a concept web and have the students present their own definitions of culture and write them on the web. When all students have written down their responses, they might read them to each other to see how different they all are and how different their responses were.

In working with Luis specifically, Ms. Carter might let him continue his successes in the ELL resource room because this seems to be a positive experience for him. But she needs to make sure he is included in the activities of his class. A home visit with a translator, in which Ms. Carter sits down with Luis and his parents, could be useful in identifying strategies for drawing Luis into the class's activities. Once he learns some English, he may feel more comfortable being in a regular, English-speaking classroom full-time.

5. Ms. Ross could have included a word bank on her study sheet. This would have ensured that Thomas understood that the word was "condensation" and not "consation." It also would have made it less likely that Thomas would mistake the side discussion on acid rain for a formal part of the lesson, because terms related to acid rain would not appear in the word bank.

Ms. Ross also could have given students a chance to compare notes in pairs. This would have given Thomas a chance to get missing pieces of answers from a peer. More importantly, it would have let Ms. Ross circle the room and visually inspect student answers. This would provide a more accurate assessment of the class's understanding than simply asking whether they have questions—she would know that Thomas (and possibly other students) needed assistance in understanding parts of the lesson.

6. Ms. Ross can make a safer environment for students by offering praise for behaviors other than asking questions. By singling out vocal students for praise, she may have worsened Thomas's impression that she is playing favorites in her classroom. If she had complimented Thomas for excellent work on a paper or homework assignment, her praise would have let Thomas know that Ms. Ross did value his contributions, and would likely appreciate his questions and comments as well.

    Ms. Ross could have gotten more value out of her praise of Carlos by eliciting from him that he was having trouble with the material, rather than pointing it out herself. Carlos might have been less embarrassed this way. But more importantly, Thomas would have seen a more popular student admit to having trouble with the material. This would have let him know that many students found the material challenging, and that there was nothing wrong with asking questions and admitting imperfect understanding.

7. I would ask how Johnny behaves doing group work with other advanced students. If Johnny follows instructions and engages with his advanced peers, then changes related to the difficulty of the assignment—such as giving Johnny a specific, challenging task when he works in a group—will alleviate the problem. However, if he works on his own and ignores even partners who can work at his level, Mr. Fayerwether might consider that the problem is one of socialization and is best addressed with the help of guidance.

    I would ask whether Lucy is more productive during group activities that actually require conversation as part of the assignment. As Mr. Fayerwether pointed out, Lucy earns As in English. If she chats with her friends because she is primarily a verbal/auditory thinker, then giving her more opportunities to discuss problems will help her understand the mathematical concepts that are challenging her. If she won't talk about math problems even when instructed to, the root of her behavior probably lies elsewhere.

8. When reviewing answers on the test sheet, Mr. Fayerwether could put them on the overhead projector. This large image could be easier for students with visual difficulties to read—especially if Mr. Fayerwether used assigned seating to ensure Karl was close to the front of the class. Additionally, Mr. Fayerwether should move several students to a new seating assignment in the room—and not just Karl. Moving other students as well as Karl to different areas of the room removes the focus from Karl and instead explains the situation as an instructional change for the benefit of the entire class—and not just a special-needs adjustment for Karl.

    Mr. Fayerwether could further modify group activities in his class to include more conversation and collaborative work than occurred in this case. If he did so, Karl might be willing to ask his peers for the help he refuses from his aide.

PLT Grades K–6 Practice

Directions: For selected-response questions 1–25, choose the response that best answers the question or completes the statement. Then follow the directions provided for constructed-response questions 1–2.

A teacher wants to effectively manage and accommodate students from varying cultures while supporting their development of English language skills.

1. Which of the following strategies would best support that goal?

    A. Instructing students not to speak their native language while completing classroom tasks

    B. Setting up daily cooperative learning activities with mixed groups of boys and girls

    C. Allowing students to communicate understanding through writing, drawing, or speaking

    D. Supporting English language learners by correcting most errors in their speech so that they learn faster

2. Ms. Lane, a second-grade teacher, notices that many of her pupils come to class with their homework incomplete. Ms. Lane plans an activity in which her students will fill out an after-school schedule, detailing tasks to be done at half-hour intervals from 3:30 until 9:00 PM each day of the school week. Which of the following student capabilities does this activity promote?

    A. Awareness of consequences

    B. Risk-taking behavior

    C. Self-regulation

    D. Pro-social behavior

3. A kindergarten teacher is concerned with helping students make positive progress through the "initiative versus guilt" stage of development, as described by Erikson. Which of the following student activities would most likely help students meet the goals associated with this stage of development?

    A. Memorizing a poem and reciting it in front of the class

    B. Engaging in independent play each day

    C. Watching a cartoon and discussing it together

    D. Playing a supervised game together

4. In a sixth-grade French class, some students are successfully writing letters in French, while other students labor to write even a single sentence. Previous test results indicate these students have a similar level of French vocabulary knowledge. How could the teacher use Vygotsky's zone of proximal development theory to help all students write paragraphs more successfully?

    A. The class could write a paragraph together, then write in small groups, then write individually.

    B. Students could write paragraphs in English and then translate them into French.

    C. The teacher could show examples of well-written paragraphs in French for students to model.

    D. Students could write paragraphs in French about events occurring in their own lives.

Luz, a student in Mr. Lipnicki's classroom, typically completes in-class assignments very quickly. Her answers are usually correct and well written. After she has finished her work, she often tries to strike up conversations with students who are still working on their own assignments. On occasion, she also loudly complains that the work in class is "boring."

5. Which of the following would be an appropriate strategy for Mr. Lipnicki to use in light of Luz's pattern of disruptive behavior?

    A. Refer Luz to a school administrator for disciplinary measures.

    B. Create a reward structure in which students can win prizes like candy and toys for sitting quietly after all of their work is completed.

    C. Tell the other students in Luz's class that they are encouraging her misbehavior when they respond to the things she says, and advise them to ignore her.

    D. Create appealing and intellectually challenging lesson-related "bonus activities" for students who finish work early.

Upon completion of a unit, students must describe those learning activities that helped them and those that did not. Students are also asked to infer what this information reveals about their own learning styles and preferences.

6. Which of the following cognitive processes does this assignment encourage?

    A. Problem solving

    B. Concept learning

    C. Transfer

    D. Metacognition

A first-grade teacher is teaching comparison word problems during math time in a classroom that includes several English language learners (ELLs).

7. Which of the following is the most effective strategy the teacher can use to support the ELLs in her class?

    A. Exempting ELLs from word problems, having them focus instead on number comparisons

    B. Having ELLs work on addition with pictures while the rest of the class does word problems

    C. Having ELLs read the problems aloud to the class to make sure they understand the words

    D. Having the class retell the word problems and discuss any unfamiliar vocabulary to give ELLs multiple ways to access the content

A teacher begins a unit on the American Revolution with his sixth-grade social studies class by conducting a preassessment to determine students' understanding of the term *revolution* and its significance in the historical development of nations. He then plans instruction to build upon the base knowledge demonstrated by his students in the preassessment.

8. Which of the following learning theories does the strategy described above most closely adhere to?

    A. B. F. Skinner's classical conditioning

    B. Lev Vygotsky's zone of proximal development

    C. Jerome Bruner's constructivist theory of learning

    D. Benjamin Bloom's taxonomy

9. According to Piaget, a first-grade student who is unable to recognize that two differently shaped balls of clay have the same mass is most likely in which of the following stages?

    A. Sensorimotor stage

    B. Preoperational stage

    C. Concrete operational stage

    D. Formal operational stage

10. Which of the following approaches most effectively reinforces students' self-regulatory skills while assisting the teacher in communicating information about student progress to parents and other caregivers?

    A. The teacher establishes a system in which students know that any test grade of F or A+ will result automatically in the teacher placing a phone call to the student's parents.

    B. The teacher instructs students to regularly update their parents about their performance in school, as well as about upcoming projects and other major assignments.

    C. Two times during each grading period, students write "progress letters" to their parents identifying recent successes and areas for future improvement.

    D. The teacher requests that parents tether positive and negative incentives at home to students' academic performance and behavior in the classroom.

11. Which of the following lesson plan excerpts includes observable and measurable educational objectives?

    A. By the end of the lesson, students will be able to describe the difference between a whole note and a half note and demonstrate the difference through rhythmic clapping.

    B. By the end of the lesson, students will grasp the fundamentals of badminton and develop an appreciation of the importance of fair play and good ethics on the court.

    C. By the end of the lesson, students will understand literary symbolism.

    D. By the end of the lesson, students will be able to pass a multiple-choice test on the makeup of plant cells.

An earthquake occurs outside a small community. When students arrive at school the following day, they begin to ask their teacher all types of questions. Though the subject is not part of the lesson plan, the teacher uses this opportunity to teach the students about the causes of earthquakes.

12. What is the situation described above an example of?

    A. Off-task behavior

    B. Storytelling

    C. Socratic questioning technique

    D. A teachable moment

13. A teacher is planning a unit that will include student-generated presentations to the whole class. Which of the following is the best technique that the teacher could use to increase student attentiveness to their classmates during the presentations?

    A. Giving a surprise quiz after the presentations to test students' retention of what the presenters said

    B. Sitting in the front of the classroom to remind students that the teacher is watching them

    C. Creating a new classroom rule that insists that students be polite to the speakers

    D. Giving students a graphic organizer in which to take notes during the subsequent presentations

14. Which of the following is the best strategy to use when implementing an experiential instructional model to support students in memorizing multiplication tables?

    A. Having the class complete a set of practice problems in a computer program that targets multiplication tables

    B. Having students pair off to play a game that requires them to use multiplication tables

    C. Having students pair off to read a fictional selection in which the main character uses multiplication tables to resolve a conflict

    D. Having the whole class perform a choral recitation of the multiplication tables

15. Allowing "wait time" for student thinking, helping students reshape or sharpen verbal explanations, and establishing a noncritical classroom environment are all important aspects of

    A. written assessment

    B. instructional objective setting

    C. IEP development

    D. effective questioning

16. A school with a fine-arts emphasis wishes to enroll students who have the potential to excel in musical studies. The admissions director plans to use a test to help identify students with strong musical potential. Which choice below serves as the best example of a test designed to measure what the student is capable of accomplishing musically?

    A. Ability test

    B. Achievement test

    C. Aptitude test

    D. Selected-response test

17. Which of the following is the best rationale for peer assessment processes for essay assignments?

    A. Peer assessments lessen the need for teacher-created feedback, giving teachers more time to focus on lesson planning.

    B. Peer assessments can help students think more deeply about their weaknesses as writers.

    C. Peer assessments can create opportunities for writers to receive and consider a variety of viewpoints and solutions.

    D. Peer assessments give students time to talk to one another, providing a break from listening to the teacher.

18. Which of the following scoring systems would best indicate whether a student has developed the content knowledge and mastery deemed appropriate to the student's age?

    A. Stanine

    B. Raw score

    C. Grade-level equivalent

    D. Percentile rank

19. Which of the following is an accurate description of analytical scoring?

    Select all that apply.

    A. Analytical scoring provides a separate score for each targeted skill, thus making clear a student's areas of strength and weakness.

    B. With analytical scoring, a single skill deficit is less likely to dominate the teacher's assessment of a student's work.

    C. Analytical scoring improves grade reliability by requiring that the grader assign a number of scores to a single piece of work.

    D. Analytical scoring focuses on the total effect of student work, rather than on the success of individual aspects of the work.

20. A fifth-grade teacher notices that one of her students performed at the 24th percentile in reading on a standardized achievement test given to all fifth graders. Which of the following inferences can the teacher make from these results?

    A. Either this teacher or the student's previous teacher did not teach reading in the most effective way possible.

    B. The student did not perform as well on the assessment as would a typical fifth grader.

    C. The student performed at a grade-appropriate level on the exam.

    D. The student performed better on the exam than most fifth-grade students.

21. Which of the following classroom activities is/are acceptable under fair use?

	Acceptable	Unacceptable
Showing a copyrighted motion picture for instructional purposes		
Scanning a legally purchased textbook and posting it on the class website		
Copying poems from copyrighted books to make a class anthology		
Incorporating a 10-second music clip into a student-generated multimedia presentation		

22. Which individual among the support personnel listed below would most likely be responsible for coordinating services for a child who felt unsafe at home?

    A. Guidance counselor

    B. Assistant principal

    C. IEP team leader

    D. Occupational therapist

23. Which of the following actions would best support a teacher seeking to deepen social studies content knowledge?

    A. Perusing the blog posts of teachers working on similar content

    B. Reading historical works set in the period during which the class's next unit takes place

    C. Joining a national organization of history teachers

    D. Searching for and watching video reenactments of historical events online

24. A schoolteacher in a geographically isolated rural community wants to obtain a broad range of perspectives on lesson planning and classroom management problems on a daily basis. Which of the following professional resources would be most helpful for this purpose?

    A. A conference on behaviorist-oriented classroom management strategies

    B. Education-focused, news-aggregating web applications

    C. A series of one-on-one meetings with a more experienced teacher of the same grade level at the same school

    D. Online educator forums and study groups

25. A teacher struggles with disruptive students in class. Which of the following responses would provide the best demonstration of reflective practice?

    A. The teacher discusses his struggles with two of his senior colleagues, and with their help, he formulates a plan of action.

    B. The teacher contacts the parents of the disruptive students and recommends disciplinary measures.

    C. The teacher rearranges the classroom to separate the disruptive students.

    D. The teacher writes down his struggles in a journal.

Approximate time: 25 minutes

Directions: The case history below is followed by two short-answer questions. Your responses to the questions will be evaluated with respect to professionally accepted principles and practices in teaching and learning. Be sure to answer all parts of the questions. Write your answers on the pages indicated in your answer sheet booklet.

Scenario:

Naima is a student in Mr. Traister's fifth-grade class. While Naima gives indications of being highly capable—she participates in the school's Gifted and Talented program and routinely scores at or above the 95th percentile on standardized math and reading tests—she rarely participates in class discussions and frequently fails to submit required homework assignments. Recently, Mr. Traister has noticed that the quality of Naima's participation in certain collaborative classroom activities has declined sharply.

Document 1

Excerpt from a conference between Mr. Traister and Naima's mother, Ms. McCarron

Mr. Traister: On this recent math quiz, for instance, Naima left half of the questions unanswered and neglected to show her work as required.

Ms. McCarron: But these questions are too basic for her. I thought she was in the "high-math" group. Is this what the high-math group is doing? I used to play a computer game with her on a tablet that had problems like these.

Mr. Traister: If she's mastered the skill, she should be able to complete the quiz quickly and accurately. Notice that she missed a number of problems here.

Ms. McCarron: But I've seen her answer questions like these a million times! If she's not getting them right, it's because she's not paying attention.

Mr. Traister: Even on open-ended, creative assignments, I have trouble getting Naima engaged. Here, for instance, is a sheet of drawing paper on which Naima was supposed to illustrate her essay about dinosaurs. She drew one tree in the corner and then stopped working on it. Her quizzes often come back to me covered in little pictures, so I know that she enjoys—and has a talent for—drawing. When we break into groups, Naima often won't participate in the work her group is doing until I goad her.

Ms. McCarron: Is it her job to teach the other children?

Mr. Traister: The group work is about exploring new concepts collaboratively. It isn't about one student teaching the others.

Ms. McCarron: Well, I'll tell her to do a better job with her work in school. But I worry, Mr. Traister, that some of this work is not worth her time.

Document 2

Excerpt from a transcript of a whole-class reading exercise in Mr. Traister's class

Billy: "Thanks to this magic . . . potion, I will soon have . . . "

Mr. Traister: Sound it out. The first syllable is—

Billy: ffff . . . ffrrr . . . *freckles.* "Freckles, just like"—

Mr. Traister: Nice job, but start again at the beginning of the sentence, Billy.

Billy: "Thanks to this magic potion, I will soon have freckles just like my best . . . friend."

Mr. Traister: Great. Naima, please take over. Naima?

Naima: What page are we on?

Mr. Traister: Naima, I need you to follow along with us.

Naima: I read this book in first grade. It's dumb.

Andrew: You did not read it in first grade! Liar!

Mr. Traister: Andrew, that's inappropriate. Naima, we're on page 21. "I will soon have freckles like my best friend."

Please resume the reading.

Document 3

Conversation between Mr. Traister and Ms. Benson, a Gifted and Talented resource teacher at the school

Mr. Traister: It's frustrating, because I know that Naima has the skills to be a real leader in our classroom.

Ms. Benson: She may have the skills, but we also need to make sure we give her the opportunities.

Mr. Traister: In small groups, I've asked her many times to use her abilities and her understanding to help the students who are struggling. I can't seem to cajole her into taking on that role.

Ms. Benson: She needs to get a chance to explore her own interests as well.

Mr. Traister: When the students were researching their book reports on biomes, she said that she had already read all of the books we were using, so I let her work with the librarian, Ms. Upshaw, to find some books she hadn't read. But when it came time for her to report back, she simply read undigested passages from a complicated book; she wasn't making any effort to paraphrase or synthesize.

Ms. Benson: It may be that she's shy, as well. I know that she enjoys our weekly GT small-group sessions in the resource room—but even there, she isn't particularly talkative.

Mr. Traister: I can see that. She doesn't seem to get along with the other kids in the class. At recess, for instance, I often find her sitting by herself reading a book, even though I've told her that recess time is for playing, not reading.

Constructed-Response Questions

Question 1

Mr. Traister's student Naima appears increasingly disengaged and unmotivated in the classroom.

- Identify TWO ways in which Naima's needs may currently be going unaddressed in Mr. Traister's classroom.
- Discuss a strategy that Mr. Traister could use to address EACH of Naima's two unaddressed areas of need. Base your response on the principles of teaching gifted and talented students.

Question 2

Mr. Traister works at a school that employs a number of educational paraprofessionals.

- Identify TWO ways in which Mr. Traister could collaborate with other professionals at the school to provide beneficial educational opportunities to Naima.
- Discuss how EACH of the collaborative relationships you identify would improve the quality of the education offered to Naima. Base your response on the principles of collaboration with instructional partners in instructional planning.

PLT Grades K–6 Practice Answers and Explanations

1. C

Allowing English language learners (ELLs) to use nonverbal and verbal means of communicating helps the teacher assess their understanding. Therefore, choice (**C**) is correct. Creating a classroom community is crucial to helping ELLs learn, and prohibiting the use of their native language (A) could lead to frustration or resentment. Daily use of mixed-gender groups (B) does not necessarily advance learning, and this strategy is not logically connected to the teacher's goal of creating the best environment for English language learners. Correcting most errors directly (D) will discourage students and interrupt the flow of spoken words; the teacher could instead wait until the student is finished and restate the response with the correct language for the student to model in the future.

2. C

By guiding her students to set up a schedule, Ms. Lane is encouraging students to regulate their own use of after-school time. Choice (**C**) is correct. Ms. Lane is not instituting consequences, as suggested by choice (A), nor is she addressing students' behavior toward one another, as suggested by choice (D). She is prompting students to think about how they spend and structure their time once they have left school. This is quite distinct from choice (B), which suggests that she is telling students to take more risks and thus think less carefully about how to structure their time.

3. B

Erikson's theory of initiative versus guilt states that children of kindergarten age need to learn by exploring the world and initiating their own activities without too much guidance or restrictions from adults. Independent play allows a space for children to engage with one another and devise their own methods and solutions to problems. Choice (**B**) is therefore correct. Choices (A) and (D) both suggest that adults would be determining all of the children's actions and intervening frequently with overt guidelines. In choice (C), the children would have slightly more autonomy, but the activity would still be determined by an adult.

4. A

The zone of proximal development (ZPD) theory, when applied to education, is much like scaffolding: challenging students to accomplish with assistance what they may lack the skill and experience to accomplish independently. By writing paragraphs together before attempting to do so separately, struggling students can improve their French writing skills in stages with meaningful assistance. Choice (**A**) is therefore correct. Translating entire paragraphs into French (B) might, at this point, be extremely challenging for some of the students in this class; the activity therefore does not reflect the tenets of ZPD theory. Showing students well-written examples (C) could offer some benefits, but the activity does not require them to take on challenges with assistance. The personal essay-writing assignment in choice (D) also lacks ZPD theory's crucial element of letting students take on challenges at the edge of their competence with assistance.

5. D

Luz seems to be struggling with her behavior in class, but she tends to do well on her assignments, suggesting that she can easily keep pace with the work. Her declaration that work is "boring" indicates that she may be a gifted student and that more challenging options for her, as described in choice (**D**), may be the solution. Enforcing punishments, as in choices (A) and (C), is unlikely to serve Luz's best interests or get to the root of the issue. Choice (B) works on extrinsic motivation rather than building Luz's intrinsic motivation or addressing her desire for more challenging assignments.

6. D

Reflecting on how one learns best and why one might have gained more from different activities is a hallmark of metacognition (**D**), or "thinking about thinking." This is distinct from problem solving (A), in which students are presented with an issue to resolve rather than asked to reflect; concept learning (B), in which students are guided to understand a new idea rather than to reflect on how and why they learned; and transfer (C), in which students use concepts from one area of study in another and make connections.

7. D

English language learners (ELLs) can be expected to perform the same work as other students so long as they have sufficient scaffolding to understand the concepts on which they are working. This includes clarifying vocabulary and discussing the ideas behind the word problems as a class so that the language does not present a barrier to the math content. Thus, choice (**D**) is correct. Allowing ELLs to skip the more complex work the class is doing (A) or work on addition (B) ensures that these students will fall further behind the class in math without advancing in the development of their English language skills. Asking these students to read problems aloud (C) not only does not reveal whether they understand what is being asked (as there may be no correlation between their pronunciation and their comprehension), but also may make them feel uncomfortable if they encounter unfamiliar words.

8. B

Vygotsky's zone of proximal development includes all tasks that a learner is unable to accomplish alone but can accomplish with assistance. Vygotsky argued that teachers can facilitate student growth by helping students as they work within their zones of proximal development—thus enabling students to do more and more things independently. By beginning his instruction right at the point at which his students need help, the teacher is focusing his instruction within his class's zone of proximal development. This means choice (**B**) is correct. Classical conditioning is a behaviorist strategy in which a certain stimulus comes to be associated with a certain result. The teacher is not using conditioning, so (A) is incorrect. Constructivism is a theory of learning under which the teacher acts as the facilitator of student-driven exploration and experiential learning. Nothing in the situation suggests that the teacher is planning to use student-directed learning, so (C) is incorrect. Finally, (D) is incorrect; Bloom's taxonomy is a system of educational objectives (broken into "domains") and is not obviously related to the teacher's current lesson plan.

9. B

According to Piaget, children in the preoperational stage fail on tasks that require them to solve conservation tasks, such as recognizing that two differently shaped balls of clay have the same mass. It is not until the concrete operational stage that children can reliably supply logical justifications, such as reversibility, for conservation. Thus, choice (**B**) is correct. (A), the sensorimotor stage, refers to Piaget's first stage of development, in which infants are discovering relationships between their bodies and the environment. (C), the concrete operational stage, refers to the stage in which children develop logic and rational thought, which Piaget says usually happens around age 7 to 11. (D), the formal operational stage, refers to the stage from age 12 through adulthood, in which adolescents acquire the use of abstract thinking.

10. C

Correct choice (**C**) meets the two goals of promoting students' self-regulatory skills and keeping parents informed of student progress. The students write letters to their parents, summarizing their own progress to date. Students can identify reasons for their successes and areas in which they need to improve. It is probable that parents will discuss these letters with their children, along with any implications for their progress in school. Choice (A) would give parents information on student progress only in rare situations. Additionally, the system described in (A) lacks any element of student self-evaluation, which is important in developing self-regulation. It is helpful for students to discuss projects and progress with parents, but choice (B) would not provide parents with definitive statements related to students' strengths, achievements, and areas for improvement. (B)'s vague instruction to "regularly update parents" also makes it likely that students will not really keep their parents informed about their progress. Choice (D) ties together student behavior and academic progress, and it may punish or reward students regardless of their level of effort, thus possibly serving as a disincentive for students to develop their self-regulatory skills.

11. A

Educational objectives are explicit statements that clearly express what students will be able to do at the conclusion of a lesson. Choice (A) requires students to describe and demonstrate knowledge of full and half notes. Because this objective includes tasks that the teacher can observe and thus use to clearly measure whether learning has taken place, choice (**A**) is correct. While it is important for lessons to allow students to "grasp the fundamentals" and "develop an appreciation," as in choice (B), or "understand," as in choice (C), such goals can be difficult to observe and measure. Because neither (B) nor (C) includes any method of observing whether students have met those goals, both are incorrect. Finally, administering a multiple-choice test, as in choice (D), is one way of measuring attainment of educational objectives, but the ability to pass a test is not in and of itself an educational objective.

12. D

In this scenario, the teacher makes use of an opportunity to engage students with a topic made especially relevant by a real-world situation that affects them inside and outside the classroom. This is a classic example of a teachable moment, making choice (**D**) correct. The teacher recognizes that, while this topic is not part of the planned lesson, it is still a valuable learning opportunity for students, meaning it is not off-task (A). The students and teacher are reflecting on a true local event, rather than storytelling (B), and the teacher is not using the Socratic method (C), as the teacher is not leading the questioning and does not have a specific conclusion in mind for students to reach.

13. D

One highly effective strategy for holding students accountable for their learning is to require measurable and observable activities, such as using graphic organizers or taking notes during presentations. Therefore, choice (**D**) is correct. While administering a surprise quiz after the presentations (A) may help the teacher determine who was listening and who was not, this strategy is ineffective because it does not curtail the inattentiveness before it happens. Having the teacher watch students from the front of the room (B) will

not guarantee their attention to the presenters and may be distracting. Classroom rules are essential, but in this case, adding a new rule (C) is not nearly as effective as providing students with a productive activity that requires their attention and directs it to the presentations.

14. B

The experiential instructional model is centered on the learner's experience with the concepts being taught. It is characterized by the active participation of the learner in constructing knowledge through a concrete activity and using that knowledge as a basis for future decisions. The only strategy that fits both criteria is having students play the game described in (**B**).

15. D

All strategies listed in the question stem correspond to laying the groundwork for effective questioning. Choice (**D**) is therefore correct. Students must feel comfortable and supported as they work to express themselves. Verbal explanations by students are not present in written assessment (A). While establishing a noncritical classroom environment will support all students as they learn, allowing "wait time" does not apply to objective setting (B), as teachers engage in this activity separately. IEP development (C) is also an activity that adults will primarily work on in a distinct group, perhaps with the input of the individual student in question, and thus does not require the establishment of any particular type of classroom environment.

16. C

An aptitude test measures potential rather than achievement. Admissions exams are often measures of aptitude, since schools are interested in finding out what applicants are capable of accomplishing in the years ahead. Choice (**C**) is therefore correct. Ability tests (A) and achievement tests (B) are not always designed to predict future achievement, so these choices are incorrect. A selected-response test (D) is a multiple-choice assessment. Such a test would not allow the applicant to demonstrate potential in the expressive arts.

17. C

Choice (A), which focuses on freeing up teacher time for lesson planning, does not express a rationale for incorporating peer assessments. Teachers should still provide feedback on student work, even when peer assessments are included. Focusing on students' weaknesses, as in choice (B), is not the point of conducting peer assessments. Choice (C), especially when combined with teacher feedback, highlights a strong benefit of peer assessment and is correct. While students may enjoy talking to one another, choice (D) is not a strong reason to conduct peer assessments.

18. C

A grade-level equivalent score demonstrates the representative grade level at which a student is currently performing. Choice (C) is therefore correct. A student's stanine score, (A), and percentile rank, (D), both reveal how a student performs in relation to peers, while a raw score, (B), shows how many of the questions a student answered correctly on a given assessment.

19. A, B, C

Analytical scoring measures a learner's proficiency by considering the essential elements of the key learning skills involved. Therefore, the only incorrect choice is (D) because it describes holistic grading, which focuses on the effect of an entire work. Analytical scoring assesses the student's strengths and weaknesses in each targeted skill, as in (A), making it less likely that only one skill will become the focus of an assessment, (B). Analytical scoring also improves grade reliability, (C), because it considers a variety of criteria.

20. B

A percentile score shows how well a student performed on an assessment compared to peers taking the same assessment. A student scoring in the 24th percentile has been outperformed by 76 percent of test takers, making choice (B) correct. This is the opposite of (D), which suggests that the student outperformed most others, and also does not fit (C), which says that the student performed on par with others at the same grade level. Choice (A), which implies that one of the student's teachers is at fault for the student's reading performance, does not necessarily follow from the information provided.

21.

	Acceptable	Unacceptable
Showing a copyrighted motion picture for instructional purposes	✔	
Scanning a legally purchased textbook and posting it on the class website		✔
Copying poems from copyrighted books to make a class anthology		✔
Incorporating a 10-second music clip into a student-generated multimedia presentation	✔	

Due to the educational purpose and the fact that no one will be charging admission, showing a copyrighted motion picture in class to support instruction is acceptable. Distributing an entire book through the internet deprives the owner of revenue and is thus not considered fair use. Collecting copyrighted works to create anthologies is not acceptable under fair use due to the amount of material being copied. Incorporating short music clips into educational multimedia presentations is considered fair use because of the brief nature of the clips and the educational purpose of the presentation.

22. A

A school guidance counselor has extensive training in responding to allegations of or concerns about abuse or neglect in students' homes. Choice (A) is therefore correct. (B) is incorrect; while an assistant principal is someone with whom a teacher might share concerns about a student's welfare, it is the guidance counselor who, by training and job description, is primarily responsible for coordinating a response to those kinds of concerns. The IEP team leader's job is to tailor curricula and the school environment to the special needs of particular students; a person with this role would likely report abuse allegations to a counselor rather than coordinate the school's response, so (C) is incorrect. An occupational therapist is there to help students with special needs navigate and adapt to the challenges of the school environment, not to coordinate services for a student in an unsafe home environment; (D) is therefore incorrect.

23. C

A national organization of history teachers has a wide range of resources for both educators and their students on diverse topics. Choice (**C**) is therefore correct. Choice (A) is not likely to gain the teacher new content knowledge, and (B) and (D), while entertaining, may not provide the deep or accurate content knowledge that best supports students' education.

24. D

Selective use of online educator forums and study groups would most effectively allow the teacher to consider a variety of perspectives on these educational issues. These forums would likely include educators and individuals with educational experiences from diverse backgrounds. Choice (**D**) is therefore correct. Choice (A) focuses on one classroom management approach, rather than a variety of approaches, and it might not

include lesson planning. The information available from news-aggregating web applications, as described in (B), might include topics that do not relate to the teacher's study goals, and the intended audience for the readings might be the general public rather than schoolteachers in particular. Developing a relationship with a more experienced educator, as suggested in (C), could be beneficial, but this one-to-one orientation in the school where the teacher is located would limit the perspective of these meetings to that of the mentor and school involved.

25. A

Key components of reflective practice include reviewing one's successes and areas for growth, seeking guidance about how to improve, and formulating a plan for improvement. Choice (**A**) demonstrates these components as the teacher actively reflects on his actions and experiences, consults with more experienced mentors, and creates a plan for the future. Choice (B) places responsibility on students and their families, rather than exploring what the teacher can do to improve his practice. Taking action without thoughtful consideration or only reviewing the situation without formulating a plan to address it, such as in (C) and (D), leaves out critical components of reflective practice.

Constructed-Response Questions

Sample Response to Question 1

Naima appears to fall into the category of "gifted and talented (GT)," a flexible term that applies to highly capable students whose needs may not be addressed by the standard curriculum. GT students often already have accomplished the learning goals the teacher has set for the class, or they are able to learn the content more quickly than other students and therefore become bored. GT students are not covered by the IDEA, so they are not guaranteed the right to accommodations to meet their special abilities. However, these students do have "special needs"; if these students' needs are not addressed, they may be denied an equal opportunity to learn. Given Naima's performance on standardized tests and her comments to Mr. Traister in class, it appears that she is not being challenged by his assignments. One partial solution would be for Mr. Traister to incorporate an element of choice into classroom assignments: students could opt to complete the standard assignment or do a more challenging and open-ended version. Mr. Traister could also "compact" Naima's curriculum, allowing her to skip lessons she does not need and use that time to work independently on intellectually challenging assignments.

On the other hand, it appears from Mr. Traister's comments to Ms. Benson and from Naima's own behavior in class that Naima also needs to be brought into the life of the classroom more. One solution would be to modify small-group instruction so that Naima can join other students without serving as a de facto teacher's aide. Assigning each group member a discrete role—reporter, connection finder, math solver—can bring each student into the group work without allowing any one student to take over or be unduly burdened.

Sample Response to Question 2

Ms. Benson, the school's GT resource teacher, directs small-group GT sessions outside of the general classroom—but she is also a potentially valuable resource in helping Mr. Traister make decisions about his own classroom instruction. By consulting with Ms. Benson, Mr. Traister may gain insight on ideas for lesson plans that serve the needs of gifted students like Naima along with the others in the class.

The school librarian, Ms. Upshaw, is another paraprofessional whom Mr. Traister can bring into his instructional planning process. Ms. Upshaw should be able to identify reading materials that Naima would find challenging and interesting. By consulting with Ms. Upshaw, Mr. Traister may be able to craft compelling and challenging individualized assignments for students like Naima who have unusual needs.

PLT Grades 5–9 Practice

Directions: For selected-response questions 1–25, choose the response that best answers the question or completes the statement. Then follow the directions provided for constructed-response questions 1–2.

Sarah, an outgoing student who is well-liked by her peers, is not doing well in a social studies class in which her teacher uses videos, lectures, and worksheets to cover the material. She is doing well in math and English classes in which her teachers use hands-on activities to teach concepts.

1. Which of the following is most likely a variable that is affecting how Sarah is learning and performing?

    A. Learning disability

    B. Self-confidence

    C. Learning style

    D. Maturity

A student has recovered from head trauma. However, the student's eyesight is permanently affected, resulting in the need for larger fonts on copies when available. The student also needs additional time to complete on-level assignments.

2. Which one of the following documents would best ensure that proper educational accommodations will be in place for this student?

    A. 504 plan

    B. IEP with modifications

    C. IEP without modifications

    D. Healthcare documentation signed by physician

A ninth-grade literature student with a learning disability in reading comprehension has been assigned the book *To Kill a Mockingbird*.

3. Which of the following accommodations would be beneficial in helping the student read the book successfully?

    Select <u>all</u> that apply.

    A. Giving the student extended time to complete the reading assignments

    B. Placing the student in a group with high-performing peers during independent reading time

    C. Allowing the student to read along with an audio book

    D. Having the student take turns reading aloud with a teacher or peer tutor

4. Which of the following activities is characteristic of a constructivist learning approach?

    A. Students work in groups to compare contemporary music lyrics to the lines of a Shakespearean sonnet.

    B. Students work at their own pace to view a series of videos about World War II and complete a set of comprehension questions for each video.

    C. Students watch the teacher quote a PowerPoint presentation about the atomic bomb and then write an essay summarizing key points of the presentation.

    D. Students take a field trip to an artist's studio and listen to the artist describe his process.

5. Which of the following strategies could a math teacher use to increase students' intrinsic motivation most significantly?

A. Allowing students with a stronger understanding of math concepts to have fewer homework problems

B. Having students present examples of how math concepts in a unit apply to their own hobbies

C. Holding a pizza party for all students who earn an A on the semester exam

D. Allowing students to complete assignments with a partner during class time

A science lesson requires students to memorize details related to certain biological concepts. In the same lesson, students also analyze science data to reach conclusions.

6. Which of the following terms most closely represents the thinking skill in which the students are engaged?

A. Planning

B. Problem solving

C. Questioning

D. Metacognition

7. In which of the following activities do students have an opportunity to demonstrate synthesis of new concepts?

A. Using colored pencils, crayons, scissors, construction paper, and other craft tools, students trace models to vivid posters featuring and illustrating formulas such as $p = mV$ and $F = ma$.

B. Students complete word-search worksheets that include key terms from a unit on momentum, looking up each new word in a scientific dictionary.

C. After students silently read a textbook chapter on momentum, work, and energy, the teacher explains the practical importance of each of these concepts in modern industry.

D. Students drop balls of four different weights from a certain height, measure the height of each ball's bounce, and draw conclusions concerning the impact of weight on the height of a ball's bounce.

8. Which of the following practices would most likely contribute to effective classroom management?

A. Posting behavior expectations in the classroom

B. Consistently using the same instructional strategy throughout the class period

C. Homogeneous grouping of students for reading activities

D. Heterogeneous grouping of students for math activities

9. A teacher wants to use schema theory to help students learn most effectively. Which strategy would provide the teacher with the most information about students' schema related to a biology topic?

    A. Having students complete an individual brain-storm activity related to the biology topic

    B. Having students write a 10-word main-idea summary based on an article related to the biology topic

    C. Having the teacher lead a whole-class discussion, comparing and contrasting a video and article that discuss a similar biology topic

    D. Having students make predictions about the content of an article related to the biology topic, based on the article's title and illustrations.

This week, the seventh graders at Chavez Middle School will be learning about Egyptian history, geography, and culture in their social studies classes. In their language arts classes, they will read and discuss *The Secret of the Pharaoh*, a contemporary young-adult novel set in ancient Egypt. During their math classes, they will learn about Egyptian numerals as part of a broader lesson on nonstandard units of measurement.

10. Which of the following instructional processes is embodied in the lesson plans described above?

    A. Creating lesson plans that reflect the major contributions of a variety of educational theorists

    B. Creating practical opportunities for students to apply acquired knowledge outside of the classroom

    C. Accommodating differences in students' learning styles and creating a comfortable environment for English language learners

    D. Developing lesson plans within the framework of a thematic, interdisciplinary unit

11. Handing out a rubric along with the instructions for an assignment is an effective scaffolding aid for students because

    A. the rubric articulates the assignment prompts

    B. the rubric clarifies expectations

    C. the rubric sets a serious tone

    D. the rubric provides needed background information

12. Which of the following teaching behaviors best exemplifies the assistive strategy of modeling?

    A. In her intermediate woodworking class, Ms. Hinton has students break into small groups, each of which will be responsible for creating a different part of a multi-hinged wooden toy.

    B. In his advanced chemistry class, Mr. Finch mixes chemicals in a beaker, causing them to fizz, and then asks students to describe the chemical process that produced the fizzing reaction.

    C. In her introductory French language class, Ms. Mignot greets students in French and encourages them to return the greeting.

    D. In her studio art class, Ms. Dawson projects photographs of a dog onto a screen and asks students to use their pencils to create sketches of the dog.

13. Which of the following techniques for equalizing student participation in whole-class discussions is most appropriate and constructive?

    A. The teacher provides a reward—such as a piece of candy or a drink—to the "top participant" in the discussion each week.

    B. The teacher spends part of each discussion period calling on students at random by drawing names out of a hat.

    C. The teacher deducts daily discussion points from "overparticipating" students, who too frequently raise their hands.

    D. The teacher assigns additional homework to "underparticipating" students, who too rarely raise their hands.

A teacher gives students untimed quizzes, which include a mix of multiple-choice and open-ended mini-essay questions, to complete at home every weekend. The quizzes cover material reviewed over the previous week but also include questions designed to help shape the teacher's instruction for the upcoming week.

14. The weekly quizzes described above are

    A. formative assessments

    B. summative assessments

    C. diagnostic assessments

    D. informal assessments

Results from a pre-test indicate that students are weak in multiplication skills. These same students have been previously identified as either kinesthetic or visual learners.

15. Which of the following instructional strategies would best suit the students' educational needs and learning strengths?

    A. Demonstrating on the blackboard how to solve the multiplication problems, providing a hands-on activity, and following up with a formative assessment

    B. Saving multiplication for a later unit, having the students draw graphic organizers reviewing previously studied addition concepts, and following up with a summative assessment

    C. Giving a brief lecture on how to work multiplication problems and following up with a formative assessment

    D. Providing a video on solving the problems, engaging the students in a discussion related to the math concepts involved, and following up with a summative assessment

16. Students gave presentations at the conclusion of a unit on biomes. Afterward, the teacher instructed each student to write down one thing he or she did well in the presentation and one thing to improve. Which of the following capabilities is this writing assignment likely to promote?

    A. Performance skills

    B. Physical manipulation

    C. Self-regulation

    D. Pro-social behavior

Ms. Petrie, an eighth-grade language arts teacher, is interested in using informal formative assessment methods to complement the formal diagnostic, summative, and formative assessments she is already using.

17. Which of the following is an example of the type of assessment Ms. Petrie is interested in adding to her class?

   A. Interviews with students, in which they evaluate their own work, discuss difficulties they have encountered, and set expectations for coming weeks

   B. Timed essay examinations, in which students identify connections between events portrayed in the course texts and events in daily life

   C. Collage projects that require students to demonstrate what they have learned about particular places and periods in world literary history

   D. Multiple-choice tests given at the end of instructional units that determine how closely students read the course texts and how well they listened during class

A student received test results indicating that his level of reading comprehension was higher than that of 80 percent of students at his grade level.

18. What sort of test would provide this result?

   A. Criterion-referenced assessment

   B. Norm-referenced assessment

   C. Standards-based assessment

   D. Holistic assessment

19. Which of the following describes an appropriate time and reason for a teacher to use a summative assessment?

   A. At the beginning of an educational unit, to assess preexisting knowledge of the material

   B. At the beginning of an educational unit, to encourage creative thinking about the material coming up

   C. In the middle of an educational unit, to aid in student comprehension of the material

   D. At the end of an educational unit, to judge how much students learned

20. Which of the following activities would best exemplify an interactive instructional model in teaching cell division?

   A. Showing students a short video that uses a blend of sophisticated microscopy and computer-generated imagery to illustrate mitosis

   B. Assigning a project in which students independently produce cartoons depicting the various stages of mitosis, meiosis, and binary fission

   C. Conducting a thorough lecture, accompanied by a timeline, on the history of the study of binary fission

   D. Inviting pairs of students to engage in Lincoln-Douglas–style debates on a variety of questions pertaining to mitosis, meiosis, and binary fission

21. Which of the following interactions between educators describes a collaborative relationship that is likely to provide the greatest educational benefit to students?

    A. Advised by a colleague, Mr. Small uses free lesson plans from a website to cut down on planning time.

    B. A school's technology teacher, Mr. Crumb, shares some entertainment sites from the school staff's mailing list so students can visit them as a reward.

    C. Mr. Grimm, an English teacher, stores up a secret trove of unique "five-star" lesson plans that he created and only uses on days when his class is visited by a school administrator.

    D. Before giving students their first research assignment, Ms. Wise invites the school's librarian to give a short presentation in which she introduces tools for library research.

22. Which of these strategies is most beneficial to a teacher in improving cross-cultural communication in the classroom?

    A. Maintaining universally applied rules about what kinds of communication are welcome in the classroom

    B. Communicating regularly with parents and treating them as collaborators in a program of instruction

    C. Grouping students homogeneously by culture and language to improve the clarity of intra-group communication

    D. Learning the basic grammar of every language spoken by a student in the class

23. Which of the following materials would be most useful in helping a new sixth-grade science teacher to shape appropriate instructional units for this subject and grade level?

    A. A district pacing guide

    B. A biology textbook from the teacher's undergraduate program

    C. Biographies of famous scientists

    D. Science books that the teacher used in a science teaching position in a different state

24. Which approach should a teacher planning a genetics unit follow to ensure that students have the most effective materials to help them achieve the unit objectives?

    A. Identifying the outcomes students should achieve and selecting textbook readings, Internet resources, and video clips that serve most effectively to help students achieve those goals

    B. Identifying a variety of interesting and up-to-date materials related to genetics, finding specific readings within these resources, and creating class activities based on those readings

    C. Giving lectures to share personal learning about genetics and then testing students on the knowledge they obtained from those lectures

    D. Focusing on the textbook's coverage of the genetics unit and allowing students with different reading levels to work in groups to understand the readings most effectively

Two teachers collaborate to develop a lesson on Japanese culture. Then, each teacher observes the other teacher as she teaches the lesson. The observing teacher identifies strengths and areas for improvement in the observed teacher's approach.

25. Which of the following are the teachers practicing when they provide feedback on each other's teaching?

    A. Peer observation

    B. Incident analysis

    C. Reflective listening

    D. Multiculturalism

Approximate time: 25 minutes

Directions: The case history below is followed by two short-answer questions. Your responses to the questions will be evaluated with respect to professionally accepted principles and practices in teaching and learning. Be sure to answer all parts of the questions. Write your answers on the pages indicated in your answer sheet booklet.

Scenario:

Jenny Carmichael is an eighth-grade student in a heterogeneous urban classroom. It is the beginning of the year, and Mr. Koppel is getting to know his eighth-grade language arts class, which includes Jenny. Concerned about Jenny's responses to an introductory survey on the first day, Mr. Koppel is gathering documents to attempt to discern whether he needs to take any particular action regarding Jenny's education.

Document 1

Jenny's answers to Mr. Koppel's introductory survey (including errors):

What is your favorite subject in school, and why?

I don't like any but I guess science is okay because sometimes we look at pretty animals and plants.

What is your least favorite subject in school, and why?

English. I don't get grammer and reading.

What were three things you had fun doing as part of English class last year?

I liked cutting up magazines to make a poem colage.

I liked when we found that the author messed up about how snakes are, so the detective was totally wrong when he said who did it.

I liked watching other people do sharades and act out parts of books. But I hated doing it myself.

What was something that was very hard for you in last year's English class?

I don't like long books because I can't remember who the characters are or what happened.

Document 2

Jenny's end-of-term evaluations from the final term of seventh grade:

English: D+

Jenny has been struggling in this class from the beginning of the year, but her performance has declined this term. Her earlier difficulties seem to have discouraged her, and she has left her last few assignments incomplete.

Math: B

Jenny generally doesn't participate in class unless called upon. However, she completes most assignments and performs adequately on quizzes.

Physical Education: A

Jenny participates in all activities and passes all basic fitness requirements. She is sometimes hesitant to be involved in competitive games.

Science: B+

Jenny's performance has improved substantially this term. She still has trouble with reading assignments from the textbook, but her performance has improved noticeably since I've started providing her with visual organizers. This has also improved her motivation, and she has not missed a homework assignment this term.

Social Studies: B

This term, the majority of student grades were based on students' composing a report and presentation on a country of their choosing. Jenny's written report received only a C, but her presentation was excellent. In particular, she demonstrated a strong aptitude for making slides in the computer lab, even though she does not have a computer at home.

Document 3

Note from Ms. Moran, Jenny's seventh-grade English teacher, to Mr. Koppel:

I'm glad you're reaching out to me about Jenny. She's a good student, and she's occasionally shown glimmers of brilliance with regard to English. In particular, she wrote a very interesting story about horseback riding during a creative writing unit, even though she didn't seem to understand the importance of proofreading and revision.

Jenny's biggest challenge is with reading. She is very slow when we read aloud together in class; she also gets so focused on pronouncing individual words and sentences that she'll often be completely lost about what actually happened in the text she just read. I've tried to introduce her to metacognitive strategies such as making predictions while she's reading, organizing things in terms of cause and effect, and listening to her "internal voice" to see if it's talking to her or just reciting text. So far, they have been unsuccessful.

Finally, she left multiple assignments incomplete during the last term of the year, which nearly caused her to fail. I think the frustration is getting to her, and I'm hoping a fresh approach will make English accessible to her.

Document 4

Note from Jenny's guidance counselor to Mr. Koppel

According to my records, Jenny's parents are both blue-collar workers. Neither has a college degree, and her mother was a college dropout. Jenny's standardized test scores have been consistently low. She needed remedial literacy education in elementary school, and her reading level remains two grades below expectation.

She hasn't had any major disciplinary concerns. Past progress reports indicate that she has not always been thorough about completing assignments, but never to the point of failure. Meanwhile, teachers consistently describe her as well-behaved, if withdrawn.

Constructed-Response Questions

Question 1

Ms. Moran mentioned that she attempted to introduce Jenny to metacognitive techniques to help her focus on reading. However, those techniques were unsuccessful.

- Suggest TWO reasons why the strategies Ms. Moran used might not have been effective for Jenny.
- For EACH of those reasons, propose an alternative that addresses the reason and is more likely to help Jenny understand challenging reading. Base your responses on the principles of modifying instruction for diverse learners.

Question 2

Throughout the case study, Jenny demonstrates indifference or frustration toward academics and toward language arts in particular.

- Briefly describe TWO activities that Mr. Koppel could plan to engage Jenny's interest.
- Explain how EACH of those activities could help Jenny become more involved in class material. Base your response on the principles of encouraging student motivation.

PLT Grades 5–9 Practice Answers and Explanations

1. C

Sarah's success in math and English shows that she is likely not affected by a learning disability. Likewise, maturity and self-confidence do not factor into her educational abilities in a negative manner. Given her success with hands-on manipulatives, Sarah is most likely experiencing a learning-style issue. Choice (**C**) is therefore correct.

2. A

A 504 plan requires healthcare documentation and will then ensure the student has appropriate access to grade-level curriculum with medically necessary accommodations. Choice (**A**) is correct. Merely providing the healthcare documentation itself, (D), will not ensure access to accommodations. Individualized Education Plans (IEPs), as in choices (B) and (C), are for students with diagnosed cognitive learning disabilities. This student does not have a cognitive processing disorder; therefore, an IEP is not appropriate.

3. A, C, D

The student will benefit most from supplementary curricula, such as audio books, (**C**), and curricular supports, including extended time, (**A**), and one-on-one help from a teacher or peer, (**D**). Combined, these supports will provide appropriate access for this student. While priority seating may be a necessary accommodation in some cases, it is not beneficial for individual reading time, making (B) the only incorrect answer.

4. A

A constructivist learning approach is driven by student-led, rather than teacher-led, inquiry. Constructivism is characterized by students actively constructing their own understanding of the world through experience, often through interaction with others, rather than by a teacher telling them what to think. (**A**) is the only choice with these qualities.

5. B

In order to boost intrinsic motivation, students need to be able to relate the curriculum to real-world situations. Given their developmental maturity at this age, real-world situations need to include things that directly affect the students. Incorporating their own hobbies into the examples, as in choice (**B**), will give the students buy-in to the curriculum to increase their intrinsic motivation.

6. B

Data analysis is a higher level of cognitive processing. It requires the students to synthesize information and determine how it applies to the question posed. This would be considered a form of problem solving. Choice (**B**) is therefore correct.

7. D

A crucial step in the synthesis of new concepts is the application of those concepts to real-world situations. Therefore, the activity needs to go beyond recall skills, direct instruction, and replication. Students need to be able to analyze what the new skills mean and how they apply to a problem. Choice (**D**) is an appropriate activity for this purpose.

8. A

The first requirement for effective classroom management is to set and consistently reinforce clear expectations. Choice (**A**) is correct. And while using a variety of teaching methods and grouping students may help students stay engaged and motivated, they will only work once clear expectations have been set.

9. A

Schema theory includes chunking information to help commit it to memory. Brainstorming is a great activity that helps students synthesize what they think will happen or want to learn. This promotes the free flow of ideas to allow students to better process and commit new information to memory. Therefore, choice (**A**) is correct.

10. D

When thematic units of study from one subject can be implemented across multiple subjects, then teaching is considered thematic and interdisciplinary. This approach requires careful planning and, when more than one teacher is involved, thoughtful collaboration. Choice (**D**) is correct.

11. B

A rubric clarifies the expectations for an assignment as it will be evaluated, so (**B**) is correct. While the teacher will likely want to include the prompts and background information for her students, as in (A) and (D), the rubric is not the place to do this. While the teacher may prefer a serious tone for her classroom, (C), a rubric is an assessment tool and is not used to set a tone.

12. C

Modeling occurs when the teacher demonstrates the skill she wants her students to learn. Ms. Mignot in choice (**C**) accomplishes this by demonstrating the language frame she desires of her students.

13. B

Ensuring that students find a reason to pay attention and be ready to participate in discussions is key to preventing a "monopolized" lesson, in which a small group of students make most of the contributions. Random selection, as in (**B**), ensures a higher percentage of students will contribute and be engaged in the lesson.

14. A

The quizzes are assessments designed to help students identify areas of strength and learning opportunities. This fits the definition of formative assessment, and (**A**) is correct.

15. A

Students with visual and kinesthetic learning styles require a varied teaching approach. Visual learners benefit from seeing notes, problems, data, and pictures to help them process the information. Kinesthetic learners require a hands-on approach to be able to interact physically with the curriculum. Therefore modeling and hands-on activities provide the strongest links for these learners. Choice (**A**) is correct.

16. C

Allowing students time to reflect on their successes as well as develop a plan to work on improvement gives them more control over their education. This, in turn, teaches them to self-regulate through intrinsic motivation. This activity has a greater impact than simply telling students what their perceived strengths and weaknesses are. Choice (**C**) is correct.

17. A

An informal assessment does not generally have grading criteria, though it may have a rubric to follow. In addition, Ms. Petrie is already using formal assessments to assign class grades. The informal assessment described in choice (**A**) works as a supplement and, in this case, will allow the students to determine the strengths and weaknesses they see in their own work. This type of analysis and goal setting is important, but it is still considered informal.

18. B

Results that tell students where they rank in terms of other students at their grade/age level come from norm-referenced tests. The phrase "higher than 80 percent" refers to a percentile score, because the student scored better than 80 percent of the other students who took the test. Choice (**B**) is correct.

19. D

Summative assessments are appropriate for the final, or summary, portion of a unit. They belong at the end of the instructional unit. Choice (**D**) is correct.

20. D

An interactive instructional model is characterized by groups of students constructing meaning in partnership with one or more other students in a collaborative way, as described in (**D**). Videos, independent projects, and lectures do not feature this collaborative quality.

21. D

It is important for educators to utilize all the resources available to them. To ensure that students are receiving the highest level of instruction, experts in other areas of the school play a crucial role. Using these professionals allows students to make cross-curricular connections that will assist them in success in multiple subject areas. Choice (**D**) is therefore correct.

22. B

Garnering parent participation is a challenge for most educators but is also highly beneficial. Choice (**B**) is correct. The first step in achieving this goal is to make sure parents know what is going on with their child. The teacher should communicate with each set of parents in whatever way works best for them. For example, the teacher should not rely solely on email to communicate with families who lack easy access to the Internet.

23. A

Subject curricula will vary not only by state, but also by district. State standards provide a foundation on which the district will build its pacing guide. District-developed resources should always be the first go-to resources for any new teacher. Choice (**A**) is correct.

24. A

As teachers prepare new lessons, professional best practices include using a variety of resources to develop their lessons. The foundation of developing any new unit is determining the desired outcome: this includes learning objectives, standards, and skills to be mastered. From there, teachers should choose a diverse base of educational materials, including readings and technology. Choice (**A**) is therefore correct.

25. A

By collaborating to evaluate and improve their teaching through observing one another and providing feedback, these teachers are practicing peer observation. Choice (**A**) is correct.

Constructed-Response Questions

Sample Response to Question 1

Ms. Moran notes that Jenny is having serious reading comprehension problems. The strategies the teacher tried with Jenny in seventh grade would tend to promote comprehension, but they focused on written responses, while Jenny's past work and preferences indicate she is a strong visual learner. Instead of asking Jenny to think about the "voice in her head" as she reads, it might be more helpful for her to form a "picture in her head."

Another reason Ms. Moran's techniques might not have worked is that Jenny was told to try them while reading out loud. Jenny does not speak out in other classes and does not like to compete. Mr. Koppel might consider having students read aloud in small groups, rather than in a whole-class, "round robin" fashion, which is considered less effective. Students such as Jenny who are not comfortable speaking in front of the class may develop anxiety during this activity, while other students may lose focus when it is not their turn to read aloud. Mr. Koppel should have Jenny focus on prereading metacognitive techniques, such as making predictions and looking at illustrations. These are tasks she can perform while she's not in the spotlight.

Sample Response to Question 2

Mr. Koppel could pair Jenny up with a student with stronger verbal skills and have the two of them collaborate on making a comic related to the week's reading. Jenny became involved in designing slides for her social studies class, and she would likely be engaged in designing visuals for a comic. Her classmate with strong verbal skills would likely model to Jenny the strategies he uses when reading and writing, and this approach could encourage Jenny to use some of these same effective techniques.

Mr. Koppel could collaborate with the eighth-grade science teachers to do a joint unit. Jenny has demonstrated an interest in zoology and biological sciences—her survey response noted that she enjoyed a reading activity involving snakes, and she was very successful in her seventh-grade science class. Perhaps a "detective investigation," in which students find factual errors in the textbook, would be helpful. Such activities can remind students that authors are human, and they can also make even challenging texts seem less intimidating.

PLT Grades 7–12 Practice

Directions: For selected-response questions 1–25, choose the response that best answers the question or completes the statement. Then follow the directions provided for constructed-response questions 1–2.

1. An English-language arts teacher is concerned with helping his students make positive progress through the identity-versus-role-confusion stage of development, as described by Erikson. Which of the following classroom activities would most likely help students meet the goals associated with this stage of development?

   A. Students memorize a series of lines spoken by Romeo or Juliet in Shakespeare's play and recite them in front of the class.

   B. Students choose among different responsibilities to create a modern version of a scene from *Romeo and Juliet*.

   C. Students research one character from *Romeo and Juliet* and explain that character's motivation.

   D. Students compare and contrast two film versions of *Romeo and Juliet* and discuss their findings with a partner.

2. Which approach to math instruction is best tailored to help the teacher engage a kinesthetic learner?

   A. The use of manipulatives such as blocks and geoboards to teach and reinforce mathematical concepts

   B. The use of colorful visual models and vivid animated displays to illustrate new mathematical concepts

   C. The use of engaging lectures and Socratic class discussions in which students summarize key information

   D. The use of complex logical problems to draw students into new math concepts and illustrate math's practical importance

3. Which of the following describes a challenge particular to English language learners in any classroom in which instruction is given primarily in English?

   A. Students have difficulty picking up on different uses of nonverbal cues and their implied meanings related to expected classroom behavior.

   B. Students have trouble understanding the meaning of idioms and expressions, including the use of slang by teachers and students in the classroom.

   C. Students have less background knowledge of the subject matter, and as a result, they are not familiar with concepts the teacher refers to when teaching new material.

   D. Students are accustomed to a didactic teaching approach and are not accustomed to the group work and student-centered approach used in their classroom.

4. Vygotsky's scaffolding technique includes breaking a complex task into smaller tasks and modeling the desired learning strategy. What is the ultimate goal of this scaffolding process?

   A. Learners will be able to accomplish the task without assistance.

   B. Students will learn to monitor their own behaviors to increase their attention to the task.

   C. Participants will be able to use a visual image of a scaffold to track their learning progress.

   D. Students will use scaffolding to identify their own learning style preferences.

5. Which of the following is an application of Skinner's behavioral theory?

   Select all that apply.

   A. Group instruction is effective because students enjoy competing with their peers.

   B. Providing feedback as students work helps them more than providing feedback after they complete a task.

   C. Teachers must ensure that students have mastered necessary skills before going to the next level.

   D. Rewarding positive behaviors is more effective than punishing negative behaviors.

Before her 10th-grade biology class begins its unit on water ecology, Ms. Zehner asks students to write down everything they know about water issues in the Great Lakes. Then she asks them to spend time talking to other students and reading a relevant article in order to add items to and revise the list. For homework, she asks them to write a reflective essay in which they discuss what they have learned and how their conversations with peers impacted their understanding.

6. What are Ms. Zehner's writing assignments designed to foster?

   A. Creative thinking

   B. Deductive reasoning

   C. Metacognition

   D. Critical thinking

7. Troy is a student in Ms. Devine's eighth-grade class. Ms. Devine is concerned because Troy's performance has been repeatedly low, but his records show that he has above-average abilities. Ms. Devine wants to adjust her practice to increase Troy's self-efficacy in her class. Which of the following would be most likely to support Troy?

   A. Pairing Troy with another student who also has low performance

   B. Reprimanding Troy whenever she notices he is off task

   C. Ensuring she is grading each piece of Troy's work

   D. Providing immediate feedback and chunking work

8. Which of the following purposes could iPad note-taking applications and "smart whiteboards" best achieve when used in the high school classroom?

   A. Enhancing communication

   B. Facilitating portfolio assessment

   C. Assisting with behavior management

   D. Serving as a counseling tool

9. Mr. Glee is preparing his eighth-grade class for their end-of-quarter essay. He plans to give students checkpoints throughout the assignment to monitor their own progress. Which of the following best describes this instructional strategy?

   A. Effective questioning

   B. Scaffolding

   C. Differentiating

   D. Self-regulation

10. Which of the following objectives best targets the highest level of Bloom's taxonomy?

    A. Students will be able to identify the proper use of an adverb in a given sentence.

    B. Students will be able to evaluate the use of rhetoric in a given essay.

    C. Students will be able to describe the use of similes and metaphors.

    D. Students will be able to demonstrate understanding of text structure through use of outlining and graphic organizers.

11. Which of the following domains of learning includes the skills involved in a flute player's adept physical manipulation of her instrument?

    A. Affective

    B. Cognitive

    C. Psychomotor

    D. Synthesis

12. On an individual student's summative math assessment, the data analysis reveals the following:

Topic	Correct/Total Number
Fractions	8/10
Algebraic Equations	11/15
Word Problems	4/10

Which of the following would be an appropriate follow-up activity for the teacher to use, based on these assessment results?

    A. Allowing the student to progress to the next unit

    B. Giving the student an additional quiz with six math problems to see whether the student can now answer them correctly

    C. Having the student use a computer program that provides tutorial help with word problems

    D. Working with the student individually to determine what aspects of word problems are causing the student difficulty

A teacher identifies seven students in her class who need additional help in order to get up to grade level in mathematics. She identifies a different group of eight students who are significantly below grade level in reading. Finally, she identifies two groups of five students each who are performing well above grade level in math and reading, respectively. Each day at recess, she calls in one of these four groups (choosing a different group each day) and takes them to the library, where the students collaborate on teacher-directed math and reading challenges tailored to their ability levels.

13. Which of the following instructional grouping techniques does this teacher use?

    A. Homogeneous grouping

    B. Heterogeneous grouping

    C. Dyad grouping

    D. Round-robin grouping

At the end of their unit on the ecosystem, Ms. Sterling creates cooperative learning groups in her 11th-grade earth science class and gives the students an assignment to investigate ways they could make an ecological improvement in their school or community. After Ms. Sterling discusses several ways to gather information and shares a rubric that outlines her expectations for their final presentations, the learning groups work independently. The teacher guides the groups by asking the learners questions related to the information they have gathered, and she suggests additional resources they may wish to consult.

14. Which learning concept does the teaching-and-learning strategy described above exemplify?

    A. Vicarious learning

    B. Problem-based learning

    C. Mapping

    D. Direct instruction

After a test in an American literature class, Mr. Sullivan returns the written essays to his 11th-grade students and gives them a few minutes to look at his comments and corrections. He then tells the students to spend 10 minutes writing a reflection describing what they feel they did well on and what specific target they have for improvement on the next essay.

15. Which of the following abilities is the activity described above most likely to promote in Mr. Sullivan's students?

    A. Abstract reasoning

    B. Classical conditioning

    C. Collaborative learning

    D. Self-regulatory skills

Ms. Leffingwell is creating a rubric that she will make available to students as they begin work on a new research and writing project. Each area of the rubric includes descriptions of "exemplary," "acceptable," and "unsatisfactory" work. She will use this rubric to give students targeted feedback on interim drafts of their papers and, later, to generate grades for the final drafts of the essays.

16. Which of these descriptions of "acceptable" work in the area of "source selection" is most appropriate and useful?

    A. Selected sources are good but not great—could be improved.

    B. Selected sources are solid, but essay could be improved with more research and more rigorous selection process.

    C. Selected sources include a relevant library book, magazine article, and website.

    D. Selected sources are acceptable—work was neither exemplary nor unsatisfactory.

17. A teacher models how to create an outline for an essay. Which of the following instructional models best describes this teaching approach?

    A. Experiential

    B. Interactive

    C. Direct

    D. Independent

18. Which of the following would be most likely to encourage more students to participate and to allow all students to develop more thoughtful responses during class discussions?

    A. Tracking the number of students who respond and how often they respond

    B. Partnering students during group work in a way that encourages peer tutoring

    C. Developing hand signals that allow students to indicate whether they are raising their hand to participate in the discussion or to ask a logistical question, such as whether they may use the bathroom

    D. Extending wait time before calling on students

19. Which of the following types of scores results from statistically adjusting a raw score on a standardized test to account for discrepancies on different versions of that standardized test?

    A. Age-equivalent score

    B. Scaled score

    C. Percentile score

    D. Grade-equivalent score

20. Which of the following distinctions should a teacher consider when using anecdotal notes (a record of student accomplishments, learning progress, learning lapses, and behavior) as a method of understanding the whole child?

    A. Student inner live vs. outer life

    B. Knowledge vs. intelligence

    C. Questions vs. answers

    D. Observations vs. interpretations

To teach the causes of the Civil War, a history teacher paired up students and had them read an excerpt from the textbook together to learn the material. After reading the students' essays on the Civil War, the teacher realized that the students did not fully understand the causes of the war. The teacher retaught this material to his students and made a note in his lesson plans to emphasize this detail the following year and to try a different instructional strategy.

21. Choose the answer below that best describes the teacher's actions.

   A. Analysis of and reflection on instruction

   B. Metacognition

   C. Effective use of learning styles

   D. Think-pair-share work

22. Which of the following would provide the greatest opportunity to involve stakeholders in a high school?

   A. Inviting community members to participate in the school's collection for a local food pantry

   B. Inviting school administrators to run a mock election in a social studies class to promote citizenship

   C. Approving funding to take band, orchestra, and choral students to state competitions

   D. Sponsoring both extracurricular activities and student membership in honor societies

Ms. Benzi has noticed that one of her seventh-grade students has been coming to class with suspicious bruises on his face and arms. On two occasions several days apart, when she asked the student for an explanation, he said, "I fell down." Ms. Benzi does not believe that the boy's pattern of injuries is consistent with a fall. She lives in a state in which teachers are mandatory reporters to Child Protective Services in cases of "suspicion based on facts that could cause a reasonable person in a like position, drawing on his or her training and experience, to suspect child abuse or neglect."

23. Which of the following statements best describes Ms. Benzi's legal obligations?

   A. She is permitted to make a report to Child Protective Services, provided that she has first alerted the student's parents to her suspicions.

   B. She is permitted to make a report to Child Protective Services, provided that she has obtained the permission of a school administrator.

   C. She is permitted to make a report to Child Protective Services or to school administrators, although she is not required to make such a report.

   D. She is required to make a report to Child Protective Services, even if she has been denied permission to do so by a school administrator.

24. Which of the following would be the best resource for a new teacher interested in improving his reflection about his teaching practice?

    A. Peer observation

    B. Independent research

    C. Subscription to an educational journal

    D. Technology workshop

25. A class includes students with varying levels of background knowledge and literacy skills, as well as several English language learners. Which educational partner could most appropriately and effectively assist the teacher in the classroom on a daily basis?

    A. ELL teacher

    B. Bilingual-certified counselor

    C. Media specialist

    D. Language pathologist

Approximate time: 25 minutes

Directions: The case history below is followed by two short-answer questions. Your responses to the questions will be evaluated with respect to professionally accepted principles and practices in teaching and learning. Be sure to answer all parts of the questions. Write your answers on the pages indicated in your answer sheet booklet.

Scenario:

Davis Budde is a popular member of his suburban school's football team. His teachers report that he is friendly and polite, but seldom puts effort into his academics. His grades are consistently low, but passing. He has several offers of athletic scholarships to notable universities.

Davis is in Ms. Kohl's senior elective class, Movies as Literature. Ms. Kohl is a second-year teacher. This is her first year teaching this elective. The class was taught for the past 10 years by Ms. Adams, who recently retired. Ms. Kohl is planning the first unit of the class, based on the film *Citizen Kane*.

Document 1

Lesson plan for Ms. Kohl's unit on *Citizen Kane*, Friday to Wednesday:

Goals:

- Students will understand why *Citizen Kane* is considered by many critics to be the greatest film of all time.
- Students will understand the connection between the character Kane and the real-life William Randolph Hearst.
- Students will be able to identify basic cinematographic techniques by name and by appearance.

Activities:

- Students will read a short biography of Hearst for homework, then have an in-class discussion about what sort of legacy he left.
- Students will see short excerpts of films with examples of techniques like crosscut, ellipsis, and montage.
- Students will watch *Citizen Kane* for homework.
- Students will read critical reviews of *Citizen Kane*, both contemporary with the film and modern, and then write their own review in the style of a movie critic.

Assessment:

- Students will be graded on the quality of their reviews.
- Students will be given a quiz on the techniques used in the film, and on the similarities and differences between Kane and Hearst.

Planning note:

Several students have expressed concern that they would have to watch movies on their own time. I was disappointed to find that most of the class signed up to watch movies in class and expected to coast by. However, the student body is strong here, and I'm confident they will adjust to the challenges and learn to appreciate film as literature, even if it takes them more effort than they expected.

Document 2

Email conversation between Davis and Ms. Kohl, Thursday evening:

Email 1

Dear Ms. Kohl, I got a D on my quiz. I don't understand what happened. It's very important that I get at least a C in your class so I can stay on the football team. I thought we would watch movies in class, that's why I chose the class.

Davis

Email 2

Davis, This class used to have a reputation as an "easy A," but you are a senior and I don't think it's unreasonable to expect students in this class to work for their grades. I mentioned this at the beginning of class, so this should not come as a surprise. As for why you got a D, you got very few of the answers correct. In particular, I was disappointed to see that you got every question related to Kane and Hearst incorrect. I have to wonder whether you watched the movie at all.

Best,

Ms. Kohl

Email 3

Dear Ms. Kohl

I did watch the movie but it was very hard because of training. I watched most of it while I was on the treadmill. I guess I wasn't paying attention.

Davis.

Document 3

Note from Davis's coach to Ms. Kohl:

Hi Ms. Kohl,

Davis spoke to me about your Film in Literature class. I've emphasized to him the importance of doing well in his classes, but I'm concerned about the workload for your class. In addition to football practice, he is working with a tutor for his math grades three nights a week, which leaves very little time for him to watch all the movies listed on your syllabus.

Davis's role on the football team is essential; I will work with him to get as much of his schoolwork done as possible, but any allowances you can make would be appreciated.

Coach Malory

Document 4

Davis's weekly after-school and weekend schedule, as prepared by his coach

Monday, Wednesday: 2:15–5:45, football practice; 6:00–7:30, travel home and dinner; 7:30–9:30, homework.

Tuesday, Thursday: 3:00–5:00, math tutoring; 5:15–6:15 gym; 6:30–7:00 dinner; 7:30–9:30, homework.

Friday: 5:00–7:00, football practice, team building; 7:00–10:00, free time.

Saturday: morning, run; afternoon, math tutoring; evening, free time.

Sunday: morning, church; afternoon, gym; evening, homework.

Document 5

Ms. Kohl's self-evaluation for September

This class has proven challenging. The students have strongly resisted the current structure of the class, and I get requests to watch films during school hours almost daily. It's important to me that class time be spent interacting and thinking; the last thing I want to do is have my students sit staring at a screen for an hour. But it's clear that as it stands, the "flipped classroom" model is not working—quiz grades and enthusiasm are low among almost all of my students.

Constructed-Response Questions

Question 1

Ms. Kohl attempted to change the structure of the Movies as Literature class, assigning the movies for homework and spending class time completing activities the teacher planned. Despite her interaction with the students each day, Ms. Kohl was not aware that Davis had little understanding of the movie until after he had failed his quiz.

- Suggest TWO ways that Ms. Kohl could alter her lesson plan to address this problem.
- Explain how EACH of those alterations would help students understand the film and enable Ms. Kohl to assess that understanding. Base your response on the principles of teaching in a flipped classroom.

Question 2

Davis, like many other seniors in his school who are involved in extracurricular activities, has responsibilities that take up a great deal of his time.

- Suggest TWO strategies that Ms. Kohl could recommend to Davis to help him complete all of his assignments.
- Explain how EACH strategy would allow Davis to complete his homework in a meaningful way, while still fitting it into a busy schedule.

PLT Grades 7–12 Practice Answers and Explanations

1. B

Choosing responsibilities is an activity that helps students assess the roles that best fit them as individuals. Therefore, the activity in (**B**) would help them meet the goals of the identity-versus-role-confusion developmental stage. (A), which focuses on memorization and recitation, may help students build confidence before a group but does not focus on self-identity. (C) focuses on understanding a dramatic character rather than understanding oneself. (D) develops the analytic skill of comparison and develops the understanding of genre, but it does not directly clarify identity or role issues.

2. A

Kinesthetic learners respond to movement and hands-on activities. Choice (**A**) is correct because it allows the student to manipulate objects to learn math principles. Colorful visual models and displays (B) will attract visual learners. Lectures and discussions (C) meet the needs of students who respond to verbal activities. Choice (D) relies on abstract reasoning and providing intrinsic motivation for that reasoning, and it is not particularly suited to kinesthetic learners.

3. B

The English language is rich in idiomatic expressions that do not use literal word meanings. Because idioms can be misinterpreted easily, even by students who have a good understanding of standard English, choice (**B**) is correct. Nonverbal cues, (A), such as when the teacher demonstrates a procedure or points to the object being named, are typically understood regardless of English fluency. The background knowledge and abilities of English language learners, (C), can vary widely, but this challenge isn't "particular" to ELLs; assessing prior knowledge is an important step to teaching any and all students. Finally, didactic approaches to teaching, (D), are neither universal among, nor unique to, ELLs. Some students may not speak English at home and may qualify as ELLs despite having spent their lives in American schools; meanwhile, students from some parts of Africa, Asia, or Europe may be native English speakers whose

national education systems rely on didactic teaching. For these reasons, (D) is incorrect.

4. A

The final step of successful scaffolding occurs when targeted skills have been transferred directly to the learner, who then no longer needs support from others. Therefore, choice (**A**) is correct. Although monitoring one's own learning, as in (B), is a valuable skill, it is not the ultimate goal of scaffolding. The term *scaffolding* is a metaphor for educators—educational supports, as in the construction of a building, are dismantled once the structure (learning) is complete—but it is not something that students need to visualize, so (C) is incorrect. Although scaffolding is particularly useful for meeting the needs of students with varied learning styles, it is not a tool for students to discover their own learning styles; (D) is not the correct choice.

5. B, C, D

Skinner's behavioral theories do not deal with competition, so (A) is incorrect. Choices (**B**) and (**D**) deal with reinforcement, which is key to operant conditioning, a central part of Skinner's behavioral theory. Choice (**C**) relates to sequencing, a concept key to learning as understood through Skinner's theories.

6. C

Metacognition requires understanding one's own thought process, which is what Ms. Zehner's assignments are designed to promote. Choice (**C**) is correct. Creative thinking, (A), encourages students to look at situations from a new perspective. Deductive reasoning, (B), involves logically combining multiple statements to come to a new conclusion. Critical thinking, (D), involves analysis and evaluation of an issue.

7. D

Both providing immediate feedback and chunking Troy's work into smaller pieces, as in choice (**D**), would allow Troy to feel a greater sense of achievement and would be the most appropriate way to encourage Troy.

8. A

Both note-taking applications and smart whiteboards are communication tools by definition. Furthermore, note taking is an activity that records information that is being communicated. Choice (**A**) is therefore correct. Choices (B) and (D) involve assessment and counseling, respectively. While software applications for assessment and counseling are available, they are not specifically mentioned here. And finally, while behavior management, (C), may be facilitated by electronic-communication applications that hold students' attention, such management is incidental, not the primary focus of iPad note-taking apps and smart whiteboards.

9. D

Mr. Glee is providing his students with an opportunity to self-regulate through opportunities to monitor their own progress throughout the assignment. Thus, choice (**D**) is correct. While questioning, scaffolding, and differentiating are all valuable practices, they are not illustrated here; eliminate (A), (B), and (C).

10. B

Evaluating an essay focuses on level 6 of Bloom's taxonomy, so choice (**B**) is correct. Identification is in level 1; eliminate (A). Description is in level 2, involving comprehension; eliminate (C). And demonstration is an application of the concept, as in level 3; eliminate (D).

11. C

The term "domains of learning" refers to the ways in which a person acquires knowledge. The psychomotor domain includes skills related to the physical manipulation of objects such as tennis rackets, woodworking tools, and musical instruments. A skilled flutist possesses excellent psychomotor skills, so choice (**C**) is correct. The affective domain, (A), encompasses attitudes and motivations; a person with high affective skill is able to empathize and get along with other people. The cognitive domain, (B), includes skills such as problem solving and critically evaluating facts. Synthesis, (D), is a subcategory of cognitive development that has to do with creatively combining information and ideas or finding new applications for ideas.

12. D

The assessment suggests that the student needs remedial help with word problems. Working individually with the student is an important first step toward identifying whether these test results are actually representative of the student's comprehension and, if so, what sort of remedial help would be most effective. Choice (**D**) is therefore correct. Choice (A) is incorrect; the summative assessment indicates that the student is having difficulties that, if left unaddressed, could impede his or her progress in future instructional units. (B)'s phrase "math problems" is too vague, and simply giving the student additional test problems is not likely to be helpful or revealing. (C) is incorrect because it is not certain from one test that the student has difficulties, nor is it clear that this computer program would remedy such difficulties; the teacher must find out exactly what caused these discrepant test scores before proceeding.

13. A

Homogeneous grouping is an instructional technique whereby students are grouped by a trait that they have in common. In the example above, students are grouped by their performance level in mathematics and reading. Choice (**A**) is correct. Heterogeneous grouping, (B), is a technique whereby students are grouped in mixed levels. Dyad grouping, (C), is strategic pairing. Round robin, (D), is a strategy that can be implemented within groups but is not a technique by which teachers group students.

14. B

Ms. Sterling is engaging her class in problem-based learning because the students are directly collaborating to solve a real-world problem. Choice (**B**) is correct. In vicarious learning, (A), students observe but do not engage directly in an activity. Mapping, (C), allows students to make connections between ideas. Direct instruction, (D), is explicit, teacher-led learning.

15. D

Self-regulatory skills allow students to monitor and control their own behavior. By allowing the students to reflect on their performance and set a target for their next essay, Mr. Sullivan helps them gain insight into and practice with refining their behavior. Choice (**D**) is correct. Abstract reasoning, (A), involves thinking that extends beyond concrete, tangible ideas into mental concepts. Classical conditioning, (B), pairs one stimulus with another. Collaborative learning, (C), involves students working together in a way that mutually benefits their learning processes.

16. C

The description in choice (**C**) is most useful for the student because it gives concrete examples. This description makes clear to the student what sort of sources were to be included, and it confirms that the student selected them appropriately. Choice (A)'s description—"good but not great"—is subjective and does not let the student know what he did well or could have improved upon. Similarly, (B) and (D) do not provide specific examples related to the sources selected.

17. C

Direct instruction is characterized by explicit instruction by a teacher, rather than by students constructing understanding through experience. Choice (**C**) is correct.

18. D

Wait time is a critical practice that stimulates more complex thinking and encourages more students to participate in the discussion. Choice (**D**) is correct. Choice (A) would give the teacher data on her students but would not stimulate additional participation. (B) and (C) both illustrate commonly used teaching practices that are designed for other activities, not specifically for class discussions.

19. B

A scaled score is a raw score that has been modified in some way to add consistency to results or to fit results to a certain format. Choice (**B**) is therefore correct. Age-equivalent scores, (A), compare individual test takers' performance to performance averages for test takers of certain ages; an age-equivalent score of 9, for instance, means that the test taker did as well as a typical 9-year-old would have done on the same test. That is not what's happening here, so (A) is incorrect. Percentile scores, (C), state which percentage of test takers performed below the test taker; a percentile score of 56, for instance, means that the test taker's score was better than that of 56 percent of test takers. There are no percentiles in the above description, so choice (C) is incorrect. Grade-equivalent (GE) scores, (D), are very similar to age-equivalent scores, except that the scores refer to grades instead of ages; a GE score of 9 would mean that the student's performance matched that of a typical student entering high school. No grade equivalences are mentioned here, so (D) is incorrect.

20. D

Observations are objective; they document what is visible. Interpretations are how the teacher might integrate and apply the information in his diary to draw conclusions about his students. Only observations are included in the anecdotal notes to ensure that the notes accurately capture student achievements. Interpretations are subjective and should be omitted from anecdotal notes. Choice (**D**) is correct.

21. A

Having the ability to reflect on one's own pedagogical practices is a key component of competent, effective teaching. With adequate reflection, teachers may assess whether learning objectives have been achieved, and they can change their strategies as needed. Therefore, choice (**A**) is correct. Metacognition, (B), refers to an awareness of one's own thinking processes; merely reflecting on an unsuccessful lesson plan and making changes is not necessarily a metacognitive practice. Learning styles, (C), are different ways in which individual students most successfully learn. In this example, the teacher does not clearly incorporate attention to diverse learning styles in the design of his lesson. Although students were paired up, the activity the teacher originally used was not a think-pair-share as in (D). Think-pair-share is a strategy that requires students to briefly consider a question or problem individually, then talk with a partner to discuss their thoughts, and finally share with the whole group.

22. A

The first choice is the only one that involves stakeholders. Inviting members of the community to participate directly endows them with ownership in the work of the school. Choice (**A**) is correct. The other three choices all limit involvement to members of the community within the school walls.

23. D

Mandatory reporting is a law that requires a teacher or other caregiver to report suspected child abuse. Since the teacher suspects the bruising might be the result of abuse, choice (**D**) is correct. Parents are not to be alerted before a call to Child Protective Services, (A), because it is the agency's job to determine whether abuse has occurred and, if so, who is responsible. The mandated reporter's legal responsibility supersedes the decision of any school official, so (B) is incorrect. Reporting under this law is not an option, as in (C), but rather a legal requirement.

24. A

Peer observation allows teachers to share with each other and engage in a cycle of feedback and discussion about teaching practices. Choice (**A**) is correct because it would be the most effective.

25. A

An ELL teacher would be best qualified to assist the teacher daily, so choice (**A**) is correct. A bilingual-certified counselor, (B), would be effective at supporting bilingual students in their mental health and well-being. A media specialist, (C), would assist the teacher in integrating information resources into her classroom. A language pathologist, (D), would assess and provide intervention support for language and communication difficulties.

Constructed-Response Questions

Sample Response to Question 1

Ms. Kohl could assign students tasks during viewing, intended to ensure the students' more active involvement when watching the films. She could prepare study guides for students to complete, related to the instructional objectives associated with the films. Ms. Kohl could then use class time to review student answers before moving on to further discussion of the film.

Ms. Kohl could arrange for students to view the film together. The logistics would depend on student availability and technology, but encouraging the students to watch the video in pairs or groups—even if they were sharing a streamed video feed or watching the video independently at home while chatting online—would encourage student interaction and collaboration. Ms. Kohl could allot some class time for the student groups to conduct a follow-up discussion in which they could share ideas and questions related to the movie.

Sample Response to Question 2

Ms. Kohl could advise Davis to begin watching the movies early and over a period of time, rather than all at one sitting. Any type of long reading, research, or video assignment can be overwhelming when taken all at once, but if Davis plans ahead, he can probably manage 20 minutes of a movie every day for a week. Davis could be responsible for completing an organizer or review sheet related to the film, so as to demonstrate his progress throughout the week.

Ms. Kohl could arrange some sort of check-in system with Davis. Davis has previously emailed Ms. Kohl—he could be required to send two short emails every week, in which he could briefly describe his progress in watching the film and let her know when he was having trouble with assignments. This information would help Ms. Kohl gauge Davis's progress and plan supporting instructional activities as needed. It would also help her provide recommendations to Davis concerning how to prioritize his homework time effectively.

CHAPTER 6

PRINCIPLES OF LEARNING AND TEACHING PRACTICE TESTS

Taking Your Practice Tests

Now that you're more familiar with the concepts and issues tested on the Praxis Principles of Learning and Teaching (PLT) tests, it's time for some full-length practice. The official PLT will be administered on computer, and you have additional practice tests to take in your online resources (more on those shortly). For your convenience, Kaplan has included two full-length PLTs—one for Grades K–6 and one for Grades 7–12—in this book.

The best practice is to take these tests under timed, test-like conditions. On the official test, you won't be allowed to have a cell phone or any other electronic items with you. So, during your in-book practice tests, turn off your phone and computer or tablet. Find a quiet environment where you will not be interrupted while taking the test. Time yourself using a watch or kitchen timer. To get used to the test day experience, take any notes on plain scratch paper.

When you're done, review the entire test, question by question, using the Kaplan explanations. While it's important to build up your concentration and stamina by taking full-length tests, reviewing the explanations is where much of your learning and improvement actually take place. Review even for the questions you got right. The explanations often point out patterns and strategies you can use to tackle the questions more efficiently and confidently on your official exam.

Remember that while the individual PLTs are targeted to different grade-level bands, they test many of the same overarching theories and concepts. Make sure you take the Practice Tests for the grade levels you'll be required to take, but don't hesitate to take PLT Practice Tests outside your grade level bands if time permits.

In your online resources, you have the following additional practice materials:

- One additional full-length PLT (Grades K–6) Practice Test with complete answers and explanations

- Two full-length PLT (Grades 4–9) Practice Tests with complete answers and explanations (By the way, we put in two Grades 4–9 Practice Tests because while far fewer states require this grade-level band, these tests provide excellent additional practice for both the elementary and high school versions.)

- One additional full-length PLT (Grades 7–12) Practice Test with complete answers and explanations

GO ONLINE

kaptest.com/login

Keep in mind the exhortations above about creating a test-like environment for your full-length practice. The same goes whether you're testing from your book or on a laptop.

PLT Grades K–6 Practice Test

2 Hours: 70 Selected-Response Questions and 4 Constructed-Response Questions

Directions: On test day and on this practice test, standard time to complete this test is 120 minutes, and there are 74 questions. You are not penalized for wrong answers on the Praxis. Your score is calculated by the number of questions you answer correctly, so select an answer for every question, even if it is a guess.

Joaquin, a student in Ms. Babbage's language arts class, has been diagnosed with ADHD. When Ms. Babbage gives her students timed reading and writing assignments, Joaquin rarely finishes his work, sometimes leaving more than half of it unfinished. Joaquin also has a habit of tapping his pencil on his desk while others are working, which can create a distraction. When Ms. Babbage met with Joaquin to talk about his trouble completing in-class assignments, Joaquin said that the other students make noises that "make it hard [for him] to think."

1. Which of the following adaptations or strategies would be appropriate and effective for Ms. Babbage to use in helping Joaquin and other students remain focused throughout the class period?

   Select all that apply.

   A. Letting Joaquin keep a noiseless "squishy ball" at his desk to squeeze when he feels restless.

   B. Keeping a set of noise-cancelling headphones in the classroom so any student can use them to minimize distractions during independent work.

   C. Instituting a "three strikes" system in which a child, if he or she continues to distract other students after receiving three warnings, will be sent to the principal's office.

   D. Encouraging Joaquin to use a silent timer to keep track of the passing minutes during timed assignments.

2. Goal setting, self-monitoring, and self-evaluation are all examples of:

   Select all that apply.

   A. Motor impulses

   B. Executive functions

   C. Habits beneficial to independent learning

   D. Metacognitive regulatory processes

3. A second-grade creative writing student with dyslexia is engaged in writing a poem that highlights his favorite color. Which of the following accommodations is most likely to be effective in helping the student write with a sense of confidence?

   A. Reteaching the lesson to the student during lunchtime

   B. Assigning an aide to mark misformed words for correction

   C. Allowing the student to dictate certain words or lines

   D. Giving the student a pocket dictionary in which to look up particularly difficult words

4. As her third-grade class undertakes its unit on states of matter, Ms. Zehner guides her students to create a KWL chart on the topic. As students review the "L" column, Ms. Zehner encourages them to compare their previous knowledge and predictions to what they have learned. Which of the following is this process most likely to encourage?

   A. Inductive reasoning

   B. Metacognition

   C. Deductive reasoning

   D. Automaticity

5. Mr. Rohmann is incorporating critical thinking skills into a science unit for his fourth-grade class. Toni, a student in the class, has a hearing impairment. She is having trouble grasping cause and effect as it relates to the unit, even though she has a signing aide to help her. Mr. Rohmann soon realizes that Toni probably does not have the background experiences needed to readily understand some of the examples he has been sharing with the class (for example, the relationship between thunder and lightning). After doing some research, Mr. Rohmann decides he can best help Toni by

   A. including varied example types, particularly when discussing difficult concepts

   B. transferring the student to a special classroom for those with impaired hearing

   C. using brain-teaser activities to stimulate the student's thinking

   D. using chart plans as a self-monitoring activity to engage the student

6. Which of these problems, if experienced by a sixth-grade student, would offer the clearest indicator of an atypical variance in cognitive development?

   A. The student often confuses letter sequences, reading "expect" as "except" and "felt" as "left."

   B. The student often argues with her friends and sulks when assigned tedious or undesirable school assignments.

   C. The student is less dexterous than many of her classmates and demonstrates less skill at games like volleyball and tennis.

   D. The student's mastery of content areas varies significantly; the student is above grade level in math, but slightly below grade level in social studies.

7. Which of the following describes a strategy that would be appropriate for Ms. Ruiz, a fifth-grade teacher, to use in the course of mathematics instruction in a classroom that includes several English language learners (ELLs)?

   A. Exempting ELLs from responsibility for learning math concepts that involve challenging or esoteric words like "scalene" and "ordinal"

   B. Having ELLs sit in a separate part of the classroom, reading silently from math textbooks written in their native languages, while the rest of the students are working on collaborative problem-solving exercises

   C. Treating all students in exactly the same way and imposing identical requirements on students during classroom instruction, to avoid the appearance of favoritism

   D. Guiding the class through a quick review of the place value system before introducing more complex decimal concepts, to account for the fact that decimal points are used differently across cultures

8. Kohlberg's "conventional" level of moral development, in which the individual desires to live up to societal conventions and will adhere to social norms even in the absence of immediate approval from others, is most strongly associated with which of the following stages of physical development?

   A. Toddlerhood

   B. Early childhood

   C. Late childhood

   D. Adolescence

9. After evaluating the special needs of a student who is entering a public high school for the first time, a team of educators develops an Individualized Education Plan (IEP) for her. Which of the following is a legally required component of this student's IEP?

   Select all that apply.

   A. Listing instructional goals and objectives in the IEP and updating and revising them as needed

   B. Providing the student with copies of all materials listed as "recommended readings" in her course textbooks

   C. Sharing the plan with each of the student's teachers and clarifying that teachers must provide stipulated accommodations

   D. Reviewing the IEP at least once per year in order to update its content and notifying parents of meeting dates well in advance

10. Mr. Pierce is helping Ms. Nicole identify intellectually gifted students in her classroom. Which of the following characteristics would be good cognitive indicators for her to watch for?

    A. Students' preferring to choose their own learning activities

    B. Students' exhibiting lower expectations for their peers

    C. Students' having a strong sense of awareness

    D. Students' thinking at abstract levels earlier than their peers

11. Ms. Hall regularly works with her students on generating and tracking SMART goals in her class. Which of the following is Ms. Hall likely working to develop in her students?

    A. Extrinsic motivation

    B. Metacognition

    C. Self-efficacy

    D. Collaboration

12. Which of the following describes Piaget's cognitive stage at which students' thoughts are largely egocentric and they are not yet able to understand concrete logic?

    A. Sensorimotor stage

    B. Preoperational stage

    C. Concrete operational stage

    D. Formal operational stage

Steven is a new student who just transferred here from another school. According to his records, he recently exited English language learner (ELL) services. However, his teacher has noticed that Steven is struggling in his history class. While Steven is able to converse easily with his peers, he is having difficulty participating in class discussions and providing written responses to class questions.

13. Which of the following would be the most appropriate strategy to support Steven's achievement?

    A. Providing Steven with scaffolding until he is able to complete the tasks independently

    B. Using a different grading scale for Steven that allows more leeway

    C. Meeting with Steven's family to discuss study strategies

    D. Advocating for Steven's readmission to ELL services

14. Which of the following is an example of a statement that is positively extrinsic?

    A. Teacher: If you do your homework all week, you get to pick a prize.

    B. Student: I don't want to do this homework.

    C. Teacher: If you don't do your homework, you will have detention.

    D. Student: I really want to do this homework.

15. Which of the following is a required component of an Individualized Education Program (IEP)?

    A. Physical exam findings, as completed by a physician

    B. A list of trusted adults and role models, as identified by the student

    C. Current dietary and fitness data

    D. Current levels of academic achievement and functional performance

16. Raven is a student who receives special education services. Which of the following might be an appropriate curriculum accommodation for her Individualized Education Program (IEP)?

    A. Extended lunch time

    B. Use of graphic organizers

    C. Use of a computer as a positive incentive

    D. Minimized transitions

17. Which of the following best illustrates a way in which a teacher might apply schema theory in his or her classroom practice?

    A. Allowing students to choose their groups for a cooperative activity

    B. Using student choice to increase motivation during math stations

    C. Using analogies and comparisons to support students in drawing connections to prior knowledge

    D. Analyzing student assessment data to create homogeneous groups for literature circles

18. Ms. Farmer and Ms. Denos are collaborating to create a socially supportive environment for their students. Which of the following strategies is most likely to create an inclusive classroom culture?

    A. Facilitating small-group and whole-class meetings

    B. Leaving all questions for the end of a lesson, so as not to interrupt the flow

    C. Encouraging parent involvement in the PTA

    D. Arranging desks in neat, orderly rows

19. Which of the following strategies would best integrate cognitive learning theory into a teacher's practice?

    A. Organizing classroom furniture to allow for easy movement between activities

    B. Permitting student choice to increase motivation

    C. Using concept maps to help students understand relationships

    D. Creating flashcards to provide students with repetitive practice

20. Farrah has asthma and needs accommodations in her elementary school. Which of the following protects her?

    A. Americans with Disabilities Act

    B. Individualized Education Program

    C. No Child Left Behind Act

    D. Section 504 of the Rehabilitation Act

21. Ms. Nelson is a fourth-grade classroom teacher. Which of the following would best illustrate the application of Maslow's hierarchy of needs in her classroom?

    A. Students are given severe consequences for not turning in their homework.

    B. Parents are regularly invited to events that highlight students' academic achievements.

    C. Special guests are invited to read their favorite story in class and talk about why they love reading.

    D. Students are provided with access to a full breakfast in the morning if they are hungry.

22. **Use a check mark or X to indicate the educational theory associated with each instructional activity listed below.**

	Cognitivism	Constructivism	Behaviorism
Using schema theory to connect a student's prior knowledge of gardening to a lecture about evolution			
Using stickers to reward students who completed the previous night's homework			
Using problem-based learning to engage students in generating solutions to community needs			

23. In which of the following domains would a flute student be considered highly proficient once she goes beyond playing directly from sheet music to improvisation?

    A. Affective

    B. Cognitive

    C. Psychomotor

    D. Synthesis

Ms. Jimenez's third-grade class has recently read a series of versions of the Cinderella fairy tale from different cultures. Ms. Jimenez is considering which questions she will ask her class to stimulate a discussion of these texts.

24. Which of the following questions is designed to promote the highest level of thinking based on Bloom's taxonomy?

    A. Can you retell your favorite version of the story?

    B. If you wrote your own version of the Cinderella story, what would you have to include from the other versions and what would you leave out?

    C. What words did the authors of each version of the story use to describe the main character?

    D. Where did each of the stories take place? Can you find them all on a map?

Mr. Patel has just finished a social studies unit with his sixth-grade class. When he grades the unit assessments, he is disappointed to learn that his students received average scores of 50 percent on several of the key unit objectives.

25. Which of the following steps should Mr. Patel take to help students master these objectives?

    A. Reteach the objectives with which students struggled, using different teaching methods.

    B. Review the lessons, covering only the objectives on which students performed poorly.

    C. Begin the next unit with a review of essential study skills.

    D. Hold mandatory lunch tutoring sessions for the lowest-performing students until they perform above 50% on the unit assessment.

26. **In each row, identify whether the statement about interdisciplinary units is true or false.**

True	False	Statement
		If a teacher is not prepared to teach an interdisciplinary unit, he or she should not try teaching interdisciplinary lessons.
		Interdisciplinary units help students uncover preconceptions.
		It is appropriate for an interdisciplinary team to assess students using a culminating activity that integrates skills and approaches from each content area.

In anticipation of the Day of the Dead holiday, Ms. Halliwell is working with her grade-level team to develop a thematic unit involving aspects of Latin American culture and history. The team plans to incorporate the content into art, history, geography, and language arts lessons.

27. Which of the following steps should Ms. Halliwell and her team take first?

    A. Determine which activities will accomplish each learning objective.

    B. Design an interactive lesson that teaches students how to make art traditionally seen during the celebration.

    C. Make a map showing where the Day of the Dead is observed and hang it in classrooms.

    D. List all the stories the classes will read during language arts lessons and identify their themes.

A month after finishing a unit on geology, Mr. Allen asks his students to partner up and discuss how to list the layers of the earth. Before they begin, Mr. Allen encourages them to think of the clay models of the earth they made last month.

28. Which of the following types of memory is Mr. Allen stimulating?

    A. Procedural

    B. Institutional

    C. Academic

    D. Episodic

After breaking playground safety rules, a student badly scrapes her arm and requires bandages. Once the student has sufficiently recovered and returned to class, Ms. Najdi engages her class in a previously unplanned discussion about why the playground rules are in place and how students can ensure their own safety.

29. Which of the following best describes Ms. Najdi's action?

    A. Adjusting instruction due to student needs

    B. Following school safety protocols

    C. Taking advantage of a teachable moment

    D. Reviewing previously taught content

Mr. Caputo is leading his sixth-grade class in a discussion as a way of concluding a social studies unit. He presents his students with a proposition based on the unit's content and encourages them to agree or disagree with the statement. Mr. Caputo has his students jot down their responses and evidence and then share their thoughts with a neighbor. He then pairs students with others who have taken the opposite stance and asks each student pair to present their own arguments and question one another's arguments. Mr. Caputo encourages each student to defend his or her point of view with new evidence if necessary.

30. What is the most likely reason Mr. Caputo has set up the class discussion in this manner?

    A. To encourage students to engage in conversation with different classmates

    B. To improve students' debate performance

    C. To demonstrate that there are two sides to every story

    D. To develop students' critical-thinking skills

31. Which of the following is an example of experiential learning?

    A. Students engage in calculating the measure of angles through peer practice, then share their answers on the board.

    B. The media center specialist shows students resources for finding information about leaders in mathematics.

    C. After conducting a school survey, students compile data and create a variety of charts to illustrate the results.

    D. Students work on learning-activity packets the teacher compiled to individualize lessons for the current unit.

Mr. Kealoha tells his fourth-grade math class to follow his progress on the whiteboard as he divides one fraction by another and simplifies the quotient. As he works, he says, "In step one, I will flip this fraction. In step two, I'll multiply across—like so. Then in step three, I'll reduce this fraction by finding a common denominator. Presto!"

32. Which of the following instructional techniques is Mr. Kealoha using?

    A. Concept mapping

    B. Inquiry

    C. Demonstration

    D. Drill-and-practice

33. Which of the following is an appropriate research prompt for an inquiry-based instructional unit in a third-grade classroom?

    A. "Predict what the high and low temperatures will be in our town this year on January 15, April 15, July 15, and October 15."

    B. "State how you think the seasonal barometric pressure ranges will differ this year between our town and Seaville Beach."

    C. "Take an educated guess as to whether this sheet of notebook paper will feel smoother to the touch than this sheet of sandpaper."

    D. "Use an almanac to look up the average high and low temperatures in our town in the winter, spring, summer, and fall."

Ms. Barnes is setting up reading groups in her fourth-grade classroom. She plans to meet with each group once a week, during which time she will guide the group in reading a text she chooses based on the group's most recent reading assessment.

34. What type of grouping should Ms. Barnes use to produce the best outcomes for student learning, and why?

    A. Grouping by gender, because it will reduce distractions

    B. Heterogeneous grouping, because students with stronger abilities can help those who are struggling

    C. Grouping by date of birth, because students' skills can best be approximated by their precise ages

    D. Homogeneous grouping, because it allows students to work on skills closest to their respective zones of proximal development

35. **Match each term for a grouping technique to its corresponding description in the table below.**

Description	Term
Clusters students together by skill mastery, language proficiency, or other criteria	
Places students of varying skills and ages together to maximize learning	
Uses structured learning to support a specific goal as students work together	
Intentionally places students in groups that provide a variety of perspectives	

    A. Cooperative learning

    B. Multi-age grouping

    C. Heterogeneous grouping

    D. Homogeneous grouping

36. Ms. Kim has noticed that her students are reluctant to answer questions she poses in class. One of her colleagues suggests several potential questioning techniques. Which of the following techniques are likely to be effective in promoting student participation?

    Select all that apply.

    A. Offering immediate factual corrections of students' incorrect responses

    B. Waiting for 10 to 15 seconds before expecting a student response

    C. Asking series of questions that increase in complexity

    D. Teaching students to track the speaker

37. Ms. Ali would like to increase the rigor of her questioning in the language arts portion of her second-grade class. Which of the following actions can she encourage students to use to employ higher-level thinking skills?

    Select all that apply.

    A. Identifying the settings of various stories and nonfiction narratives

    B. Making predictions based on titles and pictures and checking predictions after reading

    C. Listing instances of the spelling patterns that students find as they read books in class

    D. Suggesting alternative ways for characters to resolve their problems, based on students' readings and personal experience

Mr. Morimoto frequently leads his third-grade class in discussion. Recently, several students in the class have begun to laugh when a particular student speaks. Mr. Morimoto has spoken to the laughing students outside of class time about their behavior and has shifted his position in the classroom to be closer to the disruptive students during discussion time. Mr. Morimoto encourages each student to share opinions and participate in class discussions.

38. Which of the following goals are Mr. Morimoto's actions most likely intended to accomplish?

    A. Punishing students who disrespect their classmates

    B. Establishing a safe environment for class discussions

    C. Demonstrating the teacher's authority in the classroom

    D. Encouraging students to solve their problems on their own

While Ms. Jackson's kindergarten class is watching a cartoon together, one student seated at the front of the class tries to engage Ms. Jackson in a private conversation. The student is worried because she cannot find her book bag. Ms. Jackson makes sympathetic eye contact with the student to acknowledge the problem, but she holds one finger to her mouth in a *Shh* gesture. She then mouths the word "Wait" and directs her attention to the cartoon.

39. Which of the following does Ms. Jackson's behavior during the cartoon illustrate?

    A. Visual appreciation of an art form

    B. Deferred-gratification strategy

    C. Informal diagnostic assessment methods

    D. Nonverbal classroom management strategies

Ms. Hooper is teaching a unit on American colonial history to her fifth-grade students. She has decided to share images of colonists' dress, as well as the types of homes they lived in and the maps they used to describe the land where they lived.

40. Which of the following is the main reason to use these visual aids in this unit?

    A. To reduce Ms. Hooper's lesson planning time

    B. To give students a better understanding of the unit content

    C. To prepare students for interactive lessons

    D. To present new ideas without taking up class time

Mr. Wagner's third graders will be reading a fiction book set in the 1970s. Before they begin reading the book, the teacher shows them a short video clip about the 1970s and then takes them to the library. There, they read excerpts from books and magazines the media specialist has gathered for their use, and they explore internet sites Mr. Wagner has listed for them. He tells them to jot down some notes so they can have a class discussion the next day about what they learned.

41. Which of the following is the best rationale for having the students complete the above-mentioned activities before reading the 1970s-era book?

    A. The knowledge students obtain should help them score well on high-stakes tests.

    B. The resources students study will deepen their understanding of the book's setting.

    C. The students will recognize how far technology has advanced since 1975.

    D. The video and internet activities will satisfy local and state requirements concerning technology use.

Mr. Edat is introducing the concept of division to his third-grade class. He brings candies to the class and demonstrates how to separate them into groups so that each student receives an equal number of candies. He then illustrates this concept on the board, using two students in his example.

42. Which strategy is Mr. Edat using to support student learning?

    A. Scaffolding

    B. Developing self-regulation skills

    C. Guided practice

    D. Modeling

Mr. Penwright recently returned his fifth-grade students' book reports with his grades and comments attached. A representative grade report reads as follows:

- Synopsis: 4/5—Very comprehensive! You clearly read the whole book.

- Recommendation: 3/5—You did not take into account your audience, but you articulated feedback.

- Grammar: 3/5—Multiple errors per page, but coherent overall

- Average: 3.3/5

43. Which of the following assessment methods did Mr. Penwright use in evaluating his students' essays?

    A. Holistic scoring

    B. Analytical scoring

    C. Narrative assessment

    D. Deconstructive scoring

At the beginning of her class's unit on Mexican folk dances, Ms. Perez asks her students to raise their hand if they have ever seen a hat dance. Four students raise their hand. Then she asks her students if they are familiar with turtle dances or straw bull dances. This time, nobody raises a hand. She lifts a pair of maracas over her head and asks the students, "What are these called?" Two students volunteer incorrect answers. Ms. Perez then asks, "What family of instruments do these belong to?" Many students call out the correct reply, "The percussion family."

44. Ms. Perez's questions were most likely designed to

    A. assess progress

    B. guide thinking

    C. develop critical reasoning skills

    D. determine prior knowledge

45. Mr. Booker just received a new student into his third-grade class. What sort of assessment should he use to determine the skill level of his new student?

    A. Diagnostic assessment

    B. Formative assessment

    C. Personality test

    D. Summative assessment

A sixth-grade science teacher administers a test on the geology of the earth. She designs the test so that it tests the students' understanding of the content presented during their most recent unit.

46. Which of the following best describes the test?

    A. Criterion-referenced assessment

    B. Norm-referenced assessment

    C. Diagnostic assessment

    D. Formative assessment

At Emerson Elementary in the month of May, all of the fourth-grade students complete a standardized test that compares their performance to other testers at the same grade level and ranks the students accordingly.

47. Which of the following best describes the test that the fourth-grade students are taking?

    A. Criterion-referenced assessment

    B. Norm-referenced assessment

    C. Diagnostic assessment

    D. Formative assessment

Ms. Williams is helping her students construct their end-of-the-quarter essay. She wants to integrate time into her lessons to work with individual students on their specific needs next week.

48. Which of the following would best help her achieve her goal?

    A. Assigning homework targeted to class-wide editing needs

    B. Conducting a daily editing session

    C. Recording anecdotal notes during student revision time

    D. Having student-teacher writing conferences

Mr. Spencer wants to plan an informal, formative assessment for the end of a math lesson to assess what students learned in order to target his planning for the next day.

49. Which of the following would most help Mr. Spencer to collect formative data on each student?

    A. Having each student write a short reflection on their behavior during class today and how they feel this impacted their understanding of the lesson

    B. Writing a question on the board that requires students to apply the day's learning and asks each student to "turn and talk" to their elbow partner

    C. Having each table of students generate a summary of the day's learning that will be posted in the room for reference during the next lesson

    D. Having each student complete an "exit ticket," a quick problem based on the day's lesson that requires students to show their work and demonstrate what they do and do not know

Khalil's family is moving to a new school district. Before he moves, his father asks his teacher to administer a test that will tell the new school whether or not Khalil's math skills are on grade level.

50. Which of the following would be most likely to provide accurate information for Khalil's new school?

    A. Achievement test

    B. Aptitude test

    C. Ability test

    D. Attitude test

51. Which of the following terms describes the degree to which an evaluation accurately measures the thing it is trying to measure?

    A. Validity

    B. Reliability

    C. Norm

    D. Criterion

Ms. Kern is looking for a tool to use to evaluate her students' essays on a set of skills that they have been learning this quarter. She wants to make sure they get individual feedback on each of their skills separately.

52. Which tool would best allow her to provide this kind of feedback?

    A. Anecdotal notes

    B. Scoring continuum

    C. Analytic scoring rubric

    D. Holistic scoring rubric

Mr. Washington is putting together his materials for the upcoming parent-teacher conferences.

53. Which of the following approaches should he take in sharing data with his students' families?

    A. Providing the families with the raw data from the most recent statewide assessment

    B. Providing the families with an overview of class-wide performance that gives them an understanding of how their class is performing in relation to the standards

    C. Making a list of everything a student needs to improve, so that families understand how much work students need to do for the rest of the year

    D. Preparing data and interpretations of the data that help families understand a student's strengths and areas for improvement

Mr. Peña is planning on dividing his sixth-grade class into peer reading groups. He wants each group to read, discuss, and write about a novel appropriate to their reading level. To divide them up, he plans on giving them a reading assessment.

54. What type of scoring on the assessment will provide him with the most accurate way to divide the class?

    A. Percentile

    B. Scaled

    C. Grade equivalent

    D. Raw

55. Students in a sixth-grade science class have been conducting science experiments with gradually decreasing teacher guidance during the year. As the end of the year approaches, the teacher would like to assess the students' ability to carry out the steps of the scientific method. Which type of assessment would be most appropriate?

    A. Performance

    B. Selected-response

    C. Essay

    D. Conference

The fourth-grade team at Westview Elementary wants to conduct assessments in math. They want to give these tests at the beginning of the school year and at the end of the first semester. They are planning on writing the assessment as a team and using the fourth-grade math standards for their state.

56. What type of assessment is this?

    A. Formative

    B. Criterion referenced

    C. Informal

    D. Performance

Ms. Novack, who is in her first year of teaching science at the fifth-grade level, wants to be involved in advocating for the importance of science education in her local community.

57. Which of the following activities would best help her meet this advocacy goal?

    A. Participating in an annual conference for science educators in her state

    B. Coordinating a chemistry lab demonstration night at an elementary school

    C. Attending staff meetings in which ways to integrate science and language arts standards can be integrated

    D. Adding interactive videos and other innovative technology tools to her science lessons

Ms. Rodriguez is in her third year teaching at Keeling Elementary School. After two years of teaching third grade, she will be teaching fifth grade this coming school year.

58. How should she begin planning to teach a new grade level?

    A. She should take an online course about the developmental needs of fifth graders.

    B. She should meet with her professional learning community to review the district pacing and curriculum map for fifth grade.

    C. She should read the latest research on teaching math to upper-elementary students.

    D. She should research new science curricula based on national recommendations.

59. The second-grade team at Kennedy Elementary School wants to focus on increasing the rigor of the district science curriculum. After putting together common lesson plans for the unit on the solar system, what is the best way for them to evaluate the implementation?

    A. Inviting the principal to complete formal observations on each teacher during the new lesson

    B. Video recording themselves doing a practice teaching of a lesson

    C. Developing pre-, mid-, and post-assessments for the students to take throughout the unit

    D. Creating a school-wide display of student work based on the new unit

New teachers in the Northside School District are required to participate in biweekly induction training designed to help them succeed in their first year of teaching. The teachers receive informal visits from mentor teachers. The new teachers then meet to discuss challenging aspects of the curriculum, teaching methods, and classroom strategies.

60. What aspect of reflective practice is this an example of?

    A. Portfolio

    B. Reflective journal

    C. Critical friend

    D. Self- and peer assessment

Mr. Tripton is concerned about a student in his fourth-grade class. Alison is frequently late or absent from school, has trouble paying attention in class, has started wearing dirty clothes to school, and today came to class with visible bruises on her arm.

61. What should Mr. Tripton do first?

    A. Call Alison's parent or guardian to ask about the bruises

    B. Ask Alison if someone hit her

    C. Have his class complete a writing assignment about a time someone hurt them

    D. Report the suspected abuse/neglect to local law enforcement and/or child services

62. What is the primary role of a paraeducator?

    A. To assist students in daily activities

    B. To assess student work

    C. To communicate with parents regarding student progress

    D. To aid the classroom teacher in planning and teaching lessons

Wayside School District is located in a very socioeconomically diverse area. About 90 percent of the families in the district report having reliable daily access to the internet.

63. How should teachers best communicate with parents regarding daily student behavior and homework?

    A. They should post assignments on the class web page.

    B. They should email parents once a month to let them know how their child is doing in class.

    C. They should maintain a daily communication log to be sent home each night and reviewed and signed by the parents.

    D. They should schedule a parent/teacher conference if there are concerns with a student.

Ms. Jones has a student on an IEP with a label of Emotional Disability. She wants to learn more about this student's disability and how to best adjust her classroom environment to aide in this student's success.

64. Whom should Ms. Jones approach for help?

    A. The principal

    B. The school psychologist

    C. The school health aide

    D. The classroom teacher who had the student the prior year

65. Which of the following topics was addressed in the Equal Educational Opportunities Act of 1974?

    A. Learning disability

    B. Use of a wheelchair

    C. Transportation needs to and from the school site

    D. Segregation

Ms. Jones is in her eighth year of teaching. She wants to track her daily lesson plans to determine which teaching methods are working well and which ones need to be changed.

66. What is the best way for her to track daily lesson plans, based on reflective teaching methods?

    A. Creating a portfolio of all her class worksheets

    B. Keeping a reflective journal

    C. Discussing her plans in her annual evaluation meeting

    D. Asking another teacher to watch her teach and tell her how it went

Mr. Hanson wants to enhance a history lesson on World War II by using clips of news footage from that time period. He is unsure what public sites are considered acceptable use for his district and how to legally download the footage.

67. What or who is his best resource for help?

    A. A local newspaper office

    B. An online article on how to download media

    C. The school library/media specialist

    D. His brother-in-law, who is a history professor

Ms. Penn is a PE teacher at Smith Elementary School. She wants to start a community garden at her school to help teach her students about healthy habits.

68. What should she do after she identifies the stakeholders in her project and gains approval from her administration?

    A. Survey her students to see what they want to grow in the garden

    B. Attend a webinar on gardening techniques

    C. Apply for grants to fund the garden

    D. Research methods for creating a community garden

Samantha is in the third grade at Roberts Elementary. Her 18-year-old brother came to the school and asked for a copy of Samantha's school records because their family is moving.

69. If the school were to comply with this request, which of the following would it be violating?

    A. The right to equal access to education

    B. The Family Educational Rights and Privacy Act

    C. The right of due process

    D. Nothing; adult siblings are allowed access to the records of younger siblings

70. Which of the following is part of the collaborative process?

    A. Teachers are given daily personal planning time and are required to meet with grade levels once a month to share curriculum ideas.

    B. Teachers are given common grade-level planning time on a weekly basis, but they are not required to attend.

    C. Teachers are given common grade-level planning time on a weekly basis, and they use the time to work on common lessons, curriculum planning, or data sharing.

    D. Teachers are given common grade-level planning time only when they request it.

Approximate time: 25 minutes

Directions: The case history below is followed by two short-answer questions. Your responses to the questions will be evaluated with respect to professionally accepted principles and practices in teaching and learning. Be sure to answer all parts of the questions. Write your answers on the pages indicated in your answer sheet booklet.

Scenario: Ms. Hawke is a third-grade teacher at Smoky Hill Elementary. She is currently in her first year as a classroom instructor. Recently, in March (the seventh instructional month of the school year), Ms. Hawke's students took the BESTT, a state-mandated, three-day-long standardized test that measures students' skill in reading and mathematics. This was the students' first experience taking a standardized test and Ms. Hawke's first experience as a teacher interpreting these kinds of test results.

Document 1

BESTT Scoring Summary

Hawke, 3rd Grade, S.H.E. – BESTT Results

READING:

- Mean percentile: 72
- Median percentile: 70
- Percentile range (high and low percentile scores): 28 (87; 59)
- Mean grade equivalent (GE) score: 4.3

READING—Interpreting GE Scores:

- Below 2.5: The student struggles to use contextual clues to decipher meaning within a text. The student has difficulty identifying the thesis of an argumentative essay and may have difficulty keeping track of the plot points in a fictional narrative.

- 2.5–4.9: The student is able to infer meanings and definitions from contextual clues. The student can identify the thesis of an argumentative essay and is able to answer basic questions about the characters and plot events in a fictional narrative.

- 5 and up: The student is adept at drawing inferences about new words and unfamiliar situations, using contextual information in the text. The student is able to answer sophisticated questions about the plot, characters, themes, and style of a fictional narrative.

MATHEMATICS:

- Mean percentile: 51
- Median percentile: 47
- Percentile range (high and low percentile scores): 55 (80, 25)
- Mean grade equivalent (GE) score: 3.1

MATHEMATICS—Interpreting GE Scores

- Below 2.5: May demonstrate understanding of basic operations, but struggles with processes requiring mathematical abstraction. Has difficulty expressing the information in word problems in numeric and symbolic terms. Struggles to make inferences from simple bar graphs and pie charts.

- 2.5–4.9: Understands basic math operations and is able to convert simple word problems into statements made up of numbers and operational symbols. Can make inferences from simple bar graphs and pie charts.

- 5 and up: Understands math operations and can convert complex word problems into expressions consisting of numbers and operational symbols. Can draw valid inferences from multi-layered bar graphs and sets of pie charts.

DETAILED SKILL REPORTS

Note to educators: the next several pages show which percentage of the test takers demonstrated mastery of particular skills. For instance, the skill report "SINGLE-DIGIT ADDITION: 17/19" indicates that 17 of 19 students in a particular class have mastered single-digit addition.

Document 2

Excerpt from an observation of Ms. Hawke's classroom by Ms. Wajda, a senior faculty mentor

At the beginning of today's mathematics block—the first day of a unit introducing some new multiplication concepts—Ms. Hawke conducted a diagnostic exercise. She wrote a word problem on the board: "This morning, Steven bought three cans of tennis balls. Each can contained three balls. Later in the day, Steven took one ball out of each of the cans. Then he lost all of these balls by hitting them over a fence! How many balls does Steven have left?"

She then told the class: "For the next five minutes, I want you to try to solve this problem on your own. You may use any method you like. You may make notes on scratch paper. You may use the math blocks and abacuses at your learning stations. You may even use my calculator, which I will set down on this table for you. Please work silently. I will move around the room, watching you work. When you have finished, we will discuss the problem together."

Three of Ms. Hawke's students arrived at the correct answer quickly, either by using mental math or by drawing pictures of the balls and crossing out the ones that had been "lost." After they explained their answers to Ms. Hawke, she let them have silent reading time while the others worked. A number of her students came up with the wrong answer: "8." Ms. Hawke used questioning to direct them to the phrase "took one ball out of each of the cans," after which some children modified their answers to 6, while a few others came up with 7 (apparently because of a subtraction error). Some students struggled to deduce the original number of balls or moved blocks around without evident purpose. One student rushed to use Ms. Hawke's calculator, but then could not decide what numbers and operations to put in. Ms. Hawke observed these children both from a distance and closer up, asking them in some cases to tell her about what they were doing, or which part of the problem seemed trickiest.

When the diagnostic was over, she drew pictures of the cans and balls on the whiteboard and let students walk her through the problem step-by-step. She then told them that an operation called "multiplication," represented by an X symbol, would help them work through problems like this in the future, and that they would be learning a lot about multiplication in the coming weeks.

Document 3

Conversation between Ms. Hawke and Ms. Wajda

Ms. Hawke: The BESTT has been stressing me out, that's for sure. My kids have a long way to go before they're up to the standard of some of the other third-grade classes in the district.

Ms. Wajda: I understand the challenges, but you're off to a good start. The students seem to respond to your instruction, and they were interested in the open-ended problem-solving exercise you gave them in the diagnostic. You've got their attention.

Ms. Hawke: But they're working at such different levels. I'm not quite sure how to help students like Jennifer and Marcus interpret a phrase like "each can has three balls" without stifling the progress of students like Kenji and Austin, who already understand the basics of the math in the unit I'm starting.

Ms. Wajda: Right—the challenge is to find ways to help each student grow.

Ms. Hawke: It feels like there is a lot of pressure to bring the lowest-performing students up. I don't want my high-performing students to get lost in the shuffle.

Constructed-Response Questions

Question 1

Well-designed assessments can gauge students' learning and can also serve as instructional tools.

- Select TWO of the assessments described in the above scenario from which Ms. Hawke should be able to draw meaningful inferences about her students.

- For EACH of the assessments that you identified, describe an inference that Ms. Hawke should be able to derive. Base your response on the principles of interpretation of formative and summative assessments.

Question 2

By reflecting on testing data, educators can craft assignments that increase students' learning.

- Identify TWO instructional techniques or strategies that Ms. Hawke might wish to incorporate into her instruction in light of what the BESTT exam and diagnostic exercise have revealed.

- Describe a way that EACH of the two techniques you recommend would benefit students in Ms. Hawke's class. Base your response on the principles of formative assessment as a part of the instructional process.

Approximate time: 25 minutes

Directions: The case history below is followed by two short-answer questions. Your responses to the questions will be evaluated with respect to professionally accepted principles and practices in teaching and learning. Be sure to answer all parts of the questions. Write your answers on the pages indicated in your answer sheet booklet.

Scenario: Michael Cardamone is a student in Mr. Halpert's sixth-grade social studies class. Mr. Halpert teaches in a supported classroom; his aide is Ms. Tanaka. Mr. Halpert reports that although Michael is bright and curious, he frequently acts out in class and distracts other students. Mr. Halpert has sought the advice of his mentor, Mr. Keene, the chair of the middle-school social studies department. Mr. Keene has agreed to observe one of Mr. Halpert's classes.

Document 1

Excerpt from a transcript of audio recorded during Mr. Halpert's second-period class

(It is 10 minutes into class. Mr. Halpert is lecturing about the American Revolution. Mr. Keene and Ms. Tanaka are both observing from the back of the class.)

Mr. Halpert: And so, the colonists needed to get the word out across Massachusetts that the British were coming. Does anyone know whose job it was to send that message?

(Several students raise their hands.)

Michael: Paul Revere!

Mr. Halpert: Michael, I'm glad you know the answer, but please wait to be called on.

Michael: But I have to memorize a poem about him for English!

(Michael stands up.)

Michael: Listen my children and you shall hear/Of the midnight ride of Paul Revere.

Mr. Halpert: Michael, sit down now. You can practice after class.

Michael: But Ms. Clark said I should practice as much as possible.

Mr. Halpert: I'm sure Ms. Clark would agree that during class is not the best time to practice poetry.

Michael: Besides, Ms. Clark said Paul Revere got arrested and it was some other guy that really warned everyone. So you're not teaching right!

Mr. Halpert: That's it. Ms. Tanaka, could you please escort Michael to the front office?

(Ms. Tanaka gets up and takes Michael out of the room. Mr. Halpert continues his lesson.)

Document 2

Excerpt from the conversation between Michael and Ms. Tanaka

Michael (angry): This isn't fair! It's not my fault his lessons are boring!

Ms. Tanaka: Michael, you need to respect Mr. Halpert. He's a teacher. You also need to respect all your other classmates. When you act out, it makes it harder for them to learn.

Michael: But he's teaching things wrong. Paul Revere wasn't really the guy! Ms. Clark said!

Ms. Tanaka: And I'm sure that if you raised your hand and waited your turn to ask a question, Mr. Halpert would have been happy to talk about that.

Michael (sulking): He never calls on me when my hand is up.

Document 3

Excerpt from a conversation between Mr. Halpert and Mr. Keene

Mr. Halpert: So you see what I'm dealing with. He's like that every class.

Mr. Keene: Well, disruptive or not, he's clearly engaging with the material.

Mr. Halpert: He's very good at drawing connections between what we do in class and the real world. It's one of his most valuable skills, and if he could just focus, I know he'd be a great student. But he doesn't seem capable of filtering. He goes on and on about cartoons and comic books, just because they have a superficial similarity to the history we happen to be covering. If I tell him to be quiet, he usually listens, but not for more than a few minutes before he speaks out again. And he never waits to be called on.

Mr. Keene: How does he behave during group activities?

Mr. Halpert: He talks over the other students. But he's a clown, so they usually think it's funny. His groups tend to complete assignments poorly, if at all—even when it's a subject they're all interested in.

Mr. Keene: Are there any times when Michael does behave?

Mr. Halpert: Ms. Clark told me that he is always great when he's performing and acting out scenes or reading plays aloud. But there aren't really opportunities to do that during History lessons.

Mr. Keene: Well, have you spoken to his parents about his behavior?

Mr. Halpert: Not yet, but I suppose that I should. I'll send them a letter tomorrow.

Document 4

Letter from Michael's Parents

Dear Mr. Halpert,

Thank you for reaching out to us.

We knew that Michael had some behavioral issues, but we hadn't realized how disruptive they were. Michael often talks excitedly about the things he's studied as soon as he gets home; we assumed this was a sign that his schooling was going without incident, but apparently, we weren't getting the whole story.

At home, Michael is very animated. He does interrupt in conversations from time to time, and changes subjects rapidly. He has trouble focusing on his homework; the only times he can concentrate on one task for a long time are when he is playing video games and during his martial arts classes.

Michael clearly wants to learn, so we hope this information will help you give him the discipline he needs so that he can learn effectively. We are prepared to take any steps necessary to do what's best for him.

Best regards,

Victor and Marisa Cardamone

Constructed-Response Questions

Question 3

During Mr. Halpert's lecture, his aide, Ms. Tanaka, was observing from the back of the class.

- Suggest TWO ways in which Mr. Halpert could have had Ms. Tanaka actively assist the class during his lecture.
- For EACH of those ways, explain how Ms. Tanaka's participation could have helped students like Michael avoid disrupting the class. Base your response on the principles of teaching in a supported classroom.

Question 4

Throughout the case study, Michael demonstrates possible symptoms of a neurobehavioral or learning disorder.

- Identify TWO specific behaviors that Michael demonstrates or is reported to have demonstrated that could be symptoms of such a disorder.
- Explain how EACH behavior you identify is typical of individuals with such disorders. Base your responses on the principles of educating students with learning disorders.

IF YOU FINISH BEFORE TIME IS CALLED, YOU MAY CHECK YOUR WORK ON THIS SECTION ONLY. DO NOT TURN TO ANY OTHER SECTION IN THE TEST. | STOP

386 **K**

PLT Grades K–6 Practice Test Answers and Explanations

1.   A, B, D

As a student with ADHD, Joaquin needs assistance in keeping focused on the task at hand and avoiding possible distractions, but he may also need ways to continually keep himself occupied during lessons. To that end, taking steps to minimize distractions and allow Joaquin to burn off excess energy is likely to keep him calm and help him focus during lessons. Choices (**A**) and (**D**) can give Joaquin an outlet for his energy, while choice (**B**) can help him and other students avoid the distractions caused by others' talking or making noise. A "three strikes" system, as described in choice (C), could hinder Joaquin's progress by punishing him for his tendency to get distracted rather than helping him manage it.

2.   B, C, D

These are all examples of executive functions (**B**) because they are cognitive processes that help one plan and focus through the completion of tasks. For the same reason, these are also habits that are beneficial to independent learning (**C**). A person who is able to set, monitor, and evaluate goals is more likely to have success in independent learning, where tasks are often less structured. These processes are metacognitive regulatory processes (**D**) because they involve controlling cognitive processes. The listed processes are not motor impulses (A).

3.   C

Dyslexia is characterized by difficulty reading and understanding the written word, though those with this reading disorder tend to be of typical ability and intelligence. This student needs accommodations like those described in choice (**C**). Assigning someone to correct the student's misspellings (B) is likely to result in frustration and little progress for the student, while providing a dictionary (D) and reteaching the lesson (A) are not appropriate accommodations for the student's need.

4.   B

Metacognition is the act of thinking about how one thinks or reflecting on previous knowledge and predictions, as suggested in the prompt. Choice (**B**) is correct. Inductive reasoning, (A), is moving from specific facts or instances to general principles, while deductive reasoning, (C), is moving from general principles to specific facts or instances—neither of which is the primary reason to discuss KWL charts. Automaticity, (D), is the ability to perform a task or skill, such as walking or reciting multiplication tables, without conscious thought.

5.   A

It is always important to provide a variety of examples when teaching a new concept, but it is especially so when a student may not have access to certain shared experiences due to a learning difference or life circumstances. Choice (**A**) is therefore correct. Mr. Rohmann has identified the issue as the student's lack of familiarity with the subject matter—not a general disengagement with the content, which would be addressed by choices (C) and (D). Transferring a student with a learning difference to another classroom, as in (B), should be the last resort after all other reasonable accommodations have failed to help the student.

6.   A

Confusion with letter sequences on the scale described in choice (**A**) is more typical of an early elementary student and may indicate a learning difference in a student approaching middle school age. Variations in athletic skills, (C), and mastery of content areas, (D), are not atypical, so long as there are some areas in which a student's performance is close to or exceeds that of peers. Choice (B) may indicate an emotional need that is unmet, but it is not necessarily a sign of atypical cognitive development.

7.   D

Teachers working with ELLs strive to guide these students to master content at their grade levels while providing reasonable accommodations and additional support with the English language, all without lowering expectations. Recognizing that punctuation is employed differently in different cultures is a reasonable accommodation that will help prepare ELLs for success, so (**D**) is correct. Separating ELLs from their classmates, (B), when a reasonable accommodation could be employed or lowering expectations for these students, (A), does not serve their needs in mastering content. Avoiding any assistance based on students' unique backgrounds, (C), allows for no differentiation, which is a key component of all classroom instruction.

8.   D

Kohlberg's stages of moral development progress with a person's age. They begin with the pre-conventional stage and end with the post-conventional stage. The conventional stage, when individuals most value the opinions of peers and authorities as representatives of society at large, typically occurs during adolescence and adulthood. Choice (**D**) is therefore correct. Children younger than adolescents are typically in the pre-conventional stage of moral development. They focus on obedience and punishment as young children, (A) and (B), and move into self-interested decision making in later childhood, (B) and (C).

9.   A, C, D

(**A**), (**C**), and (**D**) are all legal requirements of an IEP as described in the Individuals with Disabilities Education Act (IDEA). (B) is not a requirement of this law.

10.   D

Choice (**D**) best illustrates a cognitive characteristic of intellectually gifted students. While not all gifted students are the same, many gifted students are able to think at more abstract levels earlier than their peers and generate atypical ways of approaching problems. They can often generate unique, creative ideas.

11.   C

Ms. Hall is working on developing her students' ability to set and reach goals, which will help them believe in their own ability to accomplish tasks. This matches the definition of self-efficacy, making choice (**C**) correct.

12.   B

Jean Piaget's theory of cognitive development states that students begin to talk and develop language skills during the preoperational stage. They often cannot understand another's perspective (egocentrism) and do not understand concrete logic. Choice (**B**) is therefore correct.

13.   A

Scaffolded instruction will help Steven transition to more difficult content and will target his specific needs. Choice (**A**) is correct. A grading scale, (B), does nothing to support his learning. Meeting with a student's family, (C), can be tremendously beneficial, but it does not seem that Steven's study strategies are his weakness.

14.   A

Choice (**A**) is extrinsic because it involves an outside incentive. It is positive because it is directed toward something desired. It would be negative if it were directed away from something to be avoided.

15.   D

Choice (**D**) is required for every student's IEP. It reflects a student's achievement levels at the time the IEP is written.

16.   B

Choice (**B**) is the only accommodation that would support Raven's curricular achievement. The accommodations in the other choices would not directly help a student learn what is being taught. The accommodations teachers choose for Raven should take into account the specific manifestation of her disability and provide the supports she needs to succeed.

17. C

Choice (**C**) illustrates the use of schema theory, which describes the way students organize information. As students interact with new information and experiences, they integrate the new information with their existing schema. A teacher who uses analogies and comparisons will make it easier for students to incorporate new information into their schema.

18. A

Facilitating meetings can help students develop appropriate strategies for resolving conflicts and learning to understand another's perspective. Meetings can give students the opportunity to make their voice hear, know their contributions are valued, and develop a sense of ownership of the classroom environment. Choice (**A**) is correct.

19. C

Cognitive learning theory specifically looks at relationships between information, so choice (**C**) would best integrate the use of cognitive learning theory into the classroom.

20. D

Section 504 is a federal law that provides protections to individuals with disabilities, medical conditions (including asthma), injuries, or other conditions that limit their participation in certain activities. Therefore, choice (**D**) is correct.

21. D

Maslow's hierarchy of needs starts with basic needs like food, water, and sleep, and it holds that students cannot focus on higher-order needs like friendship or creativity until their basic needs are met. Ms. Nelson's classroom would illustrate this best with choice (**D**), which takes care of students' hunger before addressing their other needs.

22.

Schema theory, which is associated with **cognitivism**, describes how people organize information by incorporating new information into their existing schema.

Behaviorism has a foundation in conditioning students to complete desired behaviors, including by rewarding homework completion with an extrinsic reward like stickers.

Constructivism emphasizes that learners create their own reality and that learning happens when students interpret the world based on their own experiences. Therefore, students are more likely to learn in authentic contexts, including problem-based learning.

23. C

The three learning domains described by Bloom are cognitive, affective, and psychomotor. These do not include synthesis (D), which is the process of forming a new conclusion from two separate ideas. The cognitive domain (B) refers to mental skills or knowledge; the affective domain (A) refers to emotional skills pertaining to one's attitude or sense of self; and the psychomotor domain (C) refers to manual physical skills. In this instance, playing the flute falls under the psychomotor domain because it involves considerable manual dexterity. Choice (**C**) is therefore correct.

24. B

Bloom's taxonomy classifies tasks based on the level of thinking they require. Choice (**B**) is correct because it requires students to evaluate what pieces of the Cinderella story are unique and essential, and to synthesize content from each version of the story they read. These activities involve the highest levels of thinking, according to Bloom's taxonomy. Choices (A) and (C) require recall and comprehension, while choice (D) calls for the same skills and some application. Application, comprehension, and knowledge are the three lowest levels of Bloom's taxonomy—and the related questions, while possibly promoting discussion and preparing students for further thinking, would therefore be likely to direct students to lower-level thinking.

25. A

With a class average of 50%, it is clear that Mr. Patel's students did not master all of the objectives in the unit the first time he taught it. This situation calls for remediation of the whole class, as described in choice (**A**). Remediation involves reteaching material in a different way—as opposed to simply having students review the material the same way they originally learned, as in (B). Giving additional lessons to only some students, (D), does not address the underlying issue that a majority of the class seems not to have mastered the content. Teaching students study skills, (C), is likely to be beneficial, but it does not address the underlying issue that students have not mastered the content from the previous unit.

26. The first statement is **false**. Incorporating interdisciplinary teaching into a classroom on a smaller scale can prepare the way for more expansive interdisciplinary learning later.

The second statement is **true**. Because interdisciplinary units allow students to approach content from a variety of perspectives, they help students become better equipped to discover and evaluate preconceptions. Interdisciplinary thinking is critical for students to develop a holistic understanding of content.

The third statement is **true**. A culminating activity not only allows students to see how the disciplinary approaches connect, but it also allows teachers to assess how well students have integrated the content area approaches.

27. A

In creating a thematic unit, as with any unit, the teachers' first steps should be to devise learning objectives and determine the scope and sequence of lessons. The decision on which activities to undertake during lessons should be driven by learning objectives and should come before more concrete decisions about content. This makes choice (**A**) correct. Planning for any individual lesson, (B), should only begin once the teachers have decided which lessons are essential. Likewise, the teachers will not know which stories, if any, they plan to read during lessons until they have determined their

objectives and the scope and sequence of the unit, so eliminate (D). Making any visual aids, as in (C), should be among the final steps in developing unit and lesson plans.

28. D

Episodic memory refers to personal experience. Because Mr. Allen refers to his students' personal experience of creating a model, he is triggering their episodic memory. Choice (**D**) is correct.

29. C

Ms. Najdi identifies an opportunity to teach students an impromptu lesson relating to their lived experience, also known as a teachable moment (**C**). While she is, indeed, altering instruction, (A), and reinforcing school safety protocols, (B), which may have been taught to students previously, (D), Ms. Najdi is primarily using the opportunity presented by the teachable moment—as she is adding an entirely new topic to the day based on students' direct experience.

30. D

Mr. Caputo has set up a discussion structure in which students must react to challenges to their ideas, thus using and further developing their critical-thinking skills. (**D**) is correct. While students may learn about differences of opinion, (C); gain debate skills, (B); and talk to different classmates than they might otherwise, (A), the primary purpose of this structure is to improve students' critical thinking.

31. C

In experiential learning, students undergo a process of learning by doing, or engaging in a real-world process to put into practice skills they may have developed in a more traditional classroom setting. In conducting a school survey and creating charts based on the results, as in (**C**), students are engaging in experiential learning by applying math and analysis skills to a real-world experience. Calculating angle measurements in a classroom setting, (A), and working on individualized packets in the same setting, (D), do not qualify as experiential learning, no matter how students share their results. Learning about resources for research, as in (B), occurs in a more traditional classroom setting and does not have any real-world element.

32. C

Mr. Kealoha is presenting students with a model of how to divide fractions. He is therefore demonstrating the learning objective, as in **(C)**. Concept mapping, (A), is a method of drawing connections and brainstorming related concepts, while inquiry, (B), is an open-ended process involving student research. Drill-and-practice, (D), requires students to repeatedly practice a skill or achieve understanding through memorization.

33. A

Inquiry-based work begins with an open-ended question that students then answer using research and classroom resources. Choice (D) directs students to perform a traditional and more straightforward task, and students are very likely to know the differences between notebook paper and sandpaper, as in (C)—so neither of these is inquiry. (B) is likely too advanced for third grade. But **(A)** is open-ended, intelligible to a third-grade student, and predictable based on research materials that students can access—making it the correct choice.

34. D

Ms. Barnes will choose the book she will read with students based on their reading performance, and she will be present to assist students when their groups meet. So homogeneous grouping, in which students of similar ability work together, will create the best opportunities for student learning. Choice **(D)** is therefore correct, as students will be working in their zones of proximal development and will not be unduly frustrated by working on a text that is too easy or too challenging. While gender grouping, (A), might reduce distractions, it is not likely to produce the best student outcomes because students will be grouped without regard to ability. Heterogeneous grouping, (B), or grouping together students with differing levels of ability, is more useful for tasks on which student groups work without the teacher's support and have differentiated goals. While birth order, (C), can predict some student ability in lower grades, particularly kindergarten, this type of grouping

is unlikely to resonate with reading performance in a fourth-grade classroom.

35.

Clusters students together by skill mastery, language proficiency, or other criteria	**(D)** Homogeneous grouping
Places students of varying skills and ages together to maximize learning	**(B)** Multi-age grouping
Uses structured learning to support a specific goal as students work together	**(A)** Cooperative learning
Intentionally places students in groups that provide a variety of perspectives	**(C)** Heterogeneous grouping

Teachers use a variety of grouping techniques and strategies depending on the specific instructional objectives they are targeting. No one method is universally appropriate for all tasks, so all teachers should be familiar with the strengths and limitations of each technique.

36. B, C, D

There are many important aspects of effective questioning, including allowing wait time for students to process questions and identify their responses, **(B)**; varying the difficulty of questions so that students at different levels of ability can all successfully respond to prompts, **(C)**; and encouraging active listening so that students can both understand questions and feel respected when they are speaking, **(D)**. While it is important to correct misconceptions, immediate corrections, (A), are likely to be seen as critical and are less likely to encourage students to correct mistakes on their own.

37. B, D

Higher-level thinking skills include analyzing, problem solving, and challenging assumptions, as students are guided to do in choices **(B)** and **(D)**. Identifying settings, (A), and locating spelling patterns, (C), while potentially valuable activities in a language arts setting, are not examples of higher-level thinking.

38. B

By asserting each student's right to respect, Mr. Morimoto is attempting to establish a safe environment for all of his students, so (**B**) is correct. Nothing in the scenario suggests that the offending students have been punished for their behavior, (A), or that the teacher is leaving the situation up to the students to resolve, (D). Mr. Morimoto is less concerned with his own authority, (C), than with making his students feel safe and comfortable participating in class discussions.

39. D

Ms. Jackson's use of visual cues—holding her finger to her mouth and mouthing a word, rather than speaking aloud—demonstrates the use of nonverbal management to redirect a student's attention without drawing the attention of other students. This makes choice (**D**) correct. While Ms. Jackson is encouraging students to appreciate the cartoon, her gestures to this particular student do not reflect (A). She is also not using deferred gratification, (B), which would require the child to wait for a reward or other pleasant experience. Finally, an informal diagnostic assessment, (C), would involve some means of observing a student's performance on a learning goal, which is not the case here.

40. B

The use of visual aids should always be directly related to the lesson and should help students better understand the content, as in choice (**B**). The goal is not convenience for the teacher, (A), nor taking shortcuts in the introduction of concepts, (D). While students may use visual aids for interactive lessons, (C), this should not be the first consideration in using visual aids.

41. B

This scenario describes the steps that Mr. Wagner takes prior to having his students read a book set in a time period with which they are unfamiliar. In this case, sharing audiovisual and textual information relevant to the time period will familiarize students with the setting of the book before they begin reading. This matches choice (**B**). This instructional choice is not directly related to high-stakes testing, (A), or local and state learning requirements, (D). Though students may incidentally learn about changing technologies, (C), this learning is not the goal of the activities Mr. Wagner undertakes with his students.

42. D

The process of demonstrating how to perform a task, as Mr. Edat does with grouping as a way to divide, is called modeling, so (**D**) is correct. Scaffolding, (A), is the support that the teacher provides and slowly removes to help students complete a task on their own, while guided practice, (C), describes the portion of the lesson during which students use scaffolding and the teacher's support to practice the objective. Self-regulation skills, (B), which may be in play to help students avoid eating their candy, are not the focus of Mr. Edat's actions.

43. B

Analytical scoring, (**B**), provides different scores for multiple categories of performance, as described in the question stem. Holistic scoring, (A), describes a system in which the teacher gives one score for an entire piece of work, using a rubric that describes proficiency on all learning outcomes as a single category. Narrative assessment, (C), involves observation of student interactions, performance, and results in a narrative format. Deconstructive scoring, (D), is not a standard type of assessment.

44. D

In asking questions related to content she will teach during the present unit, Ms. Perez is assessing students' prior knowledge of that content, so (**D**) is correct. Since this discussion takes place at the beginning of the unit, it would be difficult for her to assess progress, (A), on material that students have not yet learned. The questions that Ms. Perez asks are based on recall, so she is neither developing critical reasoning skills, (C), nor guiding students' thinking, (B).

45. A

Teachers use diagnostic assessments as pre-assessments to determine what students know and don't know. Choice (**A**) is correct.

46. A

The test the teacher has designed is a criterion-referenced assessment because it is written to ascertain a student's mastery of predetermined objectives. Choice (**A**) is correct.

47. B

Because the students are being compared to other students and ranked, this is an example of a norm-referenced assessment. Choice (**B**) is correct.

48. D

Choice (**D**) would best allow Ms. Williams to work individually with her students. Writing conferences help teachers learn about what students are thinking and provide them with one-on-one guidance.

49. D

Having each student complete an exit ticket is an easy way for Mr. Spencer to gather informal data on each of his students to plan for the next day's learning. Choice (**D**) is correct.

50. A

Khalil's results on an achievement test could tell his new school whether or not he is on grade level, as an achievement test would provide an evaluation of Khalil's mastery of skills. Choice (**A**) is correct.

51. A

Validity describes the degree to which a test accurately measures the thing it is trying to measure. Reliability is a measure of how consistent an evaluation is. A test can have high reliability without having high validity. Choice (**A**) is therefore correct.

52. C

Using an analytic scoring rubric would allow Ms. Kern to evaluate each of the targeted skills individually so that students receive feedback on each skill. This is especially useful for scoring tasks such as essays, where a teacher is likely assessing more than one competency. Choice (**C**) is correct.

53. D

If families are to have an accurate picture of their child's performance, they should understand what their child has already mastered and what their child can continue to work on. Providing this information is the most productive way to make a positive plan for improvement. Choice (**D**) is correct.

54. C

When giving an assessment, the first thing to consider is the desired outcome. If Mr. Peña is looking for data to help determine reading levels, then grade equivalent scores would be most appropriate, as that data would allow Mr. Peña to identify the appropriate reading group placement as well as novel selection for each group. Choice (**C**) is correct.

55. A

A performance assessment related to a lab or project would be most appropriate to measure the level of mastery of the objective described, since the teacher is interested in measuring how well students perform a task. Choice (**A**) is correct.

56. A

Formative assessments are based on what the students have learned and still need to learn. They are intended to serve as diagnostic data tools teachers can use to aid in planning their teaching. Choice (**A**) is correct.

57. B

In order to address the importance of science education to the local community, Ms. Novack needs to focus her efforts on ideas that impact parents and community members in her school (as opposed to the state). The choice with the correct focus and scope is (**B**).

58. B

The professional learning community and district resources are always the first place to begin. All planning needs to meet district standards, which are already aligned with state and national requirements. Each district and PLC team is responsible implementing those standards, and the pacing guide set forth by them is the foundation for any grade/subject level. Choice (**B**) is correct.

59. C

In order to use data to assess instruction, teachers need to develop appropriate assessments to be given at key points during a unit. This will allow them to enhance reflection on their teaching and then adjust the unit or reteach the standards as needed. Choice (**C**) is correct.

60. D

Reflective practice encompasses many aspects to enhance teaching methods. Peer mentoring, induction training, and informal classroom visits all work together to help teachers with reflective practice in their teaching. Self- and peer assessment are key to guiding the new teacher into the reflective-practice mindset. Informal visits quickly followed by collaborative reflection time allow for strong implementation of this portion of reflective practice. Choice (**D**) is correct.

61. D

Anytime they suspect child abuse or neglect, teachers are bound by mandated reporting laws to notify the proper authorities. A teacher should never confront the child or the parent about his or her suspicions. Immediately notifying law enforcement or child services—based on the requirements of the locality—is the only option. Choice (**D**) is correct.

62. A

Paraeducators provide invaluable support to students and classroom teachers, but they are not meant to replace the certified teacher. Assigning grades, discussing academic progress with parents, and delivering content are all responsibilities of the certified classroom teacher. Paraeducators—under the supervision of the classroom teacher—are able to assist students with all classwork, either one-on-one or in small groups. Choice (**A**) is correct.

63. C

Teachers should take access to resources into account when it comes to familial communication. If any family is lacking in reliable internet access, then it is not appropriate to use email as the primary means of communication. Likewise, timeliness of communication is essential to providing parents with the best information possible.

The communication should be daily and trackable. So, sending a simple log home with each student maintains timely communication in a way that is accessible to all families and that makes sure any issues are swiftly addressed. Choice (**C**) is correct.

64. B

When a teacher is looking for specific information on a type of special-education disability, a member of the special education faculty is the best resource. The school psychologist can provide specific information on the student, as well as best-practice needs for the classroom environment. While the previous classroom teacher is certainly a good resource for insight on the student, he is probably not an expert on disabilities. Choice (**B**) is correct.

65. D

The first three choices are covered under the Americans with Disabilities Act (ADA), which came into law in 1990. The Equal Educational Opportunities Act (EEOA), signed into law by President Nixon in 1974, addressed civil rights issues in education, barring states from discriminating against students based on gender, race, color, or nationality and requiring public schools to provide for students who do not speak English. In many ways an extension of the Civil Rights Act of 1964, the EEOA was specifically aimed at the segregation of public schools. (**D**) is correct.

66. B

Ms. Jones should choose a method of reflection to which she can refer in subsequent years as she plans lessons. Keeping a journal would best suit that objective. Choice (**B**) is correct.

67. C

Teachers have the responsibility to follow federal copyright laws and district policies for media use in the classroom. The school librarian/media specialist is the expert resource help in these areas. While the other choices may be valid resources, they are not the best options for ensuring that the teacher follows federal and district guidelines. Choice (**C**) is correct.

68. C

Once stakeholders have been identified and approval secured, the next step in a community collaboration project would be to secure the methods for implementation. This means identifying, applying for, and obtaining funding. Choice (**C**) is correct.

69. B

The Family Educational Rights and Privacy Act protects student education records. Samantha's records can only be released with written permission from the custodial parent(s). All other requests would violate this policy. Choice (**B**) is correct.

70. C

Teachers need frequent, consistent, and well-planned time with their professional team. The meetings need to be planned in advance so that teachers have enough time to complete their collaborative work. Choice (**C**) is correct.

Sample Response to Question 1

The BESTT score report is a rich source of data about Ms. Hawke's students' abilities. From the BESTT data, for instance, Ms. Hawke can see that her students are working slightly above grade level in reading, and are at grade level, or slightly below, in mathematics. Because "above grade level" is abstract, Ms. Hawke can use the test's interpretation guide and skill reports to get a fine-tuned sense of her students' skills in specific areas. Ms. Hawke can also use her students' percentile scores to see how their performance compared to that of other students around the country; her class's mean mathematics percentile score of 51 indicates that her students scored higher than 51 percent of students nationally. Ms. Hawke should be able to use these math and reading results to help shape whole-class and individual learning opportunities that best meet her students' skill levels.

The diagnostic exercise—a type of formative assessment—also provides a wealth of information for Ms. Hawke to consider. By observing individual students' problem-solving processes, Ms. Hawke can judge how well they understand the fundamentals of multiplication and also, perhaps, what kinds of learners they are (kinesthetic, visual, etc.). As a result of these observations, Ms. Hawke should be able to shape effective math instructional activities suitable for the needs and skill levels of her students.

Sample Response to Question 2

Given the very wide variation in percentile scores reported in the BESTT scoring summary, Ms. Hawke will need to avoid a "one-size-fits-all" approach to reading and mathematics instruction. Ms. Hawke should be especially careful in developing appropriate math content and instructional strategies, as results indicate that students' learning levels vary from considerably below grade level to significantly above. There are several ways, however, for a teacher to include students of diverse skill levels in an assignment with a common content focus. One approach would be to use a mix of whole-class instruction and ability-grouped instruction. Ability-based small-group instruction, when it is used effectively, gives the most skilled students opportunities to grow on a daily basis. During whole-class instruction, Ms. Hawke could give high-achieving students opportunities to share their expertise and guide her work on the board, thus bringing them into the activities.

Ms. Hawke can also use the diagnostic exercise to determine what kind of instruction is likely to work best for each student. To give one example: the students who tried to solve the multiplication problem using blocks may be kinesthetic learners; if Ms. Hawke finds that these students are continuing to struggle with the math concepts she is teaching, then she may wish to work with them one-on-one or in learning-style groups in ways that reflect the approaches they prefer.

Sample Response to Question 3

If Mr. Halpert cannot answer all student questions during lecture, he could have Ms. Tanaka write down the names of everyone whose hands went up but were not called on. She could then address those questions on an individual basis, either quietly during lecture, or while students are working on activities and writing later in the class. Taking note of all students who had questions would let students know that every question was valuable, and getting their questions answered individually would make it less likely that students like Michael would interrupt the class by shouting out their questions.

Sample Response to Question 4

Michael stands up from his seat repeatedly, interrupts the class by calling out answers, and focuses for a long period of time only when in constant motion, such as in his martial arts class. Fidgeting, inability to stay still, and lack of focus while stationary often characterize ADHD and similar disorders associated with hyperactivity.

Michael switched topics from history to English, a behavior that Mr. Halpert describes to Mr. Keene as typical. Students with attention disorders have trouble focusing on one task and often switch between thoughts rapidly. This example is less clear-cut than the first, however; Michael appears to be at least attempting to stay on task, as Mr. Halpert reports that Michael's responses are at least tangentially related to the topic at hand.

PLT Grades 7–12 Practice Test

2 Hours: 70 Selected-Response Questions and 4 Constructed-Response Questions

Directions: On test day and on this practice test, standard time to complete this test is 120 minutes, and there are 74 questions. You are not penalized for wrong answers on the Praxis. Your score is calculated by the number of questions you answer correctly, so select an answer for every question, even if it is a guess.

A seventh-grade science teacher started a lesson on erosion by asking students how powerful they think water is. The students agreed that since they can drink water, it must not be very powerful. The teacher then contrasted this by showing the students a picture of the Grand Canyon and telling them it was formed by water.

1. Which of the following strategies was this teacher using to motivate her students?

   A. Transfer

   B. Negative reinforcement

   C. Cognitive dissonance

   D. Metacognition

2. Which of the following terms best describes the application of learning from one context to a new situation?

   A. Schema

   B. Self-determination

   C. Attribution

   D. Transfer

3. The chemistry team at Rickford High School is working on a common summative assessment for a unit on chemical structure. Which of the following will provide the best data to demonstrate that each student has learned the required standards of the unit?

   A. An individual project on an assigned chemical element

   B. A group project on an assigned chemical element

   C. A test based on the key standards of the unit

   D. An individual paper on three types of chemical elements

4. Ms. Evans is designing a science project for her class. She wants to be able to evaluate their projects efficiently and group the characteristics of the assignment together to give each student one overall score. Which of the following best describes the type of evaluative tool Ms. Evans is seeking?

   A. Anecdotal notes

   B. Scoring continuum

   C. Analytic scoring rubric

   D. Holistic scoring rubric

5. Which of the following is an acceptable assessment format for a teacher who wants to include student input?

    A. Observation

    B. Performance

    C. Rubric

    D. Conference

6. As part of a science unit, Ms. Trisan presents her students with polluted water and encourages them to develop their own ways of purifying it. Which of the following theories is Ms. Trisan using in her classroom?

    A. Constructivism

    B. Behaviorism

    C. Cognitivism

    D. Socialism

7. **For each instructional strategy, identify the instructional model with which it is most associated.**

	Direct instruction	**Experiential instruction**	**Independent instruction**
Role-play			
Research projects			
Learning contracts			
Demon-strations			

8. Which of the following best describes an example of a teacher using an indirect instructional strategy?

    A. Students are presented with a complex geometric shape and must work with a partner to compute its area.

    B. Students use a teacher-generated study guide to take notes on a video demonstration of how to use watercolor paint in art class.

    C. The teacher models how to construct an outline for an essay.

    D. Students visit a natural history museum and take a guided tour through the dinosaur exhibit.

9. What type of measurement is obtained by administering the same test two or more times to the same group of students?

    A. Validity

    B. Standard deviation

    C. Scaled score

    D. Reliability

10. Hillside High School is located in a rural farming area. The community is small but active within the school. Which of the following would NOT be considered a primary stakeholder in this school?

    A. Local business owner

    B. Parents

    C. Students

    D. Textbook company

11. Which of the following statements conveys most accurately how standards should be considered in developing units and lesson plans?

    A. Standards documents should be set up so teachers can use them to create lists of terms for students to memorize.

    B. Standards should be suggested resources, like additional reading material in the classroom library.

    C. Teachers should be responsible for ensuring that students demonstrate understanding of concepts addressed in the standards.

    D. Teachers should take the initiative and choose which learning standards they feel students will most need to understand.

12. Mr. Jameson wants to ensure he is integrating his understanding of schema theory into his science planning. Which of the following would apply schema theory to support his students' learning?

    Select all that apply.

    A. Using a concept map to draw connections between the topics in the unit on evolution

    B. Allowing a student who missed yesterday's lesson to turn in the homework at a later date

    C. Describing a virus by comparing its functions to a monster in a movie with which the students are familiar

    D. Creating a "city" cell that draws an analogy between the functions of the organelles in a cell to those of jobs in a city

13. Which of the following strategies is most closely associated with independent instruction?

    A. Concept mapping

    B. Field trips

    C. Demonstrations

    D. Learning contracts

14. Which of the following terms describes whether an evaluation can be expected to consistently produce the same results?

    A. Validity

    B. Reliability

    C. Norm

    D. Criterion

15. A ninth-grade language arts teacher is planning a research unit for her students. She wants to begin by introducing her students to the tools they can use to conduct their research. Which of the following instructional planning partners might be able to collaborate effectively to support this unit?

    A. Library media specialist

    B. Special-education teacher

    C. Paraeducator

    D. Assistant principal

16. Which of the following refers to an area of learning that a student is not yet able to do independently but is able to do with support or guidance?

    A. Zone of proximal development

    B. Classical and operant conditioning

    C. Cognitive dissonance

    D. Intrinsic motivation

17. Which of the following is the best illustration of Erikson's stage of psychosocial development called identity vs. role confusion?

    A. Being assertive and initiating activity with others

    B. Initiating control in determining appropriate actions

    C. Considering a future job and role in the world

    D. Gaining an understanding of cause and effect

18. The English department at Kennedy High School is planning to teach a different set of novels in the upcoming school year. Which of the following are appropriate ways to inform the stakeholders of this change?

    Select all that apply.

    A. Newspaper announcements

    B. School newsletters

    C. Academic journal articles

    D. No announcements at all, since this change does not require stakeholder notification

19. Which of the following situations illustrates peer assessment used effectively in the classroom?

    A. Ms. Whittier's ninth-grade English class takes a vocabulary quiz. When the students have finished, they grade each other's papers.

    B. Ms. Jackson's ninth-grade English class is working on personal narratives. She has students read them aloud to the class and then score their peers using a rubric.

    C. Mr. Eli has his ninth-grade English class students pair up and read each other's essay rough drafts. Then the partners give each other feedback on their writing.

    D. Mr. Shoemaker has his ninth-grade English class write the test questions for their upcoming summative assessment on *Great Expectations*.

20. Mr. Burge is a history teacher at North High School. He is teaching a unit on World War II and wants his students to gather newspaper articles from that time period. The students will then write their own newspaper articles as if they were reporting on that time period. What would be considered the best assessment tool for him to use for this assignment?

    A. A rubric

    B. A continuum

    C. Anecdotal notes

    D. An analytical checklist

21. Which of the following are likely to contribute to an inclusive and positive classroom environment?

    Select all that apply.

    A. Allowing students to sit with whomever they want from Day 1

    B. Engaging families in curriculum activities and after-school events

    C. Spending time teaching students how to interact positively during cooperative work

    D. Collaboratively creating a classroom code of conduct

22. Ms. Baretto has been making an effort to use precise vocabulary when leading discussions in her tenth-grade history class. For example, instead of asking students what might have happened if President Lincoln had not been assassinated, she asks them to *speculate*. She also uses verbs and phrases such as *analyze*, *compare*, and *provide evidence*. Which of the following describes the primary way in which Ms. Baretto's approach helps students?

    A. It encourages appropriate behavior.

    B. It introduces a variety of critical thinking skills.

    C. It encourages creative ways of writing reports.

    D. It emphasizes the role of language in decisions.

23. Ms. Trebon is planning her math lesson. Which of the following objectives would best engage her students at a high level on Bloom's taxonomy?

    A. Students will be able to describe what an outlier is.

    B. Students will be able to evaluate which experimental design would produce the most generalizable results.

    C. Students will be able to summarize how to estimate the square root of an imperfect square.

    D. Students will be able to perform operations using numbers written in scientific notation.

24. Which of the following is an example of a formative assessment?

    A. Ms. Wheeler has her twelfth-grade economics students complete exit tickets at the end of each class session.

    B. Mr. Hill's tenth-grade geometry class takes a chapter test on special triangles.

    C. Ms. Rodriguez has her ninth-grade child development class watch a video on the learning stages of toddlers.

    D. Mr. Huntington has his tenth-grade English class complete a reading guide while reading *The Grapes of Wrath*.

25. Ms. Leakey is a biology teacher at Canyon High School. She is teaching an advanced class on genetics and assumes her students will have some basic knowledge in the subject before beginning the class. What is the best way for her to determine what her students already know compared to what she wants to teach in the class?

    A. Giving students a pre-test on the first day of class, based on key standards for the course

    B. Having students complete a survey about what they want to learn in the class

    C. Meeting with community members to determine what resources are available to her class

    D. Researching what other high school genetics classes in her state are learning

26. David's teachers have noticed that he has had difficulty building and maintaining personal relationships and often exhibits impulsive reactions. Which of the following areas of exceptionality is David exhibiting?

    A. Cognitive

    B. Auditory

    C. Behavioral

    D. Speech/language

27. Which of the following best describes an observable and measurable instructional objective for a unit on early American history?

    A. Students will learn the importance of agriculture to the colonies.

    B. Students will understand the major differences between early and modern American society.

    C. Students will recognize the value of trade and knowledge sharing with Native American tribes.

    D. Students will compare and contrast the lifestyles of American colonists with those of people who remained in their countries of birth.

28. Mr. Mindela is determining the standards that his history class will cover in their next unit. Which of these is he working to determine?

    A. Sequence

    B. Theme

    C. Scope

    D. Topic

29. Which of these assessment methods is or are appropriate for a modern dance performance class?

    Select <u>all</u> that apply.

    A. Portfolio

    B. Performance

    C. Research paper

    D. Selected-response

30. Several English, social science, and science teachers at a high school have expressed interest in developing interdisciplinary thematic units. All of the teachers have taught thematic units previously, but none has taught on an interdisciplinary team. They each have done some background reading on interdisciplinary teaching. Which of the following steps should the teachers tackle together first in order to decide whether or not to proceed in a collective effort to provide a successful interdisciplinary thematic unit?

    A. Choosing a theme and developing a timeline for the interdisciplinary unit

    B. Collaborating by discussing learning benefits and possible pitfalls of interdisciplinary teaching

    C. Sharing lesson plans and teaching materials from various thematic units they have taught previously

    D. Developing the scope and sequence of the content and instruction of the interdisciplinary thematic unit

31. Which of the following are elements of successful teacher collaboration?

    Select <u>all</u> that apply.

    A. Building professional relationships

    B. Building student relationships

    C. Shared collaboration time

    D. Shared responsibility

32. Which of the following is an example of a teacher complying with copyright laws and fair use guidelines?

    A. A teacher instructs students that they may include a 10- to 20-second music clip in their multimedia presentation.

    B. A teacher purchases and shows a recent box office hit movie in class as a reward for good behavior.

    C. A teacher scans a novel and posts each chapter on the class website as she assigns that chapter.

    D. A teacher copies workbook pages and distributes them to students.

33. A teacher preparing a unit on plant biology plans a lesson in which students work in groups to observe, identify, and classify plants growing near their campus, and then reflect together on their work. Which of the following instructional models does this plan reflect?

    A. Experiential

    B. Direct

    C. Indirect

    D. Independent

34. Which of the following would be considered a formal evaluation?

    A. A weekly, non-graded vocabulary quiz

    B. A year-end final mathematics exam

    C. An impromptu science project with a lab report

    D. A chapter summary of the class concerning Archduke Franz Ferdinand

35. When beginning to plan a lesson using the reflective teaching model, which of the following is the best first step for a teacher to follow?

    A. Using the data from last year's assessment on the lesson

    B. Determining what the students need to know by the end of the lesson

    C. Asking other teachers how they plan for the same/similar lesson

    D. Writing the final assessment first and then planning the lesson

36. Ms. Prez is a new teacher at Mr. Embiid's school and is struggling to get her students settled and started on work when they arrive in the morning. What advice should Mr. Embiid give to Ms. Prez to help her productively start her lessons each day?

    A. Adjust her expectations to meet the students where they are.

    B. Allow students five minutes at the beginning of class to chat and get settled before beginning instructional material.

    C. Try a different routine each day for a month to see what students respond to best.

    D. Establish a simple entry routine for students to follow and practice it with the students to ensure they understand the expectation.

    Mr. Filsaime, an eighth-grade history teacher, calls on students at random during class discussions. During today's class, he calls on a student named Oceane and says, "In the early 1920s, Warren G. Harding's administration was rocked by a sensational corruption scandal. Please tell the class what that scandal came to be called." Oceane has had humiliating public speaking experiences in other classes, which have left her very uneasy about answering questions aloud. Startled and suddenly short of breath, she mumbles, "The one with the funny name." Mr. Filsaime says, "Exactly: the Teapot Dome scandal. Nice work!"

37. The shortness of breath Oceane suffered in response to Mr. Filsaime's question was most likely an effect of which of the following kinds of conditioning?

    A. Classical conditioning

    B. Operant conditioning

    C. Olfactory conditioning

    D. Inadequate conditioning

38. Which of the following are examples of transfer of learning?

    Select all that apply.

    A. Reciting the atomic masses of different elements through a song

    B. Writing letters to a local paper to practice elements of logical structure and debate

    C. Applying concepts of recursion learned in math class to draw fractals in art class

    D. Writing personal memoirs based off of a memoir read in class

39. Mr. Franklin is teaching his high school government class about speech and debate. He is planning on holding a mock debate on the pros and cons of the Electoral College. This is an example of

    A. intellectual freedom

    B. a Fourth Amendment right

    C. equal access

    D. due process

    Ms. Anderson informs her tenth-grade students they will soon be reading a novel set in the northeastern United States in the 1920s. She asks students to recall what they have learned or seen about the region and the time period in order to both assess their familiarity with the setting of the novel and prepare them for concepts they may encounter while reading.

40. Ms. Anderson is most likely attempting to access her students'

    A. scaffolds

    B. schemas

    C. zones of proximal development

    D. memories

41. Mr. Vance has noticed that some of the students in his algebra class learn better by working with physical manipulatives, while others prefer virtual manipulatives. Knowing this, Mr. Vance intentionally plans his next lesson to include both physical and virtual manipulatives. Which of the following is Mr. Vance doing?

    A. Scaffolding instruction

    B. Modeling skills

    C. Differentiating instruction

    D. Coaching

42. Which of the following are considered parts of the role of a mentor?

    Select all that apply.

    A. Maintaining confidentiality

    B. Providing lesson plans to mentees

    C. Reporting on mentees to a supervisor

    D. Aiding in the development of teaching skills

43. After Jackie and Amanda both performed poorly on a recent exam, Jackie decided to make a new study schedule, while Amanda wrote a letter to the principal about her teacher. Which of the following might explain their differing responses to the situation?

    A. Attribution theory

    B. Cognitive dissonance

    C. Zone of proximal development

    D. Bloom's taxonomy

A ninth-grade teacher begins a unit on speech writing and public speaking by assigning students a 10-minute quickwrite in which they describe their past experiences and personal feelings regarding public speaking.

44. Which of the following best explains the teacher's rationale for choosing this activity?

    A. The teacher is providing scaffolding while students learn to communicate thoughts in a narrative form.

    B. The teacher is testing students' public-speaking abilities before beginning instruction.

    C. The teacher is motivating students to actively engage in the material to be presented.

    D. The teacher is assessing students' backgrounds to understand their preliminary attitudes and expectations in order to customize instruction.

45. Ms. Friedman teaches composition at Westvale High School. She wants her students to improve on sentence variation in their latest writing assignment. She has a specific set of criteria that students need to meet to achieve a specific score. She makes notes on their papers, telling them whether they meet these criteria and also providing suggestions on how to improve. This is an example of

    A. holistic grading

    B. analytical scoring

    C. norm-referenced assessment

    D. performance

46. Which of the following would NOT function as a component of reflective practice?

    A. Reflective journal

    B. Online webinar

    C. Incident analysis

    D. Portfolio

47. Joel, a student in Mr. Hinkie's math class, has low self-efficacy. If Mr. Hinkie wants to improve Joel's self-efficacy, which of the following strategies would be most likely to help?

   Select <u>all</u> that apply.

   A. Planning a lecture that requires no student input and therefore no opportunities for failure

   B. Comparing Joel's performance to that of his sister, who consistently won awards for high achievement in Mr. Hinkie's class last year

   C. Working with Joel to set, track, and evaluate attainable and measurable goals

   D. Providing Joel with frequent, focused feedback

48. Hannah, a tenth-grade student, has been consistently achieving high marks in her math class this year, but she struggled in her math class last year. On the other hand, she is receiving poor marks in her English class this year but did very well in her English class last year. Which of the following learning variables most likely explains this discrepancy?

   A. Socioeconomic status

   B. Learning style

   C. Culture

   D. Cognitive development

Mr. Herrera has noticed that a student in his social studies course who has special needs has begun to experience a drop in his course grade. The student participates in class discussions of videos relevant to the day's lesson, but he does not join in when the class discusses readings, especially of primary-source documents. This student has also been inconsistent with homework, particularly writing assignments. When Mr. Herrera meets with the student to better understand the issue, the student tells him, "These readings are just boring and stupid. What are they even talking about?"

49. Which member of Mr. Herrera's school staff should he seek out for advice about helping this student improve his class performance?

   A. A paraeducator

   B. A special-education teacher

   C. A counselor

   D. An intervention specialist

50. Which one of the following questions best stimulates complex thinking?

   A. What are three differences between poetry and prose?

   B. How is the period of a signal related to its frequency?

   C. Do you agree with George's decision to kill his friend? Why or why not?

   D. Can you provide an example of a metaphor?

51. Ms. Collins was told she will be getting a new student, Chelsea, in her tenth-grade history class. Chelsea is on an IEP with the disability of orthopedic impairment due to cerebral palsy. The school is also assigning a paraeducator, Ms. Toth, to assist in Ms. Collins' class. What should Ms. Toth's primary role in the class be?

    A. To help Ms. Collins teach lessons to make sure Chelsea understands the material

    B. To grade all of Chelsea's work to ensure she meets the standards

    C. To be the primary communicator between the school and Chelsea's parents, to keep them updated on her progress in class

    D. To assist any student in the class, but maintain a primary focus on Chelsea

52. Mr. Robin noticed very little interaction when her students worked together on a worksheet about square roots. But he noticed significant positive interaction when he provided them with square posters of different sizes and had them try to estimate the length of the sides, after providing them with the area but no measuring tools. Which of the following strategies for helping students develop self-motivation might explain this difference?

    A. Providing frequent positive feedback

    B. Deemphasizing grades

    C. Including students in instructional decisions

    D. Assigning valuable tasks

53. Ms. Khan finds that the students in her twelfth-grade social studies class have an average score of 65 percent on the unit test on economics. Which of the following is the most effective response to the results?

    A. Send the tests home and require that students get the signature of a parent or guardian

    B. Identify which objectives students did not achieve, then reteach using varied strategies

    C. Have students re-read the text that covers the material they did not master and give them the test again

    D. Offer rewards to those who come in for additional lessons about economics after school

54. Which of the following scenarios is indicative of reflective practice in teaching?

    A. Ms. Kiston is planning lessons for a new unit in her art history class. She accomplishes this by copying last year's lesson plans into her plans for this year.

    B. Mr. Jenkins finished a unit in his Spanish class with a summative assessment. He compiles the data and puts it in his professional development binder to be given to his principal at the end of the school year.

    C. Mr. Latham completed a lesson on the Civil War by having students create posters depicting key battles. He displays them in the hallway for others in the school to see.

    D. Ms. Weston is planning a lesson in English class for the novel *Great Expectations*. She refers to her notes from last year to remind her that the activities need to be changed to increase student engagement. In talking with her department members, she finds that Mr. Lyle has some ideas that she would like to incorporate. She makes arrangements to observe Mr. Lyle teaching a lesson with these new ideas.

55. Bertha says, "All eukaryotic cells have membrane-bound organelles. Therefore, since my cells are eukaryotic cells, my cells must have membrane-bound organelles." Which learning process is she engaging in when she says this?

    A. Inductive reasoning

    B. Deductive reasoning

    C. Recall

    D. Planning

During a whole-class review of the homework, Ms. Kelley asks Joe to answer a question, and Joe responds incorrectly.

56. Which of the following illustrates Ms. Kelley's best response to Joe's incorrect answer?

    A. Tell Joe that he is incorrect and ask a classmate to answer instead.

    B. Tell Joe that he is incorrect and admonish him for not completing his homework with care.

    C. Reply with a noncommittal sound and ask a classmate to answer instead.

    D. Thank Joe, tell him that he is incorrect, and ask him how he arrived at that answer.

57. Which of the following is a component of effective questioning?

    A. Allowing think/wait time

    B. Asking only definition-based questions

    C. Promoting passive listening

    D. Encouraging participation through candy rewards

58. Ms. Marnes is planning how to motivate more of her ninth-grade students to read outside of class time. Which of the following would be the most effective?

    A. Having students record the amount of time that they have read and tying it directly to their grades

    B. Working with the students and the librarian to let them choose books in which they are interested

    C. Reminding students that they will need to demonstrate strong reading comprehension skills on the SAT

    D. Holding a prize drawing for students who have read above a certain threshold each month

59. Which of the following are students most likely to develop during their adolescent years?

    A. A greater desire for peer influence and acceptance

    B. A belief that rules may not apply to them

    C. The beginnings of an understanding of what it means to feel embarrassed

    D. An interest in pretend play, but with some confusion about what is real

60. Julie, a tenth grader at Buena Vista High School, received her performance report in the state reading and math tests. Julie had a score in the 78th percentile for reading and the 67th percentile in math. What does Julie's math score indicate?

    A. She performed below 67% of her peers.

    B. She performed above 67% of her peers in her school.

    C. She performed above 67% of her peers in the state.

    D. She performed above 67% of her peers in the country.

61. Which of the following is an appropriate scenario for a professional learning community?

    A. The entire school staff meets to discuss behavior and discipline data for the school.

    B. A small group of teachers meets weekly to review student performance in the classroom.

    C. The teachers at a school receive training on how to administer a new standardized test.

    D. The principal holds a weekly staff meeting to inform teachers of ongoing news in the school and district.

62. Which of the following is an example of a statement that is negatively intrinsic?

    A. Teacher: If you do this project, you will get 10 bonus points.

    B. Student: I don't want to do this project.

    C. Teacher: If you don't complete this project, you will lose the privilege of attending Friday's field trip.

    D. Student: I really want to do this project.

63. Ms. Duane, a twelfth-grade composition teacher, is finding logical fallacies in the rough drafts of her students' research papers. She decides to teach a unit on logic. As she explains the concept of syllogism, which one of the following visual aids would prove most helpful?

    A. Pie chart

    B. Line graph

    C. Venn diagram

    D. Bar graph

64. What is the correct order of steps for successful collaboration?

    A. 1. Seeking support

       2. Identifying the stakeholders

       3. Identifying the purpose of the collaboration

       4. Developing an action plan

    B. 1. Developing an action plan

       2. Identifying the stakeholders

       3. Identifying the purpose of the collaboration

       4. Seeking support

    C. 1. Seeking support

       2. Developing an action plan

       3. Identifying the stakeholders

       4. Identifying the purpose of the collaboration

    D. 1. Developing an action plan

       2. Identifying the purpose of the collaboration

       3. Identifying the stakeholders

       4. Seeking support

65. Which of the following is an example of score interpretation using a criterion-referenced assessment?

    A. Looking at percentile scores of a student's ACT test

    B. Using grade-level equivalent reading tests to determine the level of difficulty of the novel to be used in English class

    C. Administering an end-of-unit math test to determine what concepts students have learned

    D. Administering a high school entrance exam to determine eligibility for an honors program

66. Which of the following is an example of an objective in the psychomotor domain?

   A. Students will be able to cooperate in group activities.

   B. Students will be able to use textual evidence to make predictions.

   C. Students will be able to coordinate signal use and wheel operation when driving a car.

   D. Students will be able to write a personal narrative.

Mary is a tenth-grade student at Cross High School. She has math class with Ms. Engel right after lunch. Ms. Engel has noticed that Mary seems less focused in class and that she has fallen asleep twice in the last week. From talking with Mary, Ms. Engel learns that Mary has not been eating lunch and often misses breakfast because her father lost his job and money is tight at her house.

67. Who in the school is the best resource to refer Mary to for additional help?

   A. A school resource officer

   B. A guidance counselor

   C. A school health aide

   D. The principal

Ms. Lewendowski, the eleventh-grade American history teacher, uses both direct (lecture) and indirect (problem-based) teaching methods. She notices, however, that several of her English language learners (ELLs) and a few other students are doing poorly on lecture quizzes. They do not seem to understand key words and concepts.

68. Which one of the following remediation modifications would be most appropriate for Ms. Lewendowski to employ to help these high school students understand her history lectures?

   A. Using simple (sixth-grade) vocabulary in the lecture

   B. Eliminating complex historical concepts from the lecture

   C. Assigning additional textbook questions as homework for those students who are doing poorly on the lecture quizzes

   D. Pre-teaching key vocabulary and providing a variety of visual aids to supplement the lecture

69. Which of the following is most likely to be relevant when examining protections for students with disabilities who are looking for job training?

   A. Americans with Disabilities Act

   B. No Child Left Behind Act

   C. Common Core State Standards Initiative

   D. Individuals with Disabilities Education Act

70. Which type of score compares an individual's performance to performance averages for individuals of certain ages?

   A. Age-equivalent score

   B. Scaled score

   C. Percentile score

   D. Grade-equivalent score

Approximate time: 25 minutes

Directions: The case history below is followed by two short-answer questions. Your responses to the questions will be evaluated with respect to professionally accepted principles and practices in teaching and learning. Be sure to answer all parts of the questions.

Scenario: Mr. Duncan is a first-year mathematics teacher in a suburban middle school. He has asked his team leader, Ms. Garcia, for assistance with his second-period eighth-grade algebra class. The class has 23 students, 3 of whom are seventh graders.

Document 1

Discussion between Mr. Duncan and Ms. Garcia

Ms. Garcia: I understand you would like some help with your algebra class. What seems to be giving you trouble?

Mr. Duncan: Well, class usually begins well. The students enter and review homework, but when it's time to transition to the new lesson, the simple act of turning in homework and getting out textbooks seems to eat up a third of the class time. I'm especially concerned that Duane and Julia seem to be making it difficult for everyone to focus on moving along and accomplishing the task at hand. They seem to cause a disturbance from which the class can't recover. It just seems like the rest of the class loses focus then, and many students aren't getting the new material. I guess I just don't know what to do to keep the students on task.

Mrs. Garcia: I've certainly struggled with transition times, too. Let me come and observe for a day before I offer suggestions.

Mr. Duncan: Sure. I really hope you can help me figure this out. I try to plan really exciting lessons, but I feel like it all goes to waste when the students are checked out. I'm feeling really discouraged.

Document 2

Ms. Garcia's Observation Notes

Mr. Duncan greeted students personally as they entered. He seemed to have a good rapport with the students, and they entered the room in an orderly fashion, taking their seats and getting out their homework. Some students began comparing answers while others chatted.

After about five minutes, Mr. Duncan came to the front of the room and asked the students to focus on the homework from last night. He asked what problems they would like to review as a class, and several students raised their hands. Mr. Duncan called on Julia, and the class worked through a problem together. They then reviewed four additional problems as a group, with the teacher calling on various students to provide the work. Most students followed along and even engaged with the review. There was a group of girls in the back who were quietly chatting, and Duane was playing a game on his phone under the desk, though he did contribute a step to a homework problem when asked.

When the review was complete, Mr. Duncan asked the class to pass the homework to the front of the room and get out their textbooks. Upon hearing this direction, Julia and a few girls nearby began to chat about a new clothing store that had opened nearby. Mr. Duncan immediately told the girls to stop and ready themselves for work. They lowered their voices. Duane loudly dropped his book and made a show of sighing and having to put his magazine on top of the desk to get up and groaning as he reached for the book. The class laughed loudly, and other books began to fall around the room. At this point, conversations popped up everywhere and

Mr. Duncan was visibly irritated. He raised his voice and told the class that there would be a doubled workload if they couldn't get ready for the lesson. He then leaned on his desk and indicated that he could wait. He did so for about five minutes before raising his voice again and telling them that homework would now be twice what it was, Julia whispered loudly from the back that he always says that. There were some giggles, but the class slowly opened their books to begin the lesson.

Document 3

Post-observation Conference

Ms. Garcia: How do you think the lesson went?

Mr. Duncan: Well, I think you saw what a problem it is to get the class to go from the homework review into the lesson. Every day, they come in so nicely and get started, and I feel hopeful. But then . . . Well, you saw how they were on task, and then Duane made that scene and set everybody off, and Julia and her friends just pretended I wasn't there.

Ms. Garcia: Mr. Duncan, I think we can work through this. Classroom management can be tricky, and transitions are the toughest part.

Constructed-Response Questions

Question 1

Describe at least TWO strategies that Mr. Duncan can use to settle the class down during the transition between activities.

Question 2

Explain how EACH of the two strategies will help the students to settle in and focus. Base your answers on the principles of classroom management.

Approximate time: 25 minutes

Directions: The case history below is followed by two short-answer questions. Your responses to the questions will be evaluated with respect to professionally accepted principles and practices in teaching and learning. Be sure to answer all parts of the questions. Write your answers on the pages indicated in your answer sheet booklet.

Scenario: Mr. Frederick is a third-year eighth-grade language arts teacher whose class has been reading *The Giver* by Lois Lowry. The class completed study guides that required them to answer basic questions about the plot and characters. Students have done most of the reading as a whole group or in self-selected groups, where they fill in their study guides as they move along. Mr. Frederick has chosen groups to report out on each chapter, and he reviewed the study guides with the class. He also assigned the class a short-answer homework assignment that he graded. The assignment required the students to answer two out of four questions.

Out of the 28 students in the class, 4 completed question 1, 25 completed question 2, 12 completed question 3, and 15 completed question 4.

Mr. Frederick asked for advice from his team leader because he found that the majority of the class earned a D on the final essay due to an extreme focus on the research portion and a lack of depth of analysis when comparing the communities.

Document 1

Homework Assignment

Homework Assignment: Answer two of the following questions.

1. Discuss the advantages and disadvantages of Sameness in the community.

2. After Jonas is chosen as the Receiver of Memory, why is he isolated from his friends and family?

3. In what ways does Jonas's community appear to be a utopia? Why do the things you list contribute to creating perfection?

4. Why have feelings and memories been eliminated in the community?

Document 2

Final Essay Topic

Utopian communities have been previously established in the United States. Research one of these communities and compare it to Jonas's community.

Constructed-Response Questions

Question 3

Describe TWO ways in which the teacher could use instructional strategies to support the learner's achievement on the final task.

Question 4

Describe TWO ways in which the teacher can utilize the homework assignment as a formative assessment to create scaffolding prior to assigning the essay.

IF YOU FINISH BEFORE TIME IS CALLED, YOU MAY CHECK YOUR WORK ON THIS SECTION ONLY. DO NOT TURN TO ANY OTHER SECTION IN THE TEST. | STOP

412 K

PLT Grades 7–12 Practice Test Answers and Explanations

1. C

Choice (**C**) is correct because this teacher was creating a contrast for her students. It doesn't make sense that water is both not powerful and able to form the Grand Canyon, and students will want to resolve this discrepancy.

2. D

Transfer of learning is critical for students to be able to apply learning in one lesson or one classroom in a new context. Therefore, choice (**D**) is correct.

3. C

While most teachers desire to have students demonstrate acquired knowledge through a variety of applications, there are times when administering a test is the best practice for collecting data. Group and individual projects have value, but in this case, they are not geared toward a summative goal: understanding of multiple key standards. The listed projects do not focus on the unit as a whole—just on one component. Choice (**C**) is based on evaluating students on multiple aspects of the unit and identifying the key standards of the unit.

4. D

A holistic scoring rubric would allow Ms. Evans to give each student one score. It is a more efficient (albeit more general) evaluation that would give the students an assessment of how they did on the project as a whole. Therefore, choice (**D**) is correct. If Ms. Evans were instead looking to provide specific feedback on individual skills within the project, she would want to consider an analytic scoring rubric instead.

5. D

Asking for a student's input on his perception of skills learned can be a valuable tool for determining whether desired standards have been met. While all forms of assessment require the student to submit work, only conferencing is designed to allow the student

reflective time to add to the final assessment. Choice (**D**) is correct.

6. A

Constructivism emphasizes that learners create their own reality and that learning happens when learners interpret the world based on their experiences. Therefore, students are more likely to learn in authentic contexts. Ms. Trisan is allowing the students to generate their own solutions to an authentic problem. Choice (**A**) is correct. Both behaviorism, (B), and cognitivism, (C), often examine how to transfer knowledge to students. Socialism, (D), is a political and economic theory.

7. Role-play is an example of **experiential instruction**—which, as the name suggests, is about learning through experience.

Research projects and learning contracts are both examples of **independent instruction**, which emphasizes student initiative.

Demonstrations are examples of **direct instruction**, which is teacher directed and largely about "showing" instead of facilitating.

8. A

Indirect instruction requires a high level of student involvement in active learning; the problem-solving and inquiry activities described in choice (**A**) are typical instructional strategies of this approach. Activities that require the teacher to construct meaning for students, through demonstration, tours, or explicit teaching, do not best exemplify indirect instruction.

9. D

Test reliability is achieved by two or more administrations of the same test to the same students. Choice (**D**) is correct.

10. D

Stakeholders are people who have direct impact on and who benefit from the school. While textbook companies provide valuable resources for the school, they are not primary stakeholders in the school. Local business owners, parents, and students are all members of the direct community. They work together for the mutual benefit of the school and the students. Choice (**D**) is correct.

11. C

Standards convey what skills students should master and what knowledge they should have at certain points in their scholastic careers. It is the role of teachers to ensure that students master the skills and concepts outlined in their grade-level standards, as described in choice (**C**). Standards encompass a much broader set of skills than memorization, (A). They are also the primary benchmarks for student learning, not a suggested additional resource, (B), or a list from which teachers can pick based on personal opinion or experience, (D).

12. A, C, D

Schema theory describes how people organize information by incorporating new information into their existing schema. Choice (**A**) would help students incorporate information by directly illustrating some of the connections between what might be a student's existing schema and the new information. Choices (**C**) and (**D**) both help make new information relevant to prior knowledge, which will help the students draw connections and retain the new information.

13. D

Learning contracts, (**D**), facilitate a plan of learning between students and teachers. Concept mapping, (A), is most associated with indirect instruction; it allows students to be able to draw connections between ideas. Demonstrations, (C), are associated with direct, explicit instruction. Field trips, (B), are associated with experiential instruction.

14. B

Reliability, (**B**), is a measure of how consistent an evaluation is. Validity, (A), describes the degree to which a test is an accurate determination of what it is seeking to

measure. A test can have high reliability without having high validity.

15. A

One of the many roles of a library media specialist, (**A**), is to collaborate with teachers and other members of the school community to support information literacy. While special education teachers, paraeducators, and assistant principals serve key roles in the school building, the library media specialist is best equipped to collaborate with this teacher on this unit.

16. A

The zone of proximal development, or ZPD, is often used by teachers when they are planning instruction. By scaffolding lessons so that students are working above what they are able to do independently, teachers help students move toward being able to do more on their own. Therefore, choice (**A**) is correct.

17. C

During the identity vs. role confusion stage, children develop an idea of who they are and who they want to become. Choice (**C**) correctly illustrates this stage.

18. A, B

Whenever a change to textbooks or core curriculum happens, stakeholders need to be informed. Core content (such as novels taught in an English class) is part of this as well. However, readers of academic journals, (C), are not stakeholders in individual schools. Choices (**A**) and (**B**) are therefore correct.

19. C

Peer assessment is a valuable tool when used properly. Student activities such as grading quizzes or writing test questions do not take full advantage of the benefits of peer assessment. Instead, peer assessment works best when students exchange informal feedback to help each other improve their rough drafts. Choice (**C**) is correct.

20. A

Writing assignments are generally best handled through a rubric. This allows students to preview the criteria and ensure that they are meeting the parameters of the assignment. Choice (**A**) is correct.

21. B, C, D

Choice (A) may be counterproductive. Allowing students to sit with whomever they want may reinforce existing social groups and do little to engage students with others they may not know as well. Choice (B), engaging families, shows students and families that you value their contributions and empowers them to take ownership in their learning and their school. Choice (C) is a critical piece that new teachers often fatally omit. Students have varying background knowledge on how to interact with one another, and taking the time to teach students how to interact can set the stage for positive interaction throughout the year. Choice (D) allows students to work together to establish classroom expectations, thus giving each student ownership of the classroom space.

22. B

Using precise language in context is one way of ensuring that students understand the meanings behind that language. The words Mrs. Baretto uses—*speculate* and *analyze,* especially—denote higher-level critical thinking (B), and by employing the correct words, she reinforces her expectations of her students. The wording of her questions has little to do with student behavior, (A), or decision making, (D), and while reports, (C), may be improved by using precise language, this is not the primary reason to use such language.

23. B

Choice (B) asks students to evaluate, which requires a high level of cognitive complexity and is at a high level on Bloom's taxonomy. Describing, summarizing, and calculating basic operations require lower levels of complexity and are lower on Bloom's taxonomy.

24. A

Formative assessments are used to check for understanding so that teachers can adjust their teaching to meet student needs. The assessments can be formal as long as the teacher uses the information to aid in student learning. In this case, choice (A) provides an example of a formative assessment. Choice (B) is a summative assessment.

25. A

Determining what students know is key to reflective teaching. Teachers need to plan to cover all required elements of a unit, but gathering data on what students know will allow them to tailor the unit to meet the needs of the students. Whether it be the need to cover more information before the required elements of the unit, or just a brief review because the students have the basic standards down, giving a pre-test allows for the appropriate use of data in determining instructional needs. Choice (A) is correct.

26. C

Individual students can exhibit exceptionalities in more than one area, but those described for David are most likely to be behavioral. Choice (C) is correct.

27. D

Choice (D) provides an objective that describes students' actions and, therefore, how their learning can be measured and observed. The other objectives listed do not specify a means of measurement or observation.

28. C

Mr. Mindela is establishing the scope of his upcoming unit. Choice (C) is correct. (A) is incorrect because sequence is the order in which content will be taught.

29. A, B

An assessment for a modern dance performance class would most appropriately assess performance. Students could also compile performances into a portfolio. Therefore, (A) and (B) are correct. A research paper or a selected-response quiz would not allow a teacher to accurately gauge a student's performance mastery, making (C) and (D) incorrect.

30. B

Since none of the teachers has previously taught as part of an interdisciplinary team, their first step should be to determine whether this thematic unit will be a sensible undertaking, as in choice (**B**). Choosing a theme, (A), sharing lesson plans and other materials, (C), and developing the scope and sequence of the unit, (D), are all crucial steps to take once the team has determined that an interdisciplinary thematic unit will meet their students' academic goals and needs.

31. A, C, D

Teachers who are given the time to collaborate see tremendous benefits. This can only be done through shared time to ensure that responsibility is shared and professional relationships are built. Building student relationships, while important for student success, is not part of the professional collaboration process. Choices (**A**), (**C**), and (**D**) are correct.

32. A

According to copyright laws and fair-use guidelines, students may use short clips of videos and music in multimedia presentations for educational purposes; therefore, choice (**A**) is correct. Showing videos for noneducational purposes, scanning or copying entire novels, and copying "consumables" such as workbooks are not allowed.

33. A

Experiential learning characterizes learning through experience, rather than through more abstract classroom lessons. Observing plants in real life, rather than in the classroom, and reflecting on their progress makes this lesson an experiential one; choice (**A**) is correct.

34. B

Informal assessments are great ways for teachers to check for understanding throughout a lesson. They can be in many forms, including check-in quizzes, (A), lab reports, (C), or group shares, (D). On the other hand, formal evaluations (such as the Praxis itself) are standardized to produce reliable data, making (**B**) correct.

35. B

Teachers must determine the desired outcome—or what their students need to know—before they can do any real planning. This is the best tool to help drive planning, as it allows for a more reflective process. Choice (**B**) is correct.

36. D

Consistency is important for students, so Ms. Prez should establish a routine and stick with it. She can talk with other teachers to ask what has worked well for them in the past if she is not sure where to start. A routine can be changed farther down the line, but Ms. Prez will not be able to determine whether or not a routine will work for her classroom unless she has established the routine and practiced it with her students. This aligns with choice (**D**).

37. A

Classical conditioning, or Pavlovian conditioning, occurs when a person associates a stimulus with a given reaction. This shortness of breath is a result of classical conditioning and is often how people physically respond to phobias (such as fear of public speaking). Choice (**A**) is correct.

38. B, C

Transfer of learning involves students applying skills or content learned in one setting to a new situation. Both choices (**B**) and (**C**) ask students to apply a skill (elements of logical structure, mathematical recursion) in a new context.

39. A

Students are being given the chance to seek out and listen to varying viewpoints on a topic. This is the definition of intellectual freedom. Choice (**A**) is correct.

40. B

Schemas, (**B**), are the set of ideas people have about abstract concepts, and they can help students process new information when accessed. While Ms. Anderson may be bringing up students' memories, (D), she is primarily intending to learn about their preconceived notions and prior knowledge about the setting of the novel. Scaffolds, (A), are supports to aid students' independent mastery of a new skill or concept, while zones of proximal development, (C), describe challenges just beyond students' current levels of ability.

41. C

Differentiating instruction includes targeting the lesson format to meet the needs of all learners. By ensuring his lesson is set up to include a variety of manipulatives for his students, Mr. Vance is differentiating his instruction, making choice (**C**) correct.

42. A, D

A mentor is vital to the transition and adaptation of a new teacher. The mentee needs to feel trust in and respect for the mentor teacher. The mentor is not there to direct or report on the mentee, or to do work for the mentee, but rather to help guide the mentee and develop his or her skills so the mentee can be successful. (**A**) and (**D**) are correct.

43. A

Attribution theory often explains the differences in motivation between two people. Here, Jackie attributes her poor performance to her study habits, while Amanda attributes her poor performance to her teacher. Therefore, choice (**A**) is correct.

44. D

Learning about the unique backgrounds of students before instruction will help the teacher make informed instructional decisions, which is a key goal of any initial activity in a unit. Choice (**D**) is correct. The students are not actually speaking, so choice (B) is not correct. Although choices (A) and (C) may be secondary goals, they would not be the primary rationale for this activity.

45. B

When a teacher uses specific criteria in an assessment, she is using analytical scoring. Choice (**B**) is correct.

46. B

There are several components of effective reflective practice and several components of professional development. All are valuable tools for being an effective teacher. However, conferences and webinars are components of professional development and not of reflective practice. Choice (**B**) is correct.

47. C, D

Mr. Hinkie wants Joel to believe in his ability to accomplish tasks, meaning his self-efficacy. (**C**) would directly help Joel to see his progress and gain a sense of achievement as he works towards his goals. (**D**) can also improve Joel's self-efficacy by illustrating for Joel what he has already accomplished and giving him tangible next steps to reach his goal. (A) would not help Joel to believe in his own ability to achieve, as he would have no role in the lecture. (B) could potentially harm Joel's sense of self-efficacy, as comparing him to his sister may reinforce feelings of inferiority.

48. B

While all of the listed options are variables that can affect how students learn and perform, learning style is the option most likely to be impacted by changing teachers within the same subject area. Choice (**B**) is correct.

49. D

The student in question seems to be struggling particularly with reading and writing, but he is involved with the class when working on less literacy-focused assignments. This suggests that the student needs more support with his particular learning needs, and an intervention specialist, (**D**), can best help Mr. Herrera determine which steps to take to meet his student's needs.

50. C

Complex thinking includes cognition on the higher levels of Bloom's taxonomy, including evaluation, synthesis, and analysis. (C) asks students to evaluate the actions of a character and is therefore the correct answer.

51. D

Paraeducators are assigned to classes to help students complete daily tasks. They are not responsible for teaching class lessons, grading work, or communicating with parents about classroom progress. Those tasks are the responsibility of the classroom teacher. Paraeducators are there to assist students as needed, though they may often focus on one or two students who need specific extra help. Choice (D) is correct.

52. D

When Mr. Robin introduced the square posters, there was a tangible reason to determine the square root. Choice (D) highlights that students likely saw this as a more valuable task. It is possible that students were provided the same amount of feedback, the same grading structure, and the same level of involvement in instructional decisions here, so these are not relevant choices.

53. B

With a class average of 65%, it is clear that Ms. Khan's students did not master all of the objectives in the unit the first time she taught them. This situation calls for remediation of the whole class, as described in choice (B). Remediation involves reteaching material in a different way, as opposed to simply having students study more, as in (C). Giving additional lessons to only some students, (D), does not address the underlying issue that a majority of the class seems not to have mastered the content. Getting signatures from parents, (A), does not necessarily encourage students to learn and master the material, and it places blame on students for not learning when an average score of 65% suggests that the style the teacher used for lessons did not connect with students.

54. D

Reflective teaching means, in part, reviewing and adjusting lesson plans to better meet student needs. In addition, collaboration with colleagues, including peer observation, is a key component of the success of this model. Choice (D) is correct.

55. B

Deductive reasoning, (B), involves applying information from a general case to a specific case. Here, Bertha goes from the general case of all eukaryotic cells to her specific eukaryotic cells.

56. D

Teachers need to balance providing accurate feedback to students with sensitivity to a student's potential feelings of embarrassment at responding incorrectly. Thanking students for their participation and giving students the opportunity to fix their mistake through guided questions are ways to mitigate embarrassment while also providing clear information. Choice (D) is correct.

57. A

Allowing think/wait time bolsters the quality of responses for all students and encourages more students to participate. Thus, choice (A) is correct. Encouraging participation through external rewards, as in (D), is not a component of effective questioning. Teachers should vary the types of questions asked, rather than ask only definition-based questions as in (B), and promote active listening, not passive listening as in (C).

58. B

Choice (B) is correct here, since it ties directly into what students are already interested in and allows them some agency. External motivators such as grades, prizes, or SAT scores can be motivating to some students, but they are less powerful motivators.

59. A

Choice (A) is most likely to develop during the adolescent years, as children develop a sense of self and crave peer acceptance.

60. C

The tests are state assessments, so her scores can only be measured against other test takers in her state or a smaller sampling. Data for her school performance is not given. Choice (C) is correct.

61. B

The basis of a professional learning community is to meet with a small cohort of teachers to review student data and use that in the planning of curriculum. Choice (**B**) is correct.

62. B

Choice (**B**) is intrinsic because it is an internal desire. It is negative because it is directed away from something to be avoided. It would be positive if it were directed toward something desired.

63. C

A syllogism is a particular type of argument using reasoning to come to conclusions based on two or more true statements. A Venn diagram, (**C**), best represents this type of argument, as it is a visual representation of what two distinct concepts have in common and what distinguishes them. A line graph, (B), plots the relationship between two variables; a pie chart, (A), shows the distribution of parts within a larger whole; and a bar graph, (D), shows relative relationships between different categories.

64. B

The first step of effective collaboration is developing an action plan. From there, identify the stakeholders and then the purpose of the collaboration. Finally, seek support for the collaboration. Choice (**B**) is correct.

65. C

A criterion-referenced test measures a student's level of knowledge against established criteria, as occurs in (**C**). Norm-referenced tests measure a student's level of knowledge against that of other students as a way to determine a score.

66. C

The psychomotor domain includes motor skills and other physical actions, which makes (**C**) correct here. The cognitive domain incorporates thinking and using knowledge, including (B) and (D).

67. B

The school guidance counselor, (**B**), will be able to assist Mary in getting additional resources to help her get on a school breakfast and lunch program.

68. D

ELL students, or English-language learners, are able to understand complex concepts and learn complex vocabulary when given the appropriate supports. Choice (**D**) provides students with supports to better understand the language aspects of the lesson.

69. A

The Americans with Disabilities Act (ADA) specifically prohibits discrimination in employment for persons with disabilities. Choice (**A**) is correct.

70. A

Age-equivalent scores compare individual test takers' performance to performance averages for test takers of certain ages. An age-equivalent score of 9, for instance, means that the test taker did as well as a typical 9-year-old would have done on the same test. Choice (**A**) is therefore correct. A scaled score is a raw score that has been modified in some way to add consistency to results, or to fit results to a certain format; that is not what's happening here, so (B) is incorrect. Percentile scores state which percentage of other test takers performed below the test taker; a percentile score of 56, for instance, means that the test taker's score was better than that of 56 percent of other test takers. There are no percentiles in the above description, so (C) is incorrect. Grade-equivalent (GE) scores are very similar to age-equivalent scores, except that the scores refer to grades instead of ages; a GE score of 9 would mean that the student's performance matched that of a typical student entering high school. No grade equivalences are mentioned here, so (D) is incorrect.

Sample Response to Question 1

It seems that the students are not engaged in the homework review, despite Mr. Duncan's impression. Mr. Duncan can try changing the format of the review to engage more students initially. Reviewing in groups and reporting out to the class may be effective, as may be having the students come put some problems on the board as they walk into the room. Mr. Duncan could also move the order of the class, putting the homework after the lesson.

Alternatively, Mr. Duncan should make sure his expectations for the transition are clear before it begins. He must also be clear about the consequences for not meeting expectations and make sure he follows through every time.

Sample Response to Question 2

Regularly changing the timing or structure of the review will increase student engagement by diversifying the routine of reviewing the homework. Ms. Garcia noticed that students were quiet, but not actively engaged, so having the work start immediately upon entering will give the class momentum, and adding different review styles will increase interest by decreasing monotony.

In the class, it is clear that Mr. Duncan threatens the class with more work but does not follow through. Having clear expectations and consistent consequences is essential to good classroom management. Students then understand how they are expected to behave and what will happen if they fail to meet those expectations.

Sample Response to Question 3

The teacher must recognize that most students need more scaffolding to move from basic fact recall to analysis of how the community in the story compares to historical communities. The teacher should have made question 1 of the homework assignment a requirement. This would have provided the students a framework upon which to build their answers to the final essay. Also, the students could have been offered a list of utopian communities to research ahead of time, or the class could have researched and discussed one community and how it compares to Jonas' community before the essay was assigned.

Sample Response to Question 4

Using data from the homework assignment, the teacher could have assigned small groups of students to complete the research. He could have chosen which students to group together and then assigned each group a historical community with more or less direct connections to the community in the text. He could have based each group's assignment on the group members' understanding of the story and how well they are able to express their analysis of the concepts in the text. This teacher-provided assistance with the research portion of the project would have allowed the students to more easily focus on comparing the two communities.

Alternatively, the teacher could have provided information or source material to the students so they could have more easily focused on the comparison portion of the assignment. The teacher could have used the answers provided by the homework assignment to decide how much background information to give to each student. The teacher should recognize that if the students struggle with the analysis in the homework assignment, he should give them more practice with higher-order analysis before assigning them the essay. Also, if the students do not succeed on the homework assignment, the teacher should identify the areas in which students are lacking insight into the workings of the novel and then revisit the concepts in class.

Go Online for More Practice

Congratulations! By finishing up the Practice Tests, you've completed your work in this book for the PLT tests.

Now, continue your prep by moving on to your online resources. If you haven't yet registered your book to access your online resources, do so now using these simple steps:

1. Go to **kaptest.com/moreonline**.

2. Follow the on-screen directions. Have your copy of this book available.

GO ONLINE

kaptest.com/login

Please note that access to the online portal is limited to the original owner of this book.

Once you've registered your book, go to **kaptest.com/login** anytime to log in with your email and password.

For the Praxis PLT tests, your online resources include the following:

- One additional full-length Praxis PLT (Grades K–6) practice test with complete answers and explanations
- Two full-length Praxis PLT (Grades 4–9) practice tests with complete answers and explanations
- One additional full-length Praxis PLT (Grades 7–12) practice test with complete answers and explanations

Use your performance on the in-book practice and test material to assess your strengths and areas of opportunity on the Praxis PLT you'll be required to take. Then, find time in your study calendar for additional learning and practice. Account for the length of each practice test you want to take and block out the time required to complete it.

Take each online practice test under test-like conditions to the greatest extent possible. Turn off your phone and close all other programs and apps while you are testing. Part of becoming an expert Praxis PLT test taker is honing your concentration and building the stamina for 1 hour 20 minute to 1 hour 40 minute tests.

When you finish, review your results thoroughly, question-by-question, using the Kaplan explanations. Review is where your greatest learning and improvement will occur. Go over even those questions you got right. The explanations will help you identify patterns you can spot to more quickly and confidently handle similar questions on your official exam.

Thank you for your decision to become an educator—and thank you, too, for studying with Kaplan. We wish you all the best in your educational and professional endeavors.

GETTING STARTED: ADVICE FOR NEW TEACHERS

GETTING STARTED: ADVICE FOR NEW TEACHERS

So you've passed the Praxis with flying colors and fulfilled all the requirements for becoming a teacher in your state. Now it's time to put all of your learning into practice!

Finding the Right Position

It is common knowledge that more good teachers are needed across the country. But finding the right job can be a daunting process. Luckily, there are some simple best-practices that you can prepare to help stand out, such as following professionalism and ethics guidelines to distinguish yourself from other amateur teachers, making sure your license is up-to-date, and having ready examples of strategies and methods for instruction. Use the following tips to help narrow your focus and streamline your applications.

1. **Do Your Research**

   First, determine the grade levels and/or subjects you are most interested in teaching. Make sure you have fulfilled all the qualifications for the state in which you wish to teach. Keep in mind that different states may have different requirements for licensure, while others have license reciprocity. Some schools may even give you a provisional license to start teaching while you complete the necessary test or coursework.

   Check the testing requirements for your state at **ets.org/praxis** or by contacting the governing body directly using the *State Certification Information* that we provided in the prior section of this book.

2. **Identify Where You Would Like to Work**

   Make a list of the districts and/or schools where you would most prefer to work. Many school districts have websites on which they post job openings. In addition, you should call the district office to find out whether there are any positions open that may not have been listed yet and what the district's application procedures are.

   Use the internet as a resource. In addition to the many general websites for job hunters, there are websites devoted solely to teaching jobs. A few websites will ask you for a subscription fee, but there are many others with free listings. A list of some of these sites is included at the end of this section.

3. **Attend Job Fairs**

   While many regional schools may not attend job fairs, they are still a good way to learn about openings and to network with other education professionals. Several of the websites for job seekers listed at the end of this section also have job fair listings by state. Having a resume and broad cover letter in hand is a good idea in general, as it can make you stand out from the crowd.

Remember that you are assessing potential employers as much as they are assessing you. Consider asking the following:

- What is the first professional development opportunity offered to new teachers?
- What additional duties outside the classroom are expected of teachers?
- What is your teacher retention rate?
- When can I expect to meet my mentor? And how long is the probationary/observational period?
- What is the top schoolwide priority this year? Countywide? Statewide?
- What kinds of materials or resources would be available in my classroom? (if applicable)
- What is your policy on lesson planning?

You may also want to ask about the demographics of the student population, the unique challenges they present, and what supports the school has in place.

4. **Sign Up for Substitute Teaching**

Substitute teaching can be another good strategy for getting your foot in the door in a particular school or district, even if no permanent jobs are available. Think of this as an opportunity to impress principals and to learn from other teachers about possible openings. You can even submit your resume to the principals in the schools where you are substitute teaching and give them the chance to observe you in the classroom. While substitute teaching can be one of the most difficult jobs, it allows you to network and prove yourself in the classroom.

Your Resume and the Interview

For many people, writing down all of their accolades and crafting a thoughtful resume can be tedious and stressful. If you find a fulfilling position, though, this may be something that you'll need to update only once or twice a decade. Remember, not everything has to be in the resume and cover letter: you'll have the chance to fill in additional details during the interview. Our recommendations below are designed to help you focus on these two aspects of landing your teaching job.

Building Your Best Cover Letter

The cover letter should let prospective employers have a glimpse into your character beyond the numbers and scores and snippets from the resume. Keep it professional, but don't be afraid to use a few colloquial words or expressions that let your voice shine through.

- Read about the school you are applying to. What are its programs, policies, and mission? Specifically mention the experience you have with similar programs, how your related experience can translate to this school's environment, or how excited you are to learn more about the educational community.
- Use educational buzzwords, list other educational programs that you have used, and try to cover as many of the job description points as possible.
- Don't be afraid to name-drop. If you have been networking in the school, use your connections.
- Remember, many schools accept hundreds of applications for a teaching position. Keep your cover letter as brief and punchy as possible. Avoid formulaic phrasing or drawn-out sentences.

The Resume

There are many excellent templates to help you build your resume. Choose one that is clear and easy to follow and that isn't overly artsy or cutesy. The resume should be essentially a cheat sheet for your school to use to get an instant snapshot of your training and experience.

- Use active words that tell exactly what you did. "Developed and implemented a writing center program that trained 15 tutors" is more precise and impressive than "Participated in writing center training program."
- Narrow down accomplishments to three or four per job/position if you have many. Stay focused on the job you're applying to and which of your accolades will be most impressive relative to that job.
- Remove the fluff. If that summer waitstaff position didn't impact your ability to teach, it doesn't belong in this resume! Similarly, long-winded explanations of the programs you participated in, or language that's unnecessarily verbose, is off-putting to someone who may be reading hundreds of these.
- Try to stick to the two-pages rule. If your resume can't fit on one page (this would be ideal), cut back where possible to make it a maximum of two pages. You don't want the hiring team to have to flip through a several pages to find what school you went to.

Your Interview

So you made it through the first round and they want you to come in and speak with their team. Whether this is a one-on-one, or group, or a series of short interviews, the general recommendations are the same. Be natural and true to yourself, and be confident and clear in your answers. Remember, we are all just people; the person interviewing you was once in your shoes too.

- Project a relaxed confidence, no matter how you may feel inside. Smile, look them in the eyes, sit up straight, don't fidget, say their name when responding, speak clearly.
- When answering direct questions, such as whom you worked with at your last substitute teaching job, answer quickly to reinforce your preparedness. If the questions are more broad or conceptual, pause for a count of two or three seconds to show that you're putting real thought into each answer, even if it's a question you prepared for.
- Be ready to give specific examples of the teaching you have done. It's a good idea to bring a teaching portfolio, but don't be surprised if the selection team doesn't want to review it. Schools may ask for sample lesson plans and newsletters, or they may ask you to teach a lesson as part of the interview process.
- You are interviewing them just as much as they are interviewing you. Ask directed questions about the culture of the school, retention rate, and support systems for new teachers. Having no questions at all may make it seem like you aren't invested in learning about the school, and asking fluff questions that could have been answered by simply visiting the website comes off as amateurish.

Starting in the Classroom

Don't get disillusioned if you're not immediately comfortable in your role as a teacher. Give yourself time to adjust and don't hesitate to ask for advice from others. Be persistent about finding a mentor who can provide support during your first year and beyond. Try to find one in your subject area and determine how much experience you would like that person to have. For the sake of convenience, it's a good idea to find someone who has a similar class schedule or daily routine.

Teach Rules and Respect

With students, be friendly but firm. Establish clear routines and consistent disciplinary measures starting on Day One. This way, the students will have a firm understanding of what is expected of them and when certain behaviors are appropriate. If there is a schoolwide behavior program such as PBiS, RtI, or Responsive Classroom, make sure to follow that in your classroom for consistency. Be aware of how cliques and social hierarchies impact classroom dynamics, avoid power struggles, and don't underestimate the power of your own advice.

Although disciplinary issues vary according to grade level, there are some general tips you may find helpful in setting rules in the classroom:

- Often, misbehavior is an attempt to get your attention or avoid uncomfortable situations on work. Reduce this negative behavior by paying the least amount of attention when a student is acting out and giving that child your full attention when he is behaving.

- When it comes to establishing classroom rules, allow your students to have some input. This will increase their sense of empowerment and respect for the rules.

- Convince all of your students that they are worthwhile and capable. It is easy to assume that struggling students are lazy or beyond help; do not allow yourself to fall into this trap.

- When disciplining students, absolutely avoid embarrassing them in any way, shape, or form, especially in front of their peers. Behaviors are bad, not students.

- Double standards and favoritism will lose you the respect of all your students; always be firm, fair, and consistent. Never talk down to your students.

- Avoid becoming too chummy with your students. Young teachers often feel that they must make "friends" with students, particularly in the older grades. However, it's important to maintain some professional distance and to establish yourself as an authority figure.

- Admit your mistakes. If you wrongly accuse a student of doing something she did not do, make an inappropriate joke, or reprimand a student more harshly than necessary, be sure to apologize and explain. If a parent or administrator criticizes you for your mistake, calmly explain how you felt at that moment and why. Also, explain how you plan on handling that kind of situation in the future.

- Communicate with parents regularly. Help parents see that you are working with them and with the students to help the students succeed at the highest possible level. Parents are more likely to help address problems with students when the parents see that you are sincerely working for the students' academic success.

Do Your Homework

Any veteran teacher will tell you that you will spend almost as many hours working outside the classroom as you do with your students. Preparing lessons and grading homework and tests can take an enormous amount of time, so it's a good idea to be as organized as possible and thoughtful about the lessons and tests that you assign.

Also, consider what your expectations will be:

- Will you grade every homework assignment or just some of them?
- Will you give students an opportunity to earn extra credit?
- What kind of system will you use for grading tests?

Design Lesson Plans Early

Before you start planning, be aware of holidays off, assemblies, and similar interruptions. Design your lessons accordingly. Similarly, be sure you know your content, your state's standards, your school's expectations, and the ins and outs of child development. Be prepared with multiple learning styles and differentiated teaching strategies. Try to include some variety of activities in every lesson with valid alternate choices for completion.

Develop time-saving strategies. For example, saving your lesson plan outline as a template on the computer can be very helpful. Instead of rewriting the whole plan every day, you can just fill in the blanks.

Establish Rules for Grading Homework

Along with establishing a consistent disciplinary policy early on, it's important to know your school's grading policy or develop grading guidelines. Some teachers set the bar high at the beginning of the year by grading a little tougher than they normally would. Just as many students will underachieve if they think you are a soft grader, they will work hard to meet your expectations if your standards are high. However, it's important to assess your students' abilities and set realistic standards.

Use formative and summative assessment types. Grading every single assignment can get overwhelming; sometimes verbally assessing comprehension is enough. Rubrics are another useful tool for outlining expectations and scoring, as well as making sure you cater to the needs of all your students. Rubrics are also effective when students grade each other.

Returning graded assignments as soon as possible sets a good example, keeps your workload manageable, and prevents students' interest from waning. However, you should never use a student's work as an example of what not to do.

Consider sending grades home on a regular basis and getting them signed by parents in order to keep everyone aware of students' progress. This prevents students and parents from being blindsided by poor grades.

Don't confuse quietness for comprehension. Check in with all students because some may be afraid to admit that they don't understand what's going on. If you feel there is a problem, don't wait to address a student's needs. If you believe that a student may have an undiagnosed disability, let your principal know and follow your school's procedure.

Some teachers find that recognizing students' achievements with tangible rewards can increase students' motivation and positively influence their academic performance. These types of incentive systems work particularly well in the elementary grades.

Deal with Parents Early On

Establish a relationship with parents from the beginning. Frequent, positive communication is essential to helping the children attain the best education possible and makes conversations smoother if/when issues arise. Here are a few tips for keeping in touch with parents:

- Make phone calls, even if you're just going to leave a message. Doing so will allow you to share good news and help guardians become more familiar with you.
- Give students homework folders that frequently travel between school and home and send personal notes.
- Be ready to deal with breakdowns in communication: it may be necessary to send multiple messages home.

- Send home a short newsletter of things to come.
- Create an email mailing list or a blog, private class social media page, or other website for families to follow. Be sure to check your school's acceptable online presence standards.

Set Up Parent-Teacher Conferences

Meeting with parents can often be intimidating for new teachers, particularly if a student is not performing well; just remember that families are your greatest resource and ally for supporting your students outside of the classroom. It's a good idea to seek guidance from experienced teachers and communicate with administrators if you encounter problems. In addition, try to follow these general guidelines when talking with parents:

- Remain professional. Don't take heated words personally, have good things to say about the student, choose your words carefully, keep examples of the student's work on hand and document what is said during the meeting.
- Allow parents to ask the first question. This will help you understand their tone and their concerns.
- Be as thick-skinned as possible when dealing with problems: some parents want to vent a little before getting to the crux of the issue. Let them vent, try to put them at ease, and then look for a solution or compromise.
- If a parent becomes excessively confrontational, inform an administrator.
- Have documents available to support your statements. For example, if the student has not completed assignments, have grade book evidence to support your contention.
- Be confident. Listen to what the parents suggest, but also stand up for what you believe is the best course of action.

Building Relationships with Colleagues

Meet as many teachers in the building as you can; not only will you gain valuable insights about the inner workings of the school, but you'll also make new friends. Don't be afraid to step up and ask questions when information isn't offered. Veteran teachers are a tremendous resource for all kinds of information, ranging from labor contracts to strategies for staying sane under pressure. Also, get to know the other new teachers. These people will be valuable sounding boards and will help you feel less alone.

Earn the respect of your colleagues by stepping up to committee work and by proving yourself to be a reliable, competent teacher. You should also be polite and friendly with secretaries, custodians, and other school staff; you'll need their help for all sorts of reasons.

Finally, be professional, timely, and unafraid to calmly share your opinions or disagree with administrators. Your professionalism and enthusiasm will earn you their respect and ensure that your needs are met.

Dealing with Paperwork

Be aware of what kinds of paperwork you need to fill out and file, including the School Improvement Plan, special education forms relating to Individualized Education Plans, budget requests, reading and math benchmarks, and permanent record cards. Consider sitting with fellow teachers when filling out forms. Their companionship will make these tedious tasks more fun.